VISUAL QUICKPRO GUIDE

AFTER EFFECTS CS4

FOR WINDOWS AND MACINTOSH

Antony Bolante

 Peachpit Press

Visual QuickPro Guide
After Effects CS4 for Windows and Macintosh
Antony Bolante

Peachpit Press
1249 Eighth Street
Berkeley, CA 94710
510/524-2178
Fax: 510/524-2221
Find us on the Web at: www.peachpit.com.com

To report errors, please send a note to errata@peachpit.com
Peachpit Press is a division of Pearson Education
Copyright ©2009 by Antony Bolante

Senior Editor: Karyn Johnson
Development and Copy Editor: Kim Saccio-Kent
Technical Editor: Alex Czetwertynski
Production Editor: Cory Borman
Composition: WolfsonDesign
Proofreader: Rebecca Rider
Indexer: Jack Lewis
Cover Design: Peachpit Press

ISBN-13: 978-0-321-59152-4
ISBN-10:   0-321-59152-6

9 8 7 6 5 4 3 2 1

Printed and bound in the United States of America

For my family.

Acknowledgments

Everyone involved in creating the previous versions of this book; I hope this one does you proud.

Everyone who has let me share their lovely photos and faces.

The clever folks at Adobe Systems.

The hardworking book team: Karyn Johnson, Kim Saccio-Kent, Alex Czetwertynski, Cory Borman, and WolfsonDesign.

Shortstack.

My wonderfully supportive friends and family.

TABLE OF CONTENTS

TABLE OF CONTENTS

Chapter 1:

After Effects: The Big Picture

"It's the Photoshop of dynamic media."

Summing up Adobe After Effects often leads to a comparison to its more famous sibling, Adobe Photoshop. Just as Photoshop lends you precise control over still images, After Effects gives you startling command over moving images. And, like Photoshop, After Effects has established itself as one of the leading programs of its kind. But don't take the comparison too far: Judge After Effects for its unique merits.

After Effects brings together typography and layout, photography and digital imaging, digital video and audio editing, even 3D animation. You can edit, composite, animate, and add effects to each element. And you can output the results for presentation in traditional media, like film and video, or in newer forms, like DVD, the Web, or mobile devices.

In this sense, a more apt metaphor would be that After Effects is the opera of digital media. Just as Wagner sought to combine disparate forms of performance into a "total work of art"—or *gesamtkunstwerk*—After Effects allows you to unite various media into a unique, dynamic whole. That may sound a bit grandiose. If it's more convenient, "the Photoshop of dynamic media" works just fine.

Because After Effects draws from so many sources, it also appeals to a wide range of users. You may want to add motion to your typography or design work. Or perhaps your interest in photography and digital imaging brought you to After Effects. Maybe you're a film or video maker who requires visual effects. Or possibly you're an animator who wants to expand your repertoire of tools. Maybe you've heard that After Effects is fun. Whatever your background, whatever your goal, you're ready to get started.

This chapter acquaints you with After Effects. It explains how After Effects works and what you'll need to get started. If you're not already familiar with the QuickStart and QuickPro series, this chapter also introduces you to the book's step-by-step, visual approach to explaining After Effects. Now, let's get to *gesamtkunstwerk*.

The QuickPro Series

Chances are you're already familiar with Peachpit Press's QuickStart series of books. They're known for their concise style, step-by-step instructions, and ample illustrations.

As you might guess, the Pro appellation implies that the software under discussion appeals to more advanced users. After Effects is such a program. For this reason, this QuickPro guide is designed for intermediate to advanced users and assumes you have significant experience not only with computers, but also with using some form of digital media.

That said, the QuickPro series remains true to the essential QuickStart traditions. The approach still emphasizes step-by-step instructions and concise explanations. If the book looks a little thick for a "concise" guide, consider that literally hundreds of screen shots clearly illustrate every task. You don't have to be a beginner to find a visual, step-by-step guide appealing.

Occasionally, this guide departs from the standard layout to accommodate larger screen shots, tables, or sidebars. Sidebars set aside important background information about the task at hand. If you're already familiar with the concept, feel free to skip ahead. If not, look to the sidebars for some grounding.

Because After Effects combines assets from several disciplines—typography, design, digital imaging, animation, film, and video—it also intersects with the vast bodies of information associated with each of them. Explaining the fundamentals and background of these topics is outside the scope of this book (which, after all, includes the word *quick* in its title). And although it covers a lot of ground, it can't delve into some of After Effects' specialized features, like advanced mask interpolation or tracking. Nevertheless, this guide tries to provide enough information to keep you moving.

Adobe Creative Suite 4 Production Premium

Because After Effects brings together a range of digital media, Adobe hopes you'll use it with its other software aimed at creative professionals, known collectively as the *Creative Suite*. In fact, Adobe eschews individual software version numbers, preferring instead to state versions in terms of the suite. Hence, After Effects 9 is more commonly referred to as After Effects CS4. Even if you opt to buy After Effects separate from the other members of the Creative Suite, you'll still get additional software in the bargain: Adobe Bridge, Device Central, and (new in CS4) Mocha for Adobe After Effects, a powerful program designed for motion tracking and stabilization.

But chances are, you've acquired After Effects as part of one of the CS4 collections of software. The collection of CS4 software tailored to the production of dynamic media is called *Adobe CS4 Production Premium*. It contains After Effects, Adobe Premiere Pro, Encore, Soundbooth, Photoshop Extended, Illustrator, Flash, and OnLocation. Attractive bundled pricing makes the Production Premium edition much less expensive than the sum of its parts.

As the Creative Suite software packages mature, they also become more integrated. Over time, it has become easier to move files from one program to another without taking intermediate steps or sacrificing elements of your work. Even the programs' interfaces have grown more consistent. However, although the landscapes are similar, the customs aren't always the same: You may find that not all shared features employ exactly the same procedures or keyboard shortcuts.

Minimum Requirements

To use After Effects, your system must meet the following minimum requirements.

Mac OS

◆ Multicore Intel processor

◆ Mac OS X v.10.4.11 or later

Windows

◆ 1.5 GHz or faster processor; for AMD systems, an SSE2-enabled processor is required

◆ Microsoft Windows XP Service Pack 2 (Service Pack 3 Recommended), or Windows Vista Home Premium, Business, Ultimate, or Enterprise with Service Pack 1 (certified for 32-bit Windows XP and 32-bit and 64-bit Windows Vista)

All Systems

◆ At least 2 GB of RAM

◆ At least 2.9 GB of available storage for full installation of the software, plus 2 GB additional storage for optional content

◆ 1280 × 900 display with OpenGL 2.0-compatible graphics card

◆ DVD-ROM drive

◆ QuickTime 7.4.5 or later to use QuickTime features

◆ Broadband Internet connection for Adobe's online services

Mac OS vs. Windows

After Effects runs on both the Mac OS and Windows platforms.

With few exceptions, After Effects works the same on both systems; and apart from mostly cosmetic differences between the operating systems, the interfaces are also nearly identical. Perhaps the only notable difference between After Effects for the Mac OS and Windows is the location of the Preferences command. In the Mac OS, choose After Effects > Preferences; in Windows, choose Edit > Preferences (**Figures 1.1** and **1.2**). In the rare instances where a process or window differs between the two versions of the program, it's clearly noted. For example, this guide always includes keyboard shortcuts for both the Mac OS and Windows. The Mac OS shortcuts are given first, then the Windows keystrokes in parentheses. Otherwise, you'll find the most significant differences on the operating system level, not in the program itself.

New Features in After Effects CS4

Some of the more notable features introduced in After Effects CS4 include the following:

Interface refinements. The darker interface in After Effects CS4 is easier on the eyes and more conducive to long work sessions (and more creative breakthroughs). Other subtle yet important changes help streamline your workflow. For example, the Project panel includes a convenient button to access the useful Interpret Footage dialog.

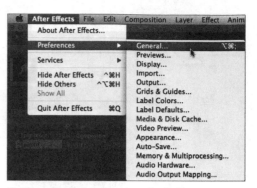

Figure 1.1 Like other programs, the Preferences command for After Effects is located in a different location on a Mac...

Figure 1.2 ...than on a Windows system. Otherwise, the Mac and Windows versions are nearly identical.

Comprehensive search features. New search fields in the Project and Timeline panels help you find a particular item in a project, while the search field in the Tools panel helps you seek guidance in After Effects Help. From the new Welcome screen, you can even search through the helpful Tip of the Day catalog.

Project navigation. Just as the new search features help you locate a particular tree in a forest of assets, other tools help you navigate the forest itself. A convenient mini-flowchart button in the Timeline panel helps you quickly check the virtual map of your project, and buttons in the Composition panel let you step through a hierarchy of comps.

Layer enhancements. Shape layers (introduced in CS3) support 32-bit HDR, include blending modes, and can "wiggle" transform properties. Text layers let you specify line joins—and you can convert text layers into masks and shape layers. Convenient commands let you flip layers horizontally or vertically without setting their scale properties manually, and layer names are no longer restricted to 31 characters in length.

3D enhancements. A new Unified Camera tool lets you use a three-button mouse to track XY, track Z, and orbit a camera without switching tools. New icons enable you to distinguish different light types in the Comp panel. And you can now animate X, Y, and Z position properties separately and create 3D animations that would be difficult to achieve otherwise. After Effects CS4 can even import 3D layers from Photoshop Extended.

New effects. Perhaps the most notable new effect is Cartoon, which automatically makes still or moving images look as though they had been produced with cel animation or rotoscoping.

Enhanced integration. Adobe has expanded the powerful Dynamic Link feature to integrate After Effects, Premiere Pro, Soundbooth, and Encore. Before Dynamic Link, to import a file into a program you would have to export it from the source program first. Dynamic Link bypasses this step; for example, you can now use a comp from After Effects in an Adobe Premiere Pro sequence directly. Any change that you make to the linked content in the program you are working in is reflected in the original program.

Expanded import and export options. In addition to accepting 3D layers from Photoshop Extended, After Effects CS4 also recognizes Time Remap settings when importing from Adobe Premiere Pro. Compositions exported from After Effects can be imported into Flash CS4 Professional as layered projects. Tight integration with Device Central lets you use After Effects to prepare and export comps for playback on a variety of mobile devices. The new Metadata panel in After Effects embodies its expanded support for XMP metadata. Finally, After Effects CS4 adds support for ProEXR, PS2 and XDCAM footage to its long list of compatible formats.

Improved preview and performance. In addition to under-the-hood performance boosts, you will notice preview improvements like 4:3 safe margin guides in 16:9 comps, and more accurate pixel aspect ratio calculations for standard-definition formats.

Closer user relationship. With a click of the mouse, After Effects CS4 connects you to Adobe's online resources and invites you to participate in its extensive community of users. Solve problems through Adobe Community Help; and get updated, educated, or inspired at Adobe Bridge Home.

NEW FEATURES IN AFTER EFFECTS CS4

Workflow Overview

Any project, it can be argued, begins at the same point: the end. Setting your output goal determines the choices you make to achieve it. Whether your animation is destined for film, videotape, DVD, the Web, or a mobile device, familiarize yourself with the specifications of your output goal, such as frame size, frame rate, and file format. Only when you've determined the output goal can you make intelligent choices about source material and setting up a project.

That established, the typical workflow might resemble the outline that follows. However, every aspect of After Effects is tightly integrated and interdependent. Between import and output, the steps of the project won't necessarily proceed in a simple linear fashion:

Import. After Effects coordinates a wide range of source materials, including digital video, audio, bitmapped still images, path-based graphics and text, and even 3D and film transfer formats. However, it doesn't furnish you with a way to directly acquire these assets—you need a video and audio capture device, a digital still camera, a scanner, or other software packages to do that. This is not to say that After Effects doesn't generate its own graphic and sound elements; it does.

Arranging layers in time. Although it's not designed for long-form nonlinear editing, After Effects ably arranges shorter sequences for compositing and effects work. You can instantly access and rearrange layers, and use the same file repeatedly without copying or altering it.

Arranging layers in space. After Effects' ability to layer, combine, and composite images earned it its reputation as the Photoshop of dynamic media. Moreover, these capabilities extend into the 3D realm.

Adding effects. Does "the Photoshop of dynamic media" refer to After Effects' ability to add visual effects to motion footage? After Effects offers many effects to combine, enhance, transform, and distort layers of both video and audio. An entire industry has grown up around developing and accelerating effects for After Effects.

Animating attributes. One of After Effects' greatest strengths is its ability to change the attributes of layers over time. You can give layers motion, make layers appear and fade, or intensify and diminish an effect. The timeline's Graph Editor makes it easy to focus on a property and control it with precision. The Brainstorm feature lets you try out and compare different choices.

Previewing. You can play back your animation at any time to evaluate its appearance and timing and then change it accordingly. After Effects maximizes your computer's playback capabilities by utilizing RAM to render frames, dynamically adjusting resolution, allowing you to specify a region of interest, and taking advantage of OpenGL. The program can fully utilize multicore and multiprocessor systems to optimize performance.

Adding complexity. Some projects require more complex structures than others. You may need to group layers as a single element or circumvent the program's default rendering hierarchy to achieve a certain effect. Or, you may need to restructure your project to make it more efficient and allow it to render more quickly. With features like Parenting and Expressions, you have the power to create complex animations with relatively little effort.

Output. When you're satisfied with your composition, you can output the result in a number of file formats, depending on the presentation media (which, of course, you planned for from the start).

Interface Overview

Before you begin exploring the program's terrain, let's take in a panoramic view.

Primary panels

Most of your work will be concentrated in three panels: the Project panel, the Composition panel, and the Timeline panel (**Figure 1.3**).

The **Project panel** lists references to audio and visual files, or footage, that you plan to use in your animation. It also lists compositions, which describe how you want to use the footage, including its arrangement in time, motion, and effects.

The **Composition panel** represents the layers of a composition spatially. The visible area of the Composition panel corresponds to the frame of the output animation and displays the composition's current frame. You can open more than one Composition panel; doing so is particularly useful when you want to compare the image in a composition to a corresponding frame in a nested composition, or view a 3D composition from different angles. It's common to call compositions *comps* and a Composition panel a *Comp panel*, for short.

continues on next page

Project panel — Composition panel —

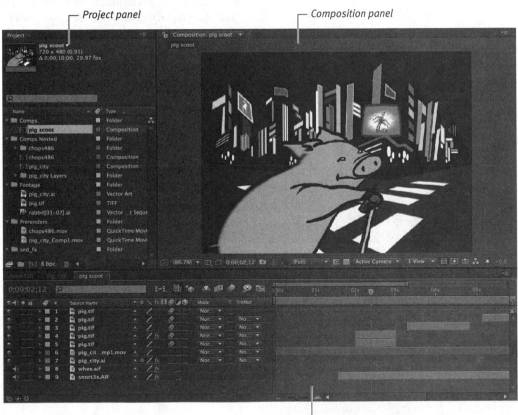

Timeline panel

Figure 1.3 Your work takes place primarily in the Project, Composition, and Timeline panels.

The **Timeline panel** represents the composition as a graph in which time is measured horizontally. When a footage item is added to the composition, it becomes a layer. The horizontal arrangement of layers indicates each layer's place in the time of the composition; the layers' vertical arrangement indicates their stacking order. You access and manipulate layer properties from the Timeline panel.

✔ Tip

- You can control the brightness and color of interface elements by choosing Edit > Preferences > User Interface Colors (After Effects > Preferences > User Interface Colors).

Secondary panels

Although the Windows menu lists them in the same group as the three primary panels, you might consider the Footage, Layer, and Effect Controls panels to be ancillaries (**Figure 1.4**). The Flowchart and Render Queue panels are also among this important ensemble.

The **Footage panel** allows you to view the source footage listed in the Project panel before it becomes a layer in a composition.

The **Layer panel** lets you view each layer in a composition individually, outside the context of the Composition or Timeline panel. For example, it can be the most convenient place to manipulate a layer's mask shape. When you paint on a layer, you do so in the Layer panel.

Footage panel

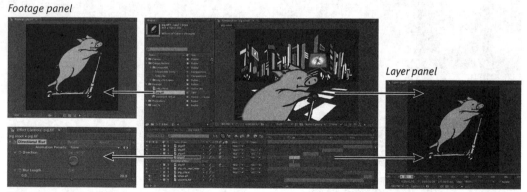

Layer panel

Effect Controls panel

Figure 1.4 The Footage panel shows the source footage listed in the Project panel. The Layer and Effect Controls panels are related to a particular layer in a composition.

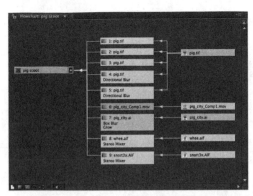

Figure 1.5 The Flowchart panel helps you analyze the hierarchical structure of a complex project.

Figure 1.6 The Render Queue panel lets you control and monitor the rendering process.

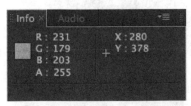

Figure 1.7 The Tools panel contains tools that help you perform special tasks using the mouse, as well as 3D axis buttons, a Workspace menu, and a way to search After Effects Help. (Typically, it extends horizontally across the workspace; this figure shows a more compact configuration.)

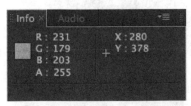

Figure 1.8 The Info panel displays pertinent information about the task at hand, such as the current position of the cursor in a composition and the In and Out points of a layer.

The **Effect Controls panel** provides separate, roomier, and often more convenient effect controls than those available in the Timeline panel.

The **Flowchart panel** lets you see your project's elements in the form of a flowchart, which can make it easier to understand the structure and hierarchies of your project—particularly a complex one (**Figure 1.5**).

The **Render Queue panel** lets you control and monitor the rendering process (**Figure 1.6**).

Specialized panels

The panels listed so far—the panels you use most often—all appear at the bottom of the list in the Windows menu, below a horizontal line. Above that separator are a host of other, more specialized panels:

The **Tools panel**, as its name implies, contains an assortment of tools that change the function of the mouse pointer. Each tool allows you to perform specialized tasks (**Figure 1.7**). The Tools panel also contains buttons for changing the 3D axis and a pop-up menu for selecting a workspace.

As in other programs, a small triangle in the corner of a tool button indicates that related tools are hidden. Click and hold the button to reveal and select a hidden tool.

The **Info panel** displays all kinds of information about the current task, from the cursor's current position in a composition to the In and Out points of a layer (**Figure 1.8**).

continues on next page

The **Preview panel** contains controls for playing back and previewing the composition. By default, setting a composition's current time also sets the time in all panels related to that composition (**Figure 1.9**).

The **Audio panel** lets you monitor and control audio levels (**Figure 1.10**).

The **Effects & Presets panel** provides a convenient way to view and apply effects. You can reorganize the list, create and view favorites, and find a particular effect in the list or on your hard drive (**Figure 1.11**).

The **Character panel** provides convenient text controls to support After Effects' direct text creation feature. It includes all the controls you'd expect—font, size, fill and stroke, kerning, leading, and the like. It also includes a few you might not expect—baseline shift, vertical and horizontal scaling, superscript and subscript, and a feature to aid in laying out characters in vertically oriented languages like Chinese, Japanese, and Korean (**Figure 1.12**).

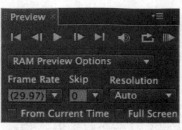

Figure 1.9 The Preview panel contains controls to play back and preview the composition.

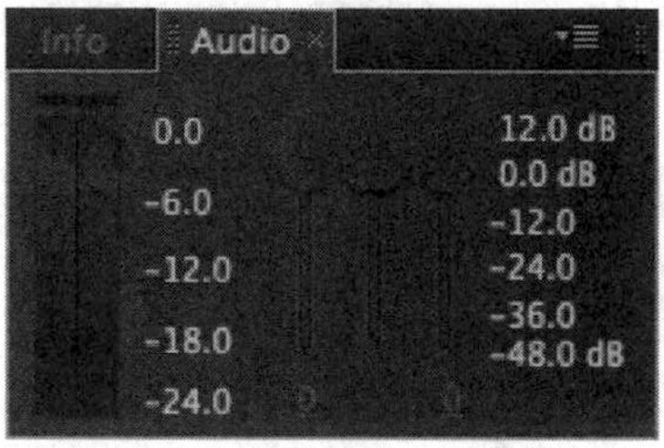

Figure 1.10 The Audio panel lets you monitor and control audio levels.

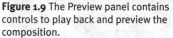

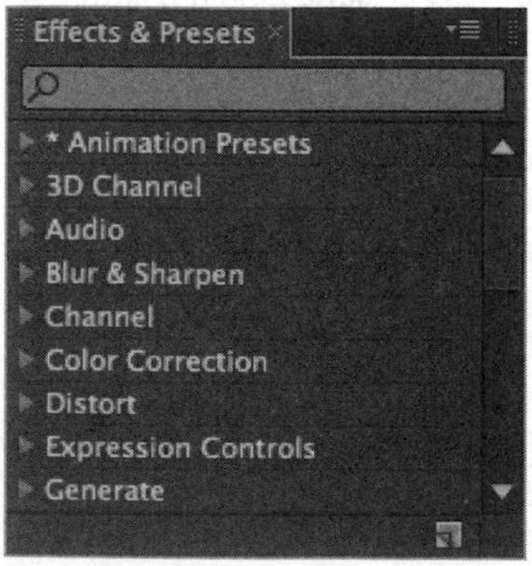

Figure 1.11 The Effects & Presets panel makes it easy to find effects and save custom presets for animation.

Figure 1.12 The full-featured Character panel lets you control the characteristics of text you create in After Effects.

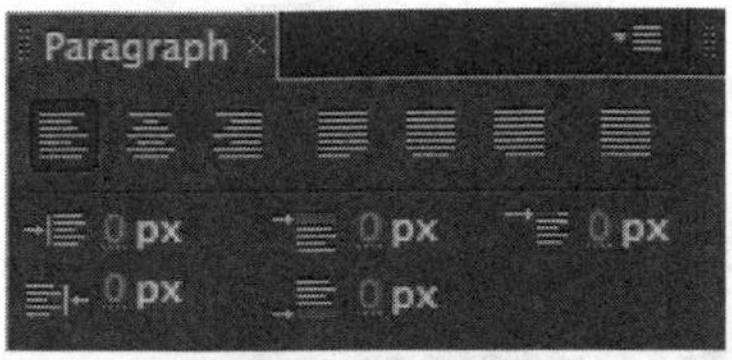

Figure 1.13 You can control blocks of text using the Paragraph panel, which lets you adjust things like alignment, justification, and indentation.

The **Paragraph panel** lets you control blocks of text as you would in a word-processing or layout program. You can specify justification, alignment, indents, and the spacing before and after paragraphs (**Figure 1.13**).

The **Paint panel** gives you full control over the characteristics of paint, such as color, opacity, and flow. You can also specify which channel you want to paint onto and whether to apply a mode to each stroke (**Figure 1.14**).

The **Brushes panel** not only provides a menu of preset brushes, but also lets you create brushes and specify their characteristics, such as diameter, angle, roundness, hardness, and so on (**Figure 1.15**).

✔ Tip

- The flexible interface in After Effects allows you to substantially alter the appearance of each panel. Don't be distracted if a figure in this book depicts a variant of a panel that differs from the one you're using.

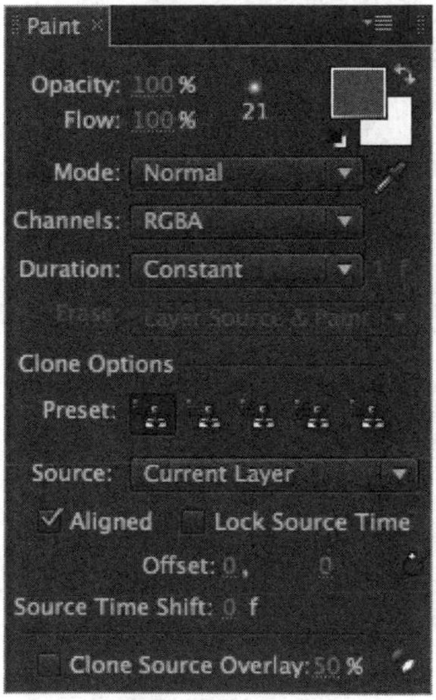

Figure 1.14 The Paint panel gives you control over After Effects' painting and cloning features...

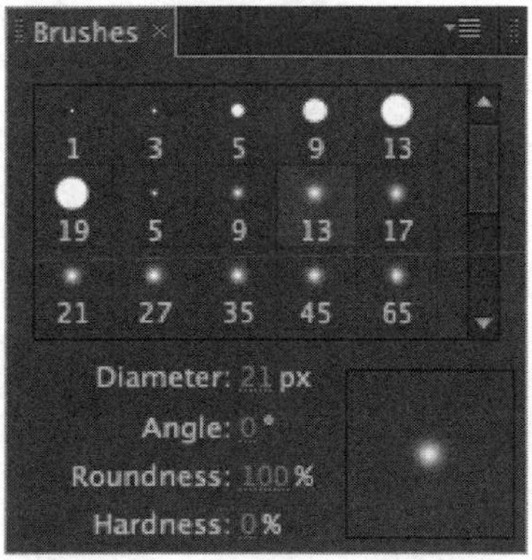

Figure 1.15 ...and its companion, the Brushes panel, lets you select the characteristics of the brush you employ.

INTERFACE OVERVIEW

Even more specialized panels

You can open the previously listed nine panels by using keyboard shortcuts. But to open the following panels, you'll have to choose them from the Windows pull-down menu:

The **Motion Sketch panel** lets you set motion keyframes by dragging the mouse (or by using a pen stroke on a graphics tablet) (**Figure 1.16**).

The **Mask Interpolation panel** helps you animate mask shapes more precisely (**Figure 1.17**).

The **Smoother panel** helps you smooth changes in keyframe values automatically to create more gradual changes in an animation (**Figure 1.18**).

The **Wiggler panel** generates random deviations in keyframed values automatically (**Figure 1.19**).

The **Align panel** helps you arrange layers in a comp vis-à-vis one another (**Figure 1.20**).

The **Tracker panel**, an advanced feature, helps you generate keyframes by detecting and following a moving object in a shot. You can use this information to make an effect track an object or to stabilize a scene shot with shaky camera work (**Figure 1.21**).

The **Metadata panel** allows you to view and edit a file's metadata—that is, information encoded into a file about the file itself. Metadata can include all sorts of data, from your personal 1 to 5 star rating of the file to critical copyright information (**Figure 1.22**).

Figure 1.16 The Motion Sketch panel lets you set motion keyframes by dragging your mouse.

Figure 1.17 The Mask Interpolation panel provides a greater degree of control when you're animating mask shapes.

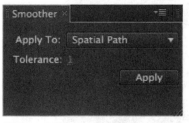

Figure 1.18 The Smoother panel helps you smooth changes in keyframe values.

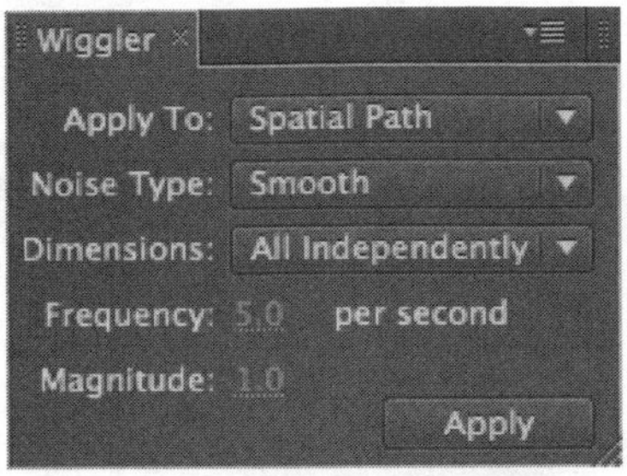

Figure 1.19 You can generate random deviations in keyframed values automatically using the Wiggler panel.

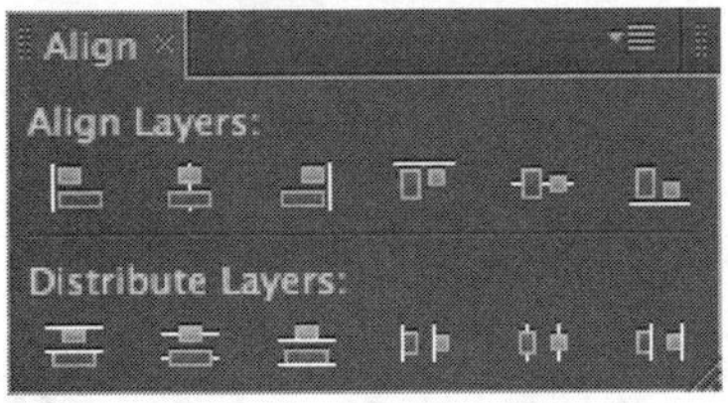

Figure 1.20 The Align panel helps you arrange layers.

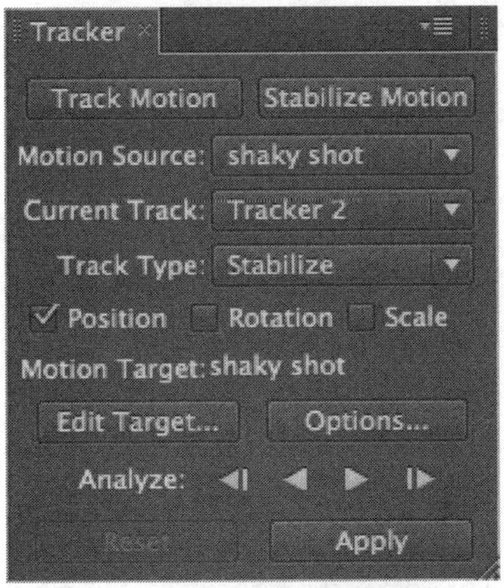

Figure 1.21 Using the Tracker panel, you can generate keyframes to follow a moving object automatically or, conversely, to stabilize a shaky image.

✔ Tips

■ Note that in addition to its own motion tracking features, After Effects CS4 ships with dedicated tracking software called Mocha for After Effects. Check out its documentation and Adobe's help resources to learn more about incorporating Mocha into your After Effects workflow.

■ You can add metadata on the project and layer level and use that information in practical ways. For example, you can render a file that retains information from the composition's markers. If you use the rendered file as a layer in a comp, then the information will appear as layer markers.

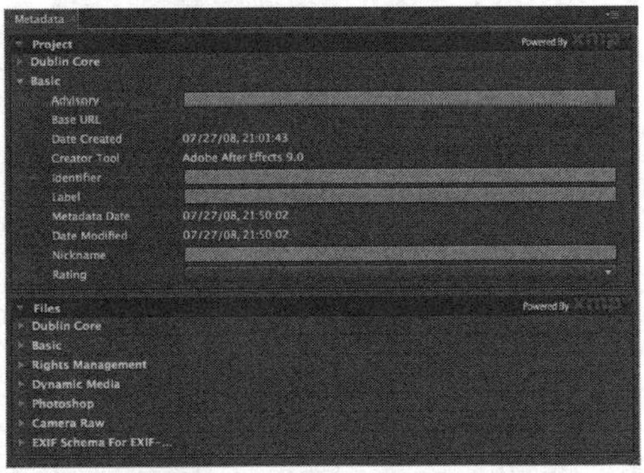

Figure 1.22 The Metadata panel lets you view and edit all sorts of information regarding a file, from a personal 1 to 5 star rating to important copyright information.

Setting a Workspace

With so many controls at your disposal, it's clear that you must arrange the panels to suit the task at hand and change the arrangement for each phase of your workflow. Conveniently, After Effects provides several preset arrangements, or *workspaces*, optimized to accomplish particular tasks, such as animation or effects (**Figure 1.23**). Selecting the appropriate workspace from a list (or using a keyboard shortcut) opens and configures the panels you need.

When you modify a preset workspace (using methods explained in the section "Customizing the Workspace," later in this chapter), After Effects maintains the changes until you reset the preset to its defaults. You can even create your own preset workspace.

Figure 1.23 This figure shows the Standard workspace.

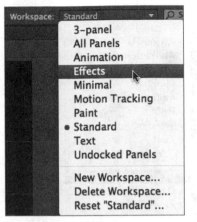

Figure 1.24 Selecting the arrangement you want from the Tools panel's Workspace pop-up menu...

To specify a preset workspace:

Do either of the following:

◆ Choose Window > Workspace, and then choose the name of the arrangement that corresponds with the task at hand.

◆ In the Tools panel's Workspace pop-up menu, choose the name of the workspace (**Figure 1.24**).

For example, changing from the preset Standard workspace to the preset Effects workspace opens the Effect Controls panel in place of the Project panel (**Figure 1.25**). The workspace retains any modifications you make to it until you reset the workspace.

Figure 1.25 ...arranges the panels according to the workspace you choose. Here, note how the Effects workspace places the Effect Controls panel where the Project panel is located in the Standard workspace (shown in Figure 1.23).

SETTING A WORKSPACE

To create a new workspace preset:

If you want, you can set the workspace that uses an arrangement on which you want to base a custom workspace.

1. In the Tools panel's Workspace pop-up menu, choose New Workspace (**Figure 1.26**).

   A New Workspace dialog appears.

2. In the New Workspace dialog, type a name for the custom workspace, and click OK (**Figure 1.27**).

   The current workspace becomes the newly named workspace preset.

3. Modify the workspace using any of the methods described in the section "Customizing the Workspace," later in this chapter.

To reset a preset workspace:

1. With the workspace set to a modified preset workspace (such as Standard), choose Reset "*workspace name*" (**Figure 1.28**).

2. When prompted, confirm that you want to discard the changes you made to the workspace.

   The workspace reverts to its original preset arrangement.

✔ Tips

- The Workspace pop-up menu also contains commands for deleting a workspace and for assigning a keyboard shortcut to a workspace.

- The Window menu (in the main menu bar) contains all the commands pertaining to workspaces.

Figure 1.26 In the Tools panel's Workspace pop-up menu, choose New Workspace.

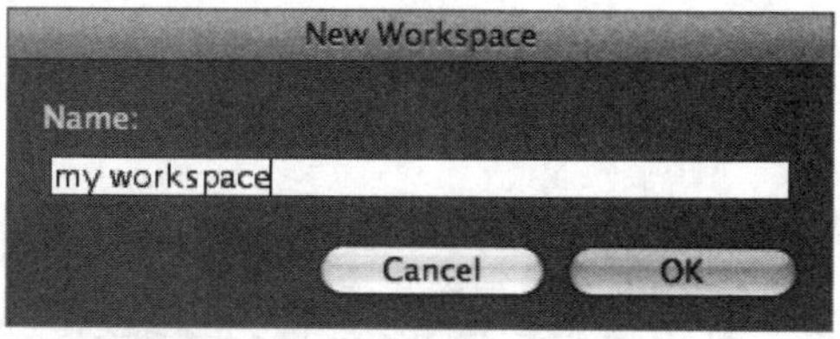

Figure 1.27 Enter a name for the custom workspace in the New Workspace dialog.

Figure 1.28 Choosing Reset "*workspace name*" in the Tools panel's Workspace pop-up menu reverts the workspace to its original state.

Customizing the Workspace

Using the preset workspaces is convenient, not compulsory. By customizing the size and arrangement of the panels, you can optimize your workspace and your workflow. You just have to know a few things about frames, panels, and tabs.

The After Effects interface consists of an interconnected system of *panels* contained within *frames*. Unlike a collection of free-floating windows that can be arranged like playing cards on a tabletop, frames are joined together in such a way that the interface may remind you of a mosaic or stained glass. Resizing one frame affects the adjacent frames so that, as a whole, the frames always fill the screen (or, more strictly speaking, After Effects' main application window, which most users maximize to fill the screen). With frames and panels it's easy to change the relative size of each part of the interface without wasting screen space. And you don't have to worry about one window disappearing behind another.

You can also customize a workspace by taking advantage of tabs. The tab that appears at the top of each panel looks a lot like its real-world counterpart in your office filing cabinet. By dragging a panel's tab into the same area as another panel, you *dock* the panels together. When panels are docked, it's as though they are filed one on top of the other. But like physical file-folder tabs, the tabs of the panels in the back are always visible along the top edge of the stack; you click a panel's tab to bring it to the front. (The Footage, Comp, and Layer panel tabs include a lock option and pop-up menu, discussed in the section "Using Viewers," later in this chapter.)

Just as docking reduces the number of spaces in the interface's mosaic of frames, dragging a panel between other panels creates an additional space, or frame.

Finally, you can separate a panel from the system of frames, creating a free-floating window. A floating window may be useful for tasks you don't perform often or when you can move it to a second computer screen.

Because the interface's design is intuitive and common to several Adobe programs, it won't be covered in detail here. However, the particular way After Effects lets you switch among images in a single panel is described in the following section, "Using Viewers."

CUSTOMIZING THE WORKSPACE

Using Viewers

As you work, you'll need to open numerous footage items, compositions, and layers. To prevent a frame from becoming overcrowded with tabs, the Footage, Comp, and Layer panels utilize *viewers*. (And because each layer can contain a set of effects, the Effect Controls panel also employs viewer system.)

Instead of opening in separate tabbed panels, multiple items of the same type (footage, comps, layers, and a layer's effects) share a single panel of that type (Footage panel, Comp panel, and so on) (**Figure 1.29**).

A pop-up menu in the panel's tab allows you to switch to another viewer. For example, you can see any composition that's open in the project by selecting it in a Comp panel's viewer menu (**Figure 1.30**).

However, you can prevent new items from opening in a viewer by *locking* the viewer. When locked, the viewer pop-up menu still works, but the panel doesn't accept new viewers. Instead, the item opens as a separate tabbed panel (**Figure 1.31**). (If another compatible panel is visible and unlocked, then new items open in it.)

Naturally, the viewer feature doesn't prevent you from using any of the methods described in the section "Customizing the Workspace". Viewers are just another feature to help you manage your workspace and your workflow effectively.

Figure 1.29 By default, all footage items open in the same Footage panel; comps share the same Comp panel; and layers share the same Layer panel.

Figure 1.30 You can view another image by selecting it in the panel's viewer pop-up menu. This Comp panel's viewer lets you select another composition in the project.

Figure 1.31 However, selecting the viewer's Lock icon prevents items from opening in the panel; instead, they open in a separate panel. Here, a locked Layer panel forces subsequent layers to open in another panel.

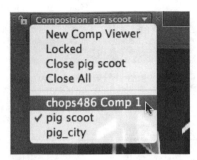

Figure 1.32 The viewer pop-up menu lists other items (note how layer names are preceded by the comp that contains them). Select the name of the item you want to view...

Figure 1.33 ...to see its image in the panel.

Figure 1.34 Click the Lock icon in the panel's tab to toggle it from unlocked...

Figure 1.35 ...to locked.

To select an item from the viewer menu:

◆ In a Footage, Layer, Comp, or Effect Controls panel, select the name of the item you want to see in the tab's viewer pop-up menu (**Figure 1.32**).

The image in the panel changes accordingly (**Figure 1.33**).

To lock or unlock a view:

◆ In a Footage, Layer, Comp, or Effect Controls panel's tab, select the Lock icon to toggle it on and off (**Figures 1.34 and 1.35**).

The icon indicates the viewer is unlocked and will let items open in the panel. The icon indicates the viewer is locked; new items must open in a separate, unlocked panel.

✔ Tips

■ Comps open as separately tabbed Timeline panels and don't utilize viewers. Typically, the frame that contains Timeline panels is wide and easily accommodates numerous tabs.

■ The Comp panel also has a View Layout pop-up menu, which allows the panel to display multiple images simultaneously. Seeing the adjustments you make to a comp from several perspectives at once is particularly useful when you're working with 3D layers. Using multiple comp views is discussed in detail in Chapter 4, "Compositions," and Chapter 15, "3D Layers."

USING VIEWERS

19

Opening Related Panels Automatically

Some tasks—specifically, creating text and painting on a layer—not only require using a particular tool, but also an associated set of panels. For example, creating text with a Type tool generally involves formatting the text using controls in the Character and Paragraph panels. If you want, you can have After Effects open the panels associated with certain tools automatically, whenever you select the tool. A button lets you toggle the panels closed. This way, you can perform the task even if you don't want to switch to a different workspace.

To open tool-related panels automatically:

1. In the Tools panel, select a tool that has panels associated with it.

   The Type tools are related to the Character and Paragraph panels; the Brush and Clone tools are related to the Brushes and Paint panels.

2. In the Tools panel, select Auto-Open Panels (**Figure 1.36**).

   Henceforth, selecting the tool makes its related panels open automatically (**Figure 1.37**).

✓ Tip

■ To toggle related panels open and closed, click the Toggle Related Panels button 🔲 (**Figure 1.38**).

Figure 1.36 With the tool related to paint or text (shown here) selected, select Auto-Open Panels...

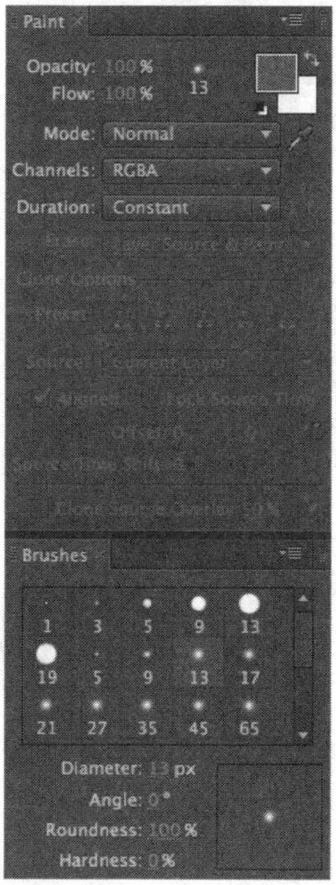

Figure 1.37 ...to make the panels associated with the tool (in this case, Paint and Brushes panels) open automatically.

Figure 1.38 Click the Toggle Related Panels button to close and open the related panels.

IMPORTING FOOTAGE INTO A PROJECT

Think of an After Effects project as a musical score. Just as a score refers to instruments and indicates how they should be played, your project lists the files you want to use and how you want to use them. The project contains neither the sources nor the end result, any more than a sheet of music contains a tuba or a recording of the concert. For this reason, a project file takes up little drive space.

Source files, on the other hand, consume considerably more storage. You need both the project and the source files to preview or output your animation, just as a composer needs the orchestra to hear a work in progress or, ultimately, to perform it in concert. Nonlinear editing systems (such as Adobe Premiere Pro and Apple Final Cut Pro) also work by referring to source files. Thus, if you're familiar with those programs, you have a head start on the concept of using file references in a project.

In this chapter, you'll learn how to create a project and import various types of footage. The chapter covers the specifics of importing still images, motion footage, audio, and even other projects. In fact, After Effects ships with a number of astonishingly useful preset project templates. And that's not all: After Effects arrives accompanied by a full-fledged asset management program, Adobe Bridge.

Don't be intimidated by the length or depth of the chapter. Importing different types of footage into your project is a simple and straightforward process. As you go through the chapter, take just what you need. As you begin to incorporate a wider range of formats in your work, revisit sections to learn the idiosyncrasies of those particular formats. To revisit the musical metaphor, if a project is like a score, start by composing for an ensemble, and then build up to an orchestra.

Starting from the Welcome Screen

When you launch After Effects CS4, you'll be greeted by a screen proclaiming, "Welcome to Adobe After Effects." Here you can get to work, get inspired, or get up to speed.

In other words, from the Welcome screen you can open or initiate a project, open a preset template via Adobe Bridge, or explore Adobe's online information resource, the Design Center. The Welcome screen also preserves an After Effects institution, the "Tip of the Day"—and it even lets you search for tips.

The Welcome screen appears only when you start up After Effects; at other times, you can open it via a menu command. Apart from using the Welcome screen, you can start and open projects and templates using the methods described later in this chapter.

To choose a Welcome screen option:

1. Launch After Effects CS4.
   The Welcome to Adobe After Effects screen appears (**Figure 2.1**).

2. In the Welcome screen, select any of the following.

   Recent Projects—Provides one-click access to projects you've worked on most recently

   New Composition—Prompts you to specify settings for a composition in a new project

   Design Center—Opens Adobe's After Effects Design Center Web page (a resource for tutorials, blogs, and the like) in your default Web browser

   Browse Templates—Opens Adobe Bridge (CS4's asset management software) and navigates to After Effects project templates

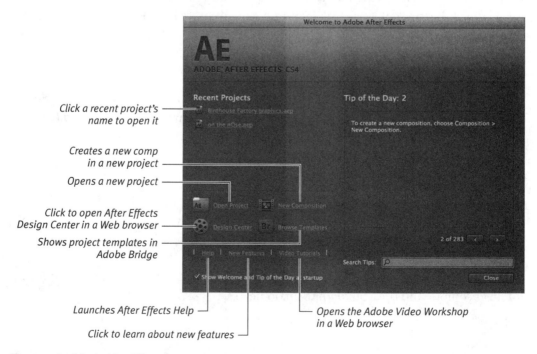

Click a recent project's name to open it

Creates a new comp in a new project

Opens a new project

Click to open After Effects Design Center in a Web browser

Shows project templates in Adobe Bridge

Launches After Effects Help

Click to learn about new features

Opens the Adobe Video Workshop in a Web browser

Figure 2.1 By default, After Effects starts up with a Welcome screen, where you can get to work, get inspired, or get up to speed.

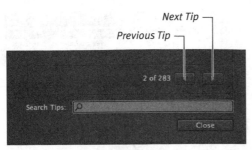

Next Tip
Previous Tip

Figure 2.2 Step through each tip by clicking the previous tip and next tip buttons...

Figure 2.3 ...or search tips by entering a keyword in the Search field.

Figure 2.4 Clicking the Show Welcome and Tip of the Day at Startup check box to deselect it prevents the Welcome screen from appearing when you startup After Effects.

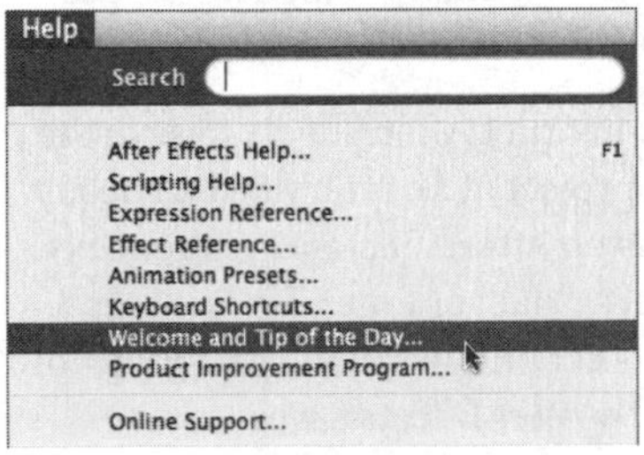

Figure 2.5 To make the Welcome screen appear any time after startup, choose Help > Welcome and Tip of the Day.

Help—Launches After Effects Help

New Features—Opens the Web page describing After Effects CS4's new features in your Web browser

Video Tutorials—Opens the Adobe Video Workshop in your Web browser

To view the Tip of the Day:

◆ In the Welcome screen, *do any of the following:*

▲ To view the previous tip, click the left arrow button.

▲ To view the next tip, click the left arrow button (**Figure 2.2**).

▲ To search for a tip relevant to a particular topic, type a keyword in the Search field.

The number of tips that can be viewed using the Previous and Next buttons are limited to those relevant to the keyword you entered (**Figure 2.3**).

▲ To clear a search, click the search field's Clear Search button ⊠.

To disable the Welcome screen:

◆ In the Welcome screen, select the Show Welcome and Tip of the Day at Startup check box to disable it (**Figure 2.4**).

Thereafter, launching After Effects opens a new, untitled project without opening the Welcome screen.

To enable the Welcome screen:

1. Launch After Effects, then choose Help > Welcome and Tip of the Day (**Figure 2.5**).

The Welcome screen appears.

2. In the Welcome screen, select the Show Welcome and Tip of the Day at Startup check box.

The Welcome screen appears the next time you launch After Effects.

Creating and Saving Projects

Creating a project is especially simple in After Effects, which doesn't prompt you to select project settings. Instead, you'll be prompted to specify settings for each composition within the project—as you'll see in Chapter 4, "Compositions."

You save After Effects projects as you would save a file in just about any program. But to more easily track changes to your work, you can instruct After Effects to save each successive version of a project using an incremental naming scheme.

Although you don't have to actively specify project settings when you start a project, you can change the default values at any time by choosing File > Project Settings. In the Project Settings dialog, you can change the project's time display style, the sample rate at which audio is processed, and color settings—which includes a color depth setting as well as color management options. You can find out more about these settings in After Effects Help.

To create a new project:

◆ With After Effects running, choose File > New > New Project (**Figure 2.6**).

If a project is open, After Effects prompts you to save it. Otherwise, a new Project panel appears (**Figure 2.7**).

To save using incremental project names:

◆ After the project has been saved, choose File > Increment and Save, or press Command-Option-Shift-S (Ctrl-Alt-Shift-S).

After Effects saves a copy of the project, appending a number to the filename that increases incrementally with each successive Increment and Save command.

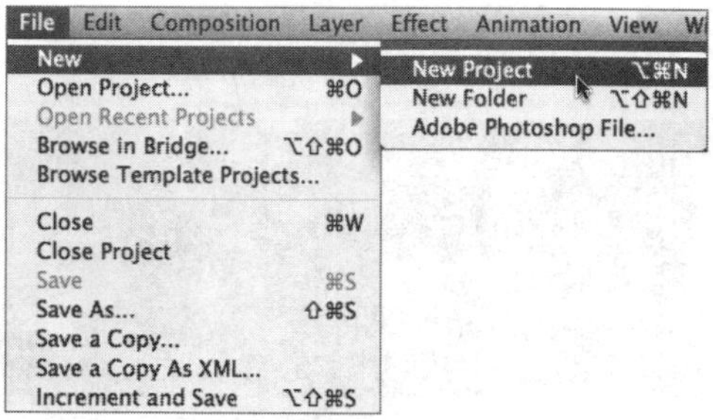

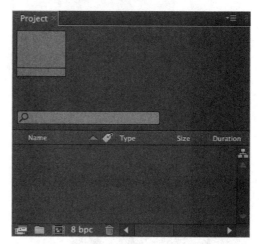

Figure 2.6 Choose File > New > New Project.

Figure 2.7 A new, untitled Project panel appears.

✔ Tips

■ A project's name appears at the top of the main application window, not the Project panel. When a project has unsaved changes, an asterisk (*) appears next to the project's name.

■ You can instruct After Effects to save the current project at an interval you specify by choosing After Effects > Preferences > Auto-Save (Mac) or Edit > Preferences > Auto-Save (Windows) and specifying how frequently After Effects saves.

■ As you might expect, the File menu also includes Save, Copy, and Revert to Last Saved commands.

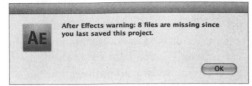

Figure 2.8 After Effects alerts you if it can't locate source files.

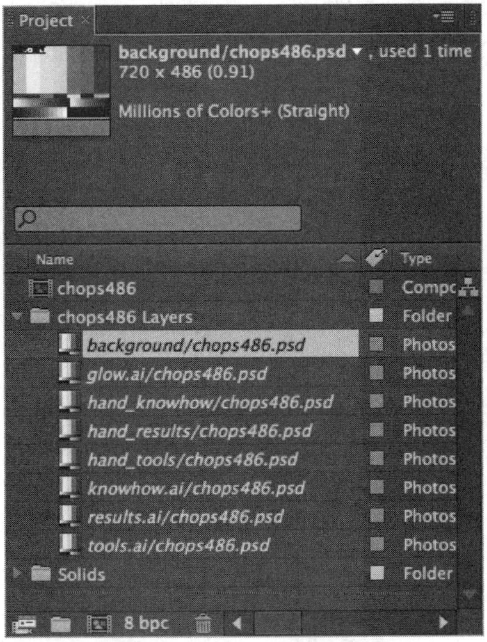

Figure 2.9 The names of missing footage items appear in italics, and the source footage is temporarily replaced by a color bar placeholder.

Opening and Closing Projects

In After Effects, you can have only one project open at a time. Opening another project closes the current project. However, closing the Project panel doesn't close the project; it merely removes the Project panel from the workspace.

As you learned in this chapter's introduction, an After Effects project contains footage items that refer to files on your system. When you reopen a project, After Effects must locate the source files to which each footage item refers. If After Effects can't locate a source file, the project considers it missing (**Figure 2.8**). (In Adobe Premiere Pro and other nonlinear editing programs, missing footage is called *offline*.) The names of missing footage items appear in italics in the Project panel (**Figure 2.9**), and a placeholder consisting of colored bars temporarily replaces the source footage. You can continue working with the project, or you can locate the source footage. For more about missing source footage, see Chapter 3, "Managing Footage."

✔ Tips

■ To open a project you worked on recently, choose File > Open Recent Projects and choose the name of the project in the submenu.

■ With After Effects running, press Shift-Command-Option-P (Shift-Ctrl-Alt-P) to open the most recently opened project (think *p* for *previous project*).

■ You can open projects and project templates, and browse tips and online resources from After Effects' Welcome screen, as described in the section, "Starting from the Welcome Screen," earlier in this chapter.

Importing Files

After Effects allows you to import a wide variety of still images, motion footage, and audio, as well as projects from After Effects and Adobe Premiere Pro. The procedures for importing footage are essentially variations on a theme, so you should get the hang of them quickly.

Although you may be tempted to speed through some sections in this part of the chapter, make sure you understand how the methods differ for each file type. Depending on the file, you may need to invoke the Interpret Footage dialog, which contains special handling options, such as how to set the duration of stills or the frame rate of motion footage. The Interpret Footage dialog also lets you properly handle other aspects of footage, such as the alpha channel, field order, and pixel aspect ratio. If you're already familiar with these concepts, go directly to the numbered tasks; if not, check out the sidebars in this chapter for some technical grounding.

You'll find that you can often use several methods to import footage: menu bar, keyboard shortcuts, or context menu. You can even drag and drop from the desktop. Once you know your options, you can choose the method that best fits your needs or preferences.

The maximum resolution for import and export is 30,000 × 30,000 pixels. However, the PICT format is limited to 4,000 × 4,000 pixels and BMP to 16,000 × 30,000 pixels.

As you've already learned, After Effects lets you import images with 16 and 32 bits per channel (bpc) —an indispensable capability if you're doing high-end work.

The maximum image size and bit depth are limited by the amount of RAM available to After Effects (see the sidebar "Wham, Bam—Thank You, RAM").

After Effects supports an extensive and growing list of file formats. Third-party plug-ins can also expand the possibilities.

Choosing the Color Bit-Depth Mode

The Project Settings dialog also allows you to set the color bit-depth mode. In addition to supporting standard 8 bits-per-channel (bpc) images, After Effects Pro lets you process images using 16 and even 32 bpc.

This means that not only can your images have higher color fidelity from the start, but they also retain that quality even after repeated color processing (for example, from transfer modes and effects).

But naturally, greater precision comes at a cost. For example, processing color in 16 bpc is twice as demanding as processing it in 8 bpc—that is, doing so requires twice the RAM and processing time. To save time, you may want to work in 8 bpc initially and then switch to 16 bpc when you're ready for critical color processing.

Although you can set the bit depth from the Project Settings dialog, it's more convenient to toggle the bit-depth mode by Option/Alt-clicking the bit depth display in the Project panel.

Figure 2.10 Choose File > Import > File, or File > Import > Multiple Files.

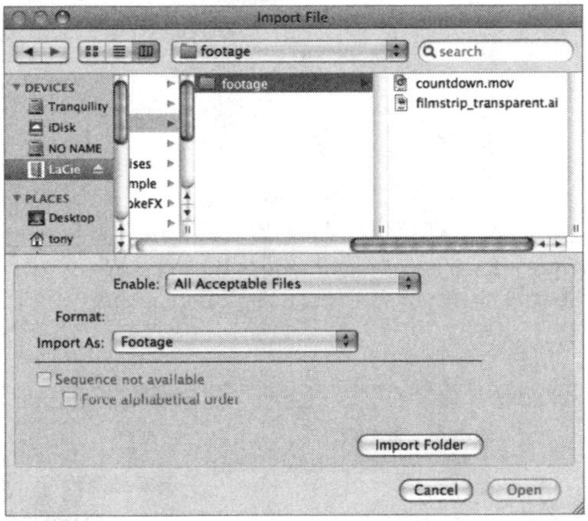

Figure 2.11 The Import File or Import Multiple Files dialog appears.

To import a file or files:

1. *Do one of the following:*

▲ Choose File > Import > File to import one item.

▲ Choose File > Import > Multiple Files to import several items (**Figure 2.10**).

The Import File or Import Multiple Files dialog appears (**Figure 2.11**).

continues on next page

Wham, Bam—Thank You, RAM

Here's the formula for calculating how much RAM an image requires:

Width in pixels x height in pixels × 4 bytes = RAM needed to display image

So, the largest file allowed would require 3.35 GB of RAM (30,000 × 30,000 × 4 bytes)—ouch!

A tall image used as an end credit roll for video output provides a less extreme example, as you can see:

$720 \times 30{,}000 \times 4$ bytes = 82.4 MB of RAM.

IMPORTING FILES

2. To expand or reduce the list of files, choose an option for Enable (**Figure 2.12**):

All Files—Enables all files in the list, including files of an unrecognized file type

All Acceptable Files—Enables only file types supported by After Effects

All Footage Files—Enables only files that can be imported as footage items and excludes otherwise acceptable file types (such as After Effects or Adobe Premiere Pro project files)

Adobe Premiere Pro, Dynamic Link, Adobe Soundbooth, and so on—Enables only files of the same file type you select

Enabled files can be selected for import, whereas other files are unavailable and appear grayed out.

3. In the Import File or Import Multiple Files dialog, choose Footage from the Import As pop-up menu.

To import files as compositions or to import projects, see the "Importing a Layered File as a Composition" and "Importing Adobe Premiere Pro and After Effects Projects" sections later in this chapter.

4. Select the file you want to import and click Open (**Figure 2.13**).

To select a range of files in the same folder, click the file at the beginning of the range to select it, Shift-click the file at the end of the range, and then click Open.

To select multiple noncontiguous files in the same folder, Command/Ctrl-click multiple files, and then click Open.

Figure 2.12 To expand or reduce the list of files, specify an option in the Enable pop-up menu.

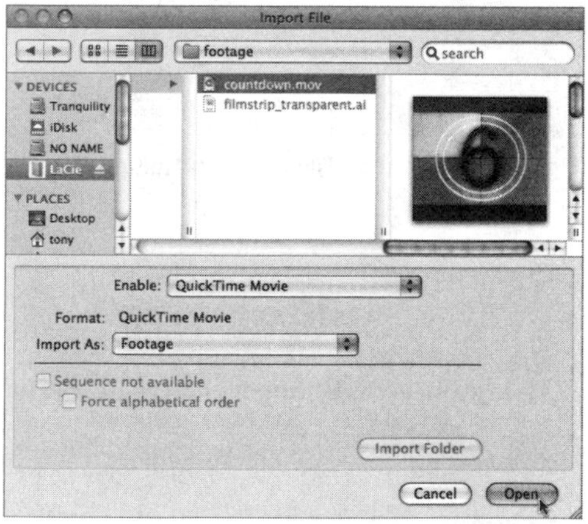

Figure 2.13 Select the file or files you want to import and click Open.

Figure 2.14 After you've selected multiple files to import, click Done to close the dialog.

Figure 2.15 Imported files appear in the Project panel.

5. If prompted, specify other options for each file you import (such as its alpha channel type or how to import a layered file).

The options for particular file types are discussed later in this chapter.

6. If you chose to import multiple files in step 1, repeat the subsequent steps until you've imported all the files you want to use; then, click Done to close the Import Multiple Files dialog (**Figure 2.14**).

The file(s) appear as item(s) in the Project panel (**Figure 2.15**).

✔ Tips

■ Double-clicking in an empty area of the Project panel is a great shortcut for opening the Import File dialog.

■ Adobe Bridge (covered later in the section "Importing with Adobe Bridge") provides yet another convenient way to browse for files to import.

■ You import audio-only files into an After Effects project just as you would any other file. Video footage that has audio can be imported as a single footage item.

Importing Still-Image Sequences

Many programs (including After Effects) can export motion footage not as a single movie file, but as a series of still images, or a *still-image sequence*. You can import all or part of a still-image sequence as a single motion footage item.

To import a still-image sequence:

1. Make sure all the still-image files in the sequence follow a consistent numeric or alphabetical filename pattern and are contained in the same folder.

2. In After Effects, choose File > Import > File. The Import File dialog appears.

3. *Do either of the following:*

   ▲ To import the entire sequence as a single motion footage item, select the first file in the sequence.

   ▲ To import part of the sequence as a single motion footage item, select the first file in the range, and then Shift-click the last file in the range.

4. Select the box for the Sequence option (**Figure 2.16**).

   The Import File dialog automatically indicates the file format for the Sequence check box. If you specified a limited range of files in the sequence to import, the dialog also displays the range next to the Sequence check box.

5. Click Open to import the file sequence and close the dialog.

   The image file sequence appears as a single footage item in the Project panel (**Figure 2.17**).

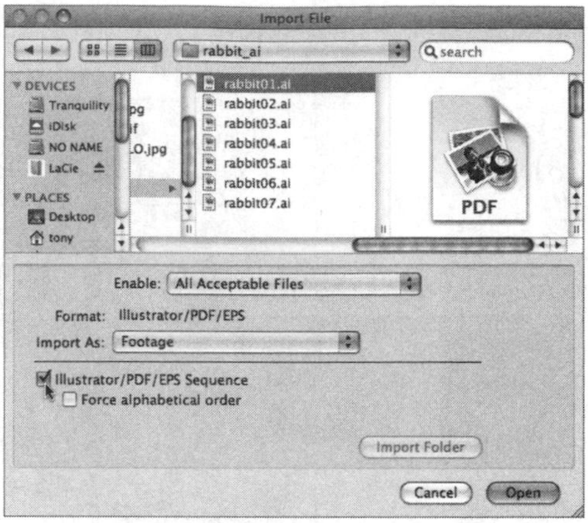

Figure 2.16 In the Import dialog, select the first image in the sequence, and select the Sequence option.

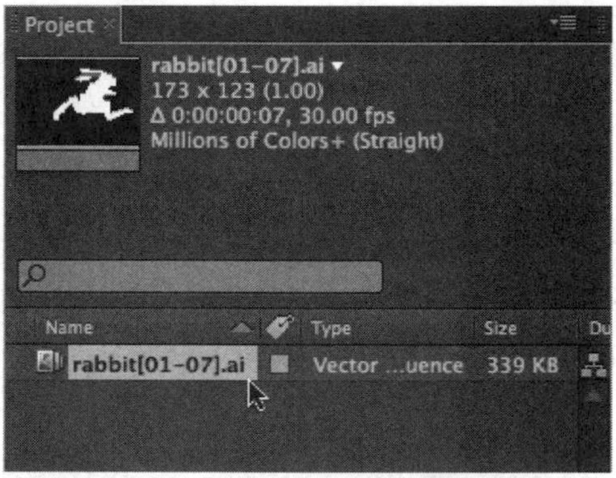

Figure 2.17 The image sequence appears in the Project panel as a single item.

✔ Tips

■ By default, a still image sequence's frame rate matches the project's frame rate. You can change the default interpretation of an image sequence's frame rate by choosing After Effects > Preferences > Import (Edit > Preferences > Import).

■ You can change an image sequence's (or any motion footage's) frame rate using the Interpret Footage dialog. See the section, "Setting a Footage Item's Frame Rate," later in this chapter for details.

Figure 2.18 Misinterpreting the type of alpha channel results in an unwanted halo or fringe around objects. Note the dark fringe around the letters and the darkness in the transparency.

Figure 2.19 Click the Interpret Footage button.

Importing Files with Alpha Channels

When you import a file containing an alpha channel, After Effects tries to detect a label (encoded in the file) that indicates whether the alpha is straight or premultiplied and then processes, or *interprets*, it accordingly. If the alpha is unlabeled, After Effects opens the indispensable Interpret Footage dialog, where you can specify how the alpha channel should be interpreted.

If its alpha channel is interpreted incorrectly, the footage may appear with an unwanted black or white halo or fringe around the edges of objects (**Figure 2.18**). Don't worry, you can reinterpret the footage item afterward by invoking the Interpret Footage dialog yourself.

To set the alpha channel interpretation for a file in a project:

1. In the Project panel, select a file containing an alpha channel and then click the Interpret Footage button 🖿 (**Figure 2.19**).

continues on next page

The Interpret Footage dialog appears (**Figure 2.20**).

2. In the Alpha section of the Interpret Footage dialog, choose an interpretation method (**Figure 2.21**).

Ignore—Disregards transparency

Straight – Unmatted—Assumes a straight alpha, which defines transparency by the alpha channel only

Premultiplied – Matted With Color—Assumes a premultiplied alpha, which blends RGB channels with a background color in transparent areas

Guess—Attempts to automatically detect the file's alpha channel type.

If the options are grayed out, the footage doesn't contain an alpha channel.

3. Click OK to close the Interpret Footage dialog.

✔ Tips

■ By default, After Effects prompts you to choose how it should interpret footage containing an unlabeled alpha channel. Alternatively, you can instruct After Effects to always interpret unlabeled alpha channels using the method you specify in the Import pane of the Preferences dialog. Choose After Effects > Preferences > Import (Mac) or Edit > Preferences > Import (Windows) to access these options.

■ You can reverse an image's opaque and transparent areas by selecting the Invert Alpha check box in the Alpha area of the Interpret Footage dialog.

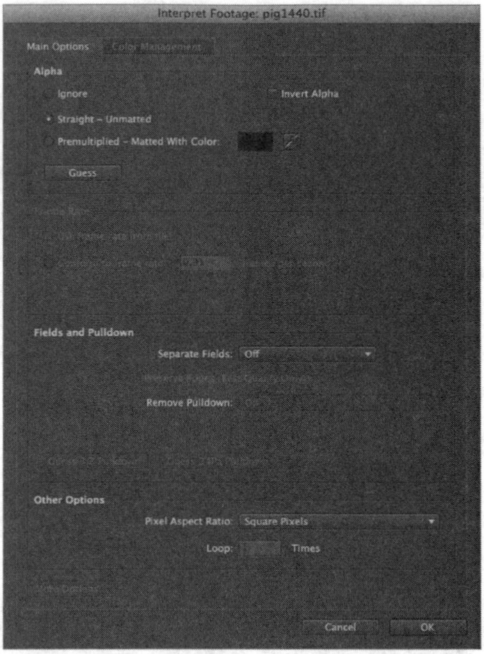

Figure 2.20 The Interpret Footage dialog appears.

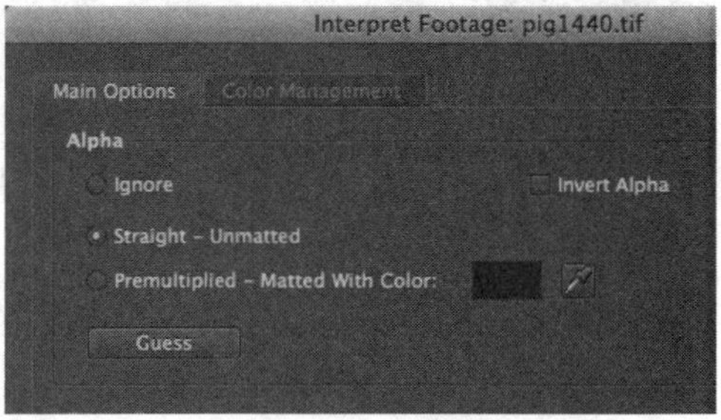

Figure 2.21 Choose an alpha channel interpretation method from the Interpret Footage dialog.

Straight and Premultiplied Alpha Channels

A file's transparency information can be saved in two ways: as straight alpha or as premultiplied alpha. Both types store transparency information in an alpha channel. But in a file with a premultiplied alpha channel, the visible channels also take transparency into account. In semitransparent areas (including smooth edges), the RGB channels are mixed—or *multiplied*—with the background color (usually black or white).

If the type of alpha is interpreted incorrectly, the transition between opaque and transparent areas may be marred by an unsightly fringe or halo.

The type of alpha channel present in a file depends on the program used to save it. In most cases, After Effects can detect and interpret it automatically. Otherwise, it treats the alpha channel according to the setting specified in the Import pane of the Preferences dialog:

Ask User—Prompts you to choose an interpretation method each time you import footage with an unlabeled alpha channel

Guess—Attempts to automatically detect the file's alpha channel type (if After Effects can't make a confident guess, it beeps at you)

Ignore Alpha—Disregards the alpha channel of imported images

Straight (Unmatted)—Interprets the alpha channel as straight alpha

Premultiplied (Matted With Black)— Interprets the alpha channel as premultiplied with black

Premultiplied (Matted With White)— Interprets the alpha channel as premultiplied with white

Importing a Layered File as a Single Footage Item

When you import a layered Photoshop or Illustrator file as a footage item, you can either import all the layers as a single merged item or import layers individually. Importing the merged file results in a footage item with the same dimensions as the source file (**Figure 2.22**).

However, when you import individual layers, you have a choice. You can import a layer at the document's dimensions so that the layer appears as it did in the context of the other layers (**Figure 2.23**). You can also choose to use the layer's dimensions—that is, the size of the layer only, regardless of the document's size (**Figure 2.24**).

When importing a Photoshop layer that has layer styles, you can specify whether to merge the layer styles into the footage or to ignore them.

After Effects can also import all the layers assembled just as they were in Photoshop or Illustrator; you'll learn that technique in the section "Importing a Layered File as a Composition," later in this chapter.

Figure 2.22 You can import a layered file so that the layers are merged into a single footage item that uses the source document's dimensions.

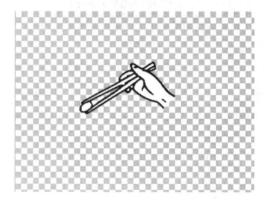

Figure 2.23 You can also import an individual layer using either the dimensions of the document (in this case, 720 x 486)...

Figure 2.24 ...or the minimum dimensions to contain the layer's image (this layer is 228 x 142).

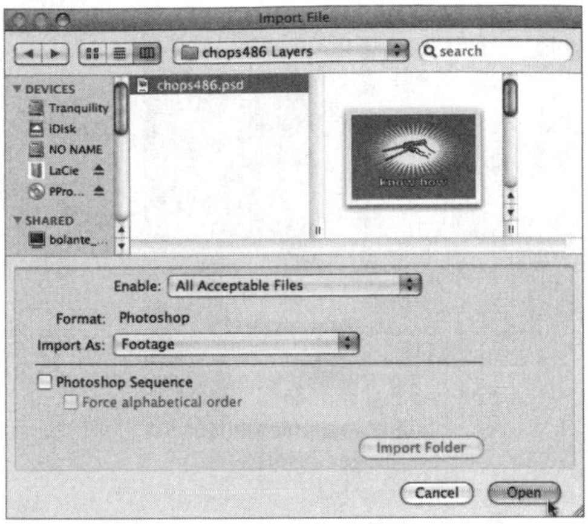

Figure 2.25 In the Import File dialog, locate a Photoshop or Illustrator file and be sure Footage is selected in the Import As pop-up menu.

To import a Photoshop or Illustrator file or layer as a single footage item:

1. Choose File > Import > File.

   The Import File dialog appears.

2. Locate and select a Photoshop or Illustrator file.

3. Make sure Footage is selected in the Import As pop-up menu, and then click Open (**Figure 2.25**).

   The Import Photoshop/Illustrator dialog appears. The dialog has the same name as the file you're importing.

4. In the dialog's Import Kind pop-up menu, make sure Footage is selected.

Photoshop Styles, Text, and 3D

After Effects retains practically every aspect of Photoshop files, including text and layer styles (such as drop shadow, inner glow, and so on). Initially, text and layer styles aren't fully editable—but you can remedy that with a simple menu command. Once you make Photoshop text a full-fledged After Effects text layer, you can employ all of After Effects' typesetting and text animation capabilities (covered in Chapter 12). By making layer styles After Effects–native, you can modify and animate layer styles as you would any other layer property (covered in Chapter 7).

In After Effects' timeline, select the layer that contains text imported from Photoshop and choose Layer > Convert to Editable Text. Similarly, you can select a layer that uses Photoshop layer styles and choose Layer > Layer Styles > Convert to Editable Styles.

Similarly, you can have After Effects recognize a Photoshop 3D layer on import, or convert it after the fact by selecting the layer and choosing Layer > Convert to Live Photoshop 3D. Whatever method you use, the layer will contain the Live Photoshop 3D effect, which allows the layer to be seen from the perspective of the comp's active camera.

5. In the Layer Options area, *do either of the following* (**Figure 2.26**):

  ▲ Choose Merged Layers to import all layers in the file as a single footage item in After Effects.

  ▲ Select Choose Layer. Then, in the pop-up menu, choose a layer to import.

6. If you chose a single layer in Step 5, specify the following options (**Figure 2.27**):

  Merge Layer Styles into Footage—Includes a Photoshop file's layer styles in the imported footage item under the property heading "Layer Styles"

  Ignore Layer Styles—Excludes a Photoshop file's layer styles from the imported footage item

  Layer Size—Imports the layer at its native size; choose this option when you plan to use the layer outside the context of the other layers in the file

  Document Size—Imports the layer using the frame size of the document that contains the layer; choose this option to maintain the layer's size and position relative to the document as a whole

7. Click OK to close the dialog.

  A footage item appears in the Project panel. When you import a single layer, the name of the footage item is the name of the layer followed by the name of the Photoshop or Illustrator file. When you import merged layers, the name of the footage item is the name of the Photoshop or Illustrator file (**Figure 2.28**).

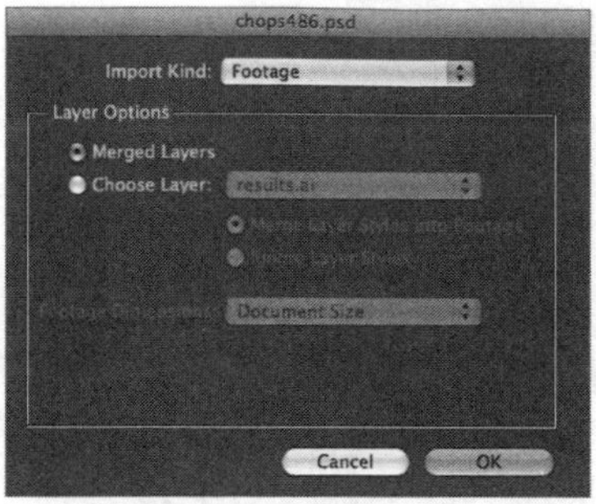

Figure 2.26 You can choose to import a single layer of a Photoshop or Illustrator file or to import merged layers.

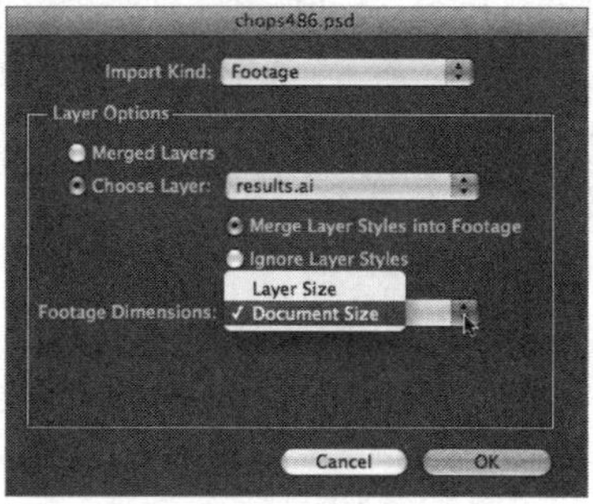

Figure 2.27 If you choose to import a single layer, specify whether to merge or ignore a Photoshop layer's layer style, and choose an option in the Footage Dimensions pop-up menu.

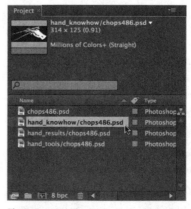

Figure 2.28 In the Project panel, single and merged Photoshop or Illustrator layers are clearly named.

LAYERED FILE AS A SINGLE FOOTAGE ITEM

Figure 2.29 After Effects can convert a layered file into a composition containing the same layers. This way, you can manipulate each layer individually in After Effects.

Figure 2.30 When you choose Composition-Cropped Layers, the imported footage includes the image only—in this case, the footage's dimensions are 314 x 125.

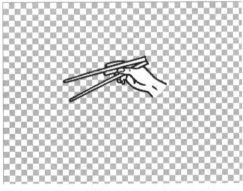

Figure 2.31 When you choose Composition, each layer uses the source document's dimensions—which, of course, match those of the imported composition. In this example, the source file's and comp's dimensions are 720 x 846.

Importing a Layered File as a Composition

One of After Effects' greatest strengths is its integration with other Adobe programs. This includes the ability to import a layered Photoshop or Illustrator file as a ready-made composition—which consists of footage items arranged in time and space. After Effects not only imports all the layers as footage items but also arranges the layers in a composition of the same dimensions. In essence, the composition replicates the layered file—suddenly transported into the world of After Effects (**Figure 2.29**).

As when you import layers separately (see "Importing a Layered File as a Single Footage Item," earlier in this chapter), you can choose whether the imported footage items (conveniently located in their own folder) use their native dimensions or share the new comp's dimensions (**Figures 2.30** and **2.31**).

To import an Adobe Photoshop or Illustrator file as a composition:

1. Choose File > Import > File.
   The Import File dialog appears.

2. Select an Adobe Photoshop or Illustrator file.

3. In the Import As pop-up menu, choose either of the following (**Figure 2.32**):

   Composition - Cropped Layers—Imports each source layer at its native size

   Composition—Imports each source layer at the document's size

4. Click Import.

5. If you are importing a Photoshop file, use the Layer Options dialog (**Figure 2.33**) to select the appropriate option:

   Editable Layer Styles—Accurately reproduces layer styles (such as blending options, drop shadow, and so on) and converts compatible styles into layer properties; however, layers may render more slowly and cannot intersect with a 3D layer.

   Merge Layer Styles into Footage—Layer styles are combined with the image; the image may render faster and intersect with 3D layers, but might not reproduce layer style effects as accurately.

   Live Photoshop 3D—Imports a Photoshop 3D layer as an After Effects 3D layer, viewed from the comp's active camera

   In the Project panel, the imported Photoshop or Illustrator file appears both as a composition and as a folder containing the individual layers imported as separate footage items (**Figure 2.34**).

✔ Tip

- After Effects imports Photoshop clipping groups as nested compositions within the main composition of the Photoshop file.

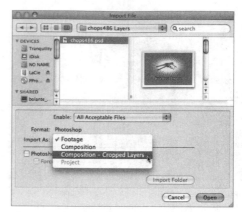

Figure 2.32 In the Import As pop-up menu of the Import File dialog, choose the appropriate option.

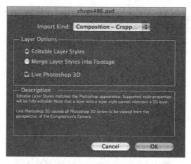

Figure 2.33 Specify your choices in the Layer Options dialog.

Figure 2.34 The Photoshop file appears both as a composition and as a folder containing individual layers.

Importing Adobe Premiere Pro and After Effects Projects

Because After Effects can import projects from Adobe Premiere Pro, it's simple to move work from Adobe's nonlinear editor for treatment in the company's advanced animation/compositing/effects program (and vice versa).

Each sequence in the Adobe Premiere Pro project appears in After Effects as a composition (in which each clip is a layer) and a folder of clips. In the composition, After Effects preserves the clip order, duration, and In and Out points, as well as marker and transition locations (**Figures 2.35** and **2.36**). Because Adobe Premiere Pro includes many After Effects filters, any effects shared by the two programs will also be transferred from Adobe Premiere Pro into After Effects—including their keyframes.

You'll learn more about compositions in Chapter 4, "Compositions"; more about keyframes in Chapter 7, "Properties and Keyframes"; and more about effects in Chapter 11, "Effects Fundamentals." For the moment, suffice it to say that you can easily integrate Adobe Premiere Pro's advantages in nonlinear editing with After Effects' superior compositing and effects features.

Similarly, you can import an After Effects project into your current project—a capability that makes it possible to combine work, create complex sequences as different modules, and repeat complex effects. All the elements of an imported After Effects project are contained in a folder in the current project.

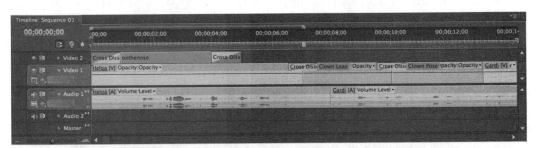

Figure 2.35 When you compare the Timeline panel of a Premiere project with one in After Effects...

Figure 2.36 ...you can see how clips translate into layers in the Timeline panel of After Effects.

To import an Adobe Premiere Pro project:

1. Choose File > Import > Adobe Premiere Pro Project.

   The Import Adobe Premiere Pro Project dialog appears.

2. Select a Premiere Pro project file (**Figure 2.37**) and then click Open.

   A Premiere Pro Importer dialog appears.

3. Select the Premiere Pro sequences you want to import as compositions (**Figure 2.38**).

4. To import the audio clips in the selected sequences as audio footage items, select Import Audio. Leave the option deselected to omit the audio.

   The Premiere Pro project appears in the Project panel as a composition. Clips appear as footage items, and bins appear as folders (**Figure 2.39**). An After Effects project appears in the Project panel as a folder containing compositions and footage items.

✔ Tips

- The Dynamic Link feature allows an After Effects project to appear as a clip in a Premiere Pro sequence and reflect any changes you make without an intermediate rendering step.

- You can embed any movie exported from After Effects with a *program link*—which is a link to the project that created it. This way, it's easy to reopen the project that created the movie. For more about embedding program links, see Chapter 17, "Output."

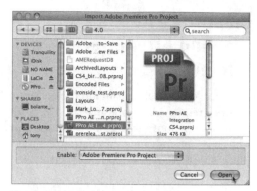

Figure 2.37 In the Import File dialog, locate an Adobe Premiere Pro project and click Open.

Figure 2.38 Specify the Premiere Pro sequences you want to import as compositions in After Effects and select whether you want to include audio.

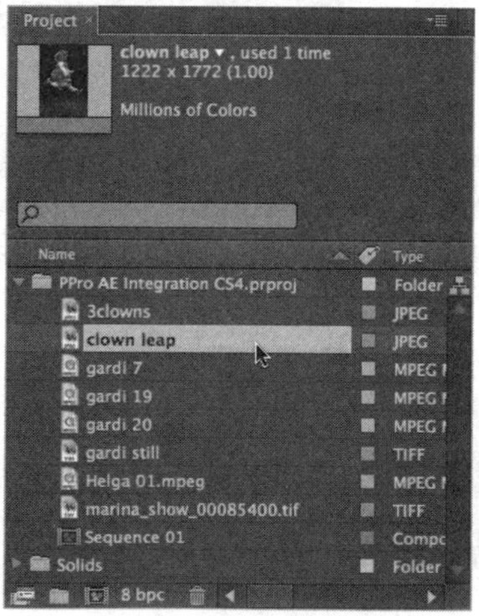

Figure 2.39 An imported Premiere Pro sequence appears in the Project panel as a composition. Clips appear as footage items, and bins appear as folders.

IMPORTING PROJECTS

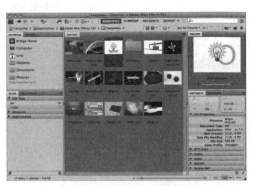

Figure 2.40 Adobe Bridge is a companion program that facilitates file management. It can help you locate and preview the file you need, including some inspiring project templates (shown here).

Importing with Adobe Bridge

Chances are, you've accumulated a seemingly countless number of assets on your hard disks. It can be a chore to find the one you need. Fortunately, After Effects and other Adobe programs ship with a companion program—a research assistant, if you will—called Adobe Bridge. Moreover, you can launch Adobe Bridge from within After Effects.

Adobe Bridge facilitates asset management by providing a convenient way to search for, sift, and preview files. Adobe Bridge also lets you see information embedded in the file, or *metadata*. You can even apply your own metadata, label, rating, and keywords to a file, adding ways to distinguish the needle from the rest of the haystack.

Adobe Bridge also provides a great access point to numerous preset project templates. Even if you don't use these ready-made projects as templates per se, they demonstrate useful techniques and provide inspiration for your own work (**Figure 2.40**).

Naturally, this book can't cover all the features of another full-fledged program; this section simply focuses on browsing and importing using Adobe Bridge. Fortunately, you should get the hang of Adobe Bridge's familiar and intuitive interface with a little experimentation and a quick visit to Adobe Bridge Help.

✔ Tip

- The Welcome screen in After Effects provides another convenient way to access the project templates folder; see the section, "Starting from the Welcome Screen," earlier in this chapter.

To import a file or project template via Adobe Bridge:

1. To launch Adobe Bridge for importing files and templates, *do either of the following:*

   ▲ To open any file, choose File > Browse.

   ▲ To navigate to the project templates folder directly, choose File > Browse Template Projects (**Figure 2.41**).

   After Effects launches its companion program, Adobe Bridge.

2. To navigate to the file you want to view, *do either of the following:*

   ▲ Use the navigation tools at the upper left of the Adobe Bridge window to select a disk volume or folder (**Figure 2.42**).

   ▲ Select an item in the Favorites or Folders tab (**Figure 2.43**).

   The selected item's content appears in Adobe Bridge's large main panel. You can also open a folder by double-clicking it in the main panel. (The appearance of items in the main panel depends on the position of the icon size and viewing mode, which you can set using controls at the lower right of the window.)

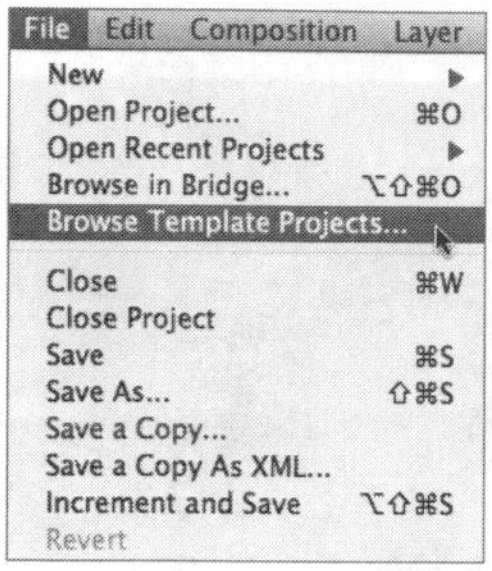

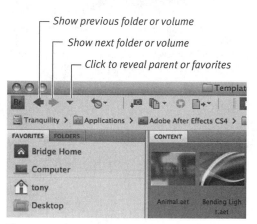

Figure 2.41 To find any file using Adobe Bridge, choose File > Browse; to go straight to the project templates, choose File > Browse Template Projects (shown here).

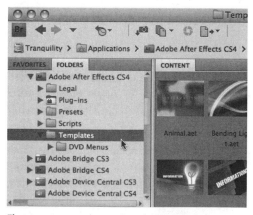

Figure 2.42 In Adobe Bridge, navigate using the browser-style navigation tools at the top of the window...

Figure 2.43 ...or select an item in the Favorites or Folders tab.

Figure 2.44 The selected item appears in the Preview tab; additional information appears in the Metadata and Keywords tabs.

3. To view a preview image and other information about the item, select the item.

The item's image appears in Adobe Bridge's Preview tab. Motion footage and templates include standard playback controls. The item's metadata and keywords appear in the corresponding tabbed areas (**Figure 2.44**).

4. In the main panel in Adobe Bridge, double-click the item you want to import (**Figure 2.45**).

After Effects may prompt you to specify options according to the type of item you import. The item appears in the After Effects Project panel (**Figure 2.46**).

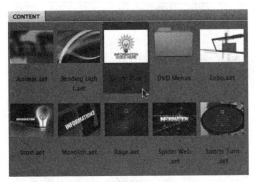

Figure 2.45 Double-clicking the item in Adobe Bridge's main panel...

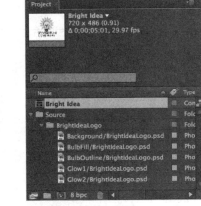

Figure 2.46 ...imports it into the After Effects project.

Motion Footage

The procedures for importing motion footage vary little from the procedures for importing other file types. But just as footage with alpha channels must be interpreted correctly, motion footage items possess unique attributes that must be processed properly. In the following sections, you'll use the Interpret Footage dialog to specify how After Effects handles frame rate, field order, and pixel aspect ratio. This way, you can avoid or correct some of the most common problems that arise from misinterpreting motion footage. You'll also use the Interpret Footage dialog to loop a footage item (without having to add it to a composition multiple times).You can also use the Interpret Footage dialog to remove 3:2 pulldown and 24P pulldown from video transferred from film, expand an item's luminance levels, and specify EPS options. The Interpret Footage dialog also includes Color Management options. For a detailed explanation of these more advanced settings, consult After Effects Help.

✔ Tips

■ Starting with After Effects CS4, you can access the Interpret Footage dialog via a button conveniently located in the Project panel.

■ In the sections to follow, you'll use the Interpret Footage dialog to help After Effects properly interpret a footage item's attributes. You can copy the settings from one footage item by choosing File > Interpret Footage > Remember Interpolation, and apply it to another item by selecting it and choosing File > Interpret Footage > Apply Interpolation.

■ If your final output is destined for computer display only (not video display) or if it will be displayed at less than full screen size, you should deinterlace the video before you import it. This will spare you from needing to separate fields in After Effects and from processing unnecessary information.

■ You can customize the rules After Effects uses to interpret footage automatically by modifying the `Interpretation Rules.txt` file (contained in the After Effects folder) in a text-editing program. This way, you can determine, for example, the default pixel aspect ratio applied to footage items of certain dimensions. For more information, see After Effects Help.

Setting a footage item's frame rate

Generally, you use the footage item's native frame rate, which also matches the frame rate of the composition. Sometimes, however, you'll want to specify a frame rate for a footage item manually.

Because features like time stretch (see Chapter 6, "Layer Editing") and time remapping (see Chapter 14, "More Layer Techniques") provide finer control over a layer's playback speed, it's more common to set the frame rate for image sequences than for movie files.

For example, some animations are designed to play back at 10 frames per second (fps). If you interpreted such a sequence to match a 30-fps composition, 30 frames would play back in 1 second—three times as fast as they were intended to play. Manually specifying a 10-fps frame rate for a still-image sequence of 30 frames would result in a duration of 3 seconds when played in a 30-fps composition.

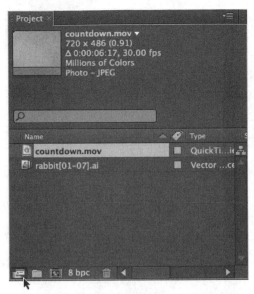

Figure 2.47 In the Project panel, select a footage item and click the Interpret Footage button.

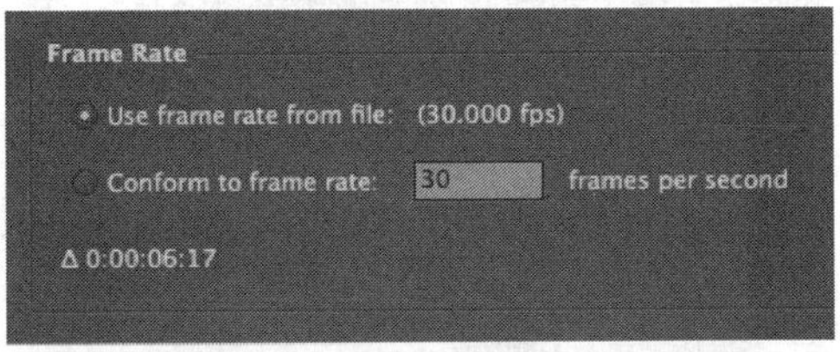

Figure 2.48 You can set motion footage to conform to a different frame rate. Note that the dialog uses the term conform when referring to motion footage.

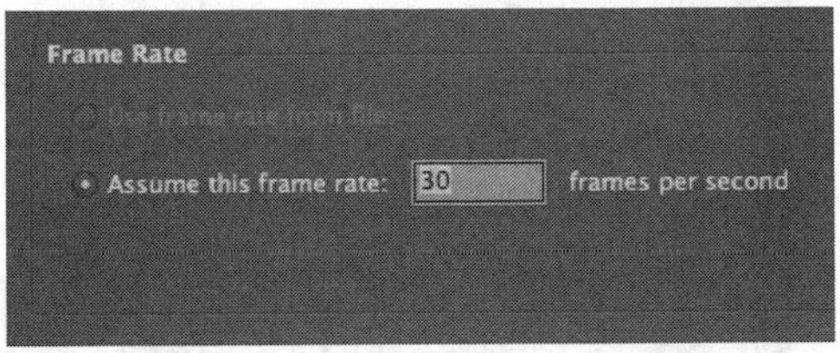

Figure 2.49 More often, you use the control to set the frame rate of still-image sequences. Note that the dialog says "Assume this frame rate" when interpreting still-image sequences.

Conversely, many programs can't render interlaced video frames. Sometimes animators choose to render 60 fps, which can be interpreted at a higher frame rate and interlaced at output.

To set the frame rate for footage:

1. In the Project panel, select a footage item and then click the Interpret Footage button (**Figure 2.47**).

   The Interpret Footage dialog appears.

2. For motion footage, choose one of the following options in the Frame Rate section (**Figure 2.48**):

   Use frame rate from file—Uses the native frame rate of the footage item

   Conform to frame rate—Lets you enter a custom frame rate for the footage

   Using a frame rate that differs from the original changes the playback speed of the movie.

3. For image sequences, enter a frame rate next to "Assume this frame rate" in the Frame Rate section of the Interpret Footage dialog (**Figure 2.49**).

4. Click OK to close the Interpret Footage dialog.

✔ Tip

- To interpret 60-fps animation sequences for output as interlaced fields, enter 59.94 in the "Assume this frame rate" field and use the footage item in a full-frame, 29.97-fps composition. Be sure to field-render the output. See Chapter 16, "Complex Projects," for more about rendering compositions.

MOTION FOOTAGE

Interpreting interlaced video

Depending on the format, the vertically stacked lines of video are displayed using either a progressive scan or as interlaced fields. Simply put, progressive video displays each line of video in succession, from top to bottom. In contrast, interlaced video divides each frame into two fields, which contain every other line of the image. The playback device presents one field first, and then the other to complete the frame.

When you import interlaced video, After Effects must correctly interpret the field order to play back the video accurately. If the fields are presented in the wrong order, movement appears staggered.

To interpret fields in video footage:

1. In the Project panel, select an interlaced video or field-rendered footage item, then click the Interpret Footage button (**Figure 2.50**).

   The Interpret Footage dialog opens.

2. In the Fields and Pulldown section, select one of the following options from the Separate Fields pop-up menu (**Figure 2.51**):

   Off—After Effects won't separate fields. Use this option for footage that doesn't contain interlaced video fields.

   Upper Field First—The fields of upper-field dominant source files will be separated correctly.

   Lower Field First—The fields of lower-field dominant source files will be separated correctly.

3. Click OK to close the Interpret Footage dialog.

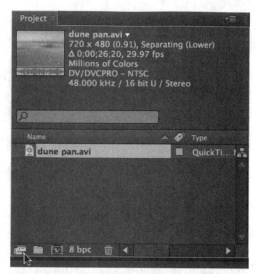

Figure 2.50 Select a footage item that uses interlaced video fields.

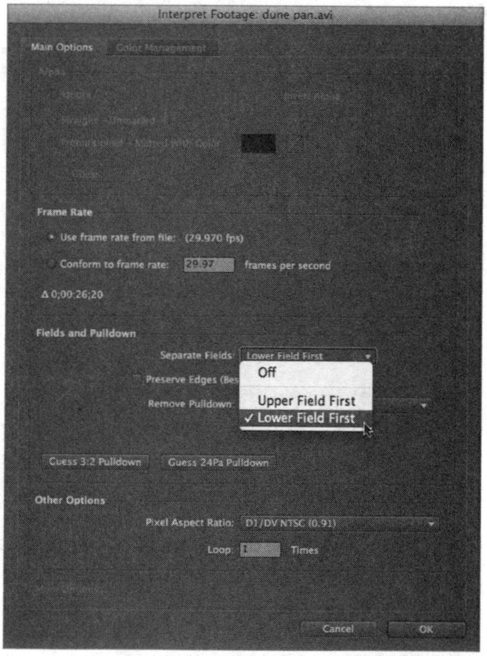

Figure 2.51 Choose the correct field dominance from the pop-up menu.

MOTION FOOTAGE

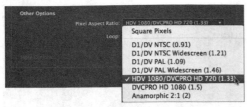

Figure 2.52 In the Interpret Footage dialog, choose the appropriate pixel aspect ratio. Most computer monitors use square pixels to represent an image with a 4:3 aspect ratio.

✔ Tips

■ Although After Effects usually sets the appropriate PAR automatically, it can be fooled. For example, if an image with a square PAR happens to have dimensions common to a format with nonsquare pixels, After Effects might interpret the PAR incorrectly.

■ To preview compositions that use nonsquare pixel aspect ratios without distortion, you can select the Pixel Aspect Correction button in the Composition panel.

■ After Effects CS4 uses more accurate PARs for standard definition formats than did previous versions. To update PAR values for projects created in After Effects CS3 and earlier, open the project in After Effects CS4 and choose File > Upgrade Pixel Aspect Ratios.

Pixel aspect ratios

In general, a video's image aspect ratio—the ratio of its width to height—is either 4:3 (standard), or 16:9 (widescreen). But the number of pixels required to achieve these dimensions varies, depending on the video format's pixel aspect ratio (PAR). For example, an image that uses square pixels (a 1:1 ratio, or PAR of 1) can create a 4:3 image that's 720 × 540 (go ahead, do the math). Yet D1 and DV footage use nonsquare pixels, so they create a 4:3 image that's 720 × 480 (a PAR of about .91). Treating an image that uses nonsquare pixels as though its pixels were square causes distortion.

After Effects sidesteps this problem by recognizing the image dimensions of common file formats and correctly interpreting their pixel aspect ratios. This lets After Effects use footage with different PARs without distorting the images. Even so, you may need to specify a footage item's PAR manually, using the handy Interpret Footage dialog.

To interpret the pixel aspect ratio:

1. In the Project panel, select a footage item, then click the Interpret Footage button.

    The Interpret Footage dialog appears.

2. In the Other Options section, choose the appropriate Pixel Aspect Ratio setting for your footage (**Figure 2.52**).

3. Click OK to close the Interpret Footage dialog.

    When you select the footage item in the Project panel, its PAR appears next to the thumbnail image.

MOTION FOOTAGE

Looping footage

Often, you need footage to loop continuously. Rather than add a footage item to a composition multiple times, you can set the footage item to loop using the Interpret Footage dialog.

To loop footage:

1. In the Project panel, select a footage item you want to loop and then click the Interpret Footage button.

   The Interpret Footage dialog appears (**Figure 2.53**).

2. In the Other Options section, enter the number of times you want the footage to loop (**Figure 2.54**).

   You can enter integers only for complete cycles, not decimals for partial cycles. When you add the footage item to a composition as a layer, its duration reflects the Loop setting.

✔ Tip

■ The Loop setting loops the content of the footage, not the movement of a layer—it's useful for turning an animation of two steps into a long walk, for example. You can't use this setting to repeat animated properties. For that, you'll need to use keyframes (Chapter 7) or expressions (Chapter 16).

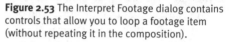

Figure 2.53 The Interpret Footage dialog contains controls that allow you to loop a footage item (without repeating it in the composition).

Figure 2.54 Enter the number of times you want the footage item to loop.

MANAGING FOOTAGE

As you saw in the previous chapter, the Project panel is essentially a list of all your footage items and compositions. The more complex the project, the lengthier and more unwieldy this list becomes. Fortunately, you can organize and sort what might otherwise become an overwhelming heap of assets using features in the Project panel—which includes several enhancements in After Effects CS4. If an item still isn't at your fingertips, you can find it with the Project panel's improved search capabilities.

In addition to using the Project panel, in this chapter you'll learn other aspects of asset management—such as how to replace missing footage and how to use placeholders and proxies to temporarily stand in for footage items. As always, taking a little time to prepare will save you a lot of time in the long run.

This chapter also introduces you to the Footage panel, which lets you not only see a footage item in a large viewer, but also magnify it, measure it with rulers and guides, overlay it with grids, and reveal its individual image channels. Most of the controls in the Footage panel are also found in the Composition and Layer panels, which means that learning how to use these controls now will go a long way toward providing the grounding you need later.

Displaying Information in the Project Panel

The Project panel (**Figure 3.1**) furnishes you with several ways to manage your footage items and compositions. Icons that resemble those used on the Mac OS desktop or in Windows Explorer provide an easy means of distinguishing between footage types. You can also view more detailed information about items in the Project panel, organize items into folders, and sort items according to categories. Depending on your needs, you can rearrange, resize, hide, or reveal the categories. And if you still need help locating an item, you can find it using the Project panel's new Search field.

To display information about a footage item or composition:

◆ In the Project panel, click a footage item to select it.

At the top of the Project panel, a thumbnail image of the footage item appears. Next to the thumbnail image, the name of the footage item appears, as well as information about the footage itself, such as frame size, color depth, codec, and so on (**Figure 3.2**).

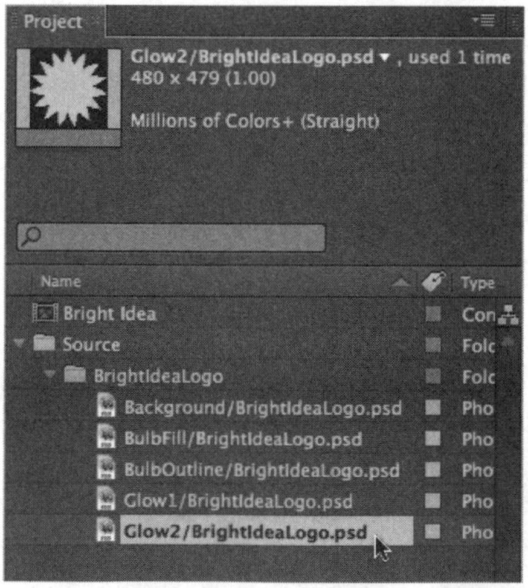

✔ Tips

■ By default, the thumbnail image displays transparency as black. To make transparent areas appear as a checkerboard pattern, choose Thumbnail Transparency Grid in the Project panel's pop-up menu.

■ Option-clicking (Alt-clicking) an item displays its file-type extension in addition to the usual information.

■ You can view additional information about a file or project in the new Metadata panel. Just select an item and choose Windows > Metadata.

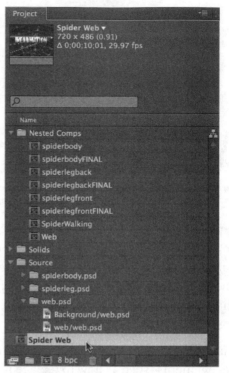

Figure 3.1 The Project panel doesn't simply list footage items and compositions; it also helps you identify, sort, and organize them.

Figure 3.2 When you select an item in the Project panel, information about the selected item appears at the top of the panel.

Figure 3.3 Entering all or part of the name of the item you're looking for in the Project panel's Search field...

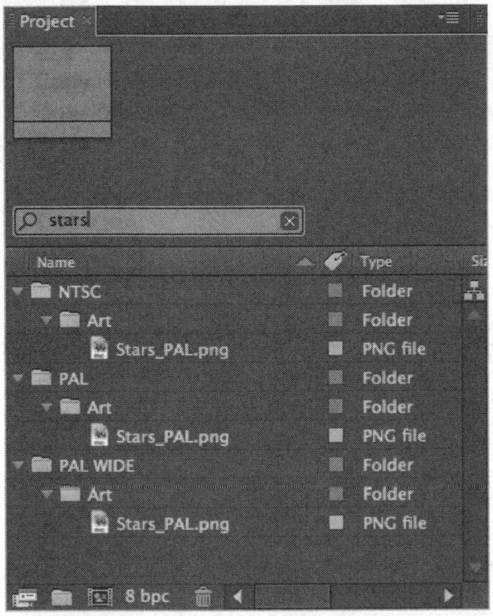

Figure 3.4 ...sifts the list to include only those items that match what you type.

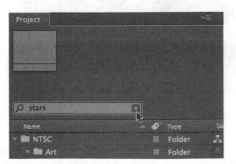

Figure 3.5 To unsift the list, click the Clear Search button (the X icon).

Finding Items in a Project

Starting with After Effects CS4, the Project panel includes a handy Search field to help you unearth items from your project that you've lost track of (or that you just want to find quickly). Using the Search field is faster and more convenient than using the Find button in earlier versions. Plus, it's consistent with the Search feature in the Timeline panel, Effects panel, and Tools panel (used for searching After Effects Help).

To find an item in the Project panel:

1. Enter all or part of the name of the item you're looking for in the Project panel's Search field (**Figure 3.3**).

   As you type, the items listed in the Project panel that don't match are hidden from view, leaving only matching items (**Figure 3.4**).

2. To unsift the Project panel and make all items visible, click the Clear Search button ⊠ in the Search field (**Figure 3.5**).

Sorting Footage in the Project Panel

By default, items in the Project panel are sorted by name, but you can sort the list by an assortment of other criteria, such as file type, size, duration, and so on. You can hide the column headings you don't want to use and rearrange their order. You can even assign a custom heading.

To sort footage items in the Project panel:

◆ In the Project panel, click a heading panel to sort the footage items according to the name, label 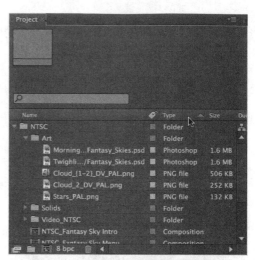, type, size, duration, comment, file path, or date (**Figure 3.6**).

By default, the Date column is hidden; you can make it visible by following the instructions in the following task.

To hide or display a heading panel in the Project panel:

1. In the Project panel, Control-click/right-click a column heading.

 A pop-up menu appears.

2. Choose an option:
 ▲ To hide the selected heading and corresponding column, choose Hide This (**Figure 3.7**). (This choice isn't available for the Name heading.)
 ▲ To hide any heading, choose Columns and a heading's name to deselect it (**Figure 3.8**).
 ▲ To show a hidden heading, choose Columns and a heading panel name to select it.

 Depending on your choice, you can hide or display headings and the columns beneath them (**Figure 3.9**).

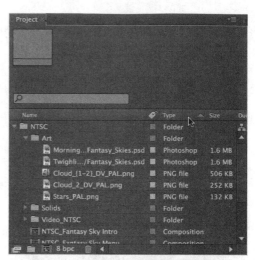

Figure 3.6 Click a heading panel to sort the items according to the information under the heading.

Figure 3.7 Choose Hide This to hide the selected heading panel.

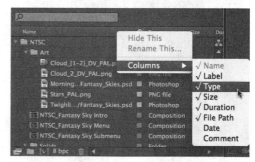

Figure 3.8 To hide a column, click a heading name to deselect it (in this case, the Type column).

Figure 3.9 The heading and the column beneath it are hidden from view.

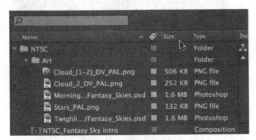

Figure 3.10 Drag the entire heading panel (in this case, for the Size column) to the right or left...

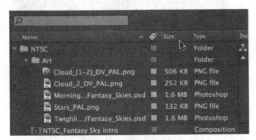

Figure 3.11 ...to change its relative position in the Project panel. Here, the Size column has been moved to the left of the Type column.

To reorder headings in the Project panel:

1. If necessary, resize the Project panel and make sure it displays the headings you want to rearrange.

2. Drag the heading to the right or left to change the relative position of the heading and column (**Figures 3.10** and **3.11**).

✔ Tips

- You can rename the Comment heading by Control-clicking (right-clicking) it and choosing Rename This in the pop-up menu.

- By default, each type of footage is associated with a color. You can sort items by color label, or reassign colors in the Label Defaults panel of the Preferences dialog. The timeline also represents layers using the color label.

SORTING FOOTAGE IN THE PROJECT PANEL

Organizing Footage in Folders

As you learned in Chapter 2, "Importing Footage into a Project," you can import an entire folder of files at once and the Project panel organizes the items automatically. But you can also create folders in the Project panel at any time and organize the items any way you see fit. Folders look and work much like they do on your operating system (particularly on the Mac's desktop). Clicking the triangle next to the folder's icon toggles the folder open and closed. The triangle spins clockwise to reveal the folder's contents in outline fashion; the triangle spins counter-clockwise to collapse the outline, hiding the folder's contents. However, the folder can't open in its own panel.

To create a folder in the Project panel:

1. In the Project panel, *do one of the following:*
   - ▲ Choose File > New > New Folder.
   - ▲ Click the Folder icon ▦ at the bottom (**Figure 3.12**).

   An untitled folder appears in the Project panel, with its name highlighted (**Figure 3.13**). If you accidentally lose the highlighting, make sure the folder is selected and press Return (Enter) to highlight the name again.

2. Type a name for the folder (**Figure 3.14**).

3. Press Return (Enter) to apply the name to the folder.

   The folder is sorted with other items according to the currently selected column heading.

Figure 3.12 Clicking the New Folder button at the bottom of the Project panel is the easiest way to create a new folder.

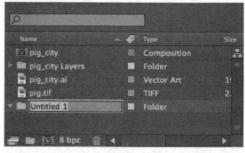

Figure 3.13 The new folder's name is highlighted.

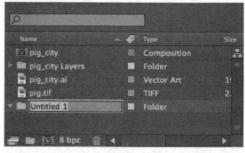

Figure 3.14 Type a new name, then press Return (Mac) or Enter (Windows).

Figure 3.15 Dragging selected items directly into a folder...

To organize footage items in folders:

In the Project panel, *do one of the following:*

◆ To move items into a folder, select and drag items into the folder (**Figures 3.15** and **3.16**).

◆ To move items out of a folder, select and drag items from the folder to the gray area at the top of the Project panel (**Figure 3.17**).

Figure 3.16 ...places the items in the folder.

Figure 3.17 To move items out of a folder, drag them from the folder to the top of the Project panel.

Renaming and Removing Items

You can rename any footage item in the Project panel. However, you'll notice that renaming items doesn't work quite like on your operating system; you have to use the Return (Enter) key.

Just as important as organizing the elements you need is disposing of the elements you don't need. You can remove individual items or have After Effects automatically discard the items that haven't been used in a composition.

To rename folders or compositions in the Project panel:

1. In the Project panel, select a folder or composition.

2. Press Return (Enter).

   The name of the item appears highlighted (**Figure 3.18**).

3. Enter a name for the folder or composition (**Figure 3.19**).

4. Press Return (Enter).

   The new name of the item is no longer highlighted and becomes the current name.

✔ Tip

■ You can also rename an item by Control-clicking (right-clicking) the item and choosing Rename from the pop-up menu. In After Effects CS4, a footage item's pop-up menu is more complete than in previous versions.

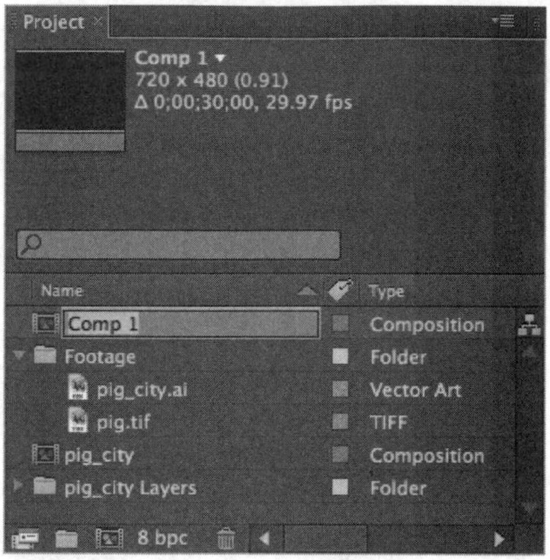

Figure 3.18 Select a folder or composition, press Return (Enter) to highlight its name...

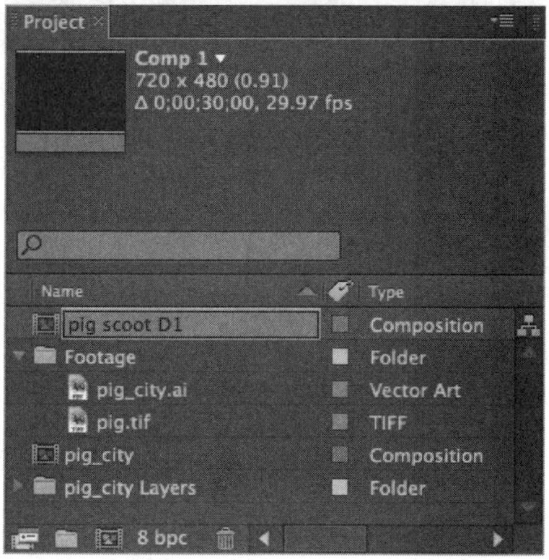

Figure 3.19 ...and then type a new name in the text box. Press Return (Enter) again to apply the new name.

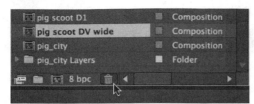

Figure 3.20 Click the Delete button at the bottom of the Project panel to delete selected items.

Are you sure you want to delete Composition "pig scoot DV wide"?

AE

Cancel   Delete

Figure 3.21 After Effects warns you if you attempt to delete an item that is in use.

File Edit Composition Layer

New ▶
Open Project...   ⌘O
Open Recent Projects   ▶
Browse in Bridge...   ⌥⇧⌘O
Browse Template Projects...

Close   ⌘W
Close Project
Save   ⌘S
Save As...   ⇧⌘S
Save a Copy...
Save a Copy As XML...
Increment and Save   ⌥⇧⌘S
Revert

Import   ▶
Import Recent Footage   ▶
Export   ▶

Adobe Dynamic Link   ▶

Find   ⌘F

Add Footage to Comp   ⌘/
New Comp from Selection
Consolidate All Footage
Remove Unused Footage
Reduce Project
Collect Files...
Watch Folder...
Scripts   ▶

Create Proxy   ▶
Set Proxy   ▶
Interpret Footage   ▶
Replace Footage   ▶
Reload Footage   ⌥⌘L
Reveal in Finder
Reveal in Bridge

Project Settings...   ⌥⇧⌘K

Figure 3.22 Choose File > Remove Unused Footage to remove items that aren't used in a composition.

To remove items from a project:

1. In the Project panel, select one or more items.

2. *Do one of the following:*
   ▲ Press Delete.
   ▲ Click the Delete button at the bottom of the Project panel (**Figure 3.20**).
   ▲ Drag the items to the Delete button at the bottom of the Project panel.

   If any of the items are compositions or are being used in a composition, After Effects asks you to confirm that you want to delete the items (**Figure 3.21**).

3. When After Effects prompts you to confirm your choice, click Delete to remove the footage from the project or Cancel to cancel the command and retain the footage in the project.

   The footage is removed from the project and all compositions in the project.

To remove unused footage from a project:

◆ Choose File > Remove Unused Footage (**Figure 3.22**).

   All footage items that aren't currently used in a composition are removed from the project.

✔ Tip

■ Other commands aid in project housekeeping, especially as a project nears completion. Consolidate All Footage removes duplicate items; Reduce Project removes deselected comps and unused footage; and Collect Files copies the project's requisite files to a single location for archiving or moving to another workstation.

RENAMING AND REMOVING ITEMS

Proxies

A *proxy* is a low-resolution version of the actual footage (**Figure 3.23**). If you're familiar with nonlinear editing applications, you might compare using proxies to using low-quality clips for offline editing (the rough cutting phase, which often utilizes relatively low-quality copies of footage). Low-quality files take less time to process, allowing you to work more quickly. Proxies may also be necessary if you have to work on a less powerful workstation—one with less RAM, for example—than you'll finish on. When you're ready, you can replace the low-quality stand-ins with the high-quality original footage.

Icons next to each item in the Project panel provide an easy way to determine whether source footage or its proxy is currently in use (**Figure 3.24**). A box containing a filled square ■ indicates that the proxy is currently in use; the name of the proxy appears in bold text. An empty box □ indicates that a proxy has been assigned but that source footage is currently in use. If there is no icon, this means no proxy has been assigned to the footage item.

Proxies aren't effective for every circumstance, however. Although they can save time when you're animating motion, other effects—such as keying—can be properly adjusted only when you're using the footage at output quality.

Figure 3.23 Low-quality proxies (top) don't look as good as the actual footage (bottom), but they have smaller file sizes and can be processed faster.

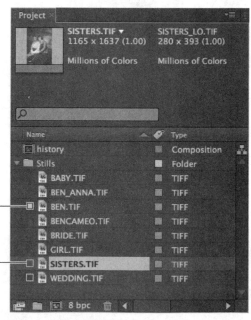

Figure 3.24 Icons indicate whether a proxy is in use or assigned to an item but not in use.

PROXIES

Figure 3.25 Choose File > Set Proxy > File to access the Set Proxy File dialog.

To assign a proxy to a footage item:

1. In the Project panel, select a footage item to which you want to apply a proxy.

2. *Do either of the following:*
   ▲ Choose File > Set Proxy > File.
   ▲ Control-click (right-click) the item, and choose Set Proxy > File in the pop-up menu (**Figure 3.25**).
   The Set Proxy File dialog appears.

3. Locate the file you want to assign as the proxy (**Figure 3.26**).

4. Click Open to select the file and close the dialog.
   In the Project panel, a Proxy icon appears next to the footage item, indicating that a proxy is currently in use (**Figure 3.27**).

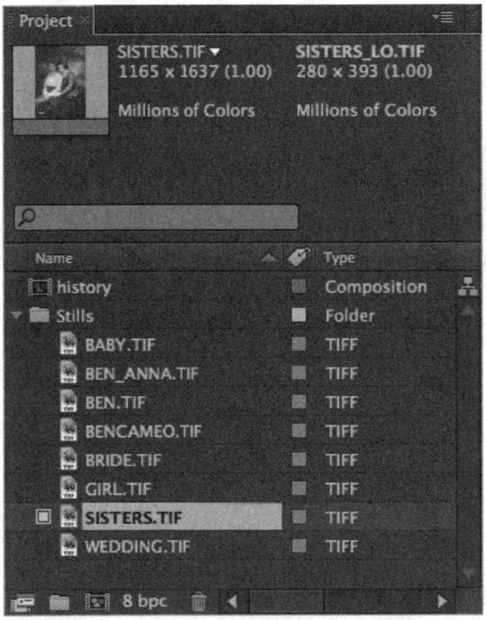

Figure 3.26 In the Set Proxy File dialog, choose a file to act as a proxy for the actual footage.

Figure 3.27 A filled box, the Proxy icon, appears next to the item, indicating that a proxy is in use.

To toggle between using a proxy and the original footage:

◆ In the Project panel, click the Proxy icon to the left of a footage item to toggle between using the assigned proxy and using the original footage (**Figure 3.28**).

To stop using a proxy:

1. In the Project panel, select a footage item that has been assigned a proxy.

2. *Do either of the following:*

   ▲ Choose File > Set Proxy > None.

   ▲ Control-click (right-click) the item, and choose Set Proxy > None in the pop-up menu (**Figure 3.29**).

   To the left of the footage item's name in the Project panel, the Proxy icon disappears.

✔ Tips

■ As pointed out in Chapter 2, After Effects automatically creates placeholders for missing footage. You can also create a placeholder manually, and then replace it with the actual footage item when it becomes available. You create placeholders by choosing File > Import > Placeholder.

■ You can create a proxy within After Effects by Control-clicking (right-clicking) a footage item and choosing Create Proxy > File or Create Proxy > Movie in the pop-up menu. Doing so places the item in a Render Queue and applies a preset template for exporting another version of the file that can serve as a proxy. For more about exporting, see Chapter 17, "Output."

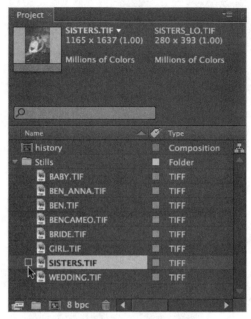

Figure 3.28 Click the Proxy icon to toggle between using the proxy and using the actual footage.

Figure 3.29 To stop using a proxy, choose File > Set Proxy > None.

Figure 3.30 Still images always open in a Footage panel.

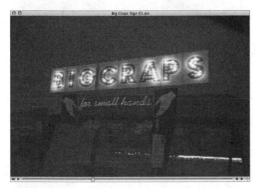

Figure 3.31 By default, motion footage opens in a panel according to the file type.

Viewing Footage

When you open a footage item in the Project panel, it appears either in an After Effects Footage panel or in the player native to its file type, depending on the file type and your preference.

Still images always open in an After Effects Footage panel. Movie footage (including audio-only files saved in a movie format), in contrast, opens in the appropriate media player by default. However, you can opt to open movie footage in an After Effects Footage panel instead.

Whereas a movie player window lets you play back motion and audio footage right away and at the full frame rate, the Footage panel relies on After Effects' frame rendering mechanism (explained fully in Chapter 8, "Playback, Previews, and RAM"). Therefore, the Footage panel won't necessarily play a movie at the full frame rate and won't play audio without rendering a preview. The Footage panel does offer a number of other viewing options (covered in the section "The Footage Panel," later in this chapter) and editing features (covered in Chapter 4, "Compositions").

Remember, the Footage panel is primarily for viewing purposes. Once a footage item becomes a layer in a composition, you use the Layer and Comp panels to arrange it in space and time, and to change its other properties.

To view a footage item:

◆ In the Project panel, double-click a footage item.

Still images open in a Footage panel (**Figure 3.30**); movie files open in the appropriate movie player (**Figure 3.31**).

To open a movie file in a Footage panel:

◆ In the Project panel, Option-double-click (Alt-double-click) a movie footage item.

The movie file opens in a Footage panel (**Figure 3.32**).

✔ Tip

■ You can open any footage item in its native application by choosing Edit > Edit Original. Any changes you make to it should be updated in After Effects. If this doesn't happen, choose File > Reload Footage.

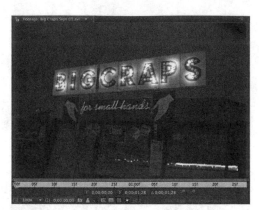

Figure 3.32 Option- or Alt-double-clicking motion footage opens it in a Footage panel.

The Footage Panel

A Footage panel has a variety of controls for viewing footage. As you might expect, it lets you play back and cue motion footage. You can magnify or reduce your view of the image, or see its individual channels. You can also show rulers, set guides, and superimpose a grid or video-safe zones. There is also a snapshot feature that lets you save and recall a frame of footage that you can use for reference (**Figure 3.33**).

As you'll see in the chapters to follow, you can also find all of these Footage panel controls in the Composition and Layer panels. If some of the controls don't seem useful now, be patient: They'll come in handy later.

The following sections cover these shared controls. Later chapters cover only the features unique to the Composition and Layer panels.

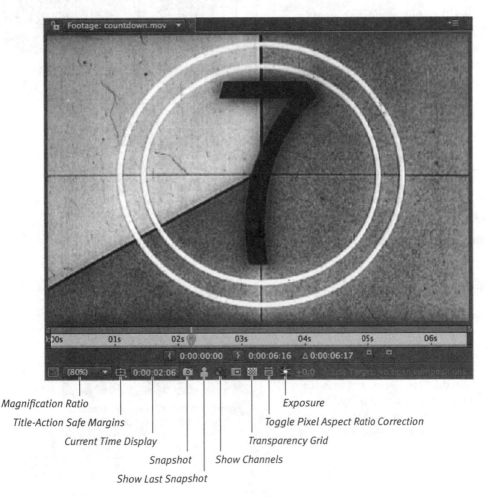

Magnification Ratio

Title-Action Safe Margins

Current Time Display

Snapshot

Show Last Snapshot

Show Channels

Transparency Grid

Toggle Pixel Aspect Ratio Correction

Exposure

Figure 3.33 The Footage panel shares several features with the Composition and Layer panels, including the snapshot feature.

THE FOOTAGE PANEL

Cueing Motion Footage

Motion footage appears in the Footage, Composition, and Layer panels with a time ruler, current time indicator (CTI), and current time display. You can use the controls to view a specific frame or to play back the footage without sound.

Figure 3.34 Drag the current time indicator to cue the footage to a particular frame.

To view a frame of motion footage by dragging:

◆ In the Footage panel, *do either of the following:*

▲ Click the point along the time ruler that corresponds to the frame you want to view.

▲ Drag the CTI to the point on the time ruler that corresponds to the frame you want to view (**Figure 3.34**).

The Footage panel displays the image at the current frame and the frame number.

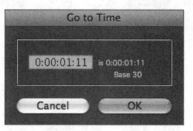
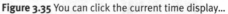

Figure 3.35 You can click the current time display...

To cue a frame of motion footage numerically:

1. In the Footage, Comp, or Layer panel, click the current time display (**Figure 3.35**).

2. Enter a time (**Figure 3.36**).

3. Click OK.

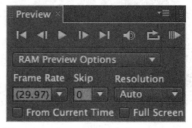

Figure 3.36 ...and enter a frame number in the Go to Time dialog.

To play and pause motion footage:

◆ Make sure the Footage, Composition, or Layer panel is active, and *do either of the following:*

▲ Press the Spacebar.

▲ Press the Play/Pause button in the Preview panel. For more on the Preview panel, refer to the "Setting the Time" section in Chapter 4.

Figure 3.37 The Preview panel provides a complete set of playback options.

Figure 3.38 Choose a magnification from the pop-up menu (shown here) or, with the mouse pointer over the viewer, change the setting with the mouse's scroll wheel.

Figure 3.39 The Footage panel displays the image at the magnification you specified.

Magnifying an Image

Sometimes, you'll want to magnify the image in the Footage, Layer, or Comp panel—the panel's viewer—so that you can closely examine details. Other times, you'll want to reduce magnification because viewing the image at 100 percent takes up too much screen space. After Effects lets you change the magnification ratio to suit your needs. However, keep in mind that this is for viewing purposes only: The actual scale of the footage doesn't change. You may be surprised to discover that no matter how much you magnify a viewer's image, scroll bars don't appear. To see different parts of a magnified image, use the Hand tool ✋.

To change the magnification of a viewer:

◆ *Do either of the following:*

▲ In the Footage, Comp, or Layer panel, press and hold the Magnification Ratio pop-up menu button to choose a magnification (**Figure 3.38**).

▲ Position the mouse pointer over a viewer's image and use the mouse's scroll wheel to change the magnification setting.

When you release the mouse button, the Footage panel uses the magnification ratio you selected (**Figure 3.39**).

To change the visible area of a magnified image in a viewer:

1. Select the Hand tool by *doing either of the following*:

   ▲ In the Tools panel, click the Hand tool (**Figure 3.40**).

   ▲ With the Selection tool active (the default tool), position the mouse pointer over the image in the Footage or Composition panel and press the spacebar.

   The mouse changes to the Hand icon 👋 (**Figure 3.41**).

2. Drag the hand to change the visible area of the image (**Figure 3.42**).

✔ Tip

■ The Comp panel includes controls not found in the Footage or Layer panels, including a control for setting the comp's viewing resolution. In After Effects CS4, changing a comp's magnification setting automatically makes a corresponding change in its resolution. You can set the magnification and resolution settings to operate independently in the Display pane of the Preferences dialog. See the section "Specifying Composition Settings" in Chapter 4.

Figure 3.40 In the Tools panel, select the Hand tool...

Figure 3.41 ...or position the Selection tool over the image and press the spacebar to toggle it to the Hand tool.

Figure 3.42 Use the Hand tool to drag the image and move other areas into view.

Figure 3.43 Use the Grid and Guides pop-up menu to specify whether to view video-safe zones or grids.

Figure 3.44 You can view Title Safe and Action Safe zones...

Figure 3.45 ...a proportional grid...

Viewing Safe Zones and Grids

You can superimpose a grid or video-safe zones over an image to better judge the placement of objects in the image. Displaying grids in a Layer or Comp panel can help you align elements or keep them within the viewable area of the screen. Obviously, these simple visual guides aren't included in the final output.

To show video-safe zones and grids:

◆ In the Footage, Comp, or Layer panel's Grid and Guides pop-up menu, choose the options you want (**Figure 3.43**):

  Title/Action Safe (Figure 3.44)

  Proportional Grid (Figure 3.45)

  Grid (Figure 3.46)

  You can display any combination of zones and guides at the same time.

✔ Tip

■ You can change the video-safe zones from the standard setting and change the color, style, and spacing of grid lines in the Grid & Guides pane of the Preferences dialog.

Figure 3.46 ...or a standard grid.

VIEWING SAFE ZONES AND GRIDS

Displaying Rulers and Guides

Like Adobe Photoshop and Illustrator, After Effects lets you view rulers as well as set guides to help you arrange and align images. As usual, you can change the zero point of the rulers and toggle the rulers and guides on and off.

To toggle rulers on and off:

Do either of the following:

◆ In a Footage, Comp, or Layer panel's Grid and Guides pop-up menu, choose Rulers (**Figure 3.47**).

◆ With a Footage, Composition, or Layer panel active, press Command-R (Ctrl-R) to toggle the rulers on and off.

To set the zero point of rulers:

1. If the rulers aren't visible, make them visible using one of the techniques described in the previous task.

2. Position the pointer at the crosshair at the intersection of the rulers in the upper-left corner of the Footage, Composition, or Layer panel.

   The pointer becomes a crosshair (**Figure 3.48**).

3. Drag the crosshair into the image area.

   Horizontal and vertical lines indicate the position of the mouse (**Figure 3.49**).

4. Release the mouse to set the zero point (**Figure 3.50**).

   The rulers use the zero point you selected.

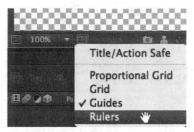

Figure 3.47 The Grid and Guides pop-up menu also lets you toggle rulers.

Figure 3.48 When you position the pointer at the intersection of the rulers, it becomes a crosshair symbol.

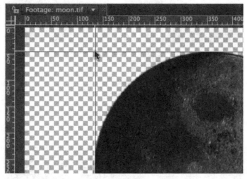

Figure 3.49 Drag the crosshair at the intersection of the rulers into the image area...

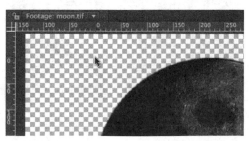

Figure 3.50 ...and release to set the zero point of the rulers.

Figure 3.51 Click and drag from a ruler into the image area to add a guide.

✔ **Tips**

■ You can hide, lock, clear, and have objects snap to guides by choosing the appropriate command in the View menu.

■ You can customize the default settings for safe zones, grids, and guides in the Grids & Guides pane of the Preferences dialog.

■ In the Comp panel, the Grid and Guides pop-up menu includes a 3D Reference Axes option. For more about 3D features, see Chapter 15, "3D Layers."

To reset the zero point of the rulers:

◆ Double-click the crosshair at the intersection of the horizontal and vertical rulers.

The rulers' zero point is reset to the upper-left corner of the image.

✔ Tip

■ Need to know the exact ruler coordinates of the mouse pointer? Just look in the Info panel.

To set guides:

1. If the rulers aren't visible, make them visible by pressing Command-R (Ctrl-R).

2. Position the pointer inside the horizontal or vertical ruler.

The pointer changes into a Move Guide icon ↔ or ↕.

3. Drag the mouse into the image area (**Figure 3.51**).

A line indicates the position of the new guide.

4. Release the mouse to set the guide.

To reposition or remove a guide:

Do one of the following:

◆ To reposition the guide, drag it to a new position.

◆ To remove the guide, drag it off the image area.

Viewing Snapshots

As you work, you'll often need to closely compare different frames. In After Effects, you can take a snapshot of a frame to store for later viewing. Then, with the click of a button, you can temporarily replace the current image in a Footage, Composition, or Layer panel with the snapshot image. The snapshot doesn't really replace anything; it's just used for quick reference—like holding a shirt up to yourself in a mirror to compare it with the one you're wearing. Toggling between the current frame and the snapshot makes it easier to see the differences.

To take a snapshot:

1. In a Footage, Comp, or Layer panel, cue the footage to the frame you want to use as a reference snapshot.

2. Click the Snapshot button ▢ (shown in **Figure 3.52**), or press Shift-F5.

   The current frame becomes the snapshot, and the Show Last Snapshot button ▢ becomes available.

To view the most recent snapshot:

1. If necessary, cue the footage to the frame you want to compare to the snapshot (**Figure 3.53**).

2. Click and hold the Show Last Snapshot button, or press F5.

   The panel displays the snapshot (**Figure 3.54**); when you release the mouse, the panel displays the current frame.

✔ Tips

- If a panel uses a different aspect ratio than that of the snapshot, the snapshot is resized to fit into the panel.

- Snapshots are stored in memory. If After Effects requires the memory that is used by a snapshot, it will discard the snapshot.

Figure 3.52 Click the Snapshot button to store the current image as a snapshot.

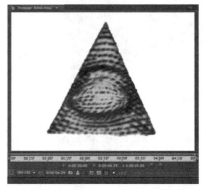

Figure 3.53 Cue to a new frame...

Figure 3.54 ...and then press and hold the Show Last Snapshot button to replace the current image temporarily with the snapshot. Release the Show Last Snapshot button to see the current frame again.

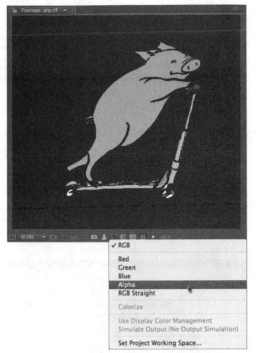

Figure 3.55 Click the Show Channel button and select the channel you want to view.

Figure 3.56 Choose Alpha to see the alpha channel.

Viewing Channels

The Footage, Composition, and Layer panels allow you to view the individual red, green, blue, and alpha channels of an image. Color channels appear as grayscale images in which the degree of white corresponds to the color value. You can also view the color channel using its own color. The alpha channel appears as a grayscale image as well, where the degree of white corresponds to opacity. You can even view the unmultiplied color channels—that is, the color channels without the alpha taken into account.

To show individual channels:

1. In a Footage, Composition, or Layer panel, click the Show Channel button ▦, and then choose the channel you want to view (**Figure 3.55**):

   RGB ▦—Shows the normal image with visible channels combined.

   Red ▦, **Green** ▦, or **Blue** ▦—Shows the selected channel as a grayscale.

   Alpha ▦—Shows the alpha channel (transparency information) as a grayscale. If active, the transparency grid is disabled while Alpha is selected (**Figure 3.56**). See the next section, "Viewing Transparency."

   RGB Straight ▦—Shows the unmultiplied RGB channels. The transparency grid is disabled while RGB Straight is selected.

2. To show the selected channel depicted in color, select Colorize.

   The Channel pop-up menu's icon changes according to the current selection.

✔ Tip

■ The Show Channel button's pop-up menu also includes options for color management. You can find out more about color management in After Effects Help.

Viewing Transparency

In the Footage panel, transparency always appears as black (**Figure 3.57**). However, if the black background isn't convenient, you can toggle the transparent areas to appear as a checkerboard pattern, or *transparency grid* (**Figure 3.58**).

Like many of the other buttons in the Footage panel, the Toggle Transparency Grid button is also available in the Layer and Composition panels. However, in those panels, you can set the background to any color. The next chapter revisits viewing transparency and other unique aspects of the Composition panel.

To toggle the transparency grid:

◆ In the Footage, Composition, or Layer panel, click the Toggle Transparency Grid button (**Figure 3.59**).

When the Toggle Transparency Grid button is selected, transparent areas appear as a checkerboard pattern; when the button isn't selected, transparent areas appear black in a Footage panel. In a Composition or Layer panel, transparent areas appear as the color you set.

✔ Tip

■ The transparency grid is disabled whenever you select the Alpha or RGB Straight viewing option in the Channel pop-up menu (covered in the section "Viewing Channels," earlier in this chapter).

Figure 3.57 In the Footage panel, transparent areas of the image appear as black.

Figure 3.58 You can also make transparent areas appear as a checkerboard pattern, or transparency grid. This also works in the Composition and Layer panels.

Figure 3.59 Click the Toggle Transparency Grid button to toggle between showing transparent areas as black (in the Footage panel, or as the specified background color in the Composition panel) and showing them as a checkerboard pattern.

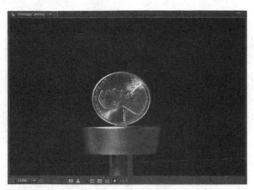

Figure 3.60 Because a DV image uses a PAR of approximately 0.91, it appears slightly squashed (or horizontally stretched) when displayed using square pixels.

Figure 3.61 The Layer, Composition, and Footage panels show an undistorted image...

Figure 3.62 ...when you click the Toggle Pixel Aspect Ratio Correction button.

Correcting for Pixel Aspect Ratios

In Chapter 2, you learned the importance of correctly interpreting an image's pixel aspect ratio (PAR) to prevent the image from appearing distorted. But because a typical computer's monitor displays pixels as square, even properly interpreted footage and comps that use a nonsquare PAR result in an image that looks distorted (**Figure 3.60**). Fortunately, After Effects can compensate for this distortion (**Figure 3.61**). As After Effects explains when you first use the Toggle Pixel Aspect Ratio Correction button, correcting the image this way is for viewing purposes only; it doesn't affect the image's actual scale.

To toggle pixel aspect correction:

1. In a Footage, Composition, or Layer panel, click the Toggle Pixel Aspect Ratio Correction button 🗔 to select it (**Figure 3.62**).

   If this is the first time you've used the button during this session, After Effects reminds you how PAR correction works and prompts you to specify whether you want to see the warning once per session or never again.

2. Select an option in the dialog, and click OK.

   If the image's PAR doesn't match your computer monitor's PAR, After Effects scales the image so that it no longer appears distorted.

Adjusting Exposure

Footage, Composition, and Layer panels have controls for the view's exposure. Just as increasing the exposure in a camera results in a brighter photograph, increasing the view's exposure value makes its image appear brighter. The exposure setting affects the view only. Even if you adjust it in a Layer or Comp panel, it won't affect the output image (to alter the output image, you need to add effects; see Chapter 11, "Effects Fundamentals"). However, the exposure setting does help you evaluate an image's brightness; it is particularly useful in identifying an image's brightest and darkest areas.

Figure 3.63 Changing a view's Exposure value doesn't alter the source or output image; it helps you evaluate its brightness. Here, increasing the Exposure identifies the darkest spots in the image. The Exposure icon turns yellow when you set a custom exposure.

To adjust a view's exposure:

◆ In a Footage, Composition, or Layer panel, set the Adjust Exposure value next to the Reset Exposure button ⬛.

Decreasing the value makes the image darker; increasing the value makes the image brighter (**Figure 3.63**). When you set the value to anything but 0, the Reset Exposure icon turns yellow.

To toggle exposure between a custom value and zero:

◆ In a Footage, Composition, or Layer panel, click the Reset Exposure button.

Clicking the button when its icon is yellow resets the exposure value to 0 (**Figure 3.64**) and the icon turns black. Clicking the button again sets the exposure value to the most recent custom setting and makes the icon yellow again.

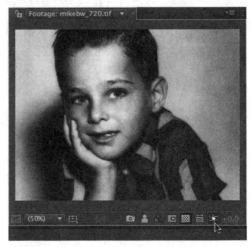

Figure 3.64 Clicking the Reset Exposure button toggles the image back to an exposure value of 0. Click it again to show the last custom setting.

COMPOSITIONS

Without compositions, a project is nothing more than a list of footage items—a grocery list without a recipe, an ensemble without choreography, finely tuned instruments without a musical score. This is because compositions perform the essential function of describing how footage items are arranged in space and time. This chapter shows you how to create a composition and define its spatial and temporal boundaries by setting frame size, frame rate, duration, and so on.

This chapter also describes the fundamental process of layering footage in compositions—and in so doing, lays the groundwork for the rest of the book, which focuses largely on how to manipulate those layers. The footage items you add to a composition become layers, which are manipulated in the defined space and time of the composition, as represented by Composition and Timeline panels. The following pages give you an overview of these panels as well as the Preview panel.

This chapter also introduces you to the idea of *nesting,* using comps as layers in other comps—a concept you'll appreciate more fully as your projects grow more complex.

Composition Settings

Because compositions describe how layers are arranged in space and time, you must define a composition's spatial attributes such as its frame size and pixel aspect ratio (PAR), as well as its temporal aspects such as its frame rate. Because frame size, PAR, and frame rate are defining characteristics of any output format, you might consider these comp settings to be fundamental. Other settings include the comp's viewing resolution, starting timecode, and duration.

A project usually contains several compositions, some of which are contained as layers (or *nested*) in a comp destined for export—the *final comp*. Although you would set a final comp's settings to match a particular output format (NTSC DV, for example), you might employ different settings (particularly for frame size and duration) for intermediate compositions.

When you create a comp, you must specify its attributes in a Composition Settings dialog, but you can change the settings whenever you want.

The Composition Settings dialog is divided into Basic and Advanced panels. With the exception of the comp anchor setting, the following sections focus on the basic settings, which are all you need to get started. Other advanced settings are addressed in later chapters, where they'll make more sense to you. And rest assured, you'll be reminded of the appropriate comp setting whenever a task or technique calls for it.

Figure 4.1 Click the Create Composition button at the bottom of the Project panel.

Figure 4.2 In the Composition Settings dialog, enter settings manually, or choose an option in the Preset menu.

Creating a Composition

A composition contains layers of footage and describes how you arrange those layers in space and time. This section explains how to create a composition; the following section describes how to choose basic settings to define a composition's spatial and temporal attributes.

To create a new composition:

1. *Do one of the following:*
   - ▲ Choose Composition > New Composition.
   - ▲ Press Command-N (Ctrl-N).
   - ▲ At the bottom of the Project panel, click the Create Composition button (**Figure 4.1**).

   A Composition Settings dialog appears (**Figure 4.2**).

2. For Composition Name, enter a descriptive title for the comp.

3. To set the comp's fundamental aspects, *do either of the following:*
   - ▲ In the Preset pop-up menu, choose the appropriate format for the comp.
   - ▲ Specify composition settings manually.

   Choosing a format from the Preset menu enters values for Width, Height, Pixel Aspect Ratio, and Frame Rate automatically; entering values manually sets the Preset menu to Custom. For more about settings, see "Specifying Basic Composition Settings," later in this chapter.

continues on next page

4. Choose a Resolution; then specify values for Start Timecode and Duration (**Figure 4.3**). Choosing a Preset does not specify these settings automatically. By default, these settings match those of the most recently created composition.

5. Click OK to close the Composition Settings dialog.

A new composition appears in the Project panel, and related Composition and Timeline panels open (**Figure 4.4**).

✔ Tips

■ It's easy to forget to name your composition or to settle for the default name, *Comp 1*. Do yourself a favor and give the composition a descriptive name. This will help you remain organized as your project becomes more complex.

■ Dragging a footage item to the Create Composition icon lets you create a comp in a single step, rather than two. The new composition uses the same image dimensions as the footage item it contains.

Figure 4.3 Specify a viewing Resolution, Start Timecode, and Duration.

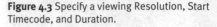

Figure 4.4 A composition appears in a Composition panel and a Timeline panel and as an icon in the Project panel (shown here).

Specifying Basic Composition Settings

In the Composition Settings dialog, you can select the settings that match video formats from a pop-up menu of presets. For a brief explanation of some common presets, see **Table 4.1**. Choosing a preset automatically enters the selected format's intrinsic attributes, including frame size, PAR, and frame rate. You just have to enter the composition name, viewing resolution, start timecode, and duration.

However, you don't always set a composition's settings to match an export format. To create an intermediate composition, for example, you might specify custom values for the following settings:

Width and Height—Enter values to set the comp's frame size (the viewing area of the Composition panel) in pixels. You may position layers outside the viewing area, but only layers within this frame are rendered for previews and export.

Lock Aspect Ratio to—Select this option to maintain the ratio of the Width and Height so that entering one value calculates the other value automatically.

Table 4.1

Common Composition Presets				
Frame Preset	**Frame Size**	**PAR**	**Frame Rate**	**Use**
NTSC DV	720 x 480	.91	29.97	DV standard for North America
NTSC D1	720 x 486	.91	29.97	Broadcast standard for North America
HDTV	1920 x 1080	1	24	High-definition standard using 16:9 image aspect ratio
Film (2k)	2048 x 1536	1	24	Film transfers
Cineon Full	3656 x 2664	1	24	Film transferred using the Cineon file format

Pixel Aspect Ratio—In the pop-up, choose the format you want the comp's pixel aspect ratio (or PAR) to match. An image's pixel aspect ratio is the ratio of each of its pixel's width to height and appears next to the format's name in parentheses. Square pixels have a PAR of 1:1, or simply 1. Other formats use nonsquare pixels, with various PARs. The DVCPro HD 720 format, for example, has a PAR of 1.33.

Frame Rate—Enter the number of frames per second (fps) displayed by the comp during playback. Usually, the frame rate you choose matches the frame rate of your output format.

Resolution—In the pop-up menu, choose the fraction of the comp's total number of pixels to be rendered in the Composition panel's viewer. The Full setting renders all the comp's pixels, ½ renders every other pixel, and so on. Smaller fractions reduce image quality and the time it takes to render the image. While you work, you can change a comp's resolution easily by using the Comp panel's Resolution pop-up menu. (Footage and Layer panels also include a Resolution pop-up menu.)

Start Timecode—Enter the number from which the time of the comp is counted. By default, a comp's time starts at 0, but you can set it to start at any number.

Duration—Enter the length of the composition. You can change a comp's duration at any time, lengthening it to accommodate more layers or cutting it to the total duration of its layers.

✔ Tips

- Individual footage items have their own frame rates, which you can interpret. (See "Setting a Footage Item's Frame Rate" in Chapter 2.) Ideally, the footage frame rate and the composition frame rate match. If they don't, After Effects gives the footage item the same frame rate as the composition.

- Whereas you can specify Start Timecode and Duration for each comp in the Composition Settings, you set the method used to count frames in all comps (for example, drop-frame timecode) in the Display pane of the Project Settings dialog. You can find the settings by choosing File > Project Settings.

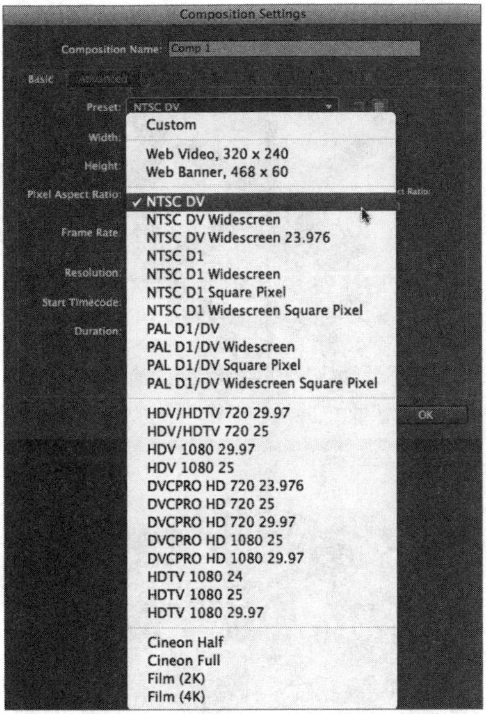

Figure 4.5 Choose an option from the Preset pop-up menu.

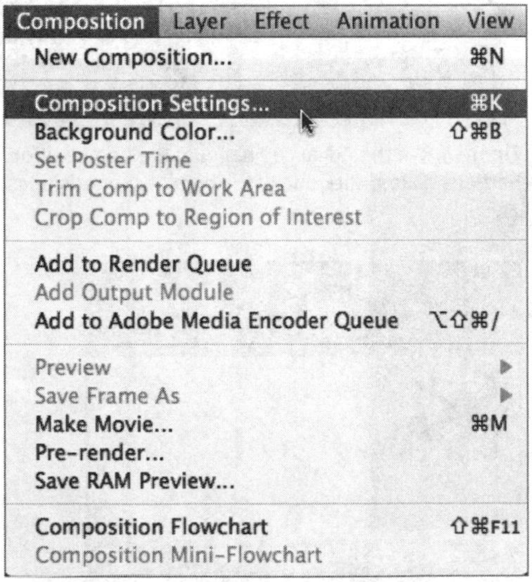

Figure 4.6 To change a comp's settings, select the comp and choose Composition > Composition Settings (or use the keyboard shortcut, Command-K [Ctrl-K]).

To select a composition preset:

1. In the Composition Settings dialog, choose an option from the Preset menu (**Figure 4.5**).

   Choose the preset that matches your needs. Presets include common settings for film, video broadcast, and multimedia projects.

2. Click OK to close the Composition Settings dialog.

   The composition appears in the Project panel.

To change a comp's settings:

1. Select a composition by clicking its icon in the Project panel or selecting its tab in the Timeline panel or its name in the Comp panel's viewer pop-up menu.

2. *Do either of the following:*

   ▲ Choose Composition > Composition Settings (**Figure 4.6**).

   ▲ Press Command-K (Ctrl-K).

   The Composition Settings dialog appears.

3. In the Composition Settings dialog, enter new values in the Basic and Advanced tabs and then click OK to close the dialog.

✔ Tips

■ To save custom settings as a preset, click the Composition Settings dialog's Save Preset button 🖫. To remove an unwanted preset from the list, select it and click the Delete Preset button 🗑.

■ You can restore the After Effects default presets by Option-clicking (Alt-clicking) the Delete button in the Composition Settings dialog.

Resizing a Comp

When you use a preset to create a comp, you probably won't go back to change any of its basic settings like the frame size, PAR, and frame rate. But it's not unusual to change a comp with custom settings, particularly its frame size. For example, you might find that you created a comp that's unnecessarily large, or too small to accommodate the layers that you need. If so, be sure to pay a visit to the Composition Settings dialog's Advanced tab. When you resize a composition, the Advanced tab's anchor setting determines how the layers are placed in the resized frame.

Figure 4.7 Before the composition is resized, it looks like this.

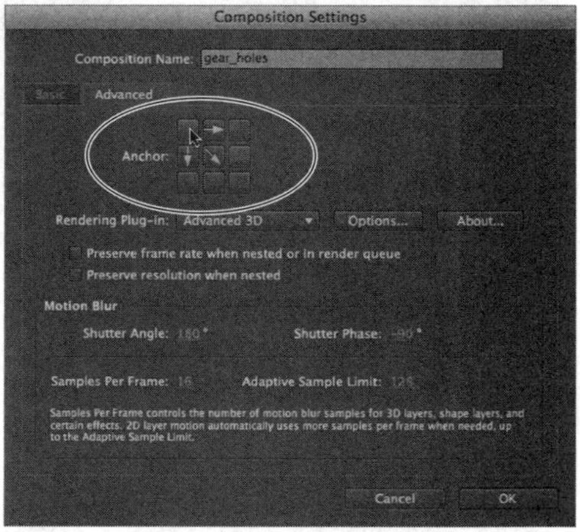

To set the anchor of a resized composition:

1. Select a composition and press Command-K (Ctrl-K) (**Figure 4.7**).

   The Composition Settings dialog appears.

2. To change the frame size of the composition, enter new values in the Width and Height fields.

3. Click the Advanced tab.

   The Advanced settings pane of the Composition Settings dialog appears.

4. In the Anchor control, click one of the nine anchor point positions (**Figure 4.8**).

Figure 4.8 In the Advanced panel of the Composition Settings dialog, click one of the nine anchor positions.

5. Click OK to close the Composition Settings dialog.

   The layers contained in the composition align to the position you specified (**Figure 4.9**).

✔ Tip

■ Don't confuse the composition's anchor with a layer's anchor point, which is something else altogether. See Chapter 7, "Properties and Keyframes," to learn about layer anchor points.

Figure 4.9 The layers are anchored to the position you specified in the resized comp.

Setting a Comp's Background Color

The default background color for compositions is black; however, you can change the background to any color you choose. Regardless of what color you make it, the background becomes transparent when you output the composition as a still-image sequence or a movie with an alpha channel. Similarly, if you use the composition as a layer in another composition, the background of the nested composition becomes transparent (**Figure 4.10**) (see "Nesting," in Chapter 16). And as with the Footage panel (see Chapter 3, "Managing Footage") and the Layer panel, you can also view the background as a checkerboard pattern, called a *transparency grid.*

Figure 4.10 The background of the comp (top image) becomes transparent when nested into another comp (middle image). The result is the bottom image.

To choose a background color for your composition:

1. Select a composition in the Project panel, or activate a composition in a Composition or Timeline panel.

2. Choose Composition > Background Color (**Figure 4.11**), or press Shift-Command-B (Ctrl-B).

   A Background Color dialog appears.

3. In the Background Color dialog, *do one of the following* (**Figure 4.12**):

   ▲ Click the color swatch to open the color picker.

   ▲ Click the eyedropper, which allows you to select a color by clicking anywhere on the screen, including the desktop.

4. Click OK to close the Background Color dialog.

   The selected composition uses the background color you specified.

✔ Tip

■ If you need an opaque background—in a nested composition, for example—create a solid layer as described in the "Creating Solid Layers" section later in this chapter.

Composition	Layer	Effect	Animation	View

New Composition...   ⌘N

Composition Settings...   ⌘K
Background Color...   ⇧⌘B
Set Poster Time
Trim Comp to Work Area
Crop Comp to Region of Interest

Add to Render Queue
Add Output Module
Add to Adobe Media Encoder Queue   ⌥⇧⌘/

Preview   ▶
Save Frame As   ▶
Make Movie...   ⌘M
Pre-render...
Save RAM Preview...

Composition Flowchart   ⇧⌘F11
Composition Mini-Flowchart

Figure 4.11 Choose Composition > Background Color to access the Background Color dialog.

Figure 4.12 Click the eyedropper to pick a screen color, or click the swatch to open a color picker.

The Composition and Timeline Panels

All compositions can be represented in the Composition and Timeline panels, which open automatically whenever you create or open a composition. These two panels furnish you with different ways of looking at a composition and manipulating its layers. This section gives you an overview of each panel, emphasizing how panels show layers along with their spatial and temporal relationships.

The Composition panel

The Composition—or Comp—panel (**Figure 4.13**) displays the layers of footage visible at the current frame of a composition. You

can use the Comp panel to visually preview the way a composition's layers are rendered within the visible frame as well as how those layers are placed outside the frame (off-screen, or if you like, in the pasteboard area).

The Comp panel is equipped with many of the viewing and time controls present in the Footage panel and Layer panel. But because the comp is where footage items become layers, the Comp panel has several unique features. For example, you can move and scale layers and masks directly in the Comp panel, and you can also view information such as layer paths, keyframes, and tangents. You can rest assured that if a button or feature isn't covered in this chapter, you'll learn about it later in the book.

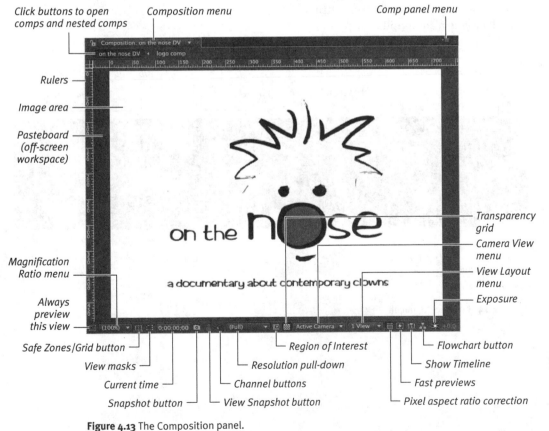

Figure 4.13 The Composition panel.

THE COMPOSITION AND TIMELINE PANELS

The Timeline panel

The Timeline panel (**Figure 4.14**) graphically represents a composition as layers in a timeline. In the time ruler, a yellow marker—called the *current time indicator (CTI)*—corresponds to the current frame pictured in the Composition panel. A vertical line extending from the CTI makes it easy to see how layers in the comp are situated in time. In the Timeline panel, each layer occupies a row and the rows are stacked vertically. (Unlike the tracks of many nonlinear editing programs, each row contains only one layer.) Layers that are higher in the Timeline panel's stacking order appear in front of lower layers when viewed in the Composition panel. The Timeline panel offers more than just an alternative view of the composition; it gives you precise control over virtually every attribute of each layer in a composition.

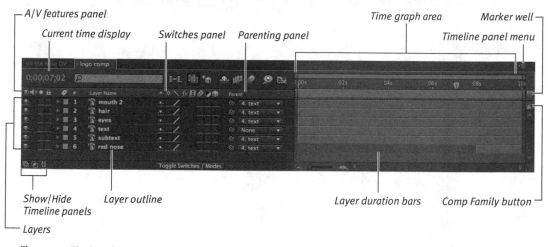

Figure 4.14 The Timeline panel.

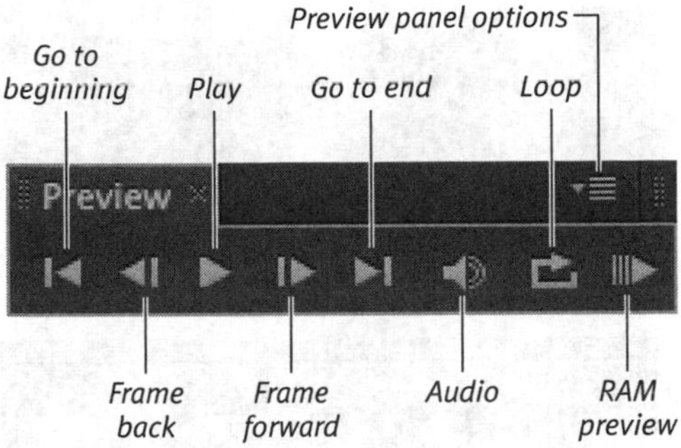

Go to
beginning   Play   Go to end   Loop
Preview panel options

Frame   Frame   Audio   RAM
back   forward   preview

Figure 4.15 The Preview panel. (In this figure, the RAM preview options are hidden.)

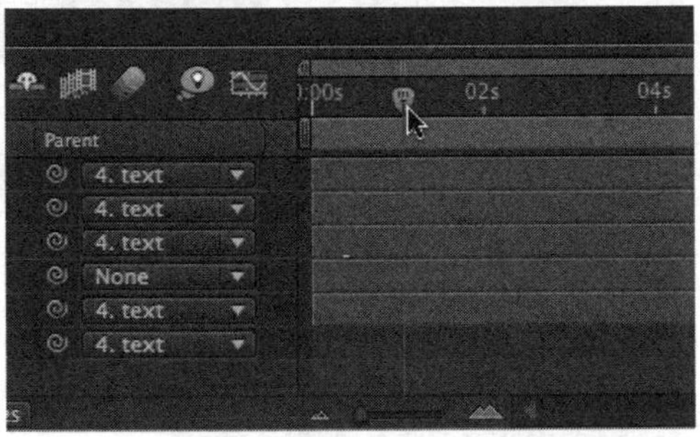

Figure 4.16 In the Timeline panel, drag the current time indicator to change the current frame (displayed in the Composition panel).

Setting the Time

Before you add footage to a composition, you must specify the time at which the layer will begin in the composition. By setting the composition's current time, you can also set the starting point for an added layer. And, of course, setting the time also allows you to view a particular frame of the composition in the Comp panel. You can set the current time via the Preview panel, the Composition panel, or the Timeline panel; you can also use keyboard shortcuts to accomplish the task.

Using the Preview panel

You can use the Preview panel to control the playback of the Footage, Composition, Timeline, and Layer panels (whichever is selected and active). **Figure 4.15** shows what the Preview panel's buttons do.

To set the current time in the Timeline panel:

◆ In the Timeline panel, drag the current time indicator to the frame you want (**Figure 4.16**).

Use the current time display to see the current time numerically.

To cue the current time of the composition numerically:

1. *Do any of the following:*

▲ In the Composition panel, click the time display (**Figure 4.17**).

▲ In the Timeline panel, click the time display (**Figure 4.18**).

▲ Press Shift-Option-J (Shift-Alt-J).

The Go to Time dialog appears.

2. *Do either of the following:*

▲ Enter an absolute time (a specific frame number) to which you want to cue the current time (**Figure 4.19**).

▲ Enter a plus (+) or minus (-) and a relative time (the number of frames you want to add or subtract from the current frame) (**Figure 4.20**). Numbers less than 100 are interpreted as frames so that entering 90 would be interpreted as 90 frames, or 3 seconds using a 30 fps timebase. Numbers greater than 99 are interpreted as seconds and frames so that entering 100 would be treated as 1 second and 0 frames.

3. Click OK to close the Go to Time dialog.

✔ Tips

■ By clicking the arrows to the left of the Preview panel's name, you can cycle through different views of the panel that include fewer or more controls.

■ Because you'll frequently need to change the current time in the Composition, Timeline, Footage, and Layer panels, you should familiarize yourself with the keyboard shortcuts that help you get around—for example (on an expanded keyboard), Page Down advances one frame and Page Up goes back one frame. Consult After Effects Help for more keyboard shortcuts.

Figure 4.17 Click the time display in the Composition panel...

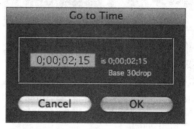

Figure 4.18 ...or in the Timeline panel...

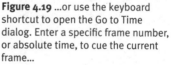

Figure 4.19 ...or use the keyboard shortcut to open the Go to Time dialog. Enter a specific frame number, or absolute time, to cue the current frame...

Figure 4.20 ...or enter a time relative to the current frame by entering a plus (+) or minus (–) sign and the number of frames.

SETTING THE TIME

Adding Footage to a Composition

When you add an item to a composition, you create a layer. A layer can be created from a footage item in the project, a synthetic layer generated in After Effects (such as solids, shapes, and text), or another composition.

You can add an item to a composition more than once to create multiple layers, or you can duplicate existing layers (using the Copy, Paste, and Duplicate commands). In this section, you'll learn to create layers in a composition. Later chapters will show you how to rearrange and modify layers. (Eventually, you'll also learn about specialized layers such as adjustment layers, guide layers, null objects, and layers used in 3D compositing: 3D layers, lights, and cameras. But first things first.)

The method you use to add layers depends on how you want to set their initial position, starting point, and layer order in your composition. You can simply drag a layer to the timeline to position it at any time or level in the stacking order.

To add footage to a composition by dragging:

1. Set the current time of the composition using one of the methods described earlier in this chapter.

2. Drag one or more items from the Project panel to any of the following (**Figure 4.21**):

   Composition panel—Dragging here places the layers in the desired position, at the current time, and layered in the order in which the files were selected in the Project panel.

continues on next page

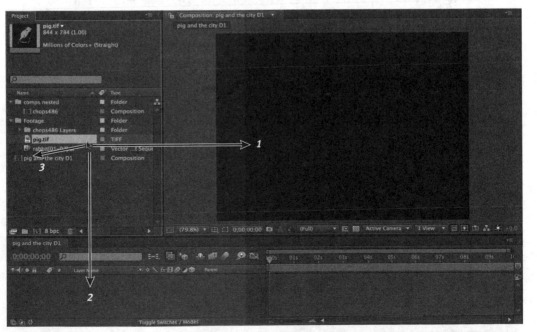

Figure 4.21 You can drag one or more items from the Project panel to the Composition panel (1), the Timeline panel (2), or the Comp's icon in the Project panel (3).

ADDING FOOTAGE TO A COMPOSITION

Timeline panel—Dragging here places the layers where you want in time and in the stacking order, and centered in the visible frame of the composition.

A composition in the Project panel—Dragging here places the layers at the current time, centered in the visible frame of the composition, and layered in the order in which you selected the items in the Project panel.

Items become layers in the composition, and their position, starting time, and layer order all depend on the method you employed to add them to the composition. Layers created from still-image footage use the default duration for stills (see Chapter 2, "Importing Footage Into a Project"). The duration of other layers is determined by the In and Out points you set in their Footage panel (see "To set source footage edit points" later in this chapter).

✔ Tips

- Another quick way to add footage to the centered composition is to select the footage item in the Project panel and press Command-/ (Ctrl-/).

- Option-dragging (Alt-dragging) footage to a selected layer in the timeline replaces the layer with the new footage.

Nesting Comps

Just as you can create layers from footage items, you can also make layers from other comps. A composition used as a layer in another comp is called a *nested composition*.

Nesting a comp lets you treat the layers it contains as a group. As a single layer, the nested comp may be more convenient to use, or it may help you achieve results you couldn't otherwise get. Like any other footage item, you can use a comp as a layer as many times as you want. Moreover, any alterations you make to a comp's contents are reflected wherever it appears nested as a layer.

Nesting can also help you achieve effects that would otherwise be thwarted by After Effects' rendering order—the sequence in which After Effects renders layers and their properties. Put simply, you can take advantage of the fact that After Effects must render the contents of the most deeply nested comp before it renders the nested comp itself (as a layer).

Similarly, you may need to use a nested comp when working with a type of effect known as a *compound effect*. Properties of a compound effect refer to a secondary layer, or *effect source*. But because a compound effect ignores property changes in the effect source, it's often best to make the source a nested comp. This way, necessary property changes can be rendered within the nested comp before it serves as an effect source layer.

If all this sounds a little confusing, don't panic. For now, it's enough for you to know that one comp can be a layer in another. You'll begin to appreciate the full implications of nesting as you progress through this book. Chapter 16, "Complex Projects," covers nesting and the rendering order in detail. Chapter 11, "Effects Fundamentals," explains compound effects.

Adding Layers Using Insert and Overlay

You can add motion footage to your composition by using tools and techniques commonly found in nonlinear editing software. Buttons in the Footage panel, for example, allow you to perform insert and overlay edits—both of which add a layer at the current time, although each affects the timeline's existing layers differently.

When you add a layer using an overlay edit, the composition's layers retain their current positions in time. The new layer is added as the topmost layer at the current time (**Figures 4.22** and **4.23**).

In contrast, adding a layer via an insert edit causes the composition's existing layers to shift in time to accommodate the new layer. In other words, if the new layer is 5 seconds long, all layers after the current time move forward 5 seconds. If the current time occurs midway through a layer, the layer is split into two layers; the portion after the current time shifts forward (**Figure 4.24**).

Figure 4.22 Note the arrangement of the layers before an insert or overlay edit, as well as the position of the current time indicator.

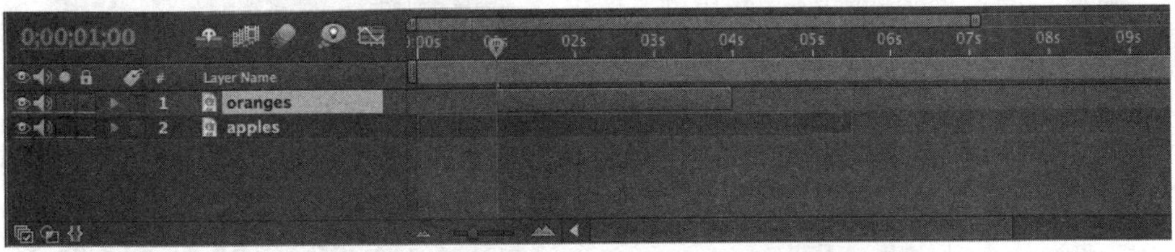

Figure 4.23 After an overlay edit, the new layer is added as the topmost layer at the current time.

Figure 4.24 After an insert edit, layers after the current time shift forward to accommodate the new layer. One of the layers is split at the edit point, and the portion after the edit point shifts forward.

To set source footage edit points:

1. Option-double-click (Alt-double-click) a motion footage item in the Project panel.

   The motion footage item opens in an After Effects Footage panel.

2. To set an In point, cue the current time and click the Set In button ▢.

   The In point display and the duration bar reflect the In point you set (**Figure 4.25**).

3. To set an Out point, cue the current time and click the Set Out button ▢.

   The Out point display and the duration bar reflect the Out point you set (**Figure 4.26**).

To insert or overlay a layer:

1. Set the current time of the composition to which you want to add the layer.

2. In the Footage panel, set the source footage In and Out points (as described in the previous task).

   Make sure the Edit Target section of the Footage panel displays the name of the composition to which you want to add a layer. If the project contains more than one composition, the panel displays the currently selected composition.

Figure 4.25 Cue the current time to the point at which you want the source footage to start, and click the Set In button to set the source In point.

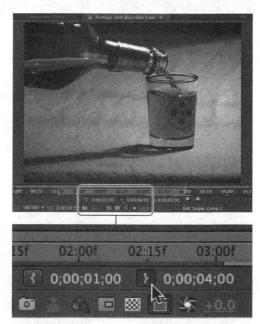

Figure 4.26 Cue the current time to the point at which you want the source footage to stop, and click the Set Out button to set the source Out point.

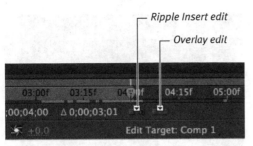

Ripple Insert edit

Overlay edit

Figure 4.27 Depending on the type of edit you want to perform, click the Ripple Insert or Overlay button.

3. In the Footage panel, click either of the following:

Ripple Insert—If you select this option, all other layers will be shifted forward to accommodate the new layer (**Figure 4.27**).

Overlay—If you select this option, other layers will retain their current positions in time.

The selected footage is added to the composition as the topmost layer at the current time. Other layers' positions in time will depend on whether you selected an insert or overlay edit.

✔ Tip

- In editing, the inverse of Overlay is Lift; the inverse of Insert is Extract. The menu command Edit > Lift Work Area removes a range of frames and leaves a gap in the timeline. Edit > Extract Work Area removes the frames and shifts subsequent layers back in time so there is no gap. For more about setting the Work Area, see Chapter 8, "Playback, Previews, and RAM". For other editing techniques, see Chapter 6, "Layer Editing."

ADDING LAYERS USING INSERT AND OVERLAY

Creating Solid Layers

As you might expect, a solid layer is a layer in the size and color of your choice. You create a solid layer when you need an opaque background for a nested composition. You can also use solids with masks to create graphic elements (**Figure 4.28**). You can even use this type of layer to create text effects within After Effects. (For more about masks, see Chapter 10, "Mask Essentials.")

Creating a solid doesn't produce an actual media file on your hard drive. But in other respects, a solid layer works like any other footage item: It has specified dimensions and PAR, as well as a color. (This is notable because older versions of After Effects didn't allow you to set a solid's PAR, forcing you to treat it a little differently than other footage items.) However, this doesn't mean the solid's settings are fixed; you can change its attributes at any time.

To create a solid-color layer:

1. Open the Composition panel or Timeline panel for the composition in which you want to add a solid layer, or make sure one is active.

2. Choose Layer > New > Solid (**Figure 4.29**), or press Command-Y (Ctrl-Y).

    The Solid Settings dialog appears (**Figure 4.30**).

3. Enter a name for the new solid.

    After Effects uses the solid's current color as the basis for the default name: for example, Gray Solid 1.

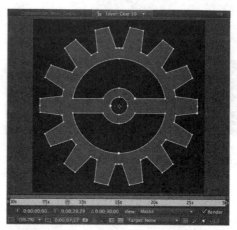

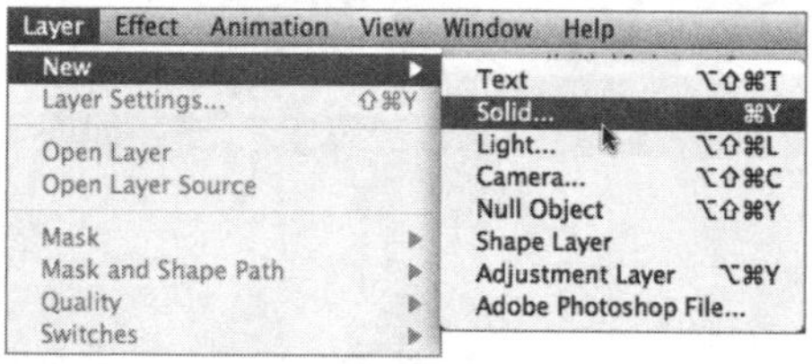

Figure 4.28 You can add text or other effects to a solid; you can mask a solid to create graphical elements (shown here); or you can use a solid as a solid-color background.

Figure 4.29 Choose Layer > New > Solid, or use the keyboard shortcut.

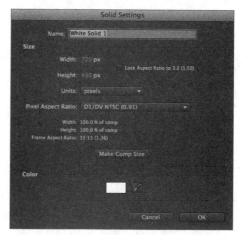

Figure 4.30 In the Solid Settings dialog, enter a name for the solid layer. Click the Make Comp Size button to make the solid the same size as the composition, or enter a custom width and height.

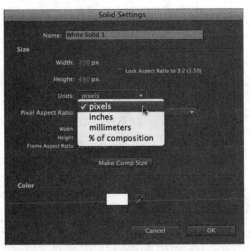

Figure 4.31 Choose a unit of measure from the pop-up menu before you enter a custom size.

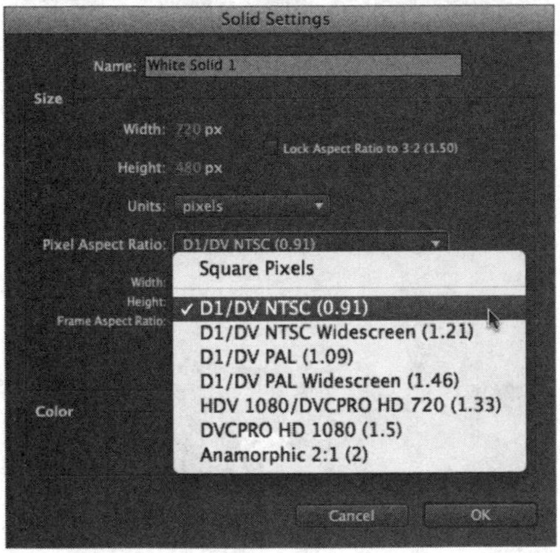

Figure 4.32 Specify an option in the Pixel Aspect Ratio pop-up menu.

4. Set the size by *doing any of the following*:
   - ▲ To make the solid the same size as the composition, click the Make Comp Size button.
   - ▲ To enter a custom size, choose a unit of measure from the Units pop-up menu, and enter a width and height (**Figure 4.31**).
   - ▲ To maintain the aspect ratio of the current width and height, click the Lock Aspect Ratio button before you change the size.

5. Choose an option from the Pixel Aspect Ratio pop-up menu (**Figure 4.32**).

6. Set the color by *doing one of the following*:
   - ▲ Click the color swatch to open the color picker, then choose a color.
   - ▲ Click the eyedropper, then click anywhere on the screen to select a color.

7. Click OK to close the Solid Settings dialog.

   The solid appears as a layer in the composition. Like any layer, the solid layer starts at the current time and uses the default duration of still images. In the Project panel, After Effects creates a folder called Solids that contains all the solid footage items you create.

To change a solid's settings:

1. *Do either of the following:*

   ▲ In the Project panel, select a solid footage item.

   ▲ In the Composition or Timeline panel, click a solid layer to select it (**Figure 4.33**).

2. *Do either of the following:*

   ▲ Choose Layer > Solid Settings (**Figure 4.34**).

   ▲ Press Shift-Command-Y (Shift-Ctrl-Y).

   The Solid Settings dialog appears.

3. Specify any changes you want to make to the solid footage, such as its name, dimensions, PAR, or color (**Figure 4.35**).

4. If you selected the solid layer from the Timeline or Composition panel in step 1, specify whether you want the changes to affect layers already created from the solid footage item by selecting "Affect all layers that use this solid" (**Figure 4.36**).

   Leave this option deselected if you want to change only this layer and not layers already created from it.

5. Click OK.

   Depending on your choices, the changes you specified are applied to the selected solid layer, solid footage item, or both.

✔ Tips

■ You can continuously rasterize a solid layer. That way, its edges remain crisp and smooth when you scale it up. This is especially noticeable when you've applied a mask to the solid. See "Continuously Rasterizing a Layer," in Chapter 5; also see Chapter 10, "Mask Essentials."

■ To create graphic objects, you might want to consider using a shape layer instead of using a solid with a mask; see "Using Shape Layers" in Chapter 14 for details.

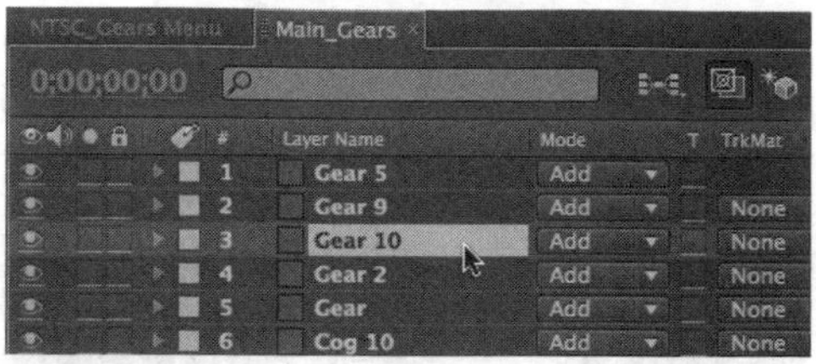

Figure 4.33 Select a solid footage item in the Project panel or a solid layer in the Comp or Timeline panel (shown here).

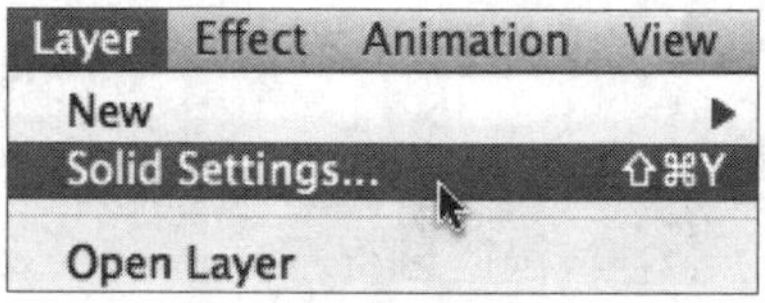

Figure 4.34 Choose Layer > Solid Settings.

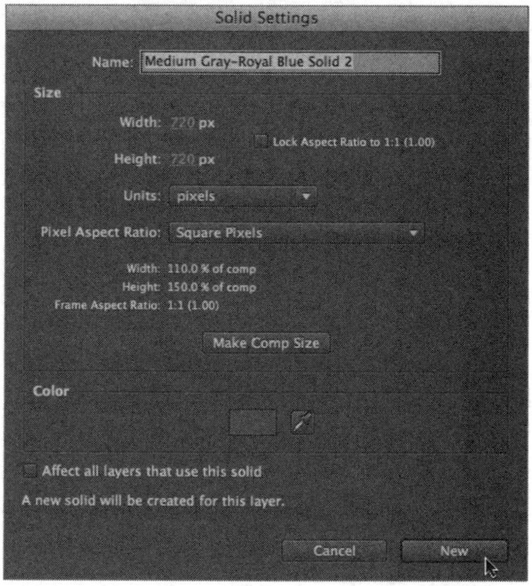

Figure 4.35 Specify new settings, and click New to modify a selected layer only...

Figure 4.36 ...or select "Affect all layers that use this solid" to modify all layers created from the solid.

LAYER BASICS

Previous chapters laid the groundwork for the central activity of your After Effects work: manipulating a composition's layers. Over the next several chapters, you'll gradually increase your command over layers. This chapter focuses on the bare essentials—describing how to select, name, and label layers. You'll also learn how to control layer quality and how to choose whether to include layers in previews and renders. In addition, you'll see how to simplify working with layers by concealing ones you're not using and by locking ones you don't want to disturb. In the process, you'll become more familiar with your primary workspace, the Timeline panel.

Selecting Layers

As you would expect, you must select layers before you can adjust them. In the timeline, a selected layer's name appears highlighted, as does its *duration bar*—the horizontal bar representing the layer under the time ruler. In the Composition panel, selected layers can appear with *transform handles* or simply, *handles*—six small boxes that demark each layer's boundaries and that you can use to transform the layer. However, you can specify whether you want these (or other layer controls) to appear in the Comp panel. See the section "Viewing Spatial Controls in the Comp Panel" in Chapter 7 for more details.

To select layers in the Composition panel:

1. If you haven't already done so, cue the current frame of the composition so that the layer you want to select is visible in the Composition panel.

2. In the Composition panel, click the visible layer to select it (**Figure 5.1**).

   The selected layer's handles and anchor point appear, unless these options have been disabled (see "Viewing Spatial Controls in the Comp Panel" in Chapter 7).

3. To select more than one layer, Shift-click other visible layers in the Composition panel (**Figure 5.2**).

Figure 5.1 You can select a layer by clicking it in the Composition panel. Here the Comp panel is set to show selected layer handles.

Figure 5.2 Shift-click to select additional layers.

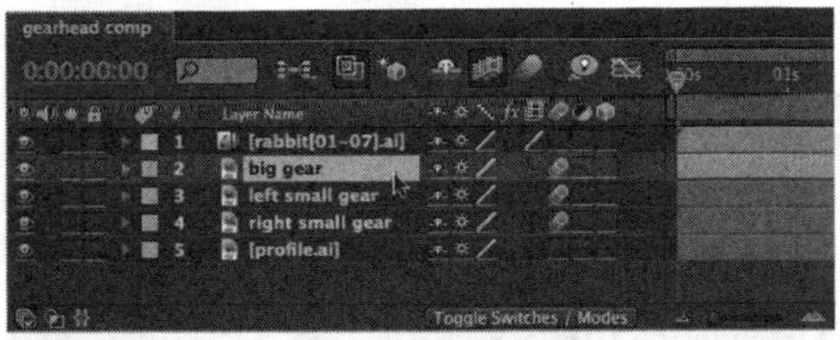

Figure 5.3 You can select a layer by clicking it in the Timeline panel or by entering the layer's number on the numeric keypad.

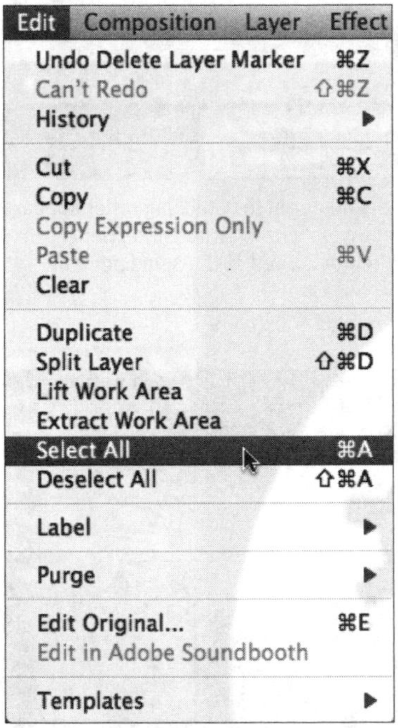

Figure 5.4 You can select all layers in the usual way by choosing Edit > Select All, or by pressing Command-A (Ctrl-A)using the keyboard shortcut.

To select layers in the Timeline panel:

In the Timeline panel, *do any of the following:*

◆ Click anywhere in the horizontal track containing a layer.

◆ To select a layer by its number, type the layer number on the numeric keypad (not the numbers on the main keyboard) (**Figure 5.3**).

◆ To add to or subtract from the selection, Command-click (Ctrl-click) layers.

◆ To select a range of layers, Shift-click other layers or drag a marquee around several layer names. (Take care not to drag a layer to a new position in the stacking order.)

To select all layers in a composition:

Do one of the following:

◆ Choose Edit > Select All (**Figure 5.4**).

◆ Press Command-A (Ctrl-A).

All the layers in the composition are selected.

To deselect all layers in a composition:

Do one of the following:

◆ Click an empty area in the Timeline panel or the Composition panel.

◆ Choose Edit > Deselect All.

✔ Tips

■ Press Command-Up Arrow (Ctrl-Up Arrow) to select the next layer up in the stacking order, and press Command-Down Arrow (Ctrl-Down Arrow) to select the next layer down.

■ If the stacking order makes it difficult for you to select a layer in the Comp panel, you can right-click in the Comp panel and then choose Select and the name of the layer you want in the pop-up menu.

SELECTING LAYERS

Changing the Stacking Order

In the Timeline panel, layers appear, well, *layered.* That is, each layer occupies a horizontal track that is stacked vertically with other layers. The horizontal position of a layer's duration bar determines its place in time; its vertical position shows its place in the *stacking order.* When layers occupy the same point in time, higher layers appear in front of lower layers when viewed in the Composition panel. You can change the relative positions of the layers in the stacking order to determine which elements appear in front and which appear behind (**Figures 5.5** and **5.6**).

A number directly to the left of a layer's name indicates a layer's position in the stacking order. The top layer is always layer 1, and the numbers increase as you go down the stack. Although layer numbers may not seem very informative, they can help you discern when layers are hidden temporarily (see "Making Layers Shy," later in this chapter) as well as provide a way for you to quickly select layers by number (see "Selecting Layers," earlier in this chapter).

✔ Tip

■ In Chapter 3, "Managing Footage," you learned that the Project panel labels each file type (motion footage, still image, and so on) using a different colored label. In the timeline, each layer's duration bar and label (the color swatch next to the layer's number) reflect the label color scheme. You can assign another color to any selected layer by choosing Edit > Label and choosing a color.

Figure 5.5 Layers higher in the stacking order appear in front of other layers in the Composition panel (provided they're positioned at the same point in time).

Figure 5.6 When a layer is moved to a lower position in the stacking order, it appears behind the higher layers in the Composition panel.

Figure 5.7 As you drag a layer in the stacking order, a line indicates where it will appear if you release the mouse.

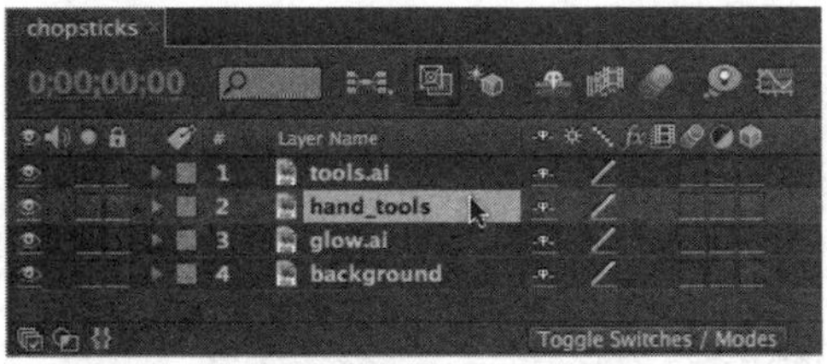

Figure 5.8 When you release the mouse, the layer appears in the new position.

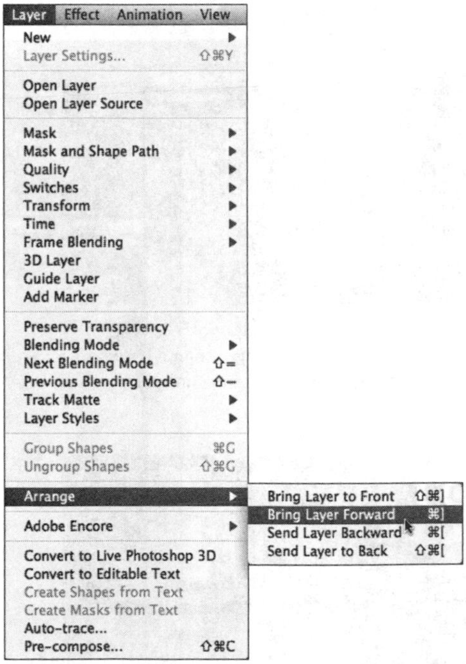

Figure 5.9 To move the selected layer using menu commands, choose Layer > Arrange > and the appropriate command.

To change the stacking order of layers in the Timeline panel:

1. In the Timeline panel, drag a layer name to a new position.

   A horizontal line appears between other layers, indicating where the layer will appear in the stacking order (**Figure 5.7**).

2. Release the mouse to place the layer in the position you want (**Figure 5.8**).

To move layers using menu commands:

1. Select a layer in the Composition or Timeline panel.

2. *Do any of the following:*

   ▲ Choose Layer > Arrange > Bring Layer to Front or press Shift-Command-] (Shift-Ctrl-]).

   ▲ Choose Layer > Arrange > Bring Layer Forward (**Figure 5.9**), or press Command-] (Ctrl-]).

   ▲ Choose Layer > Arrange > Send Layer Backward, or press Command-[(Ctrl-[).

   ▲ Choose Layer > Arrange > Send Layer to Back or press Shift-Command-[(Shift-Ctrl-[).

   The layer is repositioned in the stacking order according to the command you specified.

✔ Tip

■ You aren't restricted to adding a layer to the top of the stacking order and then moving it down in a separate step (as in older versions of After Effects). After Effects CS4 lets you drag footage items directly to any level in the stacking order.

CHANGING THE STACKING ORDER

101

Naming Layers

Because a single footage item might appear as numerous layers in a comp, you might name each instance so you can tell them apart more easily. In the Timeline panel, you can choose to view either the changeable layer name or the fixed source name. If you don't rename a layer, its layer name appears in brackets to indicate that it matches the name of the source footage item.

To change the name of a layer:

1. In the Timeline panel, click a layer to select it.

2. Press Return (Enter).

   The layer name is highlighted (**Figure 5.10**).

3. Enter a new name for the layer, then press Return (Enter).

   The layer uses the name you specified; the source name can't be changed (**Figure 5.11**).

To toggle between layer name and source name:

◆ In the Timeline panel, click the Layer/Source Name button to toggle between the layer name and the source name for the layer. When the layer name and source name are the same, the layer name appears in brackets (**Figures 5.12** and **5.13**).

Figure 5.10 To change a layer's name, select the layer and press Return (Enter) to edit the name.

Figure 5.11 Enter a new name for the layer and press Return (Enter).

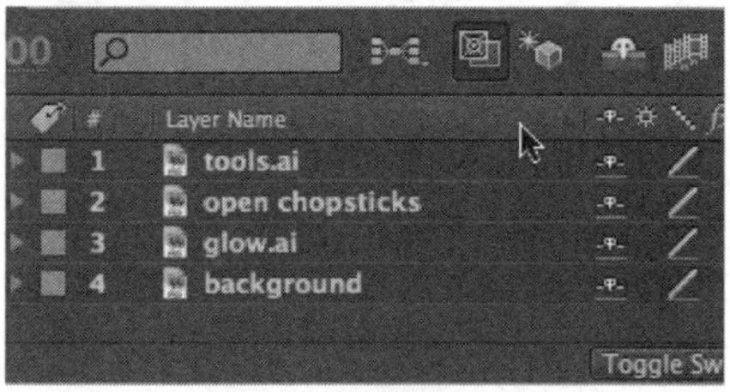

Figure 5.12 In the Timeline panel, click the Layer/Source Name button to toggle between the layer name (which you can change)...

Figure 5.13 ...and the source name (which is fixed).

Figure 5.14 When a layer's Video switch is on, the Eye icon is visible and the layer's image is included in the Composition panel.

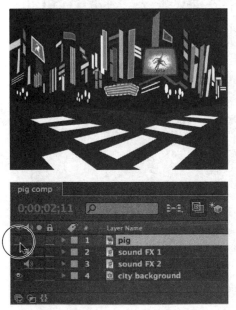

Figure 5.15 Toggling the Video switch off excludes the layer's image from the Comp panel, previews, and renders.

Switching Video and Audio On and Off

By default, the extreme left side of the Timeline panel displays the A/V Features panel. The first three columns of the A/V Features panel contain switches that control whether a layer's video and audio are included in previews or renders. (The last column of switches protects a layer from changes; see the section, "Locking a Layer," later in this chapter.)

To show or hide the image for layers in the composition:

◆ Next to a layer in the Timeline panel, click the Video switch to toggle the Eye icon on and off.

When the Eye icon is visible, the layer appears in the Composition panel (**Figure 5.14**); when the icon is hidden, the layer doesn't appear (**Figure 5.15**).

To include a layer's audio track in the composition:

◆ Next to the layer in the Timeline panel, click the Audio switch to toggle the Speaker icon ◀ on and off.

When the Speaker icon is visible, the audio is included when you preview or render the composition; when the Speaker icon is hidden, the audio is excluded (**Figure 5.16**).

To solo a layer:

1. For the layer you want to solo:
   ▲ Make sure the Eye icon is visible to solo the video.
   ▲ Make sure the Speaker icon is visible to solo the audio.

   If the layer contains both video and audio, you can select either or both. If you select neither, the Solo button ◼ disappears, and you can't solo the layer.

2. Next to the layer you want to solo, click the Solo button (**Figure 5.17**).

   If you solo the video, the Video switches for all other layers are deactivated; if you solo the audio, the Audio switches for all other layers are deactivated (**Figure 5.18**).

3. To stop soloing the layer and restore other A/V settings to their original states, click the Solo button again to deactivate it.

Icon present / audio included

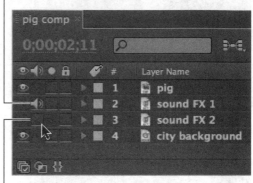

Icon absent / audio excluded

Figure 5.16 When you toggle the Audio switch (Speaker icon) off, the layer's audio track isn't included in previews and renders.

Figure 5.17 Make sure the Eye icon is visible to solo video and that the Speaker icon is visible to solo audio, and then click the Solo button.

Switching Video and Audio On and Off

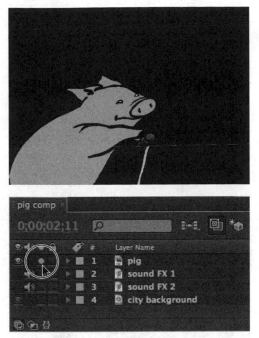

Figure 5.18 When you solo the layer's video (shown here) and/or audio, the corresponding A/V switches for other layers are deactivated.

✔ Tips

- When a blending mode has been applied to a layer, the Eye icon 👁 looks like this: 👁. For more about blending modes, see "Blending Modes," in Chapter 14.

- When a track matte is applied to a layer, the video for the layer above it is automatically switched off. Switching the video back on eliminates the track matte effect. For more about track mattes, see Chapter 14, "More Layer Techniques."

- Adjustment layers, null objects, lights, and cameras have no video component yet still have a video switch.

Locking a Layer

The fourth column of the A/V Features panel contains the Lock switch, which you can use to lock layers so that they're protected against accidental changes. When you attempt to select a locked layer, its highlight blinks on and off to remind you that it's locked and thus can't be selected or altered. You must unlock the layer to make changes.

To lock or unlock a layer:

◆ Next to a layer in the Timeline panel, click the Lock switch to toggle the Lock icon 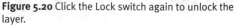 on and off.

When the Lock icon is visible, the layer can't be selected or modified (**Figure 5.19**); when the Lock icon is hidden, the layer is unlocked (**Figure 5.20**).

To unlock all layers:

◆ Choose Layer > Switches > Unlock All Layers (**Figure 5.21**), or press Command-Shift-l (Ctrl-Shift-l).

✔ Tip

■ Press Command-L (Ctrl-L) to lock selected layers. You still have to click the Lock switch to unlock layers (you can't select locked layers).

Figure 5.19 Click the Lock switch to protect a layer from inadvertent changes.

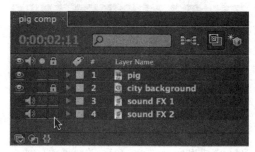

Figure 5.20 Click the Lock switch again to unlock the layer.

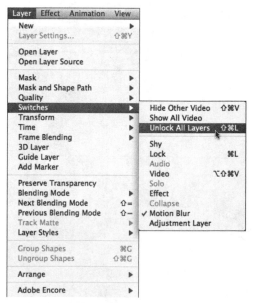

Figure 5.21 To unlock all layers, choose Layer > Switches > Unlock All Layers.

Basic Layer Switches

By default, the Layer Switches column set appears to the right of the Name column in the Timeline panel.

The Layer Switches column consists of eight switches that control various features for each layer (**Figure 5.22**). This section covers the first three layer switches: Shy, Continuously Rasterize, and Quality. Other layer switches are covered later in the book. (The Effect and Adjustment Layer switches are covered in Chapter 11, "Effects Fundamentals"; the Frame Blending and Motion Blur switches are covered in Chapter 14, "More Layer Techniques"; and the 3D switch is covered in Chapter 15, "3D Layers.")

Although you can control all of the layer switches via menu commands, the switches provide more direct access.

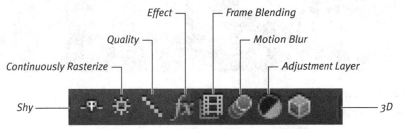

Figure 5.22 The Layer Switches panel contains eight switches.

Chapter 5

To show or hide the layer switches:

◆ In the Timeline panel, click the
Expand/Collapse Layer Switches Pane
button (**Figure 5.23**).

Clicking the button hides or shows the
Switches pane (**Figure 5.24**).

✔ Tip

■ You can toggle between the Switches
and the Transfer Controls by clicking the
Toggle Switches/Modes button at the
bottom of the Timeline panel. Transfer
Controls include options covered in the
sections "Using Blending Modes," "Track
Mattes," and "Preserving Underlying
Transparency" in Chapter 14.

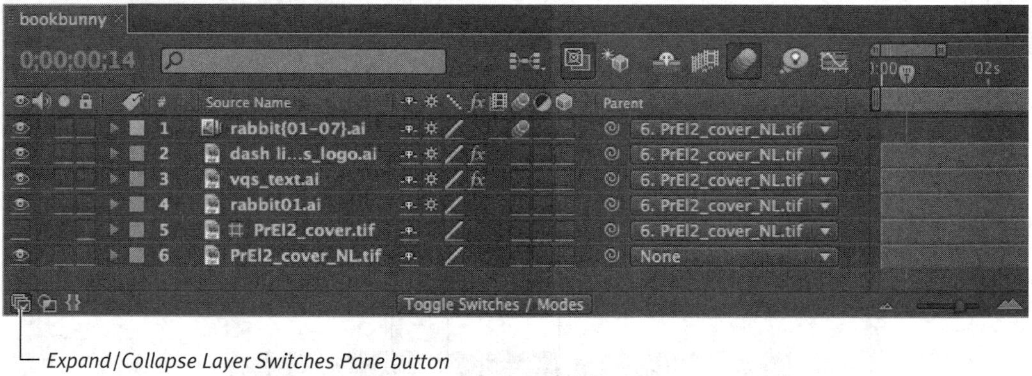

Expand/Collapse Layer Switches Pane button

Figure 5.23 Clicking the Expand/Collapse Layer Switches Pane button...

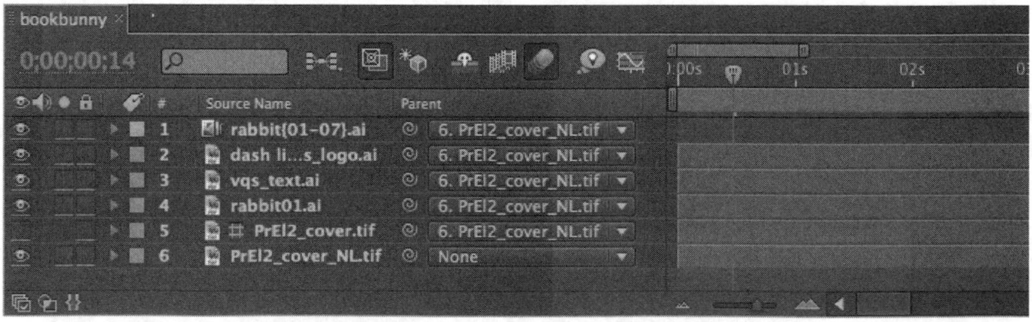

Figure 5.24 ...toggles the switches controls open and closed (shown here).

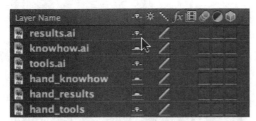

Figure 5.25 Click the Shy switch to toggle between Not Shy...

Figure 5.26 ...and Shy.

Figure 5.27 When the Hide Shy Layers button is deselected, shy layers appear in the Timeline panel.

Figure 5.28 When the Hide Shy Layers button is selected, shy layers are concealed in the Timeline panel.

Making Layers Shy

Because the Timeline panel contains so much information, you'll frequently find yourself scrolling through it or expanding it. Some users even use a secondary monitor just to accommodate a large Timeline panel. If you hate to scroll but are reluctant to buy another monitor, you may want to take advantage of the Shy Layers feature.

Marking layers you're not currently using as *shy* enables you to quickly conceal them in the Timeline panel. This way, you can concentrate on just the layers you're using and conserve precious screen space. Although shy layers may be hidden in the Timeline panel, they continue to appear in the Composition panel (provided they're visible and their corresponding video switch is on), and layer numbering remains unchanged.

To make a layer shy or not shy:

◆ Click the Shy switch for a layer in the Timeline panel to toggle the icon between Not Shy and Shy (**Figures 5.25** and **5.26**).

To hide or show shy layers:

◆ In the Timeline panel, click the Hide Shy Layers button to select or deselect it.

When the button is deselected, shy layers are visible in the Timeline panel (**Figure 5.27**).

When the button is selected, shy layers are hidden from view (**Figure 5.28**).

Continuously Rasterizing a Layer

When you import an Illustrator or EPS file, After Effects *rasterizes* it, treating the vector-based image as though it were bitmapped. As you may know from working with programs like Illustrator and Photoshop, vector-based images can be scaled up or down without regard to resolution, while bitmapped images cannot.

If you plan to use the image at its original size or smaller, the rasterization process is unnoticeable (**Figure 5.29**). But as with a bitmapped image, increasing the layer's scale over 100 percent (or changing other transform properties) makes the image's pixels apparent (**Figure 5.30**).

In this case, you should activate the layer's Continuously Rasterize switch. Instead of rasterizing the layer once, After Effects rasterizes it for each frame—after transformations such as scale have been calculated—maintaining the vector art's image quality at any scale (**Figure 5.31**).

Of course, these recalculations may increase preview and rendering time. To save time, you may choose to turn off the Continuously Rasterize switch until you want to preview or render the composition at full quality.

When a composition is used as a layer, the Continuously Rasterize switch functions as the Collapse Transformations switch. You can find out more about the Collapse Transformations option in Chapter 16, "Complex Projects."

Figure 5.29 By default, After Effects rasterizes the image at its original size.

Figure 5.30 Enlarging an image after it has been rasterized can make the pixels apparent.

Figure 5.31 When the Continuously Rasterize switch is on, the image is scaled before it's rasterized for each frame of the composition.

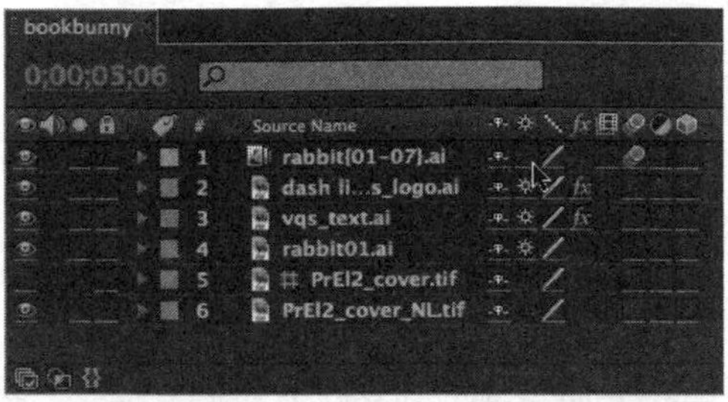

Figure 5.32 When the Continuously Rasterize switch is off, the layer is rasterized once.

Figure 5.33 When the Continuously Rasterize switch is on, the layer is continuously rasterized.

To change the rasterization method of a layer:

◆ In the Switches panel of the Timeline panel, click the Continuously Rasterize/Collapse Transformations switch for the layer.

When the switch is set to Off (no icon), the image is rasterized once (**Figure 5.32**); when the switch is set to On , the image is continuously rasterized (**Figure 5.33**).

✔ Tips

■ Regardless of the Continuously Rasterize setting, setting the quality switch to Full smoothes (anti-aliases) the edges of the art.

■ One way to avoid continuous rasterization and its slower rendering times is to steer clear of scaling the image beyond 100 percent. If you create the image in a drawing program (such as Illustrator), set its dimensions so that, when you import it into After Effects, it will appear at the proper size without increasing its scale.

■ In older versions of After Effects, you couldn't apply an effect to a layer that had the Continuously Rasterize switch on. This is no longer the case; you're free to apply effects to a continuously rasterized layer—and free to forget the workarounds you had to use in the past.

CONTINUOUSLY RASTERIZING A LAYER

Quality Setting Switches

As you'll remember from Chapter 4, "Compositions," you can set the resolution of the composition to control its image quality and thereby the speed at which frames are rendered. Just as the resolution setting controls the overall image quality of the composition, a layer's Quality switch controls the quality of an individual layer in the composition.

Figure 5.34 Set the Quality switch to Draft Quality to display the layer at a lower quality in the Composition panel.

To change the Quality setting of a layer:

◆ In the Timeline panel, click the Quality switch to set the quality for the layer:

The Draft Quality icon ▧ indicates that the layer will preview and render at draft quality in the Composition panel (**Figure 5.34**).

Figure 5.35 Set the Quality switch to Full Quality to display the layer at the highest quality in the Composition panel.

The Full Quality icon ╱ indicates that the layer will preview and render at full quality in the Composition panel (**Figure 5.35**).

The Quality switch controls the quality of individual layers in a comp. To control the quality of a comp's viewer (which displays all the layers in a comp), use the Resolution controls, as described in the "Specifying Basic Composition Settings" section in Chapter 4.

QUALITY SETTING SWITCHES

LAYER EDITING

The term *editing*, in the sense that film and video makers use it, refers to the order and arrangement of images in time. Implicit in this definition, of course, is the term's broader meaning: to include some elements while excluding others to achieve a desired aesthetic effect. This chapter focuses on editing the layers of a composition—defining which segments to include and the order in which to present them.

You'll learn basic editing functions and terms such as *In point*, *Out point*, *duration*, and *trimming*. You'll also learn other techniques common to nonlinear editing, such as setting markers and controlling the playback speed and direction of layers. In the process, you'll get acquainted with the Layer panel and take a closer look at the time graph of the Timeline panel.

Viewing Layers in the Timeline and Layer Panels

When you arrange layers in time, you work in the Layer panel and in the time graph area of the Timeline panel.

As you know, the Timeline panel lets you view all of a composition's elements as vertically stacked layers. On the right side of the Timeline panel, a *time graph* represents the layers in time (**Figure 6.1**). Each layer has a duration bar, and its horizontal position in the time graph indicates when it will start and end as you play back the composition.

You can view any layer in a composition in a Layer panel. As you'll remember from Chapter 3, "Managing Footage," the Layer panel closely resembles the Footage and Composition panels. Unlike its siblings, however, the Layer panel always includes a timeline and controls for setting the starting and ending points of the layer (**Figure 6.2**).

Compare the Timeline (Figure 6.1), Layer (Figure 6.2), and Composition (**Figure 6.3**) panels to see how the same layer appears in each panel. The distinctions between the time graph and the Layer panel are explained in greater detail in the sections to follow.

✔ Tip

- The Layer panel has a few other unique features not covered in detail here: the View pop-up menu and the Render check box. The section "The Layer Panel," later in this chapter, provides a brief explanation, but you'll learn more in later chapters. This chapter focuses on using the Layer panel's unique editing features—that is, on manipulating starting and ending points and on using layer markers.

Time graph area of the Timeline panel

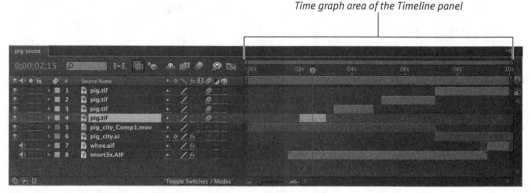

Figure 6.1 At the right side of the Timeline panel, all the layers of a composition are represented as bars in a time graph.

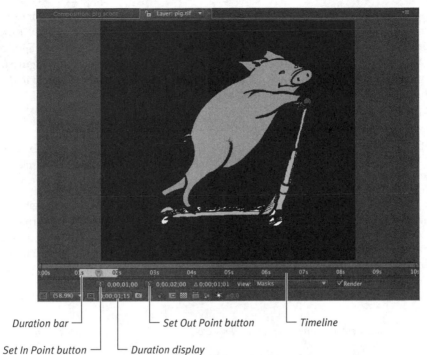

Duration bar ——

Set In Point button —— —— Duration display

—— Set Out Point button —— Timeline

Figure 6.2 You can view a single layer of the composition in a Layer panel, which includes a timeline and controls for setting the layer's starting and ending points.

Figure 6.3 In the Composition panel, you can see how the layer has been manipulated and composited with other layers.

The Time Graph

Each layer in the composition occupies a separate horizontal track, or cell, in the time graph. The vertical arrangement of layers indicates their position in the stacking order (covered in the previous chapter). Time is displayed horizontally, from left to right, and measured by a time ruler in the increments you selected in the project preferences. Layers appear as color-coded duration bars; their length and position in the time graph indicate when the layers start and end as the composition plays back.

This chapter focuses on how to view and edit layers in the time graph. Later chapters cover how to view and manipulate additional

information in the time graph (for example, keyframing attributes). Chapter 9, "Keyframe Interpolation," covers the time graph's other incarnation, the Graph Editor. **Figure 6.4** summarizes the controls covered in the following sections.

Parts of the time graph

Time ruler—Measures time horizontally (according to the time units you selected in the project preferences).

Work Area start—Marks the beginning of the Work Area bar, which determines the portion of the composition that will be rendered during previews (see Chapter 8, "Playback, Previews, and RAM").

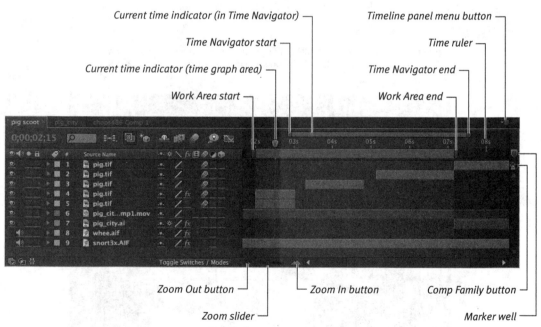

Figure 6.4 The Timeline panel's Time Graph area depicts a comp's layers in time and includes a number of special controls.

Work Area end—Marks the end of the Work Area bar, which determines the portion of the composition that will be rendered during previews (see Chapter 8).

Time Navigator start—Changes the left edge of the part of the composition visible in the main time graph. (See "The Time Navigator," later in this chapter.)

Time Navigator end—Changes the right edge of the part of the composition visible in the main time graph. (See "The Time Navigator," later in this chapter.)

Current time indicator (CTI)—Changes the current frame of the composition in the main time graph and in the navigator view. The current time is the same in all the views of the same composition.

Timeline panel menu button—Displays a menu of functions for controlling layers and keyframes as well as accessing the Composition Settings dialog.

Marker well—Adds markers to the time ruler. Drag a marker out of the well to add a marker or drag a marker back into the well to remove it.

Comp Family button—Opens the Composition panel associated with the composition displayed in the Timeline panel.

Zoom slider—Displays the time graph in more or less detail.

Zoom In button—Displays a shorter part of the time graph in more detail.

Zoom Out button—Displays a greater part of the time graph in less detail.

Navigating the Time Graph

The Timeline panel allows you to view all or part of a composition. As you arrange the layers of a composition in time, you may need to zoom into the time graph for a detailed view or zoom out for a more expansive view.

The Time Navigator

In addition to common navigation controls (like zoom buttons and the zoom slider), After Effects' Timeline panel includes another convenient tool to help view the part of the comp you want: the *time navigator*.

The time navigator is a thin bar located at the top of the time graph, above the time ruler (**Figure 6.5**). The width of the time navigator corresponds to the portion of the composition visible under the time ruler—or in other words, the scale of the time ruler. Dragging the ends of the time navigator closer together makes the area under the time ruler show a smaller portion of the comp, while extending the time navigator to its full width shows the comp's entire duration. Dragging the entire time navigator bar left or right scrolls visible portion of the comp in the Timeline.

The time navigator includes a tiny version of the current time indicator.

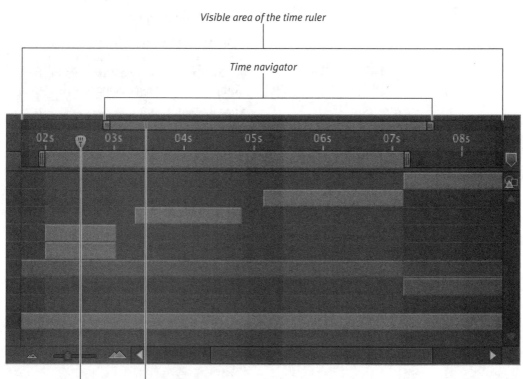

Visible area of the time ruler

Time navigator

CTI in time ruler — └ CTI in time navigator

Figure 6.5 The navigator view looks like a miniature version of the time graph. By representing the entire duration of the composition, it helps you put the area visible in the main time graph in context.

To view part of the time graph in more detail:

In the time graph area of the Timeline panel, *do any of the following:*

◆ Click the Zoom In button to view an incrementally more detailed area of the time graph.

◆ Drag the Zoom slider to the left.

◆ Drag the Time Navigator start to the right (closer to the Time Navigator end).

◆ Drag the Time Navigator end to the left (closer to the Time Navigator start).

◆ Press the equal sign (=) on your keyboard.

◆ Press Option (Alt) while scrolling up on the mouse scroll wheel.

See **Figure 6.6** for the locations of the Zoom In, Zoom Out, and Zoom slider controls; **Figure 6.7** shows the time navigator.

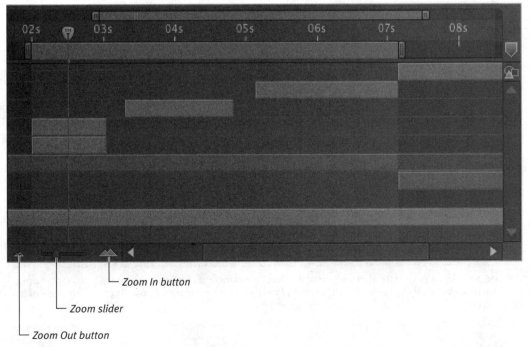

Zoom In button

Zoom slider

Zoom Out button

Figure 6.6 You can use the zoom controls at the bottom of the Timeline panel to control your view of the time graph.

To view more of the composition in the time graph:

In the time graph area of the Timeline panel, *do any of the following:*

◆ Click the Zoom Out button to view an incrementally more detailed area of the time graph.

◆ Drag the Zoom slider to the right to view more of the time graph gradually.

◆ Drag the Time Navigator start to the left (away from the Time Navigator end).

◆ Drag the Time Navigator end to the right (away from the Time Navigator start).

◆ Press the hyphen (-) on your keyboard.

◆ Press Option (Alt) while scrolling down on the mouse scroll wheel.

See Figure 6.6 for the Zoom In, Zoom Out, and Zoom slider controls; Figure 6.7 shows the time navigator.

✔ Tips

■ The shortcut for zooming out is the hyphen (-) on the main keyboard, and the shortcut for zooming in is the equal sign (=).

■ Here's another good keyboard shortcut for zooming in and out of the time graph: Press the semicolon (;) to toggle between the frame view of the time graph and a view of the entire composition.

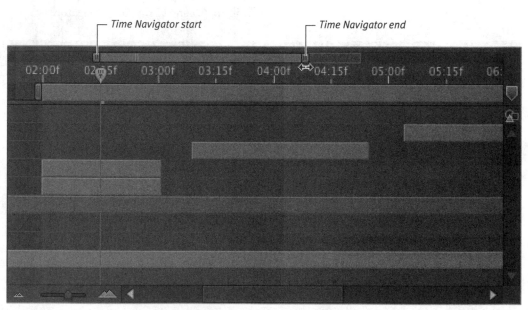

Figure 6.7 You can also drag the start and end of the Time Navigator to change your view of the time graph. Here, the Time Navigator start has been dragged to the left from its position in Figure 6.6, resulting in a wider view of the time graph.

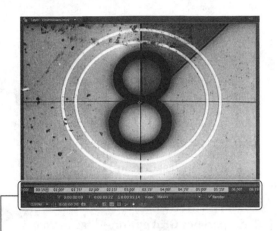

The Layer Panel

The Layer panel has many of the same controls as the Composition and Footage panels. The following sections cover the Layer panel's unique editing features, including its timeline and controls for setting In and Out points (**Figure 6.8**). Chapters 7 ("Properties and Keyframes") and 10 ("Mask Essentials") cover the Layer panel's additional features, such as its View pop-up menu and Render check box (which help you to view and manipulate layer-based attributes like anchor points, masks, and effects).

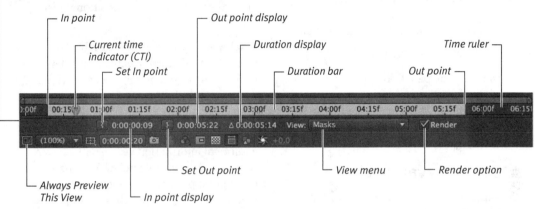

Figure 6.8 The Layer panel includes editing features not found in the Footage and Composition panels.

A Layer panel timeline corresponds to the full, unedited duration of the source footage item. The full durations of movie and audio footage are determined by the source; the full durations of still images are determined by the preferences you set (as you recall from Chapter 2, "Importing Footage into a Project").

Note that the Layer panel has its own version of the Timeline panel's time navigator, which works in much the same way as that one. (See "The Time Navigator," earlier in this chapter.)

Using the Layer panel's controls, you can set the portion of the full duration you want to use in the composition. Time displays show the exact In point, Out point, and duration you set, which are also reflected by a duration bar.

To open a Layer panel:

◆ In the Timeline panel, double-click a layer to open a Layer panel.

Double-clicking an item in the Project panel opens a Footage panel, not a Layer panel.

Parts of the Layer panel

Layer panel time ruler—Matches the full, unedited duration of the source footage.

Current time indicator (CTI)—Corresponds to the frame of the layer displayed in the Layer panel, and by default, the corresponding frame in the related composition.

Duration bar—Corresponds to the portion of the source footage included as a layer in the composition.

Set In Point button—Marks the current frame of the layer as the first frame in the composition.

Set Out Point button—Marks the current frame of the layer as the last frame included in the composition.

Always Preview This View button—Designates the view as the default for previews (playback at or near the full frame rate) rather than whatever view is frontmost. (See Chapter 8 for more information.)

Region of Interest button—Limits the area of the image in the panel for previewing. (See Chapter 8 for more information.)

Transparency Grid button—Toggles transparent areas between a black background and a checkerboard pattern, or transparency grid. (See Chapter 4, "Compositions," for more information.)

Pixel Aspect Ratio Correction button—Corrects any distortion caused by differences in the layer's pixel aspect ratio (PAR) and the display's PAR. (See Chapter 4 for more information.)

View menu—Specifies whether to make additional information visible in the Layer panel, such as masks, anchor point paths, effect point paths, and motion-tracking points. After Effects switches view options according to the task at hand. For example, selecting the Pen tool selects the layer's Mask view option automatically. (See Chapter 10, "Mask Essentials.")

Comp Family button—Makes related composition and Timeline panels appear.

Render check box—Specifies whether the window shows the layer's image only or the rendered result of any changes you make to it, such as masks and effects. (See Chapter 8, "Playback, Previews, and RAM," for more about previews.)

Figure 6.9 Note where the layer begins in the composition before trimming its In point.

Figure 6.10 Trimming the layer's In point by dragging it in the time graph is direct and intuitive; naturally, it also moves the layer's starting point in the composition.

Figure 6.11 Trimming the In point using the Layer panel controls doesn't affect the layer's starting point in the composition. It does, however, affect its duration.

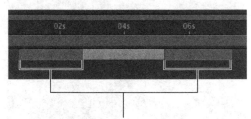

Trimmed frames (excluded from composition)

Figure 6.12 The trimmed frames of a layer appear as empty outlines extending from the layer's In and Out points. You can restore these frames at any time by extending the In or Out point again.

Trimming Layers

Changing a layer's In or Out point is known as *trimming*. Trimming a layer affects its duration; its timing in the composition depends on the trimming method you choose.

As you trim a layer in the Timeline panel, you also alter the time at which the layer starts or ends in the composition. This means you may have to shift the layer back to its original starting point after you trim it (see **Figures 6.9** and **6.10**). Although the Timeline panel provides the most direct method of trimming, it can sometimes be difficult to use with precision.

When you trim a layer using controls in the Layer panel, the layer's duration changes accordingly but its starting point in the composition remains fixed (**Figure 6.11**). This method works best if you don't want to change the layer's start time in the composition.

Whenever you *trim in* an edit point—making the layer shorter—the unused frames of the layer appear as empty outlines extending from the duration bar's In and Out points (**Figure 6.12**). You can always restore these frames by extending the In and Out points again.

To set the In and Out points in the Layer panel:

1. Set the current time to the frame of the layer you want to trim (**Figure 6.13**).

2. To set the In point, click the Set In Point button in the Layer panel (**Figure 6.14**).

   The current frame becomes the layer's In point, but the layer's starting time in the composition remains in place.

3. To set the Out point, click the Set Out Point button in the Layer panel (**Figure 6.15**).

   In the Layer panel and Timeline panel, the edit points of the Layer reflect the changes you made.

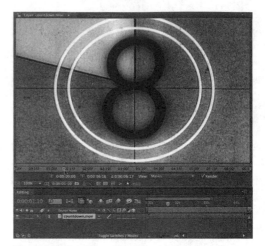

Figure 6.13 Set the current time to a frame of the layer you want to set as an edit point.

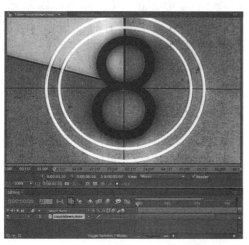

Figure 6.14 Click the Set In Point button in the Layer panel. In the Comp, the layer shifts back so the new In point starts at the same point in the comp time.

Figure 6.15 Click the Set Out Point button in the Layer panel to set the layer's Out point to the current time.

Figure 6.16 Set the current time to the frame of the layer you want to set as an edit point.

Figure 6.17 Press Option-[(Alt-[) to set the In point of the selected layer to the current time.

Table 6.1

Layer Editing Shortcuts	
EDIT	**SHORTCUT**
Move layer's In point to CTI	[(open bracket)
Move layer's Out point to CTI	] (close bracket)
Trim layer's In point to CTI	Option-[(Alt-[)
Trim layer's Out point to CTI	Option-] (Alt-])
Nudge layer one frame forward	Option-Page Up (Alt-Page Up)
Nudge layer one frame back	Option-Page Down (Alt-Page Down)

To set the In and Out points using keyboard shortcuts:

1. In the Layer panel or Timeline panel, set the current frame (**Figure 6.16**).

2. To set the In point of the layer, press Option-[(Alt-[).

   The In point of the layer is set to the current time in the composition (**Figure 6.17**).

3. To set the Out point of the layer, press Option-] (Alt-]).

   In the Layer panel and Timeline panel, the edit points reflect the changes you made. The layer's frame at the current time becomes both the layer's In point and the layer's starting point in the comp.

   See **Table 6.1** for more layer editing shortcuts.

TRIMMING LAYERS

To set the In and Out points by dragging in the Timeline:

In the time graph area of the Timeline panel, *do either of the following:*

◆ To set the In point, drag the In point of a layer's duration bar (the handle at the left end of the duration bar) (**Figure 6.18**).

◆ To set the Out point, drag the Out point of a layer's duration bar (the handle at the right end of the duration bar) (**Figure 6.19**).

Make sure you drag the ends of the layer's duration bar, not the bar itself. Otherwise, you could change the layer's position in time rather than its In or Out point.

✔ Tips

■ You can see the exact position of an edit point in time by looking at the Info panel's time display as you drag.

■ If you reach a point where you're unable to further increase a layer's duration, it means you've run out of source footage.

Figure 6.18 Drag the In point handle of a layer's duration bar to change both its In point and where it starts in the composition.

Figure 6.19 Drag the Out point handle of a layer's duration bar to change both its Out point and where it ends in the composition.

Figure 6.20 Drag a layer from the center portion of its duration bar...

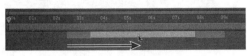

Figure 6.21 ...to shift its position in time (without changing its duration). Press Shift after you begin dragging to activate the Snap to Edges feature.

Moving Layers in Time

You can move a layer's position in time either by dragging the layer's duration bar or by using the controls in the In/Out panels of the Timeline panel.

To move a layer in time by dragging:

◆ *Do any of the following:*

   ▲ In the time graph area of the Timeline panel, drag a layer to a new position in time (**Figures 6.20** and **6.21**).

   ▲ Dragging a layer to the left causes the layer to begin earlier in the composition.

   ▲ Dragging a layer to the right causes the layer to begin later in the composition.

   Make sure you drag from the middle section of the layer's duration bar; dragging either end changes the duration of the layer.

✔ Tips

■ A layer's In point can occur before the beginning of the composition, just as its Out point can occur after the end of the composition. As you would expect, any frames beyond the beginning or end of the comp won't be included in previews or output.

■ Whether you're moving or trimming a layer, pressing Shift after you begin to drag causes the In or Out point to *snap to edges*. That is, the layer's edit points behave as though they're magnetized and easily align with the edit points of other layers, the current time indicator, and the layer and composition markers.

Showing Numerical Editing Controls

You can view and control the timing of each layer in the timeline by revealing four columns of information:

In—The layer's starting time in the comp. Enter a value to change the layer's starting point in the comp (*not* the layer's first frame).

Out—The layer's ending time in the comp. Enter a value to set the layer's ending time in the comp (*not* the layer's last frame).

Duration—The length of the layer, expressed as a corollary of *speed*. Entering a value changes the layer's playback speed and, indirectly, its Out point.

Stretch—The layer's playback frame rate expressed as a percentage of the layer's native playback rate. Entering a value changes the layer's playback rate and, indirectly, its duration and Out point. See the next section, "Changing a Layer's Speed."

The timeline lets you expand all four columns as a set or each one individually.

Because this book covers several other, more convenient ways to move and trim layers, using the In and Out panels won't be covered in detail. However, turn to the next section to find out how to use the Duration and Stretch columns.

To show and hide the In, Out, Duration, and Stretch columns:

◆ *Do either of the following:*

▲ In the Timeline panel, click the In/Out/Duration/Stretch button ⁂ to reveal the In/Out/Duration/Stretch panel. Click the button again to hide the panel (**Figures 6.22** and **6.23**).

▲ Control-click (right-click) any panel of the Timeline panel, and choose the panel you want to view from the context menu.

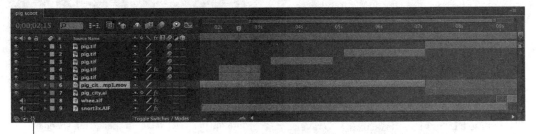

In/Out/Duration/Stretch button

Figure 6.22 Click the In/Out/Duration/Stretch button to change the In/Out/Duration/Stretch panel from hidden...

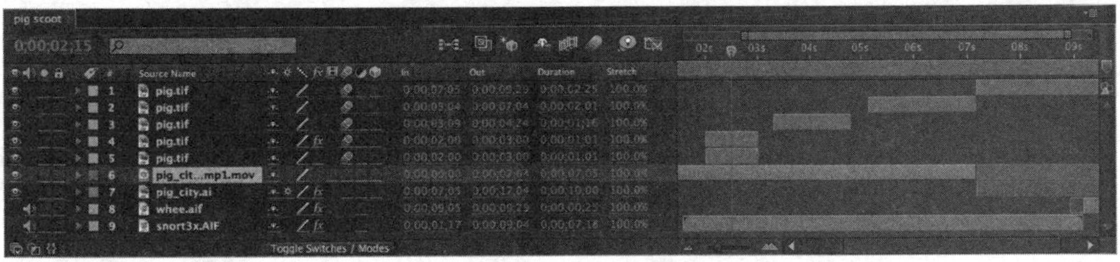

Figure 6.23 ...to visible. Click the button again to hide the panel.

Changing a Layer's Speed

Changing a layer's playback speed is yet another feature After Effects shares with typical nonlinear editing programs. However, there is a crucial difference between how you set the values in those programs and in After Effects.

In many nonlinear editing programs, you enter a *speed*: A value greater than 100 percent *increases* the speed, and a value less than 100 percent decreases the speed. In After Effects, you enter a *stretch factor* value: A stretch factor greater than 100 percent *decreases* the speed of a layer (stretching, or increasing, its duration), and a stretch factor less than 100 percent *increases* the speed of a layer. Entering a negative value reverses the playback direction of the layer—and also reverses the order of its property keyframes (see Chapter 7, "Properties and Keyframes").

To reverse a layer's speed without also reversing its keyframes, you can use the Time Remapping feature, explained in Chapter 14, "More Layer Techniques." Time remapping also lets you adjust the playback speed of a layer over time or create a freeze-frame effect.

To change the playback speed of a layer:

1. *Do one of the following:*
   - ▲ In the Timeline panel, click the Duration display or Stretch display for a layer (**Figure 6.24**).
   - ▲ In the Timeline panel, select a layer and choose Layer > Time Stretch.

   The Time Stretch dialog opens (**Figure 6.25**).

Figure 6.24 To change the speed of a layer, click its Duration or Stretch display.

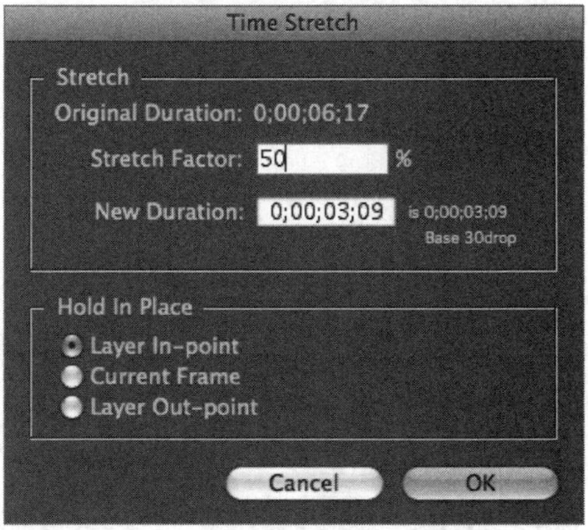

Figure 6.25 In the Time Stretch dialog, enter a new duration or stretch factor to change the speed of the layer. In the Hold In Place section, choose which frame of the layer will maintain its position in the time graph.

2. In the Stretch section, *do either of the following:*

   ▲ For New Duration, enter a new duration for the layer.

   ▲ For Stretch Factor, enter the percentage change of the layer's duration.

   To slow playback speed, enter a duration greater than that of the original or a stretch factor greater than 100 percent. To increase playback speed, enter a duration less than that of the original or a stretch factor less than 100 percent. Enter a negative value to reverse a layer's playback direction.

3. In the Hold In Place section of the Time Stretch dialog, select one of the following options to determine the position of the layer when its speed and duration change:

   Layer In-point maintains the layer's starting point position in the composition.

   Current Frame moves the layer's In and Out points while maintaining the frame's position at the current time indicator.

   Layer Out-point maintains the layer's ending point position in the composition.

4. Click OK to close the Time Stretch dialog.

   The selected layer's speed, duration, and placement in time reflect your changes. However, the range of footage frames you specified to include—the layer's In and Out points—remain the same.

✔ Tips

■ To quickly reverse a layer's playback (a stretch factor of –100 percent), select the layer and press Command-Option-R (Ctrl-Alt-R) or select Layer > Time > Time Reverse Layer.

■ You can freeze-frame the current frame of the selected layer by choosing Layer > Time > Freeze Frame. This command automatically applies the appropriate time remapping settings. See Chapter 9, "Keyframe Interpolation," for more about time remapping.

Performing a Slip Edit

After Effects includes another editing feature common to nonlinear editing programs: *slip edits*.

When you're working with layers created from motion footage, you'll find that you often need to change a portion of video without altering its position or duration in the composition. Although you can do this by reopening the Layer panel and setting new In and Out points, you must be careful to set edit points that result in the same duration. By using a slip edit, however, you can achieve the same result in a single step.

To slip a layer:

1. In the Tools panel, select the Pan Behind tool ▓ (**Figure 6.26**).

2. Position the mouse over a layer created from motion footage.

   The mouse pointer becomes a Slip Edit tool ▓ (**Figure 6.27**).

3. *Do either of the following:*

   ▲ **Drag left** to slip the footage left, using frames that come later in the footage.

   ▲ **Drag right** to slip the footage right, using frames that come earlier in the footage.

   The In and Out points of the source footage change by the same amount, which means the layer maintains its duration and position in the time ruler. As you drag, you can see the "hidden" footage extending from beyond the layer's In and Out points (**Figure 6.28**).

Figure 6.26 Select the Pan Behind tool.

Figure 6.27 When you position the mouse over a layer created from motion footage, the mouse pointer becomes a Slip Edit tool.

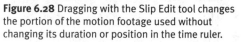

Figure 6.28 Dragging with the Slip Edit tool changes the portion of the motion footage used without changing its duration or position in the time ruler.

✔ Tips

■ You can also perform a slip edit by dragging the layer's "hidden" trimmed frames with the Selection tool. The trimmed portions of a layer appear as an outline extending beyond the solid part of a layer's duration bar.

■ Those who use nonlinear editing software know that the counterpart to the slip edit is the *slide edit*. This is also possible in After Effects. Each layer in After Effects occupies a separate track, so you can just drag a layer to a new position in the time ruler.

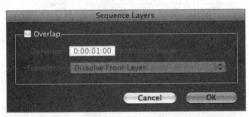

Figure 6.29 Select the layers you want to sequence.

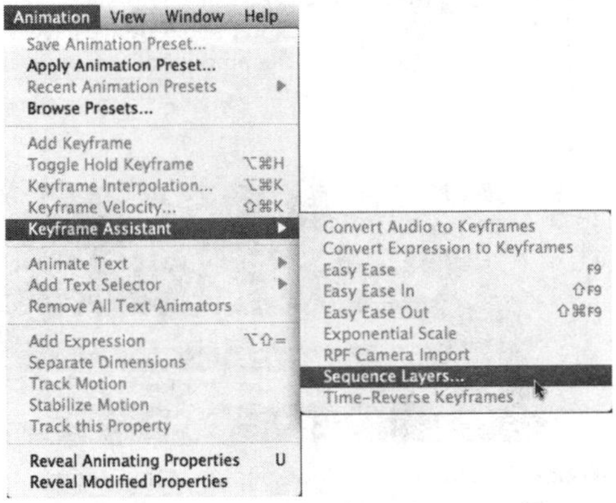

Figure 6.30 Choose Animation > Keyframe Assistant > Sequence Layers.

Figure 6.31 In the Sequence Layers dialog, make sure Overlap is not selected...

Figure 6.32 ...to arrange the selected layers into a simple sequence.

Sequencing and Overlapping Layers

Although you might not choose After Effects for editing per se, you may find yourself starting many projects by creating a simple sequence. Fortunately, After Effects automates this common request with its Sequence Layers and Overlap features.

The Sequence Layers command quickly places selected layers one after another in the time graph, seamlessly aligning their Out and In points so that the layers play back in an uninterrupted sequence. By selecting the command's Overlap option, you can make each successive layer in the sequence overlap with the last for the duration you specify. This way, they're arranged properly for creating transitions from one layer to the next. The Sequence Layers command can even create fade transitions automatically (or you can add and animate transition effects to the overlapping layers.).

You'll learn more about creating transitions and other keyframed changes in Chapter 9, "Keyframe Interpolation."

To arrange layers in a sequence:

1. In the Timeline panel, select the layers you want to sequence (**Figure 6.29**).

2. Choose Animation > Keyframe Assistant > Sequence Layers (**Figure 6.30**).
   The Sequence Layers dialog opens.

3. Make sure the Overlap check box is not selected (**Figure 6.31**).

4. Click OK to close the dialog.
   The selected layers are arranged in sequence, top layer first (**Figure 6.32**).

To arrange layers in an overlapping sequence:

1. In the Timeline panel, select the layers you want to arrange in an overlapping sequence.

2. Choose Animation > Keyframe Assistant > Sequence Layers.

   The Sequence Layers dialog opens.

3. Select the Overlap check box (**Figure 6.33**).

4. In the Duration field, enter the amount of time that the layers should overlap.

5. Choose one of the following cross-fade options from the Transition pop-up menu (**Figure 6.34**):

   Off—For no cross-fade

   Dissolve Front Layer—To automatically fade out the end of each preceding layer

   Cross Dissolve Front and Back Layers—To fade out the end of each preceding layer automatically, and to fade up the beginning of each succeeding layer

6. Click OK to close the dialog.

   The selected layers are arranged in an overlapping sequence (top layer first) and use the cross-fade option you specified (**Figure 6.35**).

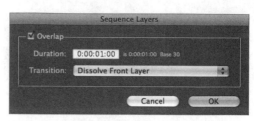

Figure 6.33 To overlap the layers of a sequence, select the Overlap check box in the Sequence Layers dialog. For Duration, enter the amount of time you want the layers to overlap.

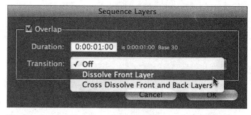

Figure 6.34 In the Transition pop-up menu, choose the appropriate option.

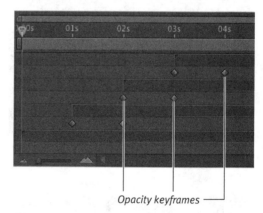

Opacity keyframes

Figure 6.35 The selected layers are arranged in an overlapping sequence. Here, you can see how the Dissolve Front Layer option generates Opacity keyframes that fade up each successive layer.

SEQUENCING AND OVERLAPPING LAYERS

Figure 6.36 To duplicate a layer, select it...

Edit	Composition	Layer	Effect	Ani
Undo Background Color Change				⌘Z
Can't Redo				⇧⌘Z
History				▶
Cut				⌘X
Copy				⌘C
Copy Expression Only				
Paste				⌘V
Clear				
Duplicate				⌘D
Split Layer				⇧⌘D
Lift Work Area				
Extract Work Area				
Select All				⌘A
Deselect All				⇧⌘A
Label				▶
Purge				▶
Edit Original...				⌘E
Edit in Adobe Soundbooth				
Templates				▶

Figure 6.37 ...and choose Edit > Duplicate, or press Command-D (Ctrl-D).

Figure 6.38 Each duplicate layer is distinguished by an incrementally higher number (in this case, "2") after its Layer name (duplicate layer's Source names are identical).

Duplicating Layers

You can add a footage item to one or more compositions as many times as you like, creating a new layer each time. However, it's often easier to duplicate a layer that's already in a composition, particularly when you want to use its edit points or other properties (such as masks, transformations, effects, and so on). When you create a duplicate, it appears just above the original layer in the stacking order. The duplicate uses the same name as the original, unless you specified a custom name for the original layer. When the original layer uses a custom name, duplicates have a number appended to the name; subsequent duplicates are numbered incrementally.

To duplicate a layer:

1. In the Timeline panel, select a layer (**Figure 6.36**).

2. Choose Edit > Duplicate, or press Command-D (Ctrl-D) (**Figure 6.37**).

   A copy of the layer appears above the original layer in the stacking order (**Figure 6.38**). The copy is selected; you may want to rename the new layer (as described in "Naming Layers" in Chapter 5).

Splitting Layers

The Split Layer command effectively cuts a layer at the current time indicator, creating two layers. You can set a preference to determine which layer—the layer before the split point or the layer after the split point—is higher in the stacking order.

To split a layer:

1. In the Timeline panel, select a layer.

2. Set the current time to the frame at which you want to split the layer (**Figure 6.39**).

3. Choose Edit > Split Layer, or press Shift-Command-D (Shift-Ctrl-D) (**Figure 6.40**).

   The layer splits in two, creating one layer that ends at the current time indicator and another that begins at the current time indicator (**Figure 6.41**). The layer that becomes higher in the stacking order depends on the preference you specify in the General Preferences dialog.

Figure 6.39 Set the current time to the frame at which you want to split the selected layer.

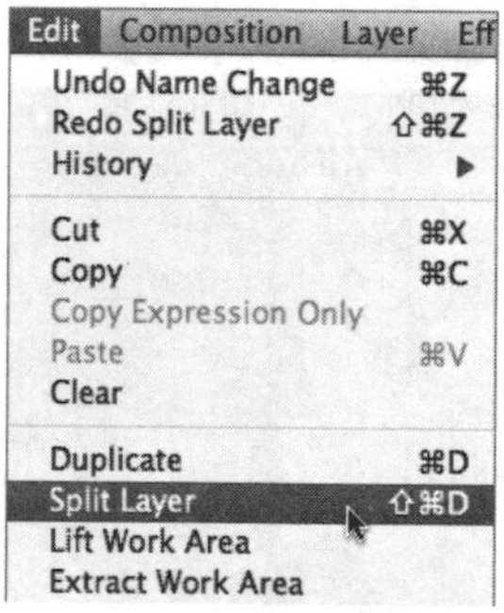

Figure 6.40 Choose Edit > Split Layer.

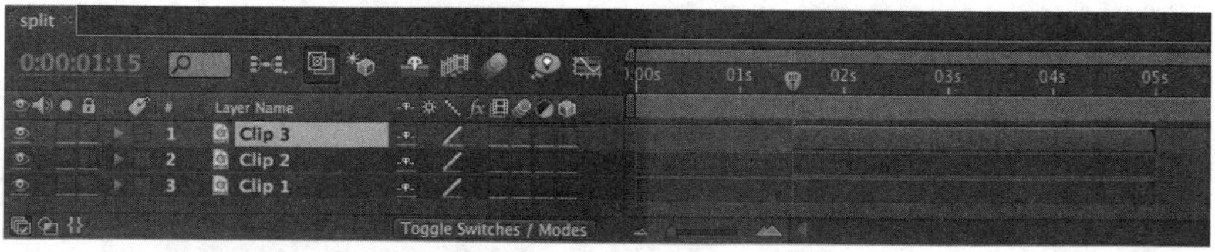

Figure 6.41 The selected layer splits into two layers at the current time.

Using Markers

Like most nonlinear editing programs, After Effects enables you to mark important points in time with a visible stamp called a *marker*. Markers allow you to identify music beats visually and to synchronize visual effects with sound effects. They can also help you quickly move the current time to particular points in the composition.

You can set composition markers and layer markers. Composition markers appear in a comp's time ruler, whereas layer markers appear anywhere in the layer's horizontal track in the time graph.

In addition to flagging a frame, markers can include informative text, called comments. By default, composition markers automatically include a comment that numbers each one sequentially, and layer markers don't include a comment. But you can enter any comment you want to appear with either kind of marker. Naturally, comments are for your reference in the Timeline panel only, and they don't appear in previews or renders.

When you export a composition to the appropriate format, markers can trigger events like opening a Web page or a DVD chapter or cue a behavior in a Flash movie. Check After Effects Help for detailed information on these specialized features.

✔ Tips

- When you nest a comp—that is, make it a layer in another comp—its comp markers appear as layer markers. (For more about nesting, see the "Nesting Comps" sidebar in Chapter 4 and Chapter 16, "Complex Projects.")

- Changing a nested comp's layer markers doesn't affect the markers in the source comp. For example, if you remove a nested comp's layer marker, the corresponding marker in the original comp remains.

- Control-clicking (right-clicking) the nested comp's layer marker and choosing Update Markers from Source makes the nested comp's layer markers match its source comp's markers.

To add a composition marker by dragging:

◆ In the Timeline panel, drag a composition time marker from the marker well (**Figure 6.42**) to the desired point in the time graph (**Figure 6.43**).

A marker appears in the time ruler of the Timeline panel.

To add a composition marker at the current time indicator:

1. Move the current time indicator to the frame you want to mark in the composition (**Figure 6.44**).

2. Press Shift and a number on the main keyboard (not the numeric keypad).

A marker with the number you pressed appears in the time ruler of the Timeline panel (**Figure 6.45**).

To move the current time indicator to a composition marker:

◆ Press the number of a composition marker on the main keyboard (not the numeric keypad).

The current time indicator moves to the composition marker with the number you pressed.

Figure 6.42 To add a composition marker, drag a marker from the marker well...

Figure 6.43 ...and drop the marker at the frame you want to mark in the time ruler.

Figure 6.44 You can also place a composition marker by setting the current time...

Figure 6.45 ...and then pressing Shift and a number on the main keyboard to place the numbered marker at the current time (in this case, Shift-2 sets a marker labeled "2").

USING MARKERS

Figure 6.46 To add a layer marker, select a layer and set the current time to the frame you want to mark.

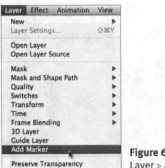

Figure 6.47 Choose Layer > Add Marker.

Figure 6.48 The marker appears in the selected layer's horizontal track at the current time indicator.

Figure 6.49 To move a marker, simply drag it to a new position in time.

Figure 6.50 Positioning the mouse pointer over a marker while pressing Command (Ctrl) makes the Scissors icon appear. Command-click (Ctrl-click) to remove the marker.

To add a layer marker:

1. Select the layer to which you want to add a marker.

2. Set the current time to the frame to which you want to add a marker (**Figure 6.46**).

3. *Do one of the following:*

   ▲ Choose Layer > Add Marker (**Figure 6.47**).

   ▲ Press the asterisk (*) on the numeric keypad (not the main keyboard).

   A marker appears on the layer's duration bar at the current time indicator (**Figure 6.48**).

To move a marker:

◆ Drag the composition or layer marker to a new position in time (**Figure 6.49**).

To remove a marker:

◆ Command-click (Ctrl-click) a composition or layer icon.

   Positioning the mouse pointer over a marker while pressing Command (Ctrl) makes the Scissors icon appear (**Figure 6.50**). Command-click (Ctrl-click) to remove the marker.

To add a marker comment:

1. In the Timeline panel, double-click a composition or layer marker (**Figure 6.51**).

   Depending on the kind of marker you double-click, a Composition Marker or Layer Marker dialog opens.

2. In the dialog, enter a comment for the marker in the Comment field (**Figure 6.52**).

   You can also add chapter links or Web links if your output format supports these features.

3. Click OK to close the dialog.

   The comment you specified appears next to the layer marker (**Figure 6.53**).

✔ Tips

- You can add layer markers on the fly as you preview audio. This makes it especially easy to mark the beats of music or other audio. Press the decimal point (.) on the numeric keypad to preview audio only. As the audio previews, press the asterisk (*) key on the numeric keypad. (Adobe Premiere Pro users should recognize this technique.)

- Adobe Premiere Pro CS4 can automatically transcribe speech from a clip's audio track. When you use the clip in After Effects, the words from the transcription can appear as layer marker comments. For details, check out Adobe Premiere Pro or refer to After Effects Help.

Figure 6.51 To add a comment to a marker (or to specify other options), double-click the marker.

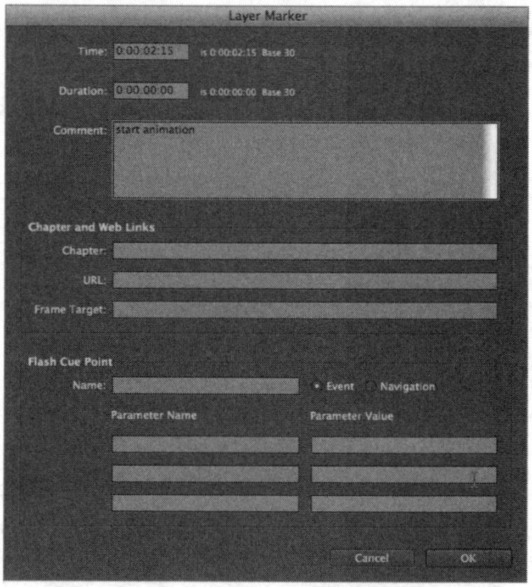

Figure 6.52 In the dialog, type a comment. You can also specify a duration, Web or chapter link, and Flash cue point.

Figure 6.53 The comment you specified appears next to the marker in the Timeline panel.

USING MARKERS

PROPERTIES AND KEYFRAMES

Once they see what After Effects can do, most folks can't wait to take a closer look at the program that produces such artful results. Upon closer inspection, however, it's easy to recoil from the cryptic array of controls that look more like the tools of a scientist than those of an artist.

But don't let a few numbers and graphs intimidate you! This chapter fearlessly unveils layer properties and demystifies animation. Once you understand how to define properties, you can extend a few simple techniques to control practically any property of any layer in a composition. Having conquered that paper tiger, you'll be ready to animate those properties using keyframes.

As any scientist or artist can tell you, it's important to have full control over the variables, but some of the best innovations are arrived at randomly. By generating random variations on specified properties, After Effects' Brainstorm feature lets you freely experiment and achieve results you might not have otherwise—in a manner not unlike a plant breeder or a Jackson Pollock. You'll find that the techniques you learn in this chapter are fundamental, and you'll be able to apply them to the features covered in subsequent chapters, from masks to effects to 3D layers. But first, you'll want to see the animation in action, using techniques covered in Chapter 8, "Playback, Previews, and RAM." And then you should build on the core keyframing techniques presented in Chapter 9, "Keyframe Interpolation." You'll realize that animating in After Effects isn't rocket science, after all—but mastering it is still an art.

Layer Property Types

A *property* refers to any of a layer's visual or audio characteristics to which you can assign different values over time. For most layers, properties fall into these main categories: masks, effects, and transform. In addition, layers that contain audio include an Audio property, and 3D layers include a Material Options property (**Figure 7.1**). For more information on the special characteristics of 3D layers, see Chapter 15, "3D Layers."

As you'll see in the next section, "Viewing Properties," clicking the small triangle next to a layer reveals its property headings in outline form. The order in which these categories are listed—masks, effects, transform—reflects the order in which the properties are rendered. Although you don't need to concern yourself with rendering order now, it does become important as your animations grow in complexity.

Masks

Like the acetate layers used in traditional compositing, masks let you include some portions of an image and exclude others. They also make it possible for you to apply effects to selected portions of layers.

You can apply one or several masks to each layer in a composition and then define the way those masks interact. Not only can you control the shape and feather of a mask, but you can also animate these attributes over time. Chapter 10, "Mask Essentials," describes using masks in more detail.

Effects

Effects include a wide range of options for modifying sound and images. You can use them to make simple adjustments—such as correcting color or filtering audio—or to make more dramatic changes, such as

distorting and stylizing. *Keying effects* help to composite images, and *transition effects* blend one layer into another. You can even use effects to generate visual elements such as text, light, and particles.

Transform properties

Although you may not choose to apply any masks or effects to the layers of your compositions, you must still define their basic properties, including position, scale, rotation, and opacity—known as *transform properties*. This chapter focuses on these essential layer properties as they relate to 2D layers. (For a detailed discussion of the transform properties of 3D layers, see Chapter 15, "3D Layers.")

Audio properties

Layers that contain audio display an Audio property in the layer outline. Because only images can have masks or transform properties, audio-only layers can contain only the Effects and Audio property categories. The Audio category includes a Levels property to control audio volume as well as a waveform display. Along with transform properties, this chapter explains how to set audio levels.

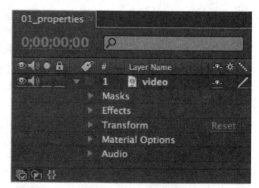

Figure 7.1 There are three major categories of visual properties: masks, effects, and transform. Layers with an audio track contain an Audio property; layers you designate as 3D have a Material Options property.

Viewing Properties

You can view any combination of layer properties in the Timeline panel in what's called a *layer outline* (**Figure 7.2**). That is, each layer works like the heading of an outline: Expanding the layer reveals property headings, which in turn can be expanded to reveal individual properties. (The property headings that are revealed depend on the layer; a layer without masks or audio won't include those headings in the outline.) Using keyboard shortcuts, you can reveal properties selectively and prevent the outline from becoming long and unwieldy.

Revealing a property also displays its current value and its *property track*, an area under the time ruler that shows the property's keyframes. Keyframes, as you'll learn, indicate points at which you define a property's values in order to make them change over time. In other words, the property track is where you can view and control animation.

To fine-tune an animation—particularly between the keyframes—you can go in for an even more detailed view using the Graph Editor (**Figure 7.3**). As its name suggests, the Graph Editor lets you see selected property values as a graph. You can manipulate the graph directly, manually changing not only the keyframes, but also how the values change between keyframes (the interpolated values).

Figure 7.2 Expanding a layer reveals its properties in outline form, or a layer outline. Appearing next to the property's name are its current value (under the layer switches) and keyframes (under the time ruler).

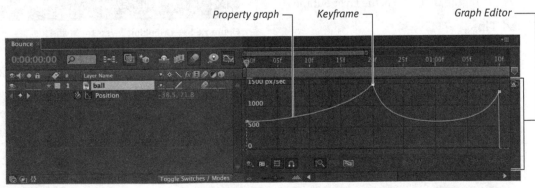

Figure 7.3 You can toggle the area under the time ruler to the Graph Editor. The Graph Editor depicts property values in graph form, allowing you to adjust both keyframed values and the manner in which After Effects calculates values between keyframes.

VIEWING PROPERTIES

But don't let yourself get overwhelmed by unfamiliar terminology or seemingly complex choices. For the moment, rest assured that the Timeline panel allows you to reveal the properties you want at the level of detail you need. This chapter covers setting property values and basic keyframing. Chapter 9, "Keyframe Interpolation," covers fine-tuning animation in the Graph Editor.

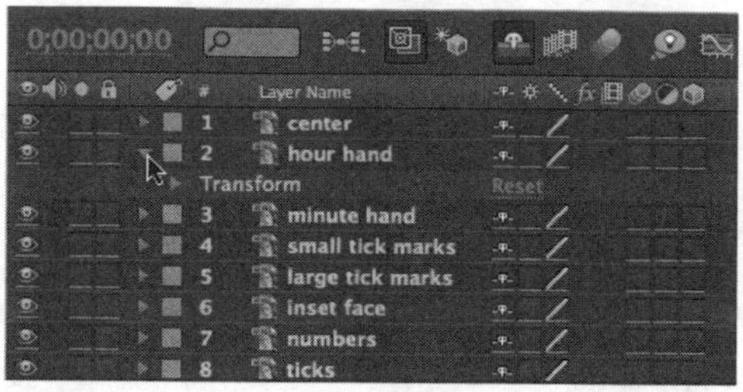

To expand or collapse a layer outline by clicking:

◆ In the Timeline panel, *do any of the following:*

    ▲ To expand the first level of property headings, click the triangle to the left of a layer (**Figure 7.4**).

    The triangle spins clockwise to point down, revealing the first level of the layer outline.

    ▲ To further expand the outline, click the triangle to the left of a property heading (**Figure 7.5**).

    The triangle spins clockwise to point down, revealing the next level of the outline.

    ▲ To collapse an expanded layer outline heading, click the triangle again.

    The triangle spins counterclockwise, hiding that level of the layer outline.

✔ Tips

■ You can expand the outline for multiple layers simultaneously by selecting more than one layer before expanding the outline. Expanding the outline for one selected layer expands all selected layers (**Figure 7.6**).

Figure 7.4 Click the triangle to the left of a layer to reveal the first level of property headings.

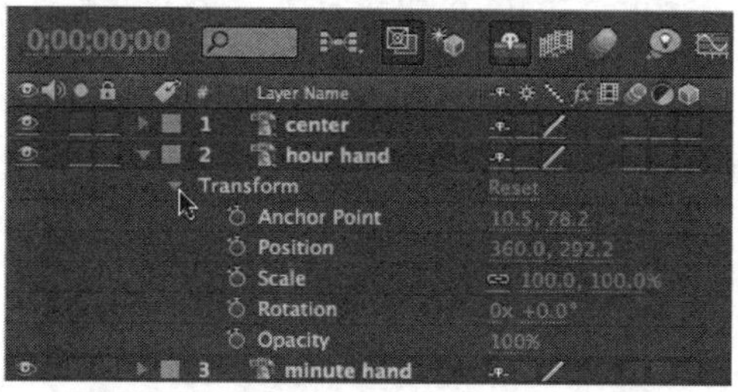

Figure 7.5 Continue to expand the outline by clicking the triangles. Click the triangles again to collapse the outline.

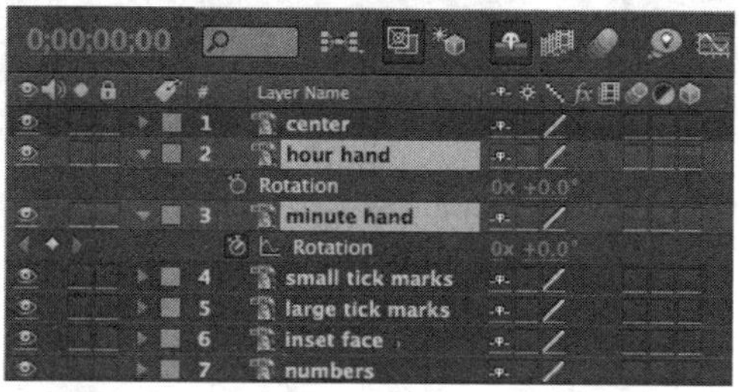

Figure 7.6 Select multiple layers to expand the outline for all of them at once.

Table 7.1

Viewing Layer Properties	
To expand/collapse	Press this shortcut
Transform	
Anchor Point	A
Position	P
Scale	S
Rotation	R
Opacity	T
Material Options	AA (3D layers)
Mask	
Mask Path	M
Mask Feather	F
Mask Opacity	TT
Mask Properties	MM
Effects	
Effects	E
Expressions	EE
Audio	
Audio Levels	L
Audio Waveform	LL
Headings	
Add/remove from outline	Shift-property shortcut
All animated	U (keyframed values)
All modified	UU

To view layer properties using keyboard shortcuts:

◆ To expand the layer outline by using keyboard shortcuts, select one or more layers and use the appropriate keyboard shortcut (see **Table 7.1**).

✔ Tips

■ Some shortcuts work differently for light and camera layers (covered in Chapter 15, "3D Layers"). Because lights aren't visible (only their effects are), pressing T reveals a light layer's Intensity property. For both lights and cameras, pressing A reveals the Point of Interest property, and pressing R reveals the Orientation property.

■ Just as 3D layers, camera layers, and light layers have unique properties, text layers and shape layers possess property categories specific to them. See Chapter 12, "Creating and Animating Text," and Chapter 14, "More Layer Techniques," for details.

VIEWING PROPERTIES

Setting Global vs. Animated Property Values

Now that you know how to view layer properties, you can set their values. The following sections describe how to set property values globally—that is, how to set a single value for the duration of the layer. Then, you'll animate properties by setting different values at different points in time. But before we continue, it may be helpful to understand a few basic differences between global and animated properties.

As you proceed, you'll notice that a property that has a *global*, or unchanging, value has an I-beam icon at its current time in the time graph, and the Stopwatch icon next to the property's name appears deselected (**Figure 7.7**).

An animated property, in contrast, displays keyframe icons, which designate values at specific points in time, and an activated Stopwatch icon (**Figure 7.8**). You can set global properties without regard to the current time, but you must always specify the current frame before setting an animated property. Although global and animated properties look different in the timeline, you always reveal and use property controls the same way.

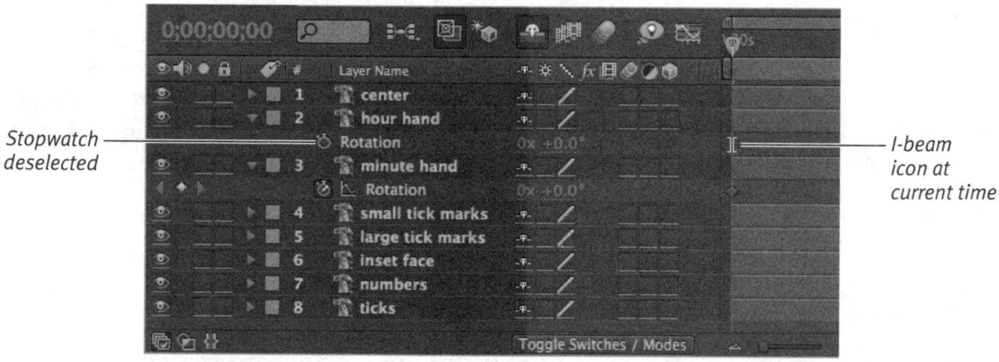

Stopwatch deselected

I-beam icon at current time

Figure 7.7 A deselected Stopwatch icon and an I-beam icon in the selected property track identify a static property.

Stopwatch selected

Keyframe

Figure 7.8 An activated Stopwatch icon and keyframe icons in the property track identify an animated property.

Viewing Spatial Controls in the Comp Panel

As you know, the Composition panel lets you view how layers will appear in your final output. It also provides controls for the spatial properties of layers, including the following:

Handles—These appear at the perimeter of the layer, at each compass point. Dragging them affects the scale of the layer.

Mask and Shape paths—You can edit these color-coded paths. Masks are covered in Chapter 10, "Mask Essentials"; Shapes are covered in Chapter 14, "More Layer Techniques."

Effect controls—These show the spatial controls of many effects, such as the end points of path text.

Keyframes—Position keyframes appear as marks in the motion path. You can move and add keyframes directly in the motion path.

Motion paths—These show a layer's position as it changes over time as a dotted line. You can't change the path directly, but you can change the keyframes that define the ends of the line segments, as well as the tangents that define the line.

Motion path tangents—You can control the curve of the motion path by using motion path tangents, which affect how the position values are calculated between keyframes. They can be extended from keyframes and dragged directly to alter the motion path.

By default, the Composition panel displays layer and effect controls whenever a layer is selected (**Figure 7.9**). You can toggle these view options on and off in the View Options dialog or, in some instances, by using buttons in the Composition panel. You'll appreciate each control more fully as you employ corresponding techniques explained later in this and future chapters.

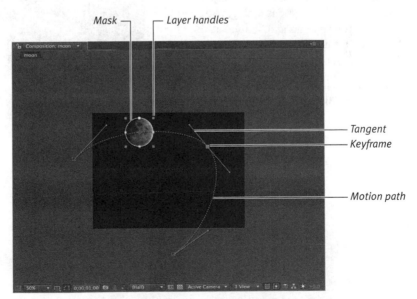

Mask — — *Layer handles*

— *Tangent*
— *Keyframe*

— *Motion path*

Figure 7.9 By default, the Composition panel displays spatial information and controls for selected layers, such as layer handles, keyframes, and the motion path.

To view layer and effect controls in the Composition panel:

1. In the Composition panel's menu, choose View Options (**Figure 7.10**).

   The View Options dialog appears.

2. Select Layer Controls, and then specify the layer controls you want to make visible in the Composition panel.

   A check indicates that the controls are visible in the Composition panel when a layer is selected; no check indicates that the controls are hidden (**Figure 7.11**).

✔ Tips

- You can specify whether the motion path is visible and how many keyframes it shows at once in the Display pane of the Preferences dialog.

- A layer's effect point controls (if present) are covered in more detail in the section "Setting an Effect Point," in Chapter 11.

- Instead of selecting Mask and Shape Paths in the View Options dialog, you can click the Toggle Mask and Shape Path Visibility button ■ at the bottom of the Composition panel.

- Cameras and lights are covered in Chapter 15, "3D Layers."

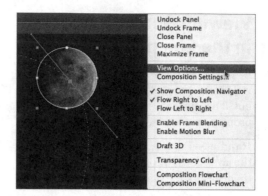

Figure 7.10 In the Composition panel menu, choose View Options.

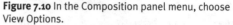

Figure 7.11 In the View Options dialog, specify the layer controls you want to be visible in the Composition panel.

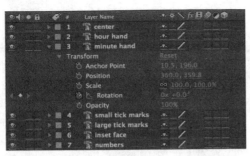

Figure 7.12 Although a layer may not use masks or effects, each of its transform properties has a value—either by default or as you choose to set them.

Anchor point in layer   Anchor point in comp

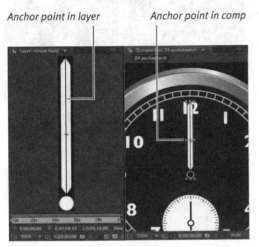

Figure 7.13 Initially, the anchor point is located at the literal center of a layer. But it's not always the best point from which to calculate the layer's transformations (as in this example).

Transform Properties

Although a layer may not use masks or effects, its transform properties—the anchor point, position, scale, rotation, and opacity—are fundamental (**Figure 7.12**). When you create a layer, you actively set its position, either by dragging to the timeline or to the Composition icon to center it, or by dragging to the Composition panel to place it manually. The other transform properties all have default initial values. The following sections describe each transform property and how to change its values.

Keep in mind that even though the following sections focus on transform properties, you employ similar techniques to set values for all types of layer properties.

Anchor point

After Effects calculates spatial transformations— position, scale, and rotation—of a layer in terms of its anchor point. By default, a layer's anchor point is positioned in the center of the layer. However, you may need to move the anchor point so that transformations are calculated from a different spot. The placement of the anchor point relative to the layer image can mean the difference between animating, say, a propeller or a pendulum, or the hands of a clock, as in **Figure 7.13**.

You can move a layer's anchor point by dragging it with the Selection tool in the Layer panel or by dragging it with the Pan Behind tool in either the Layer or Comp panels.

When you drag the anchor point in the Layer panel, it may appear that you've also changed the layer's position in the Comp panel. Actually, the layer's Position property remains the same; you simply changed the spot in the layer that determines its position in the composition. You can compensate for the shift by dragging the layer in the Comp panel, thereby adjusting its position property.

To change a layer's anchor point without disturbing the layer's placement in the composition, use the Pan Behind tool. Dragging with the Pan Behind tool moves the layer's anchor point and repositions it in a single step. In other words, it recalculates the layer's position value to compensate for the new anchor point value. This way, the layer maintains its relative placement in the composition.

To change the anchor point in the Layer panel:

1. In the Timeline panel or Composition panel, double-click a layer.

   A Layer panel appears.

2. In the Layer panel's View menu, choose Anchor Point Path (**Figure 7.14**).

   The layer's anchor point icon appears at its current position. When the anchor point's position is animated, a dotted line represents its motion path.

3. In the image area of the Layer panel, drag the anchor point to the position you want (**Figure 7.15**).

   Because the anchor point maintains its position in the Composition panel, the image in the Comp panel moves relative to the anchor point in the Layer panel (**Figure 7.16**).

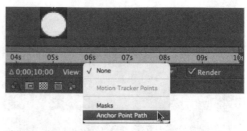

Figure 7.14 In the Layer panel's View menu, choose Anchor Point Path.

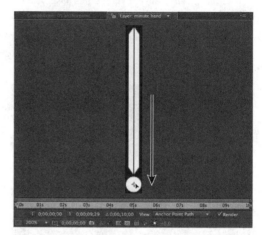

Figure 7.15 When you move an anchor point in a Layer panel...

Figure 7.16 ...the anchor point maintains its position in the comp. Here, the minute hand moves up as the anchor point is moved down to its proper point in the layer.

Figure 7.17 To move the anchor point without disturbing the arrangement of the layers, select the Pan Behind tool.

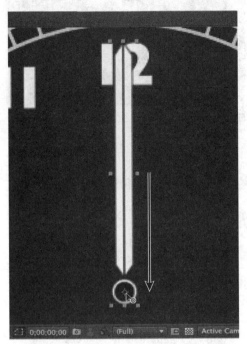

Figure 7.18 Using the Pan Behind tool recalculates the layer's position as you move the anchor point in the Composition panel.

To change the anchor point without moving the layer in the composition:

1. Select a layer in the composition.

2. If the selected layer's anchor point isn't visible in the Composition panel, choose View Options in the Composition panel menu and select Handles.

3. In the Tools panel, select the Pan Behind tool (**Figure 7.17**).

4. In the Composition panel, drag the anchor point to a new position (**Figure 7.18**). (Make sure to drag the anchor point, not the layer itself.)

   The layer's anchor point and position values change simultaneously and by corresponding amounts, so the layer maintains its relative placement in the Composition panel.

✔ Tips

- When importing a layered file as a composition, you can opt to import layers at each layer's size or at the document's size. The choice you make helps determine the anchor point's initial position relative to the layer's image. See Chapter 2, "Importing Footage into a Project," for more information.

- Just as the Pan Behind tool compensates for a layer's position as you move its anchor point, it can also compensate for a layer's position as you move its mask. In both cases, it calculates two properties at once, and avoids disturbing placement of elements in the comp. See Chapter 10, "Mask Essentials," for more about using Pan Behind with masks.

Position

Setting a layer's position places its anchor point in the 2D space of the composition. The exact position of a layer is expressed in (X, Y) coordinates, where the top-left corner of the composition is (0, 0). (Moving the zero point of the rulers doesn't change the coordinate system.) You can position a layer inside or outside the visible area of the composition. (Position and orientation properties for 3D layers are discussed in Chapter 15, "3D Layers.")

To change a layer's position in the Composition panel:

1. Select a layer in the Composition or Timeline panel.

2. In the Composition panel, drag the layer to the position you want (**Figure 7.19**).

   To move a layer off screen, drag it to the pasteboard, or workspace, outside the viewing area of the Composition panel.

   The layer is placed at the position you chose. If the Stopwatch icon hasn't been activated for the layer, the layer will remain at this position for its entire duration. If the Stopwatch is active, a position keyframe is created at this frame.

✔ Tips

- You can quickly center a layer that has been moved in a comp by selecting the layer and choosing Layer > Transform > Center in View.

- Once you start animating a layer's position property, you'll notice that multiple position keyframes are connected by a curved path (an auto-Bezier type of interpolation). You can change the default to straight lines (linear interpolation) in the Preferences. You'll learn all about manipulating the motion path in Chapter 9, "Keyframe Interpolation."

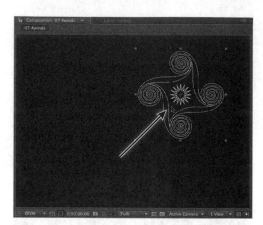

Figure 7.19 You can drag selected layers to new positions.

Subpixel Positioning

When you set a layer to Draft quality, After Effects calculates the position, rotation, and scale (or any effect that moves the pixels of an image) by using whole pixels. When layers are set to Best quality, however, these values are calculated to the thousandth of a pixel, or on a *subpixel* basis. The more you zoom in to the Composition panel, the greater the precision with which you can move a layer.

Because subpixel positioning allows layers to move with a precision greater than the resolution of the composition, movement appears much smoother than when you're not using subpixel positioning. You can see the difference by contrasting the movement of layers set to Draft quality with the same movement set to Best quality.

Subpixel positioning requires more precise calculations, which means it takes After Effects longer to render images. You may want to do much of your work in Draft quality and then switch to Best quality when you're ready to fine-tune.

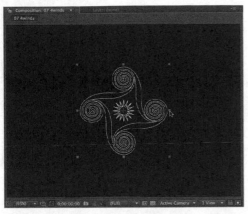

Figure 7.20 Drag a selected layer's handles to scale it...

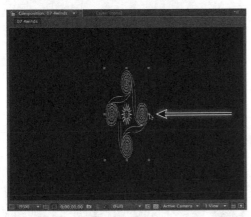

Figure 7.21 ...horizontally...

Scale

By default, a layer is set to 100 percent of its original size, or scale. You scale a layer around its anchor point. In other words, the anchor point serves as the mathematical center of a change in size. When you scale a layer by dragging, you'll notice how the handles of the layer seem to stretch from the anchor point.

Remember that bitmapped images look blocky and pixelated when scaled much beyond 100 percent. When you scale path-based images beyond 100 percent, you can use the Continuously Rasterize switch to help maintain image quality. Review "Continuously Rasterizing a Layer," in Chapter 5 if you need more information about image size and rasterization; see Chapter 15, "3D Layers," for more information about how the Scale property differs for 3D layers.

To scale a layer by dragging:

1. Select a layer, and make sure its layer handles are visible in the Composition panel (see "Viewing Spatial Controls in the Comp Panel," earlier in this chapter) (**Figure 7.20**).

2. In the Composition panel, *do any of the following:*

   ▲ To scale the layer horizontally only, drag the center-left or center-right handle (**Figure 7.21**).

continues on next page

TRANSFORM PROPERTIES

▲ To scale the layer vertically only, drag the center-bottom or the center-top handle (**Figure 7.22**).

▲ To scale the layer horizontally and vertically, drag a corner handle.

▲ To scale the layer while maintaining its proportions, select a corner handle, press Shift, and drag (**Figure 7.23**).

▲ To flip a layer, drag one side of the layer's bounding box past the other side (**Figure 7.24**).

3. Release the mouse button.

In the Composition panel, the layer appears with the scale you set. If the Stopwatch icon hasn't been activated for the layer, the layer will retain this scale for its duration. If the Stopwatch is active, a scale keyframe is created at this frame.

✔ Tip

■ You can quickly reset the scale of a layer to 100 percent by selecting the layer and double-clicking the Selection tool.

Figure 7.22 ...vertically...

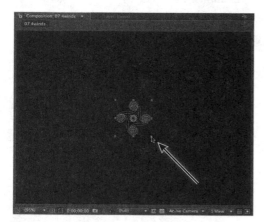

Figure 7.23 ...or by both aspects. Shift-drag a corner handle to scale the layer while maintaining its proportions.

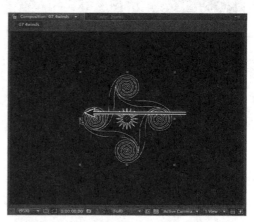

Figure 7.24 You can flip a layer by dragging one side past the other. Note how the spirals in this logo now face in the opposite direction.

TRANSFORM PROPERTIES

Figure 7.25 Choose the Rotate tool.

Figure 7.26 In the Composition panel, drag the layer to rotate it around its pivot point.

Rotational Values

Rotation is expressed as an absolute, not relative, value. You might even think of it as a rotational position. Whenever a layer's rotation is set to 0 degrees, it appears upright, with its sides parallel to the frame of the comp. This is true when you keyframe rotational values as well. For example, if you want to rotate a layer 180 degrees clockwise (upside down) and back again, the rotation values at each keyframe are 0, 180, and 0. Mistakenly setting values of 0, 180, and –180 will cause the layer to turn clockwise 180 degrees and then turn counterclockwise—past its original position—until it's upside down again.

Rotation

When you rotate a 2D layer, it rotates in two-dimensional space, using the anchor point as its pivot point. See Chapter 15, "3D Layers," to learn about rotating layers in 3D space.

To rotate a layer by dragging:

1. Select a layer.

2. In the Tools panel, choose the Rotate tool (**Figure 7.25**).

3. In the Composition panel, drag a layer to rotate it around its anchor point.

   As you drag, a bounding box represents the layer's new rotation position (**Figure 7.26**).

4. Release the mouse to set the rotation.

   In the Composition panel, the layer appears with the rotation you set. If the Stopwatch icon isn't active for the layer, this is the rotation of the layer for its entire duration. If the Stopwatch icon is active, a rotation keyframe is created at this frame.

✔ Tips

- To quickly reset a selected layer's rotation to 0 degrees, double-click the Rotate tool.

- If you want an object to turn (rotate) in the direction of its motion path (animated position), you can avoid the pain of setting a lot of rotational keyframes by using the Auto-Orient Rotation command, covered in the following section, "Orienting Rotation to a Motion Path Automatically."

- Shift-dragging one side of a layer past the other flips it both horizontally and vertically. To flip a layer horizontally only, select the layer and then choose Layer > Transform > Flip Horizontal; to flip it vertically, choose Layer > Transform > Flip Vertical.

TRANSFORM PROPERTIES

Orienting Rotation to a Motion Path Automatically

As a layer follows a motion path, its rotation remains unaffected. The layer maintains its upright position as it follows the path. Picture, for example, someone riding up an escalator, or the cabins on a Ferris wheel: They remain upright although they follow a sloped or curved path. Frequently, you want an object to orient its rotation to remain perpendicular to the motion path: Now picture a roller coaster climbing a hill.

Fortunately, you don't have to painstakingly keyframe a layer's Rotation property to ensure that it remains oriented to the motion path; After Effects' Auto-Orient Rotation command does that for you. The ant layer pictured in **Figure 7.27** looks unnatural because it doesn't turn in the direction of its movement. But by applying the Auto-Orient command, you can make the ant turn according to the path without animating its rotation—resulting in the more natural movement pictured in **Figure 7.28**.

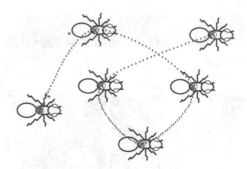

Figure 7.27 Without auto-orient rotation, objects remain upright as they follow the motion path (unless you animate rotation as well). Notice that the ant remains horizontal regardless of the direction of motion.

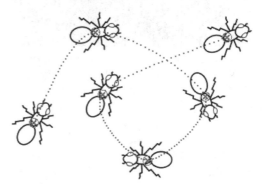

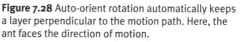

Figure 7.28 Auto-orient rotation automatically keeps a layer perpendicular to the motion path. Here, the ant faces the direction of motion.

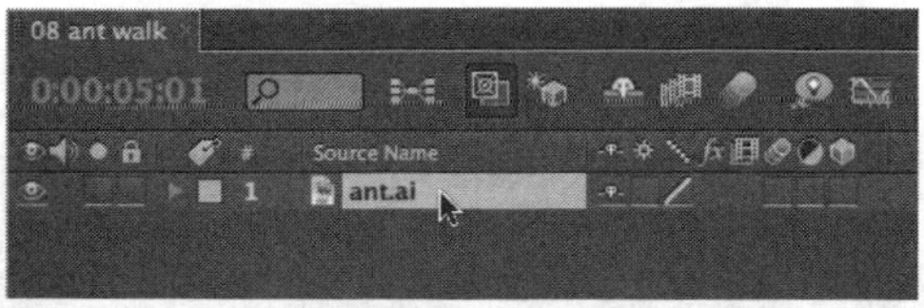

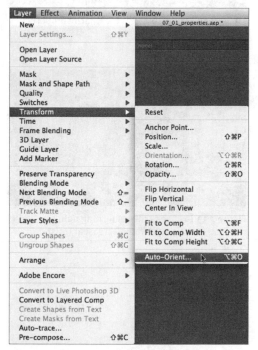

Figure 7.29 To auto-orient rotation, start by selecting a layer.

Figure 7.30 Choose Layer > Transform > Auto-Orient.

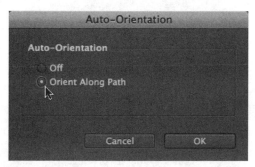

Figure 7.31 In the Auto-Orient dialog, select Orient Along Path.

To auto-orient rotation to the motion path:

1. Select a layer (**Figure 7.29**).

2. Choose Layer > Transform > Auto-Orient, or press Option-Command-O (Alt-Ctrl-O) (**Figure 7.30**).

   The Auto-Orientation dialog appears.

3. In the Auto-Orientation dialog, select Orient Along Path (**Figure 7.31**).

4. Click OK to close the Auto-Orientation dialog.

   The layer automatically orients its X-axis tangent to the motion path.

✔ Tips

■ As you'll learn in Chapter 12, "Creating and Animating Text," you don't need the Auto-Orient command to make text follow a path while remaining perpendicular to it.

■ Chapter 15, "3D Layers," covers 3D compositing, including auto-orient options for 3D layers, cameras, and lights.

ORIENTING ROTATION TO A MOTION PATH

Opacity

At any point in time, a layer can be anywhere from 0 percent opaque (completely transparent, and thus invisible) to 100 percent opaque (with absolutely no transparency).

Bear in mind that the Opacity property merely controls the layer's overall opacity. There are plenty of other ways to define areas of transparency and opacity, including transfer modes, track mattes, keying effects, and masking techniques.

Because opacity is the only transform property you can't "grab onto" in the Comp panel, you must alter it by using numerical controls.

To change the opacity of a layer:

1. Select a layer in the Timeline panel or Composition panel.

2. Press T to display the Opacity property for the selected layer.

   The layer's Opacity property appears in the layer outline, and the current value for opacity appears across from the property under the Switches column (**Figure 7.32**).

3. Under the Switches column across from the layer's Opacity property, *do any of the following:*

   ▲ To increase the current opacity value, drag the value to the right.

   ▲ To decrease the current opacity value, drag the opacity value to the left (**Figure 7.33**).

   ▲ To set the value in a dialog, Control-click (right-click) the opacity value, and select Edit Value in the context menu.

As you change the opacity value, the layer's opacity changes in the Composition panel. If the Stopwatch icon isn't active for the layer, the layer retains this opacity for its duration. If the Stopwatch icon is active, an opacity keyframe is created at this frame.

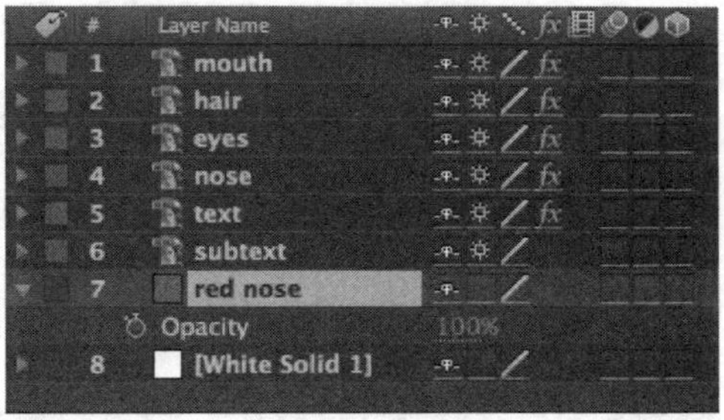

Figure 7.32 Press T to reveal the Opacity property value.

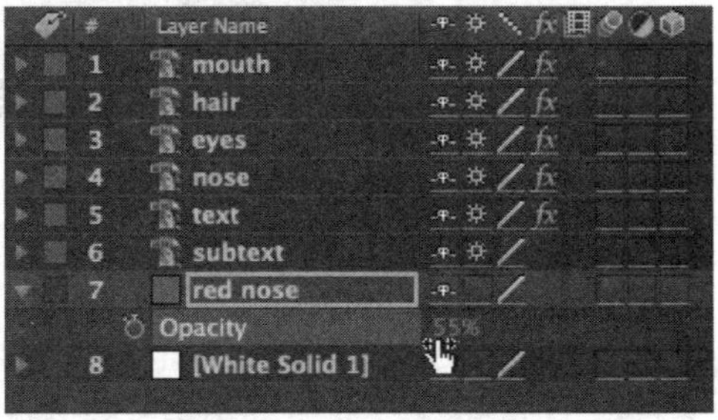

Figure 7.33 To change the value, drag right to increase the value or left to decrease it (as shown here).

✔ Tip

■ The keyboard shortcuts that display most transform properties are often the first letter of the name of the property: P for position, S for scale, and so on. However, you reveal the Opacity property by pressing T. (Pressing O cues the current time to the selected layer's Out point, the last frame included in the comp.)

Table 7.2

Property Dialog Shortcuts

To show this dialog	Press this
Anchor Point dialog	Command-Option-Shift-A (Ctrl-Alt-Shift-A)
Opacity dialog	Command-Shift-O (Ctrl-Shift-O)
Other dialogs	Command-Shift-property shortcut (Ctrl-Shift-property shortcut) (where property shortcut is P, R, F, or M)

Table 7.3

Nudging Layer Properties

To nudge this value	Do this
Nudge position one pixel	Press arrow keys (up, down, right, left)
Nudge rotation 1 degree	Press plus (+) on numeric keypad
Nudge rotation –1 degree	Press minus (–) on numeric keypad
Nudge scale 1%	Press Option-+ (Alt-+) on numeric keypad
Nudge scale –1%	Press Option-– (Alt-–) on numeric keypad
Nudge x 10	Press Shift-keyboard shortcut for nudge

Specifying Property Values

As in most other Adobe programs, numeric values in After Effects appear colored and underlined, indicating that the values are *scrubbable.* This means you can alter a property's current value by dragging, or *scrubbing,* the value display. Clicking the value highlights it so you can enter a numeric value. Pressing Return (Enter) verifies the value; pressing Tab highlights the next value display. Because these controls are familiar to most users, they won't be covered here.

Alternatively, you can open a dialog to enter property values (**Table 7.2**). Although a dialog may not offer the convenience of scrubbing or entering the value directly, it does allow you to enter decimal values or to employ different units of measurement for the property value.

You can also use keyboard shortcuts to slightly change, or *nudge,* the position, rotation, or scale of a layer. When you nudge a layer, After Effects counts pixels at the current magnification of the Composition panel, not the layer's actual size. Therefore, nudging a layer's position moves it one pixel when viewed at 100 percent magnification, two pixels when viewed at 50 percent, four pixels at 25 percent, and so on. When layer quality is set to Best, you can nudge layers on a subpixel basis (see the sidebar "Subpixel Positioning," earlier in this chapter). Therefore, a layer set to Best quality can be nudged 0.5 pixel when viewed at 200 percent, 0.25 pixel when viewed at 400 percent, and so on. **Table 7.3** lists the keyboard shortcuts for nudging properties.

Animating Layer Properties with Keyframes

Now you're ready to tackle After Effects' core feature: animation. To produce animation, you change a layer's properties over time—for example, achieving motion by changing a layer's position over time. In After Effects (as with other programs), you use keyframes to define and control these changes.

A *keyframe* defines a property's value at a specific point in time. When you create at least two keyframes with different values, After Effects *interpolates* the value for each frame in between. In other words, After Effects calculates how to create a smooth transition from one keyframe to another—how to get from point A to point B (**Figure 7.34**).

Basic keyframing

Essentially, keyframing is nothing more than repeating a two-step process: setting the current frame, and setting the property value for that frame. The specific steps are outlined in this section.

If you're new to animating with keyframes, you may want to start with one of the transform properties (such as Scale) and setting just a few keyframes. Once you grasp the process, try other properties and more keyframes. (Note that, by default, multiple Position keyframes are connected by curved motion path. If you're familiar with using Bézier curves in other programs, you know how to alter the curves in the Comp panel. If not, see Chapter 9 to learn how to manipulate the motion path—and learn about the other ways After Effects calculates values between keyframes.

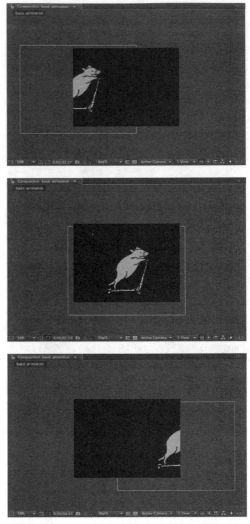

Figure 7.34 The movement depicted in this series of images is the result of After Effects calculating the layer's position between two keyframes: the first off screen to the left at one point in time, the next off screen to the right at a later point in time.

Keyframes

Keyframe is a term borrowed from traditional animation. In a traditional animation studio, a senior animator might draw only the keyframes—what the character looks like at key moments in the animation. The junior animators would then draw the rest of the frames, or *in-betweens* (a process sometimes known as *tweening*). The same principle applies to After Effects animations: If you supply the keyframes for a property, the program calculates the values in between. And you can keyframe any property, not just movement.

With After Effects, you're always the senior animator, so you should only supply the keyframes—just enough to define the animation. Setting too many keyframes defeats the purpose of this division of labor.

To set keyframes for a property:

1. In the Timeline panel, view the property of the layer (or layers) you want to keyframe.

2. Set the current time to the frame at which you want to set a keyframe.

   It's possible to set a keyframe beyond the duration of a layer.

3. Click the Stopwatch icon next to the layer property you want to keyframe to activate the icon (and the keyframe process) (**Figure 7.35**).

   The Stopwatch icon appears selected. In the property tracks of the selected layers, an initial keyframe appears; in the keyframe navigator, a check appears.

4. If the property isn't set to the value you want, set the value.

   As long as the current time is set to the keyframe, any new value is applied to the keyframe.

continues on next page

Figure 7.35 Click the Stopwatch icon to set the first keyframe for the property at the current time indicator. At the beginning of this comp, the ball layer is positioned near the left side of the comp.

ANIMATING LAYER PROPERTIES WITH KEYFRAMES

161

5. Set the current time to another frame.

6. To create additional keyframes, *do one of the following:*

   ▲ To create a keyframe with a new value, change the value of the property (**Figure 7.36**).

   ▲ To create a keyframe without changing the current property value, click the Add/Delete Keyframe button (the diamond icon) in the keyframe navigator (**Figure 7.37**).

   A new keyframe appears at the current time, and the diamond at the center of the keyframe navigator is highlighted.

7. To create additional keyframes, repeat steps 5 and 6.

8. To see your changes play in the Composition panel, use the playback controls or create a preview (see Chapter 8, "Playback, Previews, and RAM").

✔ Tips

■ There are numerous ways to generate keyframes in addition to using the keyframing process. For example, the Wiggler panel generates random values (within specified parameters), and the Motion Sketch feature lets you draw in the Comp panel to create position keyframes. What's more, you can use the Expressions feature to generate property values without using keyframes at all.

■ People often use After Effects to pan and scale large images, emulating the motion-control camera work frequently seen in documentaries. In such cases, you create pans by animating the anchor point, not the position. This technique achieves the panning you want while keeping the anchor point in the viewing area. Because the anchor point is also used to calculate scale, you'll get more predictable results when you zoom in to and out of the image.

Figure 7.36 To set a keyframe with a new value, set the current time to a new frame and change the property value. At 3 seconds into this comp, the ball's position has been moved to the right, creating a new keyframe—and animation between keyframes!

Add/Delete Keyframe button   Added keyframe

Figure 7.37 To set a keyframe without manually changing the value, select the Add / Delete Keyframe button (the diamond-shaped icon) in the keyframe navigator. Because the new keyframe uses the previously calculated position value, there's no motion between the second and third keyframes.

ANIMATING LAYER PROPERTIES WITH KEYFRAMES

Keyframe icons

A property's keyframes appear in its property track of the time graph. When a property heading is collapsed, the keyframes of the properties in that category appear as small dots. When an individual property is visible, its keyframes appear as larger icons. (**Figure 7.38**). Initially, the icons are diamond-shaped, indicating linear interpolation type, but using different interpolation methods changes the shape of the icons (see Chapter 9, "Keyframe Interpolation," for more on interpolation types). (By checking Use Keyframe Indices in the Timeline panel's pop-up menu, you can make keyframes appear as numbered boxes instead of icons.)

Keyframe icons vary according to the interpolation method used by the keyframe. The diamond-shaped icons shown here reflect linear interpolation. Regardless of its interpolation method, shading indicates that the property value either before or after the keyframe hasn't been interpolated (**Figure 7.39**). This occurs for the first and last keyframes as well as for keyframes that follow hold keyframes, which are used to suspend interpolation.

Figure 7.38 When the property heading is collapsed (as they are in the top layer), keyframes appear as small dots. When the property track is visible (as in the bottom layer) keyframes appear as diamond-shaped icons.

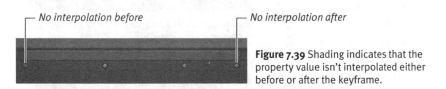

— No interpolation before

— No interpolation after

Figure 7.39 Shading indicates that the property value isn't interpolated either before or after the keyframe.

Setting a New Keyframe with the Keyframe Navigator

As you learned in the section "Basic Keyframing," you can set a new keyframe by selecting the keyframe navigator's Add/Delete Keyframe button—the diamond-shaped icon. Instead of using a value you actively specify, a keyframe created this way uses the value already calculated for that frame.

Usually, you use the check box to create keyframes when you want to modify an animation— or, when no animation exists yet, to repeat a value. Initially, the new keyframe doesn't alter the animation; it hasn't changed the property's value at that time. The new keyframe can serve as a good starting point for changing the animation by changing the keyframe's value or interpolation method (see Chapter 9, "Keyframe Interpolation").

Cueing the Current Time to Keyframes

It can be useful to quickly cue the CTI to keyframes. For example, you may want to step through your animation or create keyframes in other layers or properties that align with existing keyframes. The keyframe navigator provides the solution (**Figure 7.40**).

And as you saw in the section, "Basic Keyframing," the diamond at the center of the keyframe navigator serves as the Add/Delete Keyframe button. Because it's highlighted only when the current time is cued to a keyframe, it also provides a visual confirmation, particularly if you want to confirm that keyframes in different properties are perfectly aligned.

To cue the current time to keyframes:

1. Make sure the property with the keyframes you want to see is visible in the layer outline.

2. In the Timeline panel, *do any of the following:*
   - ▲ Shift-drag the current time indicator until it snaps to a visible keyframe.
   - ▲ To cue the current time to the previous keyframe, click the left arrow in the property's keyframe navigator, or press J.
   - ▲ To cue the current time to the next keyframe, click the right arrow in the property's keyframe navigator, or press K (**Figure 7.41**).

The current time cues to the adjacent keyframe (**Figure 7.42**). If no keyframe exists beyond the current keyframe, the appropriate arrow in the keyframe navigator appears dimmed.

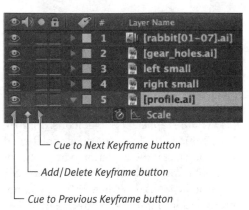

— Cue to Next Keyframe button

— Add/Delete Keyframe button

— Cue to Previous Keyframe button

Figure 7.40 Use the keyframe navigator to cue the CTI to the previous or next keyframe. The Diamond icon (aka Add/Delete Keyframe button) is highlighted only when the CTI is cued exactly to a keyframe.

Figure 7.41 Clicking an arrow in the keyframe navigator (in this case, the right arrow)...

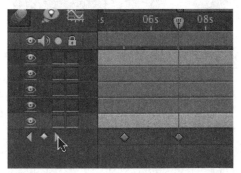

Figure 7.42 ...cues the current time indicator to the property's adjacent keyframe (here, the next keyframe). (Note that the A/V features panel has been moved closer to the time graph for the purpose of illustration.)

Selecting and Deleting Keyframes

Select keyframes when you want to move them to a different position in time, delete them, or copy and paste them to other properties or layers.

To select keyframes:

◆ *Do any of the following:*

▲ To select a keyframe, click it in the property track.

▲ To add keyframes to or subtract them from your selection, press Shift as you click additional keyframes (**Figure 7.43**).

▲ To select multiple keyframes, drag a marquee around the keyframes in the property track (**Figure 7.44**).

▲ To select all the keyframes for a property, click the name of the property in the layer outline (**Figure 7.45**).

Selected keyframes appear highlighted.

To deselect keyframes:

◆ *Do either of the following:*

▲ To deselect all keyframes, click in an empty area of the Timeline panel.

▲ To deselect certain keyframes, Shift-click an already selected keyframe.

Deselected keyframes no longer appear highlighted.

✔ Tip

■ Selecting a keyframe allows you to move it in time, delete it, or copy it. It doesn't let you edit the values of that keyframe. You can only change the value of a property at the current time.

Figure 7.43 Click a keyframe to select it; Shift-click to add to your selection.

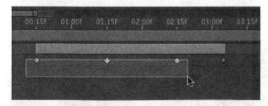

Figure 7.44 You can also select multiple keyframes by dragging a marquee around them.

Figure 7.45 Select all the keyframes for a property by clicking the property's name in the layer outline.

To delete keyframes:

1. Select one or more keyframes, as explained in the previous section.

2. *Do any of the following:*

   ▲ Press Delete.

   ▲ Choose Edit > Clear.

   ▲ With the current time cued to the keyframe, click the keyframe navigator's Add/Delete Keyframe button.

   The keyframe disappears, and the property's interpolated values are recalculated based on the remaining keyframes.

To delete all the keyframes for a property:

◆ Deactivate the Stopwatch icon for the property (**Figure 7.46**).

   All keyframes disappear. You can't restore the keyframes by reactivating the Stopwatch (doing so only starts a new keyframe process).

✔ Tip

■ If you mistakenly remove keyframes by deselecting the Stopwatch icon, choose Edit > Undo to undo previous commands, or choose File > Revert to return to the last saved version of your project.

Figure 7.46 Deactivating the property's Stopwatch icon removes all keyframes. The property uses the value at the current time.

Figure 7.47 Select the keyframes you want to move...

Figure 7.48 ...and drag them to a new position in the timeline. Shift-drag to activate the Snap to Edges feature.

Figure 7.49 Although dragging a layer also moves its keyframes, trimming a layer doesn't trim off its keyframes, which still affect property values.

Moving Keyframes in Time

You can move one or more keyframes of one or more properties to a different point in time.

To move keyframes:

1. Select one or more keyframes (as explained earlier in this chapter) (**Figure 7.47**).

2. Drag the selected keyframes to a new position in the time graph (**Figure 7.48**).

   To activate the Snap to Edges feature, press Shift after you begin dragging.

3. Release the mouse when the keyframes are at the position in time you want.

✔ Tips

■ Moving a layer in time also moves its keyframes, which maintain their positions relative to the layer. Trimming a layer, on the other hand, doesn't affect the keyframes. In fact, you can set a keyframe before a layer's In point or after its Out point (**Figure 7.49**).

■ Moving a layer's keyframes in space— by dragging them in the Comp panel— changes the keyframes' position values, but has no effect on their timing.

Copying Values and Keyframes

When you want to reuse values you set for a property, you can copy and paste them to a different point in time or even to different layers. Not only can you paste keyframes to the same property (such as from one position to another), you can also paste them to different properties that use the same kind of values (such as from a position to an anchor point). However, you can't copy and paste between properties that have incompatible values, such as position (which consists of X and Y coordinate values) and rotation (which has a single angle value).

Pasted keyframes appear in the property track of the destination in the order and spacing of the original, starting at the current time.

After Effects permits you to copy and paste keyframes one layer at a time. You can copy and paste keyframes of more than one property at a time, as long as you paste them into the same properties. If you want to copy and paste to different properties, however, you must do so one property at a time.

To copy and paste keyframes:

1. Select one or more keyframes (as explained earlier in this chapter).

2. Choose Edit > Copy, or press Command-C (Ctrl-C) (**Figure 7.50**).

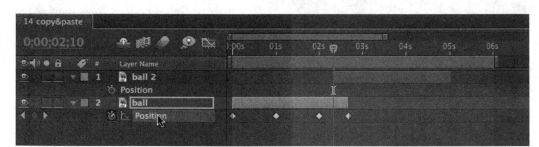

Figure 7.50 Select the keyframes you want to copy and press Command-C (Ctrl-C).

3. Set the current time to the frame where you want the pasted keyframe(s) to begin.

4. To select the destination, *do one of the following:*

▲ To paste keyframes to the same property, select the destination layer.

▲ To paste keyframes to a different property, select the destination property by clicking it in the layer outline.

5. Choose Edit > Paste, or press Command-V (Ctrl-V) (**Figure 7.51**).

The keyframes are pasted in the appropriate property in the destination layer (**Figure 7.52**).

✔ Tips

■ You can also copy and paste a global (nonkeyframed) by selecting the property's name rather than its keyframes.

■ To reuse an animation, you can save it as an animation preset. For more about effects and presets, see Chapter 11, "Effects Fundamentals."

■ As you'll see in Chapter 10, "Mask Essentials," you can copy a mask or shape path and then paste it into a layer as a motion path consisting of position keyframes.

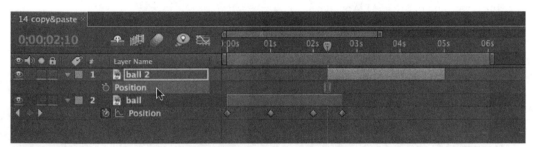

Figure 7.51 Set the current time, select the destination layer or property, and press Command-V (Ctrl-V)...

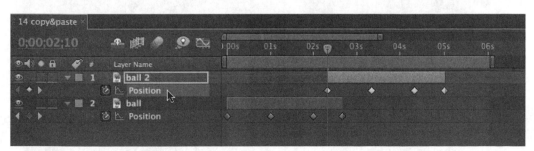

Figure 7.52 ... and the selected keyframes appear in the destination property track, beginning at the current time.

Generating Property Values with the Brainstorm Feature

At times, having full control over a multitude of property values feels like more of a curse than a blessing. Trying out even a handful of the countless combinations can be a time-consuming and potentially fruitless endeavor. The aptly named Brainstorm feature generates variations of any combination of properties automatically, and lets you preview them before committing to your favorite.

To set the frames to preview for Brainstorming:

1. In the Timeline panel, set the current time to the frame you want previews to begin and press B on the keyboard.

   The beginning of the Work Area Bar aligns with the current time indicator (**Figure 7.53**).

2. In the Timeline panel, set the CTI to the frame you want previews to end and press N on the keyboard.

   The ending of the Work Area Bar aligns with the current time indicator (**Figure 7.54**).

Work Area Bar

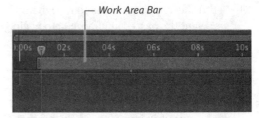
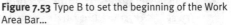

Figure 7.53 Type B to set the beginning of the Work Area Bar...

Figure 7.54 ... and type N to set the ending of the Work Area Bar. This defines the range of frames to preview—in this case, Brainstormed property values.

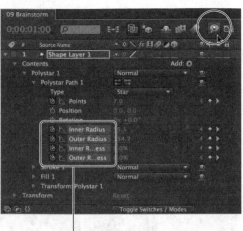

Selected properties

Figure 7.55 Select any combination of properties and keyframes for which you want to generate values and click the Brainstorm button.

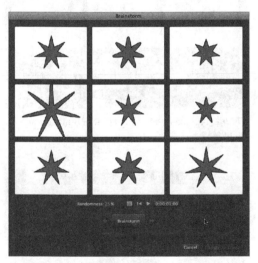

Figure 7.56 The Brainstorm panel, shows nine variations of the selected properties.

To specify the properties for Brainstorming:

1. In the Timeline panel, select any combination of global properties or keyframed property values.

2. At the top of the Timeline panel, click the Brainstorm button 🧠 (**Figure 7.55**).

   The Brainstorm panel appears. It displays nine preview images, each using a different random variant of the property values you specified in step 1 (**Figure 7.56**).

To generate new variants:

1. To specify the magnitude of variations in the Brainstorm panel, *do either of the following:*

    ▲ For multidimensional properties, specify a value for Randomness (**Figure 7.57**).

    ▲ For single-dimensional properties, specify a value for Spread.

    Specifying a relatively high value results in greater variations of the initial selected values. Properties like Rotation have a single dimension, and thus a single angle value, while properties like Position have more than one dimension (such as an X and Y value, for 2D layers).

2. Click the Brainstorm button 🧠.

    The Brainstorm panel displays a new generation of variants, using the value you specified (**Figure 7.58**).

3. To keep a variant in the next Brainstorm, hover the mouse pointer over the variant and click the Include in Next Brainstorm button 🔍 (**Figure 7.59**).

4. Repeat steps 1 through 3 as needed.

Figure 7.57 When you specify a value for Randomness (or Spread, depending on the property type), clicking the Brainstorm button...

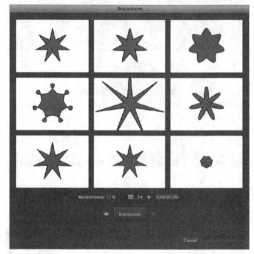

Figure 7.58 ...generates a new set of Brainstormed values.

Figure 7.59 Moving the mouse pointer over a tile makes a panel of buttons appear. Click the Include in Next Brainstorm button to retain that variant when you repeat the process.

Current time —

Play (plays Work Area) —

Rewind (cues to Work Area start) —

Toggle Transparency Grid —

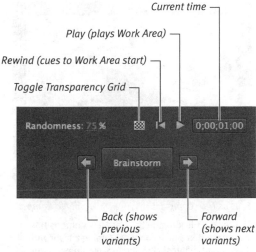

Back (shows previous variants)

Forward (shows next variants)

Figure 7.60 The Brainstorm panel's buttons help you preview the variants it generates.

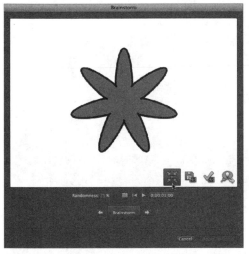

Figure 7.61 Click the Maximize Tile button to enlarge that variant. Click the button again to view all nine variants again.

To preview variants in the Brainstorm panel:

◆ In the Brainstorm panel, *do any of the following* (**Figure 7.60**):

 ▲ To toggle transparent areas between the background color and transparency grid, click the Toggle Transparency Grid button ▒.

 ▲ To preview the visible variants for the Work Area you specified, click the Play button ▸.

 ▲ To rewind playback to the beginning of the Work Area you specified, click the Rewind button ◂.

 ▲ To view the previous generation of variants, click the Back button ◂.

 ▲ To view the next generation of variants, click the Forward button ▸.

To magnify a variant:

1. Move the mouse pointer over the variant you want to view so that a panel of buttons appears, and then click the Maximize Tile button ✕ (**Figure 7.61**).

2. To restore the Brainstorm panel to nine tiles, click the button again.

To apply a variant:

1. In the Brainstorm panel, move the mouse pointer over the variant you want. A panel of four buttons appears over the tile.

2. *Do any of the following* (**Figure 7.62**):

   ▲ To create a new comp containing a copy of the layer using the selected variant, click the Save as New Composition button .

   ▲ To apply the variant's property values to the selected layer in the current comp, click the Apply to Composition button .

   The variant either appears in a new composition or its values are applied to the selected layer in the comp, according to your choice.

Save as New Comp ⎯⎯⎯⎯⎯⎯⎯⎯⎯⎯ Apply to Comp

Figure 7.62 Clicking the Save as New Composition button creates a new comp containing a layer with the variant's values; clicking Apply to Composition (selected here) applies the variant's property values to the selected layer in the current comp.

GENERATING PROPERTY VALUES

Playback, Previews, and RAM

You've already used some of the standard playback methods for each panel in After Effects. This chapter expands your repertoire and provides a more in-depth explanation of how After Effects renders frames for viewing.

You'll focus on using the Preview panel (formerly known as the Time Controls panel), which can serve as a master playback control for any selected panel. It also includes a button to render a specified range of frames (or *Work Area*) as a *RAM preview*. And you'll learn about other options, such as viewing your work on a video monitor, how to view changes you make to a layer interactively, and how to preview audio.

Whether you're using standard playback controls, rendering a RAM preview, or adjusting layers, After Effects utilizes RAM to store and more readily display frames. Consequently, the more RAM you have, the more rendered frames you can store (or *cache*) at once. After Effects makes the most of your RAM supply by retaining rendered frames as long as possible, a feature called *intelligent caching*. But you can also control the demand side of the rendering equation. Specifying RAM preview options to skip frames or reduce the resolution can lighten the rendering load—or eliminate the image altogether (along with the associated rendering delays) by previewing a bare-bones *wireframe* version of an animation. In addition, you can limit the area of the image to render by specifying a region of interest. After Effects can also reduce processing demands automatically, as needed, by employing *adaptive resolution*. Adaptive resolution reduces image resolution in exchange for increased rendering speed.

Rendering speed isn't necessarily attained at the expense of resolution; you can also utilize a compatible *OpenGL* graphics card. Because software-based processing usually can't match hardware dedicated to the same task, utilizing your OpenGL card's hardware-based graphics processing capabilities renders frames quickly, smoothly, and often without sacrificing resolution.

Rendering and RAM

Before proceeding to the tasks, you should familiarize yourself with how After Effects utilizes RAM. This section contrasts two basic methods used to display frames.

Cache flow

Adobe likes to describe the way After Effects uses RAM as "interactive" and "intelligent." Here's why.

Unless you specify otherwise, After Effects renders frames interactively. Whenever the current time is set to a previously unrendered frame, After Effects renders it and stores, or *caches*, it into RAM—which, as you're probably aware, is the memory your computer can access most quickly. Although it can take time to render a frame, once cached, the frame plays back more readily. The Timeline panel indicates cached frames with a green line at the corresponding point under the time ruler (**Figure 8.1**).

When a change (such as an adjustment to a layer property) makes a rendered frame obsolete, After Effects removes the frame from the cache. However, it intelligently retains the unaffected frames. In other words, After Effects doesn't stupidly discard the entire cache when you make changes that affect only some of the frames. When the cache becomes full, the oldest frames are purged from RAM as new frames are added. You can also purge the cache yourself using a menu command.

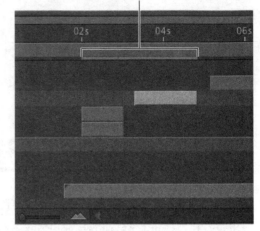

Green line = Rendered frames

Figure 8.1 Cached frames are signified by a green line in the time ruler.

Figure 8.2 Options help you balance quality and rendering speed. The Comp panel's Fast Previews button gives you access to several standard playback options...

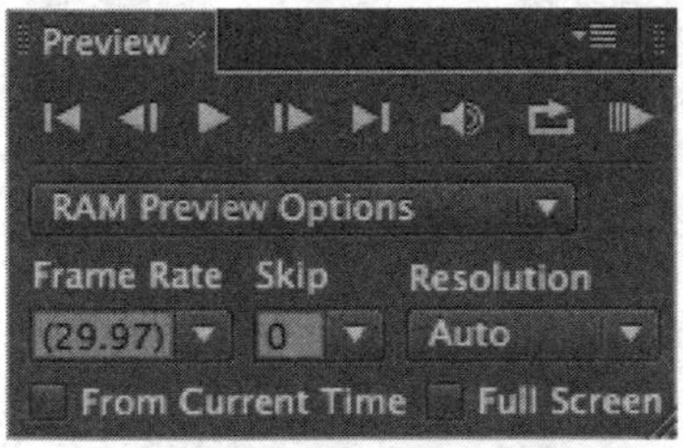

Figure 8.3 ...whereas expanding the Preview panel allows you to set options for RAM previews.

✔ Tip

- Setting the Comp panel's resolution setting to Auto links the resolution setting to the magnification setting. This way, reducing the magnification to, say, 50 percent also reduces the resolution setting to Half. For most users, it makes sense to have the resolution—and the rendering times—decrease with the magnification. But if you prefer to control the two settings independently, just change the resolution from Auto to the setting you want.

Playback and previews

Although the terms *playback* and *preview* are often used interchangeably, this book uses them to refer to two rendering methods that differ in a few important respects. Standard playback caches frames at the current time: sequentially when you click Play or nonsequentially as you cue the current time. A RAM preview, in contrast, loads a specified range of frames into RAM *before* attempting to play them back at a specified frame rate.

Both the standard playback mechanism and RAM previews utilize RAM in a similar way, caching frames and retaining them intelligently (see the previous section, "Cache flow"). But whereas standard playback respects the resolution you specified for the panel you're viewing, a RAM preview specifies resolution independent of the panel's current setting. Each method includes different options to help you balance image quality and rendering speed. In addition to the current layer quality and comp resolution settings, standard playback abides by options you set via the Comp panel's Fast Previews button (**Figure 8.2**); you set RAM preview options in the expanded Preview panel (**Figure 8.3**). Finally, standard playback options govern how After Effects depicts a frame while you make adjustments—or, in After Effects' parlance, during *interactions*. A RAM preview, in contrast, displays a range of frames at or near their full frame rate and doesn't influence the quality or speed of interactions.

No matter what method you use to view frames, processing demands are always related to the footage's native image size (and/or its audio quality) as well as any modifications you make to it as a layer in a composition: masks, transformations, effects, and so on.

Previewing to a Video Device

If your system includes a video output device (such as an IEEE-1394/FireWire/iLink connection), you can view your project on a television monitor—which is crucial for evaluating images destined for video output.

To set video preferences:

1. Choose After Effects > Preferences > Video Preview (Edit > Preferences > Video Preview) (**Figure 8.4**).

   The Video Preview pane of the Preferences dialog appears (**Figure 8.5**).

2. In the Preferences dialog, choose an option from the Output Device menu (**Figure 8.6**).

   Your choices will depend on your particular setup.

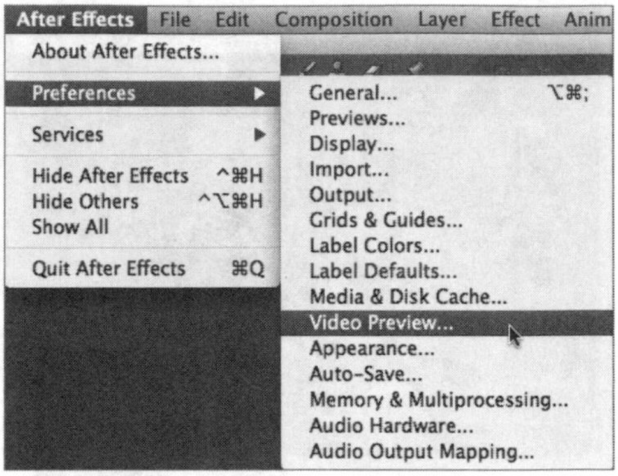

Figure 8.4 Choose After Effects > Preferences > Video Preview (Edit > Preferences > Video Preview).

Figure 8.5 The Video Preview pane of the Preferences dialog appears.

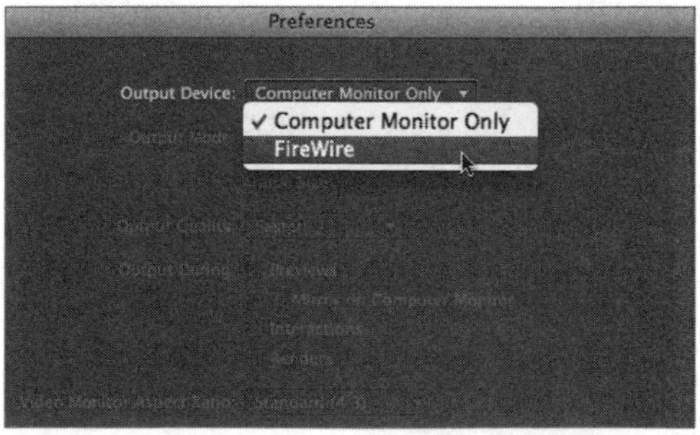

Figure 8.6 Choose an option in the Output Device menu.

Figure 8.7 Choose an option in the Output Mode menu.

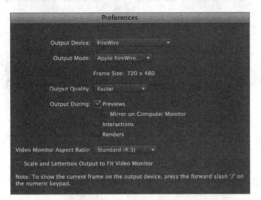

Figure 8.8 Choose an Output Quality, then select options for Output During.

3. Choose an option from the Output Mode menu (**Figure 8.7**).

Typically, you should choose an option that's equivalent to full-screen video for your output device.

4. For Output Quality, choose whether it's more important to output the video using a Faster or More Accurate method.

5. For Output During, choose any of the following (**Figure 8.8**):

▲ **Previews**—Displays RAM previews on the television monitor

▲ **Interactions**—Displays all window updates (such as while making adjustments to a layer's properties) on the television monitor

▲ **Renders**—Displays rendered frames on the television monitor

6. If you selected Previews in step 5, click the "Mirror on computer monitor" check box to display previews on your computer's monitor in addition to the video device.

To output previews to your video device only, leave this option unchecked.

7. For Video Monitor Aspect Ratio, choose the option that matches your video monitor:

Standard (4:3)

Widescreen (16:9)

8. If you wish, select "Scale and letterbox output to fit video monitor."

9. Click OK to close the Preferences dialog.

Previews appear on the connected NTSC monitor according to the preferences you set.

PREVIEWING TO A VIDEO DEVICE

Setting the Region of Interest

You can limit the portion of an image to be included in playback or previews by setting a *region of interest*. By restricting the image area to render, you decrease each frame's RAM requirements and increase both the rendering speed and the number of frames you can render.

To set the region of interest:

1. In a Comp, Layer, or Footage panel, click the Region of Interest button ▦ (**Figure 8.9**).

2. Draw a marquee in the image area to define the region of interest (**Figure 8.10**).

   The area of the image included in playback and previews will be limited to the area within the region of interest (**Figure 8.11**).

3. To resize the region of interest, drag any of its corner handles.

To toggle between the region of interest and the full image:

◆ In the Comp, Layer, or Footage panel, click the Region of Interest button.

   When the button is selected, the panel shows the region of interest; when the button is deselected, the panel displays the full image.

✔ Tips

■ To redraw the region of interest from the full image, make sure the Region of Interest button is deselected; then, Option-click (Alt-click) the Region of Interest button.

■ As always, you can reduce rendering times by reducing your composition's resolution or by setting layers to Draft quality.

Figure 8.9 Click the Region of Interest button.

Figure 8.10 Draw a marquee in the image area to define the region of interest.

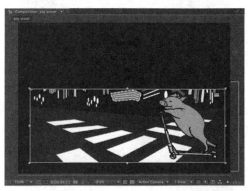

Figure 8.11 The region of interest limits the image included in playback and previews. Click the Region of Interest button to toggle between the region you specified and the full composition image.

Using the Preview Panel

Although the Footage, Layer, Composition, and Timeline panels all have their own playback controls, you can use the Preview panel to set the current frame in any selected panel. By default, the times of related panels are synchronized. For example, changing the current frame in a Layer panel also changes the current time in its related Timeline and Composition panels. You can change this setting in the General pane of the Preferences dialog.

You'll recognize most of the following buttons on the Preview panel (**Figure 8.12**); however, a few of these aren't on your home VCR or DVR remote:

First Frame—Cues the current time to the first frame in the window.

Frame Back—Cues the current time one frame back.

Play/Pause—Plays when clicked once and stops when clicked again. Playback performance depends on After Effects' ability to render the frames for viewing. During playback, the Preview panel displays two frame rates side by side: the frame rate your system is currently able to achieve and the frame rate you set for the composition.

Frame Forward—Cues the current time one frame forward.

Last Frame—Cues the current time to the last frame in the panel.

Audio—Lets you hear audio tracks when you preview a composition. Deselect it to suppress audio playback during previews. (Standard playback doesn't include audio.)

Loop—Comprises three states: Loop, Play Once, and Ping-Pong (which plays the specified area forward and backward). The frames affected by the loop setting depend on the panel selected. In a Footage panel, the entire duration of the footage loops. In a Layer panel, the layer loops from In point to Out point. In a composition—as viewed in the Composition and Timeline panels—frames loop from the beginning to the end of the Work Area (see "Previewing the Work Area," later in this chapter).

RAM Preview—Creates a RAM preview by rendering a specified range of frames, as defined by the Timeline's Work Area (explained later in this chapter).

Preview Panel—Opens a menu to show or hide RAM Preview and Shift-RAM Preview settings in the Preview panel (see the section "Rendering RAM Previews," later in this chapter).

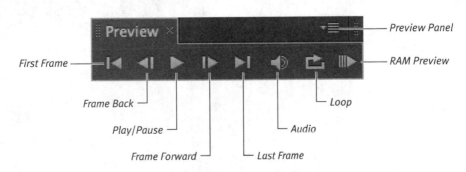

Figure 8.12 The Preview panel can control the playback of any selected window.

Using the Live Update Option

The Live Update option lets you specify how the Comp panel depicts changes during *interactions*, or while you make changes to a layer property. With Live Update enabled, you can see the layer change dynamically *while* you adjust the property. When Live update is off, the Comp panel doesn't update until *after* you alter the property (**Figures 8.13** and **8.14**).

Live Update works with the current Fast Previews setting (explained in "Specifying a Fast Previews Option," later in this chapter). With adaptive resolution enabled (either the standard option or with OpenGL), After Effects temporarily degrades the image quality during interactions until it can process and display the layer at the specified quality and resolution (see "Using Adaptive Resolution," later in this chapter).

You should choose the combination of settings most appropriate to the task at hand, the processing demands of the frame, and your system's processing capability.

To toggle Live Update on and off:

◆ In the Timeline panel, click the Live Update button 🖾 (**Figure 8.15**).

✔ Tip

■ You specify whether to view interactions on an attached video monitor separately, as explained in the section "Previewing to a Video Device," earlier in this chapter.

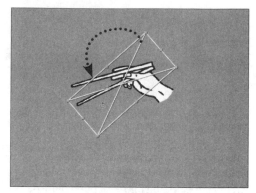

Figure 8.13 With Live Update off, the image doesn't update as you make an adjustment. Here, only the bounding box indicates the layer is being rotated…

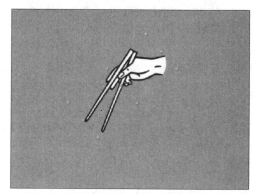

Figure 8.14 …and the layer doesn't reflect the change until you release the mouse.

Figure 8.15 In the Timeline panel, click the Live Update button.

Specifying a Fast Previews Option

As you learned in earlier chapters, the standard playback method (pressing Play or cuing the current time) is influenced by a comp's resolution as well as the quality settings of the layers it contains. (Everything else being equal, lowering quality and resolution results in shorter rendering times.) You can specify several other options to view frames as quickly as possible by using the Comp panel's Fast Previews button ⚡.

This section covers how to specify the option you want to use and summarizes each choice. Some choices (Adaptive Resolution and OpenGL options) include additional settings, which are explained fully in later sections.

To enable a Fast Previews option:

1. In a Composition panel, choose an option from the Fast Previews button's ⚡ pop-up menu (**Figure 8.16**):

   Off—Deactivates the Fast Previews option. Standard playback quality is governed by the comp resolution setting and layer quality settings.

Wireframe—Displays layer outlines only, allowing you to quickly evaluate aspects of an animation such as movement and timing by sacrificing image content.

Adaptive Resolution—OpenGL Off—Temporarily reduces the image resolution to a specified minimum setting in order to display changes to layers interactively or to maximize the frame rate.

OpenGL—Interactive—Utilizes a compatible OpenGL graphics card to process every frame requested, such as when you scrub to preview. When active, the Comp panel's Fast Previews icon appears lit.

OpenGL—Always On—Utilizes a compatible OpenGL graphics card for all previews. The notice *OpenGL* in the upper-left corner of the Comp panel indicates this mode is active.

OpenGL options are available only if you have a compatible OpenGL graphics card installed in your system and you've enabled OpenGL options in the Previews pane of the Preferences dialog.

✔ Tip

- A few more options are available for controlling the rendering quality of 3D layers; these are explained in Chapter 15, "3D Layers."

Figure 8.16 Choose an option from the Fast Previews button's pop-up menu.

Using Adaptive Resolution

If your system is slow to update the Comp panel's image, After Effects can reduce the image's resolution automatically—a feature called *adaptive resolution* (**Figures 8.17** and **8.18**). This way, you can get visual feedback even when your system can't keep up at the resolution you previously specified for the panel. You set the maximum amount by which adaptive resolution degrades images in the Previews pane of the Preferences dialog.

To set Adaptive Resolution settings:

1. In a Comp panel, click the Fast Previews button, and choose Fast Previews Preferences from the pop-up menu (**Figure 8.19**).

   The Previews pane of the Preferences dialog appears.

2. Select one of the following options from the Adaptive Resolution Limit pop-up menu (**Figure 8.20**):

   ▲ **1/2**—After Effects temporarily displays the image at no less than one-half resolution while updating the comp preview.

   ▲ **1/4**—After Effects temporarily displays the image at one-quarter resolution while updating the comp preview.

   ▲ **1/8**—After Effects temporarily displays the image at one-eighth resolution while updating the comp preview.

3. Click OK to close the Preferences dialog.

Figure 8.17 With adaptive resolution enabled, the image degrades to keep pace with your adjustments...

Figure 8.18 ...and then assumes the comp's resolution when you stop transforming the layer.

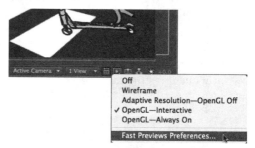

Figure 8.19 Choose Fast Previews Preferences from the Fast Previews button's pop-up menu.

Figure 8.20 Limit the amount of degradation by choosing an option in the Adaptive Resolution Limit pop-up menu.

OpenGL Graphics Cards

OpenGL is a technology utilized by many advanced video graphics cards that helps to enhance graphics processing, particularly for 3D objects and subtleties like shading, lights, and shadows. When a program is designed to recognize OpenGL, the increase in graphics performance can be substantial.

A high-end graphics card isn't necessarily a standard component in an average system configuration; instead, it's sometimes an expensive option. However, PC gamers and graphics professionals value graphics performance and are eager to upgrade to a more advanced graphics card.

Features and processing power vary from card to card. Whether your card supports features like lights and shadows in After Effects depends on the particular card.

Before you upgrade your graphics card, check Adobe's Web site to ensure the card has been certified to work with After Effects. This is also a quick way to see which features the card supports. And in addition to the card itself, make sure you install the latest software drivers, which should be available for download from the manufacturer's Web site.

Using OpenGL

Generally speaking, software processing can't match hardware dedicated to the same task. After Effects takes advantage of this fact by utilizing the graphics processing power of (After Effects-certified) OpenGL graphics cards.

After Effects detects whether your system has an OpenGL graphics card automatically and, if so, activates it as the default preview option.

When OpenGL is in effect, the Fast Previews button ⚡ becomes highlighted. By default, OpenGL kicks in whenever you drag layers in a comp, scrub a property, or scrub a comp's current time.

Overall, OpenGL provides faster, smoother screen updates than you would get otherwise, and it does so without degrading the image. But as the following task explains, you can set OpenGL to switch to adaptive resolution as you adjust effect property values (see "Using Adaptive Resolution," earlier in this chapter). This way, you can take advantage of OpenGL for most interactions and adaptive resolution when you're adjusting effects.

You already know how to specify your OpenGL card as the Fast Previews option (see "Specifying a Fast Previews Option" earlier in this chapter). This section explains how to set several options specific to OpenGL.

To set OpenGL preferences:

1. In a Comp panel, click the Fast Previews button and choose Fast Previews Preferences from the pop-up menu (**Figure 8.21**).

The Previews pane of the Preferences dialog appears.

2. Select Enable OpenGL.

3. Specify one of the following options (**Figure 8.22**):

▲ Enable Adaptive Resolution with OpenGL

▲ Accelerate Effects Using OpenGL (when possible)

4. Click OK to close the dialog.

To specify other OpenGL options:

1. In the Previews pane of the Preferences dialog, click OpenGL Info (**Figure 8.23**).

An OpenGL Information dialog appears.

2. Specify the amount for Texture Memory, in megabytes (MB) (**Figure 8.24**).

Adobe recommends allocating no more than 80 percent of the video RAM (VRAM) on your display card when using Windows; on a Mac, After Effects determines the ideal value automatically.

3. If available, specify other options, as determined by your card.

4. Click OK to close the OpenGL Information dialog, and click OK to close the Preferences dialog.

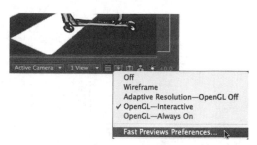

Figure 8.21 Choose Fast Previews Preferences from the Fast Previews button's pop-up menu.

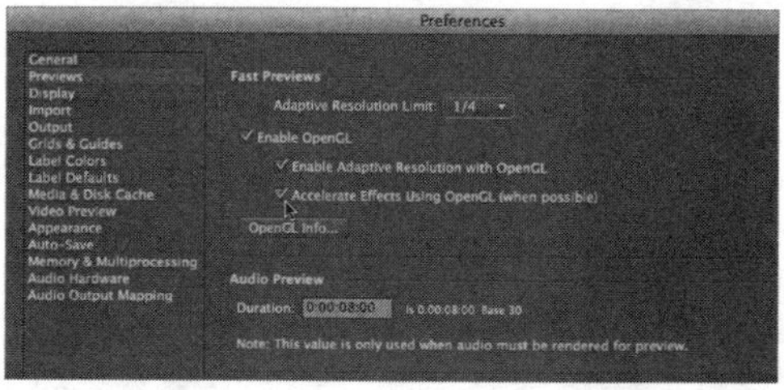

Figure 8.22 Select the OpenGL options you want.

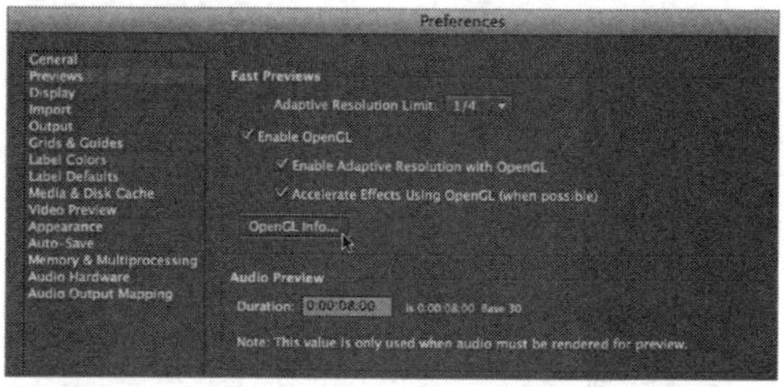

Figure 8.23 Click OpenGL Info to access more options.

Figure 8.24 In the OpenGL Information dialog, specify an amount for Texture Memory.

USING OPENGL

Figure 8.25 The Selection tool cycles between black and white as the program pauses to render frames.

Figure 8.26 When you've suppressed updates by pressing the Caps Lock key, a red outline appears around the image in the windows that would otherwise be updated. The window also displays a friendly reminder.

Suppressing Panel Updates

If frames are difficult to render, it can take time to update an image. You may have already noticed how the Selection tool cycles between black and white as a particularly difficult frame renders (**Figure 8.25**). The lower-right corner of the Composition panel also includes a small activity bar (provided the panel is sized wide enough for you to see it). When previewing gets in the way of your progress, you can prevent the Footage, Layer, and Composition panels from updating by pressing your keyboard's Caps Lock key.

When you suppress updates, panels continue to display already rendered frames. But when you alter the image in the current frame or move to an unrendered frame, a red outline appears around the image in the panels that would otherwise be updated (**Figure 8.26**). Although panel controls—anchor points, motion paths, mask outlines, and so on—continue to update, the image doesn't reflect your changes. When you're ready to update, or *refresh*, the affected panels, press the Caps Lock key again.

To suppress panel updates:

1. Press Caps Lock to suppress panel updates.

2. Press Caps Lock again to turn suppression off and refresh panels.

✔ Tip

■ If slow updates are a problem, you should consider replacing particularly demanding footage items with lower-quality proxies. See Chapter 3, "Managing Footage," for more information.

Scrubbing Audio

In After Effects, finding a particular frame based on the image is easy. Finding a particular moment based on the sound is a different matter. An audio preview plays your audio layers, but it doesn't make it easy to cue to a particular sound. When you halt an audio preview (see the next section), the current time indicator goes back to the starting point—the current time indicator doesn't remain at the moment you stop it. Viewing the audio waveform usually doesn't help you pinpoint a sound, either; individual sounds are difficult to discern in a waveform display (**Figure 8.27**).

Fortunately, After Effects allows you to *scrub* the audio—that is, play it back slowly as you drag the current time indicator. The term *scrubbing* refers to the back-and-forth motion of tape over an audio head.

Remember, you can always see audio levels—even while you scrub—in the Volume Units (VU) meter of the Audio panel (**Figure 8.28**).

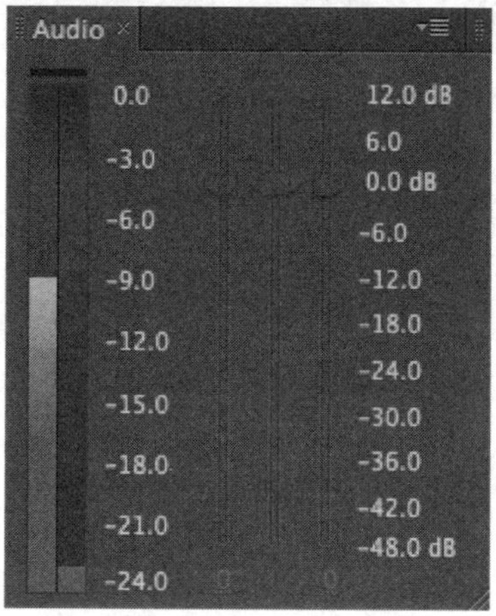

To scrub audio:

◆ In the time ruler of the Timeline panel, Command-drag (Ctrl-drag) the current time indicator.

The audio plays back as you drag.

✔ Tip

■ To hear every syllable and beat, there's no substitute for scrubbing. Once you find the sound you're looking for, you can mark the frame in the layer or the composition (see Chapter 6, "Layer Editing"). You can also set markers on the fly during audio previews by pressing the asterisk (*) key on the numeric keypad.

Figure 8.27 Scrubbing the audio provides an alternative (or an enhancement) to expanding the Audio Waveform property to cue the current time to a particular sound.

Figure 8.28 Use the VU meter of the Audio panel to see audio levels as they play.

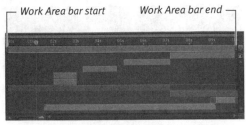

Work Area bar start   Work Area bar end

Figure 8.29 The Work Area bar defines the range of frames in the composition for previews.

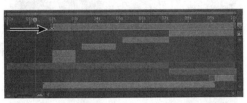

Figure 8.30 Drag the left handle of the Work Area bar to the time you want previews to start.

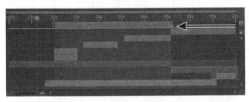

Figure 8.31 Drag the right handle of the Work Area bar to the time you want previews to end.

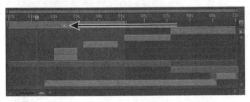

Figure 8.32 Drag the center of the Work Area bar to move the Work Area without changing its duration.

Previewing the Work Area

Until now, this chapter has focused on playback options and methods you can use to control the way the Composition panel updates when you transform layer properties. The following sections discuss previewing a specified area of the composition, a span defined by the Work Area.

The Work Area bar is an adjustable bar located just below the time ruler in the Timeline panel (**Figure 8.29**). To make it easier to identify the part of the composition that's included, the entire area under the Work Area bar is highlighted; it appears a little brighter than the area outside the Work Area.

To set the Work Area:

In the Timeline panel, *do any of the following:*

- Drag the left handle of the Work Area bar to the time you want previews to start, or set the current time and press B (**Figure 8.30**).

- Drag the right handle of the Work Area bar to the time you want previews to end, or set the current time and press N (**Figure 8.31**).

- Drag the center of the Work Area bar to move the Work Area without changing its duration (**Figure 8.32**).

  Press Shift as you drag to snap the edges of the Work Area bar to the edges of layers, keyframes, markers, or the CTI.

PREVIEWING THE WORK AREA

Previewing Audio Only

If you only need to hear the audio tracks of your composition, you don't have to wait for a time-consuming video preview.

To preview audio only under the Work Area:

1. Set the Work Area bar over the range of frames you want to preview (**Figure 8.33**).

   See the previous section, "Previewing the Work Area."

2. Choose Composition > Preview > Audio Preview (Work Area) (**Figure 8.34**).

   The audio under the Work Area plays.

To preview audio only from the current time:

◆ In the Composition or Timeline panel, cue the current time to the frame at which you want to begin your audio preview and then press the decimal point (.) on the numeric keypad (not the period on the main keyboard).

   The audio plays back from the current frame for the duration you set in the Preferences.

✔ Tips

■ You can set the quality of audio previews (and thereby the rendering times) in the Previews pane of the Preferences dialog.

■ When you preview audio from the current time, it plays for the duration you set in the General pane of the Preferences dialog.

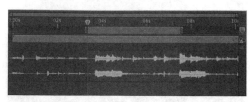

Figure 8.33 Set the Work Area bar over the range you want to preview.

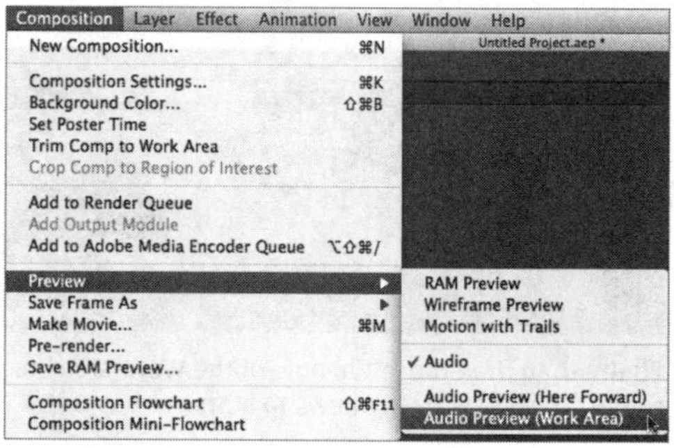

Figure 8.34 Choose Composition > Preview > Audio Preview (Work Area).

Table 8.1

Keyboard Shortcuts for Playback and Preview	
TO DO THIS	PRESS THIS
Play/Pause	Spacebar
Frame advance	Page Down
Frame reverse	Page Up
First frame	Home
Last frame	End
Scrub video	Option-drag (Alt-drag) the current time indicator
Scrub audio	Command-drag (Ctrl drag) the current time indicator
Stop panel updates	Caps Lock
Preview audio from the current time	Decimal point (.) on the numeric keypad
RAM preview	Zero (0) on the numeric keypad
Shift+RAM preview	Shift-0 on the numeric keypad
Save RAM preview	Command-0 (Ctrl-0) on the numeric keypad
Wireframe preview	Option-0 (Alt-0) on the numeric keypad
Wireframe preview using a rectangular layer outline	Command-Option-0 (Ctrl-Alt-0) on the numeric keypad
Show layers as background during wireframe previews	Add Shift to the wireframe
Preview shortcut	Shift-Option-0 (Shift-Alt-0) on the numeric keypad

✔ Tip

- To get a clear sense of motion without consuming much of your RAM or your time, you can render a wireframe preview. A *wireframe preview* represents the motion of one or more layers as an empty outline instead of a fully rendered image. Select one or more layers and choose Composition > Preview > Wireframe Preview. To get a feel for the sweep of motion, choose Composition > Preview > Motion With Trails.

Rendering RAM Previews

To see a comp at (or near) its full frame rate, you typically render a RAM preview. In contrast to using standard playback controls, a RAM preview renders frames first and then plays them back. By default, a RAM preview renders frames in the Work Area only; but you can set an option to render frames beginning at the current time (similar to standard playback). RAM previews include several options to balance rendering speed with image quality and frame rate.

You can set separate options for two kinds of RAM previews: a standard RAM preview and a Shift-RAM preview. You can customize each type according to your project's demands, choosing the best RAM preview option for the task at hand. For example, you could set the standard RAM preview to render a relatively smooth, high-resolution image, and set the Shift-RAM preview to render more quickly, at the expense of smooth motion and image quality.

By default, rendering a RAM preview (including a Shift-RAM preview) renders the active panel. But you can specify a particular panel to preview, even if it isn't the currently active panel. Doing so can streamline your workflow by freeing you from finding a particular panel to preview (especially in complex projects). For example, by designating your final comp as the panel to always preview, you can work in other panels and then quickly view your changes in the final comp.

For an overview of keyboard shortcuts for rendering a RAM preview and other playback options, see **Table 8.1**.

RENDERING RAM PREVIEWS

To show and hide RAM preview options:

◆ In the Preview panel's menu, select an option (**Figure 8.35**):

▲ **RAM Preview Options**—Expands the panel to reveal the RAM preview options

▲ **Shift+RAM Preview Options**—Expands the panel to reveal the Shift-RAM preview options

The Preview panel expands to reveal the options you selected (**Figure 8.36**). Reselect an option to hide the RAM preview options.

To set RAM preview options:

1. In the Preview panel, reveal either the RAM preview or Shift-RAM preview options, as explained in the previous task.

2. In the RAM Preview Options or Shift+RAM Preview Options area of the Preview panel, enter the following:

Frame Rate—Enter the frame rate for the preview, or choose one from the pop-up menu (**Figure 8.37**).

Lower frame rates render more quickly but at the expense of smooth motion.

Skip—Enter the frequency with which frames are skipped and left unrendered.

Skipping frames speeds rendering but results in choppier motion.

Resolution—Choose one of the following options from the pop-up menu:

▲ **Auto**—Previews use the Composition panel's current resolution setting

▲ **Full**—Renders and displays every pixel of the composition, resulting in the highest image quality and the longest rendering time

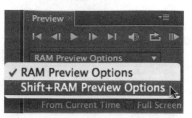

Figure 8.35 In the pop-up menu, choose the RAM preview options you want to show.

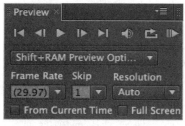

Figure 8.36 The Preview panel expands to reveal the options you selected.

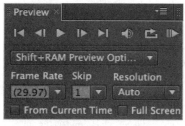

Figure 8.37 Enter a frame rate used by the preview, or choose one from the pop-up menu. Also enter the frequency at which frames are skipped.

RENDERING RAM PREVIEWS

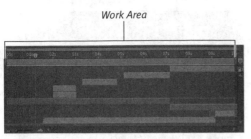

Figure 8.38 Set the Work Area bar over the range of frames you want to preview.

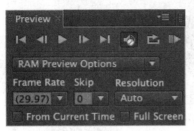

Figure 8.39 Here, the Audio button is set to exclude audio.

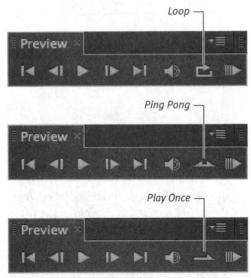

Figure 8.40 In the Preview panel, click the Loop button repeatedly so the icon corresponds to the option you want.

- ▲ **Half**—Renders every other pixel, or one-quarter of the pixels of the full-resolution image in one-quarter of the time

- ▲ **Third**—Renders every third pixel, or one-ninth of the pixels in the full-resolution image in one-ninth of the time

- ▲ **Quarter**—Renders every fourth pixel, or one-sixteenth of the pixels in the full-resolution image in one-sixteenth of the time

- ▲ **Custom**—Renders whatever fraction of pixels you specify

3. Select either of the following options:

- ▲ **From Current Time**—Renders previews from the current time (instead of the frames defined by the Work Area)

- ▲ **Full Screen**—Displays previews on a blank screen (with no panels visible)

To create a RAM preview:

1. In the Timeline panel, set the Work Area bar to the range of frames you want to preview (**Figure 8.38**).

2. To preview audio as well as video, click the Audio button in the Preview panel (**Figure 8.39**). This icon ▣ indicates audio will be included in previews; this icon ▣ indicates audio will be excluded.

3. Select an option by clicking the Loop button in the Preview panel (**Figure 8.40**).

- ▲ **Loop** ▣—Loops playback beginning to end

- ▲ **Ping Pong** ▰▰▰—Loops playback from beginning to end, then end to beginning

- ▲ **Play Once** ▰▰▰—Plays once

continues on next page

RENDERING RAM PREVIEWS

4. To use the standard RAM preview settings, *do any of the following:*

▲ Choose Composition > Preview > RAM Preview.

▲ Click the RAM Preview button in the Preview panel (**Figure 8.41**).

▲ Press 0 on the numeric keypad.

5. To use the Shift-RAM preview settings, *do either of the following:*

▲ Shift-click the RAM Preview button in the Preview panel.

▲ Hold Shift as you press 0 on the numeric keypad.

In the Timeline panel, a green line appears over the frames that are rendered to RAM. When all the frames in the Work Area have been rendered, or when the amount of available RAM runs out, the frames play back in the Composition panel.

To specify a panel to always preview:

◆ Click the Always Preview This View button  in the panel you want to designate for previews (**Figure 8.42**).

RAM previews (including Shift-RAM previews) always render the panel you specified, which becomes active for you to view.

✔ Tips

■ Choosing Composition > Save RAM preview lets you save a RAM preview as a movie file that you can use, for example, as a draft version for your own reference or for sharing with clients. For more about exporting, see Chapter 17, "Output."

■ After Effects discards cached frames as they become obsolete or as new frames are added to a full cache. But you can empty the cache manually by choosing Edit > Purge and selecting the type of cache.

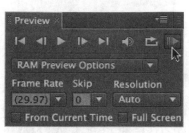

Figure 8.41 Click the RAM Preview button in the Preview panel, or press o in the numeric keypad.

Figure 8.42 In the lower-left corner of the window you want to designate, click the Always Preview This View button.

■ The Media & Disk Cache pane of the Preferences dialog allows you to specify the size and location of a disk cache. When the RAM cache is full, After Effects can move rendered frames to the location you specify. For best performance, the disk that stores source footage and the disk cache disk should use different drive controllers.

KEYFRAME INTERPOLATION

In Chapter 7, "Properties and Keyframes," you learned to animate layer properties over time by setting keyframes. By defining only the most important, or key, frames, you assume the role of head animator. After Effects fills the role of assistant animator, providing all the in-between frames, or tweens, using what's known as an *interpolation method* to determine their values.

Fortunately, you can instruct your assistant to use a range of interpolation methods. Some methods create steady changes from one keyframe to the next; others vary the rate of change. Movement can take a direct path or a curved route; an action can glide in for a soft landing or blast off in a burst of speed.

Without a choice of interpolation methods, your loyal assistant's abilities would be severely limited. If animated values always proceeded directly and mechanically from one keyframe to another, all but the most basic animations would seem lifeless and robotic. To create a curved movement would require so many keyframes you'd begin to wonder why you had an assistant at all. Calculating acceleration or deceleration in speed would present an even thornier problem.

This chapter explains how you can assign various interpolation methods to keyframes to impart nuance and variation to your animations using the Timeline panel's Graph Editor. You'll not only learn to decipher how After Effects depicts the ineffable qualities of motion, speed, and acceleration, but you'll also see how it harnesses them. In the process, you'll begin to realize that there's a big difference between animating something and bringing it to life.

Understanding Interpolation

The beauty of keyframes is that they save you work. If you set keyframes, After Effects calculates the values for the frames in between, a process known as *interpolation*. But to truly control animation, you'll need some power over the interpolated values as well. You can gain this control—without significantly increasing your work—by taking advantage of a type of calculation known as a Bézier curve.

As you'll see, mask and shape paths, spatial interpolation, and temporal interpolation are just different manifestations of the same Bézier principles. In fact, the ability to copy a mask path to a motion path attests to their shared Bézier heritage (see the sidebar, "Bézier Curves and the Motion Path," later in this chapter). And as you'll see in the following sections, most interpolation types (many of which include "Bézier in their names), calculate values in terms of both space and time: in other words, spatially and temporally.

Spatial interpolation

Spatial interpolation refers to how After Effects calculates changes in position, how a layer or its anchor point moves in the space of the composition. Does it proceed directly from one keyframe to the next, or does it take a curved route (**Figures 9.1** and **9.2**)?

As you've seen, spatial interpolation is represented as a motion path—a dotted line connecting keyframes. Changes in a layer's position value appear as a motion path in the Composition panel; changes in a layer's anchor-point value appear in its Layer panel. Effect point paths can appear in both panels. So far, you've learned how to set a layer's position at a keyframe by dragging in the appropriate panel; in this chapter, you'll learn how to adjust the path between keyframes, or the interpolated values.

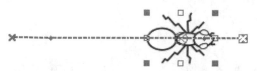

Figure 9.1 Interpolation refers to how After Effects calculates a property's values between keyframed values. Spatial interpolation determines whether movement proceeds directly from one keyframe to the next...

Figure 9.2 ...or takes a more curved, indirect route.

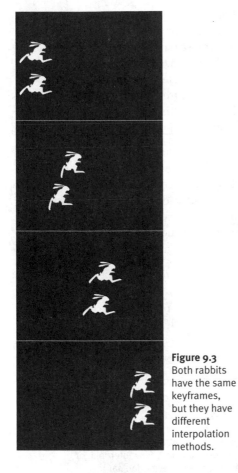

Figure 9.3
Both rabbits
have the same
keyframes,
but they have
different
interpolation
methods.

Temporal interpolation

Temporal interpolation refers to any property value's rate of change between keyframes. Does the value change at a constant rate from one keyframe to the next, or does it accelerate or decelerate?

For example, **Figure 9.3** shows two rabbits. They both travel the same distance in the same amount of time. However, one proceeds from the first keyframe to the last at a constant rate. The other gradually accelerates, starting slowly and then speeding up. As a result, the second rabbit falls behind at first and then gradually catches up. Both reach their destination simultaneously.

So far, you've viewed keyframes by expanding a layer's property values in the Timeline. The keyframes' relative timing and values give you some control of the overall speed of changes. But to see and manipulate the values *between* keyframes—the interpolated values—you must toggle the view under the time ruler to the Graph Editor. The Graph Editor represents the temporal interpolation as graphs that reflect a property's rate of change and also lets you control it (**Figure 9.4**).

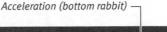

Figure 9.4 By toggling the Timeline panel to show the Graph Editor, you can see temporal interpolation represented as a graph. The straight line represents the top rabbit's speed; the curved line represents the bottom rabbit's speed.

Incoming and outgoing interpolation

Although *interpolation* refers to values between keyframes, it's important to understand that you assign an interpolation type to keyframes themselves. The interpolation type, in turn, determines how values are calculated before the keyframe and after the keyframe—the *incoming* and *outgoing interpolation*. Therefore, the values between any two keyframes (the interpolated values) are determined by the first keyframe's outgoing interpolation type and the next keyframe's incoming interpolation type. The concept is most easily understood in spatial terms. A motion path consists of at least two keyframes. A tangent extending from the first keyframe determines the outgoing interpolation, while a tangent extending from the second keyframe determines the incoming interpolation. The motion path between keyframes results from their relative positions, as well as the length and angles of their tangents (**Figure 9.5**).

Temporal interpolation also affects a property value's rate of change before and after the keyframe. In a speed or value graph, ease handles work a lot like tangents in a motion path. But because the graph lines don't trace a spatial path, they can be a little more difficult to understand and adjust (**Figure 9.6**).

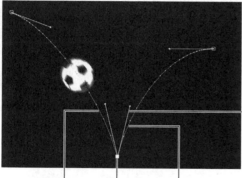

Tangent

Incoming interpolation   Keyframe   Outgoing interpolation

Figure 9.5 In a motion path, keyframe tangents define the outgoing and incoming interpolation and, hence, the curve of the motion path.

Incoming interpolation   Keyframe   Ease handle

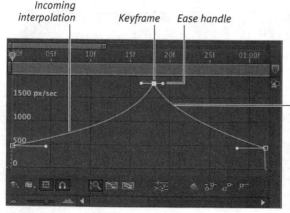

Outgoing interpolation

Figure 9.6 A value graph's direction lines and a speed graph's ease handles (shown here) define the incoming and outgoing interpolation. Here, the rate of change gradually accelerates after the first keyframe and then decelerates into the second keyframe.

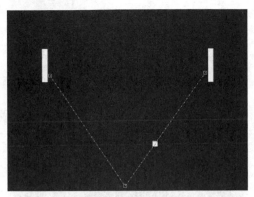

Figure 9.7 Spatially, linear interpolation defines a corner at each keyframe and a straight path between keyframes. The ball in the classic Pong game, for example, moves in perfectly straight lines and ricochets in sharp corners.

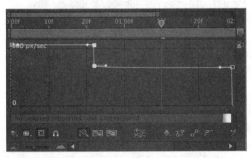

Figure 9.8 Temporally, linear interpolation results in a constant rate of change between keyframes. When speed differs between pairs of keyframes, the change is instantaneous.

Interpolation Types

With the exception of hold interpolation, After Effects uses the same methods to calculate both spatial and temporal interpolation. This section describes how each interpolation type is expressed spatially, in a motion path, and temporally, in a speed graph.

No interpolation

No interpolation is applied to properties that have no keyframes and aren't animated. Static properties display an I-beam icon (rather than keyframes) in the layer outline, and the Stopwatch icon isn't selected.

Linear

Linear interpolation dictates a constant rate of change from one keyframe to the next. Between two keyframes, linear interpolation defines a straight path; temporally, it results in a constant speed. When a keyframe's incoming and outgoing interpolation are linear, a corner is created in the motion path. Temporally, speed changes instantly at the keyframe (**Figures 9.7** and **9.8**).

Auto Bézier

Auto Bézier interpolation automatically reduces the rate of change equally on both sides of a keyframe.

Spatially, a keyframe set to auto Bézier is comparable to a smooth point, with two equal direction lines extending from it. It results in a smooth, symmetrical curve in a motion path. A satellite in an elliptical orbit, for example, takes even, round turns (**Figure 9.9**). (In addition, the satellite may auto-orient its rotation according to the direction of its movement. See "Orienting Rotation to a Motion Path Automatically," in Chapter 7.)

Temporally, auto Bézier interpolation reduces the rate of change equally before and after a keyframe, creating a gradual deceleration that eases into and out of the keyframe (**Figure 9.10**).

Continuous Bézier

Like auto Bézier, continuous Bézier interpolation reduces the rate of change on both sides of a keyframe. However, continuous Bézier interpolation is set manually, so it doesn't affect the incoming and outgoing rates of change equally. In the motion path, continuous Bézier interpolation results in a smooth and continuous, but asymmetrical, curve. Typically, the path of a thrown ball follows an arc that's continuous but asymmetrical; or imagine the ball rolling over a hill that's steeper on one side than the other (**Figure 9.11**).

Temporally, continuous Bézier interpolation reduces the rate of change unequally before and after a keyframe (**Figure 9.12**).

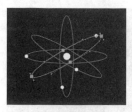

Figure 9.9 Auto Bézier interpolation creates a curved path with equal incoming and outgoing interpolation. The keyframes of an orbital path may use perfectly symmetrical curves.

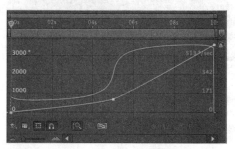

Figure 9.10 Temporally, auto Bézier interpolation yields gradual, even speed changes and a curved graph. For example, the blade of a fan goes from a lower speed to a higher speed gradually (not instantaneously).

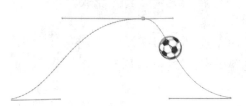

Figure 9.11 You might use continuous Bézier interpolation to show the path of a ball rolling over a hill that's less steep on one side than the other.

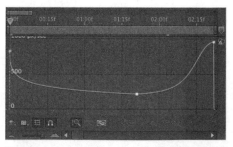

Figure 9.12 Temporally, rate of change is reduced smoothly—but unevenly—on either side of a continuous Bézier keyframe. A rolling ball may decelerate gradually as it crests a hill but accelerate more sharply on its descent.

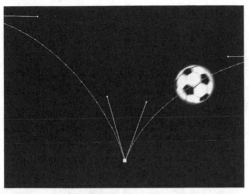

Figure 9.13 Bézier interpolation can allow the motion path to follow discontinuous curves, such as the one that describes the path of a ball's bounce.

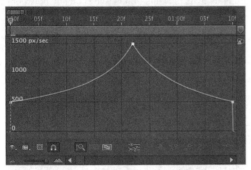

Figure 9.14 Temporally, Bézier interpolation can create sudden acceleration and deceleration. The bouncing ball accelerates until the moment of impact and then suddenly decelerates as it ascends.

Qu'est-ce Que C'est Bézier? *Qui Est* Bézier?

In case your French is rusty, *Bézier* is pronounced *bay-zee-yay*, after the late Pierre Etienne Bézier, who popularized the math behind his namesake curve in the 1970s for use in computer-aided design and manufacturing. This same math became the basis for Adobe PostScript fonts, path-based drawing, and—yes—the interpolation methods used in computer animation. Bézier died in 1999. *Merci,* Monsieur Bézier.

Bézier

Like continuous Bézier, you set Bézier interpolation manually, but the change is discontinuous. Bézier interpolation causes an abrupt decrease or increase in the rate of change on either or both sides of a keyframe.

Spatially, Bézier keyframes are comparable to a corner point in a mask path. As in a corner point, the direction lines extending from the keyframe are unequal and discontinuous. In a motion path, Bézier interpolation creates a discontinuous curve, or *cusp*, at the keyframe. Bézier interpolation can achieve the discontinuous curve of a ball's bouncing path (**Figure 9.13**).

In the value graph, Bézier interpolation can reduce or increase the rate of change before and after a keyframe (**Figure 9.14**). For example, you can use Bézier interpolation to create a sharp acceleration at a keyframe (such as when a ball falls and bounces).

✔ Tip

■ Again, the motion path and the types of spatial interpolation it uses affect motion only. For truly convincing animation, you must also adjust speed (by controlling the time between keyframes) and acceleration (via temporal interpolation). In addition, consider other physical attributes associated with motion—for example, the blurred motion of fast-moving objects, or distortion and elasticity (say, the squashing effect when a ball strikes the ground). (See Chapter 14, "More Layer Techniques," for more about motion blur.)

Hold

Although you can observe its effects both spatially and temporally, hold interpolation is a strictly temporal type of interpolation, halting changes in a property's value at the keyframe. The value remains fixed until the current frame of the composition reaches the next keyframe, where the property is set to a new value instantly. For example, specifying hold keyframes for a layer's Position property causes the layer to disappear suddenly and then reappear in different places. Instead of a dotted motion path, a thin solid line connects hold keyframes, indicating not the motion path but the order of keyframed positions (**Figure 9.15**). Similarly, nonspatial properties proceed instantly from one held keyframed value to another. Whereas using linearly interpolated keyframes to change a layer's opacity value from 0 to 100 is comparable to using a dimmer light, using hold keyframes is more like using a light switch. In the speed graph, hold keyframes appear as keyframes with a speed of 0 (**Figure 9.16**).

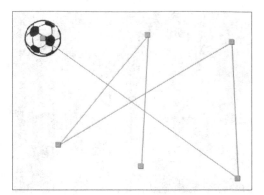

Figure 9.15 In this figure, the layer's position property uses hold keyframes. The layer remains in the position defined by a keyframe until the next keyframe is reached, at which time the layer instantly appears in its new position. A thin solid line between keyframes isn't a motion path; it indicates the order of keyframed positions.

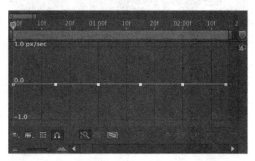

Figure 9.16 Keyframes of other properties that use hold interpolation retain their current value until the next keyframe.

Bézier Curves and the Motion Path

Motion paths consist of *Bézier curves*: the same kind of curves that define shapes in drawing programs like Photoshop and Illustrator, as well as the masks you create in After Effects. Instead of drawing a shape freehand, you can define a shape using a Bézier curve. In a Bézier curve, you define vertices (aka *control points*), which are connected by line segments automatically. (It already sounds a lot like keyframes and interpolation, doesn't it?)

In a Bézier curve, the line segments are defined and controlled by tangents, aka *direction lines* (**Figure 9.17**). Two direction lines can extend from each vertex. The length and angle of one direction line influences the shape of the curve preceding the vertex; the other influences the curve following the vertex. (Imagine that the direction lines exert a gravitational pull on the line that enters and exits a vertex.) Dragging the end of a direction line alters the line and thus its corresponding curve.

Just as a Bézier curve consists of vertices connected by line segments, a *motion path* consists of position keyframes connected by line segments—albeit dotted lines (**Figure 9.18**). The same techniques you use to draw shapes in a drawing program can be applied to creating motion paths in After Effects. (In fact, you can copy a mask path into a composition as a motion path.)

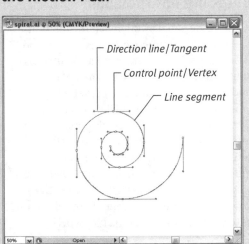

Figure 9.17 The Bézier curves you use to define a shape in a drawing program or a mask in After Effects...

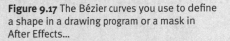

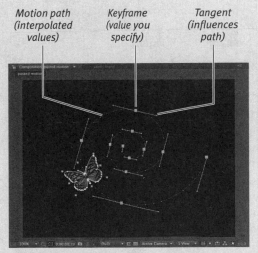

Figure 9.18 ...also define a motion path in After Effects. However, the terms used to describe the curve depend on the context.

Mixed incoming and outgoing interpolation

A keyframe can use different interpolation types for its incoming and outgoing interpolation. A keyframe's incoming and outgoing spatial interpolation can be a mix of linear and Bézier. A keyframe's temporal interpolation may use any combination of linear, Bézier, and hold for its incoming and outgoing interpolation. As usual, the shape of the motion path or graph in the Graph Editor indicates mixed interpolation. In the standard view of the time graph (rather than in the Graph Editor view), keyframe icons also indicate the temporal interpolation type.

Keyframe icons and interpolation

The Graph Editor shows interpolation explicitly in the form of a value or speed graph. Regardless of the interpolation type, keyframe icons appear as small boxes, or *control points*, on the graph. Roving keyframes always appear as small dots.

But as you saw in Chapter 7, keyframe icons look different when you're not using the Graph Editor. In the standard view of the time ruler, an expanded property's keyframes appear as relatively large icons. Because no graph is visible, each icon's shape helps indicate the incoming and outgoing interpolation (**Figure 9.19**). If you expand a heading only, any individual property's keyframes appear as small dots to indicate their presence and position.

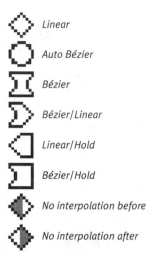

Linear

Auto Bézier

Bézier

Bézier/Linear

Linear/Hold

Bézier/Hold

No interpolation before

No interpolation after

Figure 9.19 Though the standard view of the timeline doesn't graph interpolation, the shape of each keyframe's icons indicates the type of interpolation.

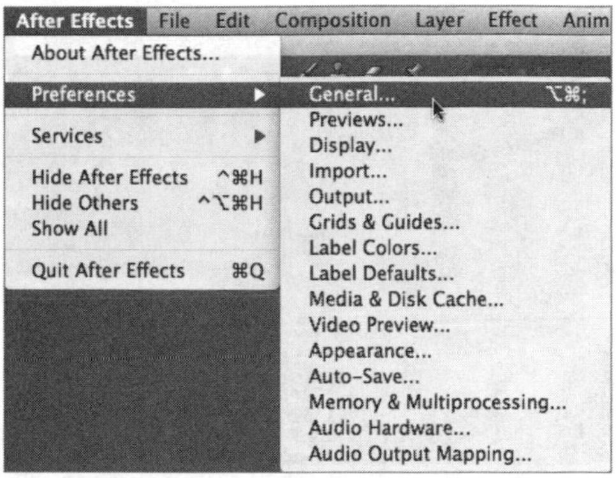

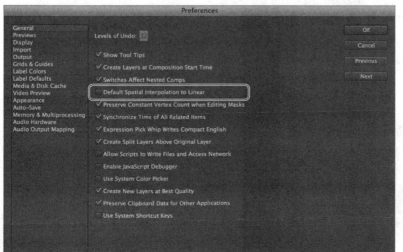

Figure 9.20 Choose After Effects > Preferences > General on the Mac, as shown here (or Edit > Preferences > General in Windows).

Specifying the Default Spatial Interpolation

Ordinarily, motion-path keyframes use auto Bézier interpolation. If most of your spatial animation requires linear interpolation (or if you simply prefer it as your initial setting), you can change the default in the Preferences dialog.

To set the default spatial interpolation:

1. Choose After Effects > Preferences > General (Edit > Preferences > General) (**Figure 9.20**).

   The General pane of the Preferences dialog appears.

2. *Do either of the following* (**Figure 9.21**):

   ▲ Click the Default Spatial Interpolation to Linear check box to make new motion paths use linear interpolation.

   ▲ Leave Default Spatial Interpolation to Linear unselected to make new motion paths use auto Bézier interpolation.

3. Click OK to close the Preferences dialog.

Figure 9.21 In the General pane of the Preferences dialog, choose whether to use linear interpolation as the default.

Specifying Spatial Interpolation in the Motion Path

In Chapter 7, "Properties and Keyframes," you learned that you can change the spatial positioning of each keyframe by dragging it directly into a Composition or Layer panel. This section focuses on using spatial interpolation to change the course of the motion path from one keyframe to the next.

To move a position keyframe:

1. Select a layer with an animated property to reveal its motion path in a Composition or Layer panel.

   Position and effect-point paths appear in the Composition panel (**Figure 9.22**); anchor-point paths appear in the Layer panel.

2. Using the selection tool, drag a keyframe to a new position (**Figure 9.23**).

   In a motion path, a selected spatial keyframe appears as small solid box, or handle; a deselected keyframe appears as an outlined box.

To toggle between auto Bézier and linear interpolation:

1. Select a layer with an animated property to reveal its motion path in a Composition or Layer panel.

   Position and effect-point paths appear in the Composition panel (**Figure 9.24**); anchor-point paths appear in the Layer panel.

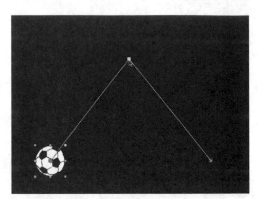

Figure 9.22 To move a position keyframe...

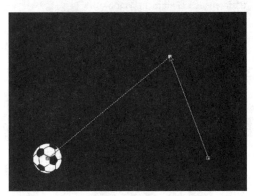

Figure 9.23 ...drag its icon to a new location in the Layer panel (for anchor point or effect point) or Comp panel (for position or effect point).

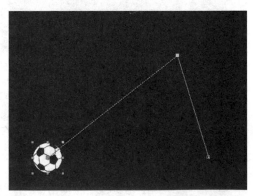

Figure 9.24 Select a layer so that its motion path is visible in the Comp panel.

Figure 9.25 In the Tools panel, select the Pen tool.

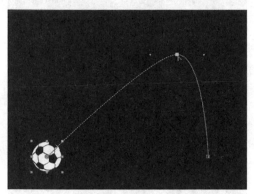

Figure 9.26 Clicking a keyframe with the Convert Vertex tool changes the keyframe from auto Bézier to linear and vice versa.

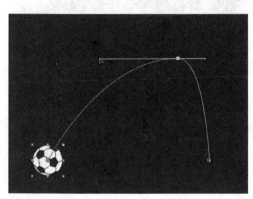

Figure 9.27 Dragging one of an auto Bézier keyframe's tangents makes it a continuous Bézier keyframe. The tangents remain continuous, but they influence the path unequally.

2. In the Tools panel, select the Pen tool ![pen] (**Figure 9.25**).

3. In the motion path, click a keyframe icon to convert it.

The Pen tool becomes the Convert Vertex tool ⋀ when you position it over a keyframe. A keyframe using linear interpolation is converted to auto Bézier, with two equal control handles (motion path tangents) extending from the keyframe. Any Bézier-type keyframe is converted to linear, with no direction handles (**Figure 9.26**).

4. In the Tools panel, choose the Selection tool ![selection].

Once you convert a keyframe, adjust it with the Selection tool. Clicking it without changing tools converts it back.

To convert auto Bézier to continuous Bézier:

1. Select a layer with an animated property to reveal its motion path in a Composition or Layer panel.

2. Using the Selection tool, drag one tangent of an auto Bézier keyframe so that it's shorter or longer than the other (**Figure 9.27**).

Both of the keyframe's tangents form a continuous line, but they influence the path by different amounts.

SPATIAL INTERPOLATION IN THE MOTION PATH

To convert continuous Bézier to Bézier, and vice versa:

1. Select a layer with an animated property to reveal its motion path in a Composition or Layer panel.

2. Select one or more keyframes in the motion path (**Figure 9.28**).

   The selected keyframe's motion path tangents (control handles) become visible.

3. In the Tools panel, select the Pen tool (**Figure 9.29**).

4. In the motion path, drag a direction handle (**Figure 9.30**).

   The Pen tool becomes the Convert Vertex tool ⋀ when you position it over a motion path tangent, also called a direction handle. Dragging a direction handle of a Bézier keyframe converts it to continuous Bézier with two related tangents; dragging a tangent of a continuous Bézier keyframe splits the two tangents, converting it to Bézier.

5. In the Tools panel, choose the Selection tool .

   Once you convert a keyframe, adjust its direction handles with the Selection tool. Otherwise, you'll convert it back.

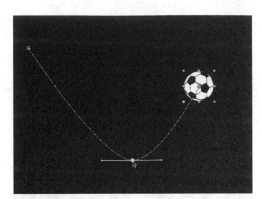

Figure 9.28 Select one or more keyframes in the motion path.

Figure 9.29 Select the Pen tool.

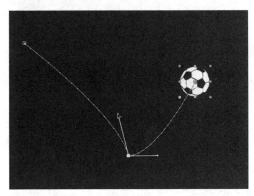

Figure 9.30 When positioned over a path tangent, the Pen becomes the Convert Vertex icon. Drag a tangent to change continuous Bézier to Bézier and vice versa.

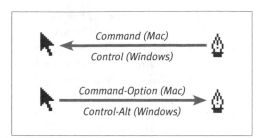

Figure 9.31 Press and hold Command (Ctrl) to toggle between the currently selected Pen tool and the Selection tool; press Command-Option (Ctrl-Alt) to toggle between the Selection tool and the Pen tool.

To toggle between the Selection tool and a Pen tool:

1. Position the mouse pointer over a motion path in a Comp or Layer panel, and *do either of the following* (**Figure 9.31**):

   ▲ To toggle the current Pen tool to the Selection tool, press and hold Command (Ctrl).

   ▲ To toggle the Selection tool to the Pen tool currently visible in the Tools panel, press and hold Command-Option (Ctrl-Alt).

2. Release the keyboard modifier to continue using the currently selected tool.

Speed in the Motion Path

In the motion path, the spacing between dots indicates speed. Closely spaced dots indicate slower speeds; more widely spaced dots indicate faster speeds. If the dot spacing changes between keyframes, this means the speed is changing—accelerating or decelerating (**Figure 9.32**). (A solid line means hold interpolation has been applied; see the section "Interpolation Types," earlier in this chapter).

Remember that the motion path gives you direct control over the physical distance between keyframes—not their timing or the temporal interpolation. As you use controls in the timeline to alter the speed or temporal interpolation of a spatial property, watch how the motion path also changes.

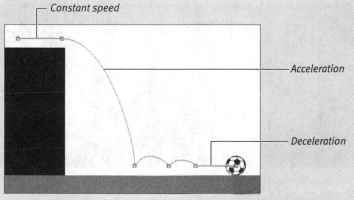

Figure 9.32 The spacing of dots in the motion path indicate speed: the more closely spaced the dots, the slower the motion. A solid line would indicate hold interpolation (and no actual motion).

Using the Graph Editor: An Overview

By taking over the area under the timeline's time ruler, the Graph Editor affords a detailed view of property changes and a spacious area in which to edit them (**Figures 9.33** and **9.34**). The number of options reflects the Graph Editor's flexibility but may also make the process seem more complex than it really is. The following task provides an overview.

Later sections cover each aspect of the process in greater detail. First, you'll learn how to adjust the timing and values of keyframes using the Graph Editor instead of the methods you learned in Chapter 7, "Properties and Keyframes." Then, you'll move on to using the graphs to adjust interpolation (the values between keyframes).

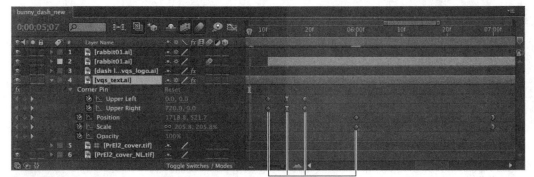

Figure 9.33 In the typical view of the timeline, you can see expanded properties' keyframe icons but no graphical representation of interpolated values.

Keyframes

Value graph (Y) — *Graph Editor* —

Value graph (X) — *Speed graph* —

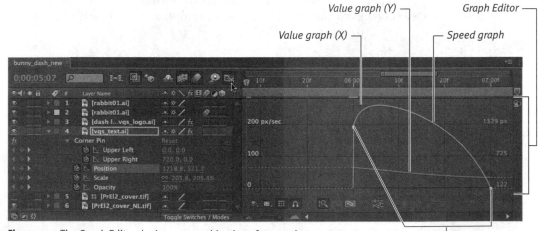

Figure 9.34 The Graph Editor depicts any combination of properties as graphs in a spacious and detailed view under the time ruler.

Keyframes

Figure 9.35 Click the Graph Editor button.

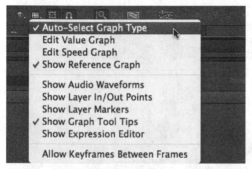

Figure 9.36 Specify the visible properties in the Show Properties pop-up menu.

Figure 9.37 Specify the graph type you want to edit and other options.

Figure 9.38 Edit a property graph by dragging its keyframe and ease handles or by using an automated method (the keyframe assistant).

To adjust properties in the Graph Editor:

1. In the Timeline panel, click the Graph Editor button ▥ (**Figure 9.35**).

2. Specify which properties are visible by choosing an option in the Show Properties menu (**Figure 9.36**).

3. Specify the graph types you want to edit for the visible properties in the Graph Type and Options menu.

4. Specify the other information you want to view by selecting the appropriate option in the Graph Type and Options menu (**Figure 9.37**).

   Optional information includes layer In and Out point icons, layer markers, and so on.

5. Edit the visible property graphs (**Figure 9.38**).

   You can select, move, add, and delete property keyframes; you can also adjust their interpolation types using either manual or automatic methods.

✔ Tip

■ Technically, you can use a keyboard shortcut to specify preset interpolation types to a keyframe without switching to the Graph Editor. Both methods are covered in the section "Setting a Keyframe's Temporal Interpolation Type," later in this chapter.

USING THE GRAPH EDITOR: AN OVERVIEW

211

Understanding Value and Speed Graphs

In the following sections, you'll use the Graph Editor to (what else?) edit a graph of a property. But first, let's take a moment to examine the two types of graphs you'll encounter: the value graph and speed graph. As you proceed with the graph-editing tasks in the following sections, note how the shape of a value graph or speed graph corresponds to the animation (**Figures 9.39** and **9.40**, and **Table 9.1**).

Table 9.1

Recognizing Temporal Interpolation

TEMPORAL INTERPOLATION	IN THE VALUE GRAPH	IN THE SPEED/VELOCITY GRAPH
No speed change	Horizontal line	Horizontal line
Constant speed	Straight line with any slope	Horizontal line
Sudden speed change	Sharp corner	Disconnected line/ease handles
Acceleration	Curve with steep slope	Upward-sloping curve
Deceleration	Curve with shallow slope	Downward-sloping curve
Holding	Horizontal line, unconnected	Horizontal line, where current speed = 0

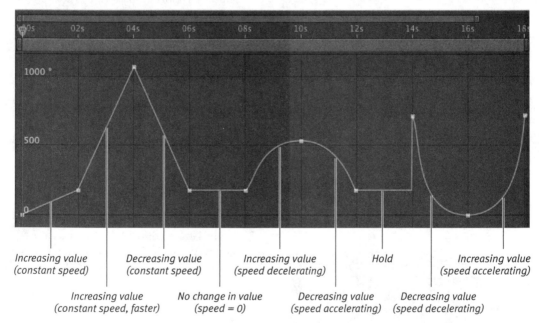

Increasing value
(constant speed)

Increasing value
(constant speed, faster)

Decreasing value
(constant speed)

No change in value
(speed = 0)

Increasing value
(speed decelerating)

Decreasing value
(speed accelerating)

Hold

Decreasing value
(speed decelerating)

Increasing value
(speed accelerating)

Figure 9.39 A value graph shows changes in a property's value (in this case, Rotation). Examine how each graph shape corresponds with certain types of temporal interpolation.

Value graph

A *value graph* measures a property's value vertically and its time horizontally. The units in which values are expressed depend on the type of property: Rotation is measured in rotations and degrees, Opacity in percentages, and so on. The slope of the line between keyframes represents the rate of change in units per second. Straight lines indicate a constant rate; curved lines indicate a changing rate, or acceleration.

A value graph is particularly easy to grasp when viewing properties such as Opacity and Audio Levels, because these properties correspond well with the "up and down" or "high and low" nature of the graph.

Note that some properties consist of more than one value, or *dimension*. For example, a Position property includes values for both an X and Y coordinate. Hence, a position value

graph includes two color-coded lines: one representing the X coordinate value and the other representing the Y coordinate value.

Speed graph

A speed graph measures rates of change in a property's values. The units measured by a speed graph depend on the property type: degrees of rotation/sec, percentage opacity/sec, and so on. Regardless of the specific property, the rate of change (units/sec) is measured vertically, and time (sec) is measured horizontally in both graphs. Therefore, the slope of the line represents acceleration (units/sec/sec). Compared to interpreting a value graph, interpreting a speed graph isn't as straightforward. For example, a property's *value* may be increasing or decreasing—but if its rate of change is constant, it results in a horizontal line in the speed graph.

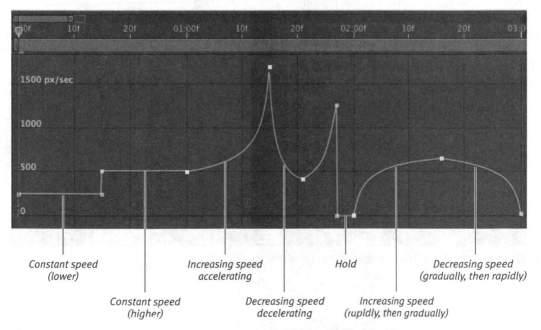

Figure 9.40 A speed graph shows changes in a property's speed (here, Position).

UNDERSTANDING VALUE AND SPEED GRAPHS

Viewing Property Graphs

To view temporal interpolation and control it manually, toggle the area under the time ruler to the Graph Editor.

The Graph Editor's flexible viewing options help you view the combination of properties you want: selected properties, animated properties, or properties you specify by including them in what's known as the *graph editor set*.

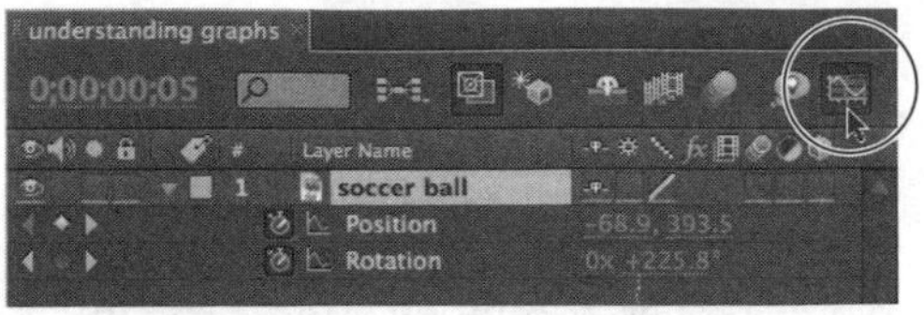

To toggle the Graph Editor:

◆ In the Timeline panel, select the Show Graph Editor button ▨ (**Figure 9.41**).

The area under the time ruler changes to the Graph Editor (**Figure 9.42**). The properties visible in the Graph Editor depend on options you specify in the Show Properties menu; the types of graphs visible depends on the options you specify in the Graph Type and Options menu. (See the next task, "To specify visible properties in the Graph Editor," and "To specify the graph types displayed in the Graph Editor," later in this chapter.)

Figure 9.41 In the Timeline panel, select the Show Graph Editor button.

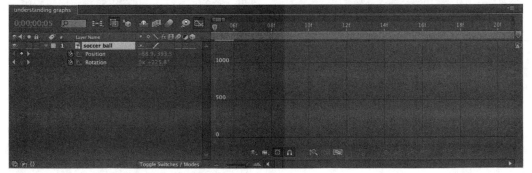

Figure 9.42 The time ruler area toggles to the Graph Editor view.

Figure 9.43 In the Graph Editor's Show Properties pop-up menu, select which properties are visible.

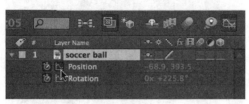

Figure 9.44 Expand the layer outline to reveal the properties you want to add to the graph editor set, and then click their Include in Graph Editor Set button.

To specify visible properties in the Graph Editor:

◆ In the Graph Editor, click the Show Properties button ☒ to access a pop-up menu, and *choose any of the following* (**Figure 9.43**):

▲ **Show Selected Properties**— Includes the property you select in the layer outline

▲ **Show Animated Properties**— Includes all of the selected layer's animated properties

▲ **Show Graph Editor Set**—Includes all properties you specify as part of the graph editor set. (See the next task, "To designate a graph editor set.")

The properties you specify appear in the Graph Editor.

To designate a graph editor set:

1. In a comp's layer outline, expand layers to reveal the properties you want to add to the graph editor set.

2. For each property you want to add to the graph editor set, click the Include in Graph Editor Set button ☒ (**Figure 9.44**).

Properties in the set appear in the Graph Editor when the Show Graph Editor Set option is selected (see the previous task, "To specify visible properties in the Graph Editor").

✔ Tips

■ Here's a reminder of something you learned in Chapter 7, Table 7.1: Press U to reveal all the animated properties of all the selected layers.

■ Keyboard shortcuts make it easy to reveal just the properties you want. See Table 7.1 in Chapter 7 for some of the most common keyboard shortcuts.

VIEWING PROPERTY GRAPHS

Specifying the Graph Type

The Graph Editor can represent any property as a value graph or speed graph. Turn back to the section "Understanding Value and Speed Graphs," earlier in this chapter, to review how the graphs work. Later sections explain how to manipulate the graphs.

To specify the graph types displayed in the Graph Editor:

1. In the Graph Editor, click the Graph Type and Options button, and then *choose any of the following options in the pop-up menu* (**Figure 9.45**):

   ▲ **Auto-Select Graph Type**—After Effects determines the most appropriate type of graph to display for editing.

   ▲ **Edit Value Graph**—After Effects displays the visible properties' value graph for editing.

   ▲ **Edit Speed Graph**—After Effects displays the visible properties' speed graph for editing.

   In the Graph Editor, the type of graph you choose appears for the visible properties (**Figure 9.46**).

2. To display the type of graph you *did not* specify in step 1 for reference, select Show Reference Graph (**Figure 9.47**).

   For example, if you chose Edit Speed Graph in step 1, then selecting Show Reference Graph makes the value graph visible. However, you can't edit the reference graph (**Figure 9.48**).

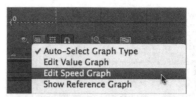

Figure 9.45 Selecting an option in the Graph Editor's Graph Type and Options pop-up menu...

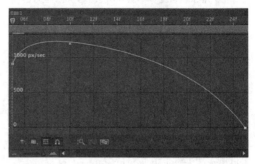

Figure 9.46 ...displays that type of graph for the visible property. Here, the property's speed graph is visible for editing.

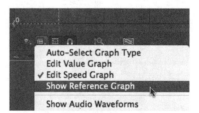

Figure 9.47 Selecting Show Reference Graph...

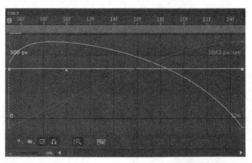

Figure 9.48 ...makes the other graph visible (in this case, the value graph). The reference graph can't be edited, but it reflects the changes you make to the other graph.

Viewing Optional Information in the Graph Editor

The Graph Editor not only lets you select which property and type of graph you want to view, but it also lets you reveal other helpful information, such as audio waveforms, In point and Out point icons, markers, tool tips, and expressions (**Figure 9.49**).

Other options help you hone in on the graph you want to work with and scale the graph when adjustments make it exceed the available space.

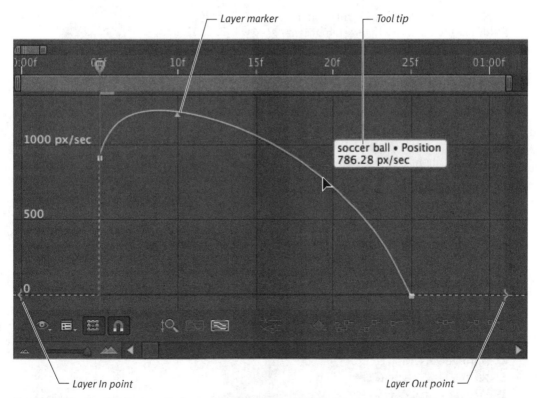

Figure 9.49 The Graph Editor can display optional information. Hovering the mouse pointer over a graph reveals a tool tip, which in this case shows the property value's speed at that point.

To specify Graph Editor options:

◆ In the Graph Editor, click the Graph Type and Options button to access the pop-up menu, and then *choose any of the following options* (**Figure 9.50**):

▲ **Show Audio Waveforms**—When you're viewing an audio layer's Audio Levels property, this option displays a waveform, or graphical representation of audio power.

▲ **Show Layer In/Out Points**—This option shows In point and Out point icons for the layer containing properties visible in the Graph Editor.

▲ **Show Layer Markers**—This option shows marker icons for the layer containing properties visible in the Graph Editor.

▲ **Show Graph Tool Tips**—This option displays a tool tip containing the current speed or value at the point where you position the mouse pointer over a graph.

▲ **Show Expression Editor**—This option shows an area to add and edit an *expression*, or script-based formula for determining the property's value (see Chapter 16, "Complex Projects," for more about expressions).

▲ **Allow Keyframes Between Frames**—Permits you to set keyframes between timebase divisions, which can be especially useful when you're synchronizing keyframes with audio.

The Graph Editor activates the options you specify.

To scale the graph automatically:

◆ In the Graph Editor, *select any of the following options:*

▲ **Auto-zoom Graph Height** 🔍

▲ **Fit Selection to View** 🗾

▲ **Fit All Graphs to View** 🗾

The view adjusts according to your selection.

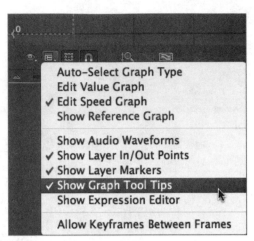

Figure 9.50 Select the options you want in the Graph Editor's Graph Type and Options pop-up menu.

Figure 9.51 Click the Graph Editor's Snap button to assist in aligning keyframes with In points, Out points, the CTI, or other keyframes.

Moving Keyframes in the Graph Editor

You select keyframes in the Graph Editor using the same methods you use to select keyframes in a motion path (or, for that matter, to select keyframes in the standard view of the time ruler). The keyframe icons differ, but the procedures are the same, and we won't review them here. However, the Graph Editor includes a couple of unique features when it comes to keyframes.

First, the Graph Editor has its own *snap* feature. As you know from other chapters (and other programs), snapping gives objects a magnetic quality so that it's easier to align them with one another. In the Graph Editor, enabling snapping helps you align keyframes with In points, Out points, markers, the current time indicator (CTI), and other keyframes.

The Graph Editor also includes a more unexpected feature, a keyframe transform box. With this option active, selecting multiple keyframes includes them in a transform box—just like the bounding box that lets you scale a layer. Ordinarily, selecting multiple keyframes lets you move all of them by the same amount. In contrast, a transform box lets you adjust keyframes *proportionally*. In other words, keyframes included in the transform box maintain their relative positions on the box.

To enable keyframe snapping in the Graph Editor:

◆ In the Graph Editor, click the Snap button (**Figure 9.51**).

When the Snap button is selected, keyframes align with other keyframes, markers, the CTI, and other elements more easily.

To move keyframes using a transform box:

◆ In the Graph Editor, click the Show Bounding Box button ▓ (**Figure 9.52**).

When you select multiple keyframes, a bounding box appears around the keyframes (**Figure 9.53**).

To move multiple keyframes using a transform box:

1. With the Show Bounding Box option selected, *do either of the following:*

   ▲ Shift-click multiple keyframes.

   ▲ Drag a marquee around consecutive keyframes.

   A bounding box appears around the selected keyframes.

2. *Do either of the following:*

   ▲ Drag any of the bounding box's handles to scale the box (**Figure 9.54**).

   ▲ Press and hold Option (Alt) to move a handle on the bounding box independently of the other handles (**Figure 9.55**).

   The keyframes contained in the bounding box move according to your adjustments, maintaining their relative positions on the box.

Figure 9.52 Selecting the Graph Editor's Show Bounding Box button...

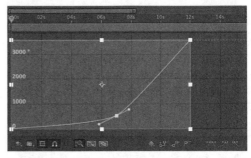

Figure 9.53 ...creates a bounding box around selected keyframes.

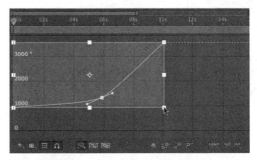

Figure 9.54 Dragging the bounding box scales the box and moves the keyframes accordingly.

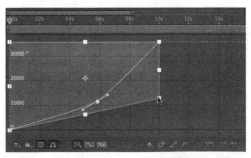

Figure 9.55 Press Option (Alt) to drag a bounding box's handle independently of other handles.

Figure 9.56 In the Tools panel, choose the Pen tool (shown here) or press Command (Ctrl) with the Selection tool.

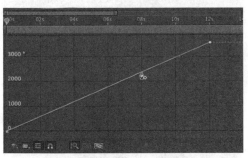

Figure 9.57 The Pen tool becomes the Add Vertex tool.

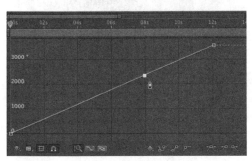

Figure 9.58 Click the value graph to create a new keyframe.

Adding and Removing Keyframes in the Graph Editor

You can add keyframes to and remove keyframes from a property graph as you would a motion or mask path. Even so, it's worth reviewing the techniques in the context of keyframing properties in the Graph Editor. Don't forget that you can still add and remove keyframes using the methods you learned in Chapter 7, "Properties and Keyframes."

To add or remove keyframes in the graph:

1. *Do either of the following:*
   - ▲ In the Tools panel, select the Pen tool (**Figure 9.56**).
   - ▲ With the Selection tool selected, press Command (Ctrl).

2. In the Graph Editor, *do any of the following:*
   - ▲ To add a keyframe, position the Pen tool over the line in a graph so that the Pen tool appears as an Add Vertex icon ⬧ (**Figure 9.57**) and then click.

     A keyframe is added on the graph where you click (**Figure 9.58**).

     continues on next page

▲ To remove a keyframe, position the Pen tool over a keyframe in a graph so that the Pen tool appears as a Delete Vertex icon and then click (**Figure 9.59**).

The keyframe is removed and the line (interpolation) reshapes accordingly (**Figure 9.60**).

3. Make sure to choose the Selection tool when you're finished.

✔ Tip

■ If you use the Pen tool to add a keyframe to the graph, dragging extends a direction line, or ease handle.

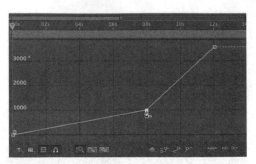

Figure 9.59 Position the Pen tool over a keyframe so that the tool becomes a Delete Vertex icon, and then click...

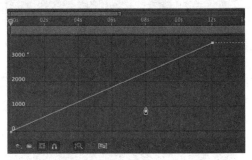

Figure 9.60 ...to remove the keyframe. The graph adjusts accordingly.

Figure 9.61 Ordinarily, a layer's position is a single property consisting of two dimensions (X and Y for 2D layers) or three dimensions (X, Y, and Z for 3D layers).

Separating a Position's Dimensions

Ordinarily, a layer possesses a single position property. If the layer is 2D, its position property consists of two components: a value defining its location along the comp's X axis, and a value defining its location on the comp's Y axis. If the layer is 3D, its position property also includes a value for its location along the Z axis. Starting with After Effects CS4, you can separate a position property's components into individual properties. Doing so lets you, for example, apply an expression to a layer's Y position while animating the X manually.

Animating separated properties can give you more control and help you achieve certain effects more easily. However, animating a single, unseparated, property is relatively straightforward, more easily achieves smooth movement, and permits you to specify roving keyframes, which smooths variations in speed. (see the section, "Smoothing Motion with Roving Keyframes," later in this chapter).

You can use the same command to toggle a layer's position between a single property and separated properties. But because information is lost in the translation, it's best to choose the most appropriate method and stick to it.

To separate position dimensions into individual properties:

1. In the Timeline panel, press P to reveal a layer's position property and then select the position property.

    You can display the position property in the Graph Editor (**Figure 9.61**).

    continues on next page

2. *Do either of the following:*

Choose Animation > Separate Dimensions (**Figure 9.62**)

In the Graph Editor, click the Separate Dimensions button  (**Figure 9.63**).

The dimensions appear as separate properties (**Figure 9.64**). You can animate them as usual, except you can't make them roving keyframes.

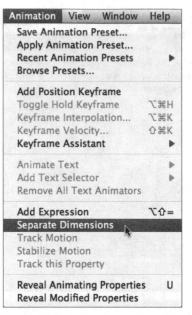

Figure 9.62 Selecting the position property and choosing Animation > Separate Dimensions...

Figure 9.63 ... or clicking the Separate Dimensions button in the Graph Editor...

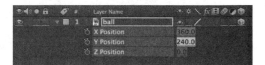

Figure 9.64 ...makes each dimension a separate property you can animate individually.

SEPARATING A POSITION'S DIMENSIONS

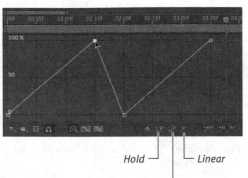

Hold ⌐ ⌐ Linear
Auto-Bézier ⌐

Figure 9.65 Select a keyframe, and select the button that corresponds with the interpolation type you want to use. Here, a keyframe that uses linear interpolation...

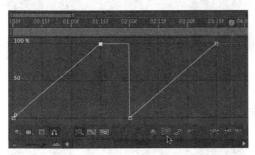

Figure 9.66 ...is converted to one that uses hold interpolation.

Setting a Keyframe's Temporal Interpolation Type

The Graph Editor includes buttons that apply hold, linear, or auto Bézier interpolation to selected keyframes.

If the automatic method doesn't yield the result you want, you can adjust the interpolation manually or apply a keyframe assistant to achieve other common effects. See the sections, "Adjusting Temporal Interpolation Manually," and "Applying Keyframe Assistants," later in this chapter.

To set a keyframe's interpolation using a button:

1. In the Graph Editor, select the keyframes you want to adjust.

2. At the bottom of the Graph Editor, click the button that corresponds with the type of temporal interpolation you want the keyframe to use (**Figure 9.65**):

   Hold 🔳

   Linear 🔳

   Auto-Bézier 🔳

   The selected keyframes use the interpolation method you specify (**Figure 9.66**).

✔ Tips

■ You can toggle a keyframe between using linear and auto Bézier interpolation by Command-clicking (Ctrl-clicking) the keyframe.

■ You can specify selected keyframes' interpolation by choosing Animation > Keyframe Interpolation or Keyframe Interpolation in the Graph Editor's Edit Keyframe pop-up menu. In the dialog, specify the type of interpolation you want.

Adjusting Temporal Interpolation Manually

As you've seen, many of the principles of adjusting a motion path apply to adjusting a property graph. Both are described by Bézier curves, although the terminology can differ. And whereas a motion path traces a literal course through space, the line of a graph corresponds to a property's value or speed. But although the techniques you use to edit Bézier curves resemble one another in principle, they differ in practice. The main difference lies in how you adjust the curves manually: dragging direction lines in a value graph or ease handles in a speed graph.

In a value graph, you can drag direction lines 180 degrees to influence the graph's curve—and, hence, its incoming and outgoing interpolation. Bézier curves closely resemble their counterparts in a motion path.

In a speed graph, ease handles influence the shape of the curve and, thereby, the interpolation. However, ease handles always extend horizontally from a keyframe; their length but not their angle helps shape the curve. Whereas a sudden change in a value plots a cusp in a value graph, a sudden change in speed splits the keyframe so that it occupies two different vertical positions on the speed graph.

To adjust a value graph manually:

1. Expand the layer outline to view the value graph for an animated layer property.

2. Select the keyframes you want to adjust (**Figure 9.67**).

3. Do any of the following to the incoming or outgoing direction lines:

   ▲ Drag a keyframe up to increase the value or down to decrease the value (**Figures 9.68** and **9.69**).

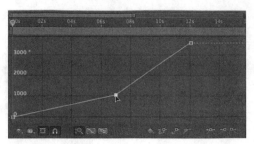

Figure 9.67 Select the keyframe you want to adjust in the Graph Editor.

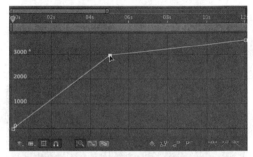

Figure 9.68 Drag a keyframe up to increase...

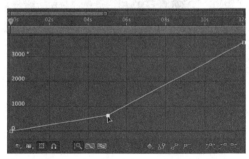

Figure 9.69 ...or down to decrease the value (shown here) or speed.

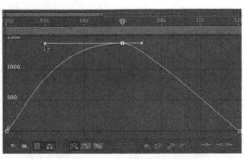

Figure 9.70 In the value graph, extend a direction line manually to use continuous Bézier interpolation.

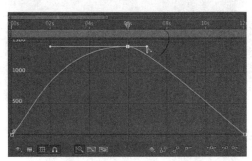

Figure 9.71 In the value graph, Option (Alt)-drag a direction handle.

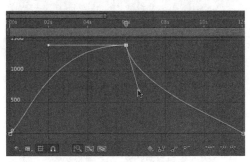

Figure 9.72 Dragging a direction handle of a continuous Bézier keyframe splits the direction handles, converting it to Bézier.

▲ To convert auto Bézier to continuous Bézier, drag one direction line so that the direction lines are unequal but retain their continuous relationship (**Figure 9.70**).

▲ To toggle between continuous Bézier and Bézier, Option-drag (Alt-drag) a direction handle (**Figure 9.71**).

The Selection tool becomes the Convert Vertex tool when you position it over a direction handle. Dragging a direction handle of a Bézier keyframe converts it to continuous Bézier with two related direction handles; dragging a direction handle of a continuous Bézier keyframe splits the direction handles, converting it to Bézier (**Figure 9.72**).

✔ Tip

■ Avoid converting a keyframe unintentionally: Invoke the Convert Vertex tool only when you want to convert a keyframe; otherwise, use the Selection tool.

To adjust a speed graph manually:

1. Expand the layer outline to view the speed graph for an animated layer property.

2. Select the keyframes you want to adjust (**Figure 9.73**).

3. Do any of the following to the incoming or outgoing ease handles:

   ▲ Drag an ease handle up to increase the incoming or outgoing speed at a keyframe (**Figure 9.74**).

   ▲ Drag an ease handle down to decrease the incoming or outgoing speed at a keyframe.

   ▲ Drag the left ease handle to change its length and influence on the preceding curve (**Figure 9.75**).

   ▲ Drag the right ease handle to adjust |its length and influence on the following curve.

   ▲ Option-click (Alt-click) a keyframe to toggle it between linear and auto Bézier.

Figure 9.73 Select the keyframes you want to adjust.

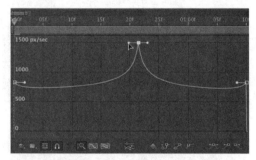

Figure 9.74 Drag an ease handle up to increase the incoming or outgoing speed at a keyframe.

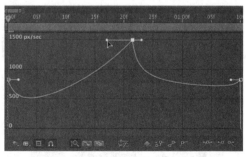

Figure 9.75 Here, dragging an incoming ease handle to the left increases the influence of the previous keyframe's value.

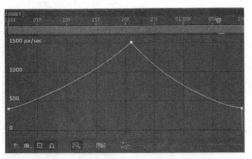

Figure 9.76 An abrupt shift from acceleration to deceleration, or bounce, looks like this in a speed graph.

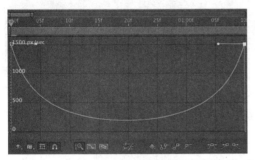

Figure 9.77 A gradual deceleration followed by a gradual acceleration (as when a rising object slows at its apex) looks like this in a speed graph.

The shape of the graph and the corresponding property's speed change according to your adjustments (**Figures 9.76** and **9.77**). When the incoming and outgoing speeds differ, a keyframe's icon splits, occupying two different vertical positions on the graph.

✔ Tip

■ You can adjust a graph with numerical precision by selecting the keyframe and choosing Keyframe Velocity from the Edit Keyframe button's pop-up menu.

ADJUSTING TEMPORAL INTERPOLATION MANUALLY

Applying Keyframe Assistants

Adding slight deceleration to soften or ease the speed into and out of keyframes is such a commonly used technique that After Effects has provided the following *keyframe assistants* to automate the task:

Easy Ease—Smooths both the keyframe's incoming and outgoing interpolation.

Easy Ease In—Smooths the keyframe's incoming interpolation.

Easy Ease Out—Smooths the keyframe's outgoing interpolation.

Try employing a keyframe assistant and observing its effects on a layer's property graph and animation.

To apply a keyframe assistant in the Graph Editor:

1. In the Graph Editor, select the keyframes to which you want to apply a keyframe assistant (**Figure 9.78**).

2. At the bottom of the Graph Editor, click the icon that corresponds to the keyframe assistant you want to use (**Figure 9.79**):

   Easy Ease

   Easy Ease In

   Easy Ease Out

   The icons and graphs associated with the selected keyframes reflect your choice, and the animation plays accordingly (**Figure 9.80**).

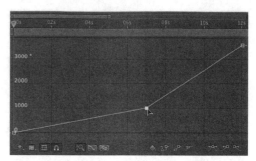

Figure 9.78 Select the keyframes you want to ease with a keyframe assistant. This keyframe uses linear interpolation.

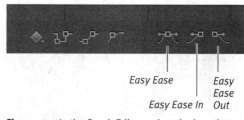

Easy Ease *Easy Ease In* *Easy Ease Out*

Figure 9.79 In the Graph Editor, select the icon that corresponds to the keyframe assistant you want to apply.

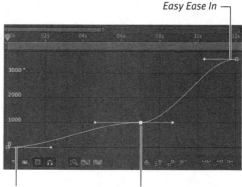

Easy Ease In

Easy Ease Out *Easy Ease*

Figure 9.80 The selected keyframe's interpolation is adjusted according to your choice. The linear interpolation pictured in Figure 9.78 looks like this after you apply keyframe assistants.

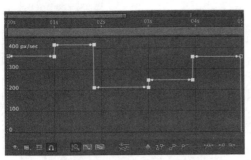

Figure 9.81 Select a range of keyframes between two keyframes. This uneven speed graph indicates sudden changes in speed between keyframed positions.

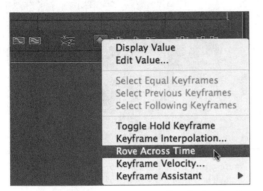

Figure 9.82 Selecting Rove Across Time in the Graph Editor's Edit Keyframe pop-up menu...

Smoothing Motion with Roving Keyframes

Frequently, adjusting a motion path causes drastic and unwanted fluctuations in timing. The layer goes where you want in terms of space, but its movement lags and lurches from one keyframe to the next. In the speed graph, these abrupt changes look like steep hills and chasms. You can try to adjust the speed and timing of the problem keyframes manually, or you can convert them into roving keyframes.

Roving keyframes retain their values; but their position in time is adjusted automatically so that the property's speed becomes consistent, and the property's speed graph flattens out. The adjustments are derived from the values of the standard, time-bound keyframes before and after the roving keyframes. Moving the first or last keyframe automatically readjusts the roving keyframes in between. This way, you can change the duration of the animation without having to carefully adjust the speed between each part.

If you don't want a keyframe to rove, you can convert it back to a standard keyframe, which is *locked to time*.

To smooth motion with roving keyframes:

1. Reveal a property's speed graph in the Graph Editor.

2. Select a range of keyframes other than the first or last keyframe for the property (**Figure 9.81**).

   The keyframes preceding and after the range must be locked to time. That is, they must be standard, nonroving keyframes.

continues on next page

3. In the Graph Editor, click the Edit Keyframe button, and then choose Rove Across Time from the pop-up menu (**Figure 9.82**).

The selected keyframes become roving keyframes, moving in time so that the speed is constant (as evidenced by the speed graph). The roving keyframe icons appear as small dots (**Figure 9.83**).

To convert a roving keyframe to a standard keyframe:

1. Reveal a property's speed graph in the Graph Editor, and select one or more of its roving keyframes (**Figure 9.84**).

2. Click the Graph Editor's Edit Keyframe button, and deselect Rove Across Time in the pop-up menu (**Figure 9.85**).

The keyframe is converted from a roving keyframe to a standard keyframe that is locked to time. Its keyframe icon changes from a small dot to its standard icon (a small box in the Graph Editor, or a diamond icon in the standard view of the time ruler).

✔ Tip

■ You don't have to view the Graph Editor to toggle between standard and roving keyframes. After selecting keyframes in the standard view of the time ruler, choose Animation > Keyframe Interpolation, and then specify whether the keyframes Rove Across Time or are Locked to Time.

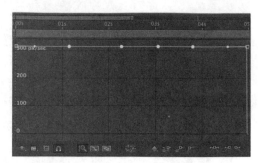

Figure 9.83 …converts the selected keyframes to roving keyframes, which shift in time to create constant speed between the standard keyframes. Contrast this speed graph with the one in Figure 9.76.

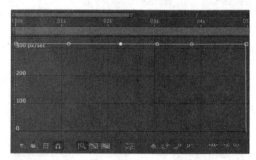

Figure 9.84 Reveal the speed graph of a property, and select one or more of its roving keyframes…

Figure 9.85 …and deselect Rove Across Time to convert the selection to standard keyframes, which are locked to time.

10

MASK ESSENTIALS

A *mask* is a shape, or path, that you create in a layer. Masks are essential to compositing images and to creating many other effects.

You can draw a mask manually with a tool, define it numerically using a dialog, copy and paste it from Adobe Illustrator or Photoshop, or use a menu command to create one from a text layer or other image. A mask can be a closed shape (such as a circle) or an open path (such as a curved line).

A closed mask modifies or creates an alpha channel—which, as you recall, defines the opaque and transparent areas of an image. The image within the masked area remains visible; the area outside the mask reveals the layers below. An open path, in contrast, consists of a curve, or path, with two endpoints. By itself, an open path can't define areas of opacity, but it can be used to achieve a variety of other effects. For example, you can use the Stroke effect to trace a mask with a color. Or, you can paste a mask path into the Comp panel to use it as a motion path. A mask can also define a curved baseline for path text. You can apply these techniques to both open and closed masks, but you can imagine how an open mask is sometimes the more appropriate choice.

This chapter is devoted to the fundamentals of mask making. You can apply what you learn in other chapters to animate mask properties, apply effects to masks, and combine masks with other techniques, such as layer modes. Later, you'll discover that the same tools that apply masks to layers can also be used to define a new type of layer, graphical objects called *shape layers*. (See the section, "Creating Shape Layers," in Chapter 14.)

Understanding Paths

Generally speaking, a *path* is a series of line segments, generated using Bézier curves. In a Bézier curve, you define two endpoints—called vertices or control points—which are connected by a curve. You can control the curve's shape by manipulating the length and angle of a direction line, or tangent, that extends from each vertex (**Figure 10.1**).

Motion, Mask, and Shape paths

In After Effects, you use some of the same tools and techniques to create and edit different types of paths.

As you saw in Chapter 7, "Properties and Keyframes," a *motion path* consists of a series of Bézier curves, though the curves describe motion instead of a visible line.

A *mask* is a kind of path you apply to a layer to define areas of opacity or to dictate the placement of other effects.

In Chapter 14, "More Layer Techniques," you'll see how the same tools that can create a mask on a layer can also generate a layer, called a *shape layer*. But unlike masks, shape layers can be defined either by Bézier curves or parametrically—in other words, by a number of parameters, or geometric property values.

As you become adept at creating and modifying motion, mask, and shape layer paths, you'll see that each represents a different application of a similar set of principles. This chapter focuses on creating mask paths.

Figure 10.1 The mask path (top), shape layer path (center), and motion path (bottom) shown here are all made up of Bézier curves. Here, the vertices are selected so you can see their tangents.

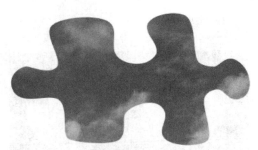

Figure 10.2 A closed path creates a typical mask, which defines the opaque areas of the layer image.

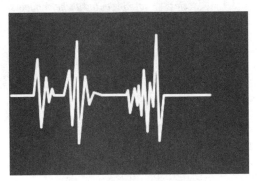

Figure 10.3 An open path doesn't create a mask per se, but it can be used for other effects, such as creating stroked lines. Open paths can also be used to create motion paths.

Open and closed paths

Strictly speaking, the term *mask* refers to a closed shape that defines areas of opacity. You can draw closed paths with any of the drawing tools (**Figure 10.2**). By default, the interior of a closed mask shape defines the opaque area of a layer; the exterior defines transparency. However, you can manipulate the transparency in numerous ways.

You can create open paths with the Pen tool, or you can open a closed path by using a menu command. Open paths aren't used as masks per se, but they can serve as the basis for path text and path-based effects (**Figure 10.3**). For example, they can serve as the baseline for text or be pasted into a motion path.

Bezier and RotoBézier curves

To create a path you can use the standard method of creating Bézier curves, or a simpler RotoBézier option (**Figure 10.4**).

You can control the shape of a Bézier curve by specifying the position of its vertices as well as the length and direction of the tangents extending from each vertex. Standard Bézier curves offer a high degree of control, but they can be tricky to master.

When you create a mask using the RotoBézier option, you set vertices only, not tangents. Instead, After Effects calculates the curves automatically; you might think of each vertex as using the Auto-Bézier spatial interpolation you learned about in Chaper 9, "Keyframe Interpolation"). However, you can adjust each point's *tension* to change the relative amount of curve in the corresponding line segments. Because you don't have to define tangents manually, it can be easier to draw smooth shapes with the RotoBézier option—but it's also impossible to create shapes with uneven curves or cusps.

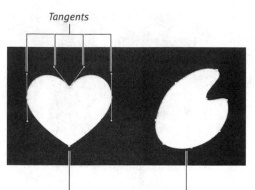

Tangents

Bézier   *RotoBézier (no visible tangents)*

Figure 10.4 It's easier to create shapes like the palette using the RotoBézier option, but manually adjusting tangents in a Bézier shape lets you create cusps like the ones at the top and bottom of the heart.

✔ Tips

■ Bézier curves should be a familiar concept by now; the same math used to calculate curves also applies to keyframe interpolation, covered in Chapter 9, "Keyframe Interpolation." When you think about it, vertices on a mask path are analogous to keyframes, and line segments on a mask are comparable to interpolated values.

■ Option-clicking (Alt-clicking) a vertex in a Bézier curve converts it from a smooth point to a corner point and vice versa; the same shortcut changes the tension of selected RotoBezier vertices from an automatically calculated value to 100 percent and vice versa. Although the result is equivalent, this action doesn't convert the mask from one type to another.

Figure 10.5 The Layer panel shows masks in the context of the layer; it also lets you see the image outside the mask.

Figure 10.6 The Comp panel shows the layer after masks and other property changes have taken effect.

Viewing Masks in the Layer and Comp Panels

Although you mask a layer, you can create and work with masks not only in the Layer panel but also in the Composition panel. The panel you use will depend on the task at hand as well as your personal preference. A Layer panel shows masks in the context of a single layer, letting you view the image outside the masked areas (**Figure 10.5**). In addition, the Layer panel shows you the layer before any property changes (Scale, Rotation, and so on) are applied. In contrast, the Composition panel shows only the masked portions of a layer and places them in the context of all the layers that are visible at the current time. By the time you're able to view a layer in the Comp panel, Mask, Effect, Transform, and 3D properties have all been applied (**Figure 10.6**).

When you want to create or modify a mask in the Comp panel, you must select the layer that contains the mask. Tasks throughout this chapter assume you have done so.

Viewing Masks in the Layer Outline

Each mask you create appears in the layer outline of the Timeline panel under the Mask property heading. The Target menu in the Layer panel also lists the layer's masks. The most recent mask appears at the top of the stacking order (**Figure 10.7**).

When you expand the Mask property heading, it reveals four properties: Mask Shape, Mask Feather, Mask Opacity, and Mask Expansion. The following sections deal with these properties as well as other ways to control layer masks.

Because you can rename, reorder, and lock masks just like layers, that information won't be covered here (**Figure 10.8**). (See Chapter 5, "Layer Basics," to learn the analogous procedures for layers).

You can also hide and apply motion blur to masks much as you can with a layer as a whole. But instead of clicking a button in the Timeline panel, you access these commands in the Layer > Mask menu (**Figure 10.9**). For example, masks don't have a video switch, but you can hide locked masks via the Layer > Mask > Hide Locked Masks command. Again, these commands won't be covered in detail here.

✔ Tip

■ Although locked and hidden masks are invisible in the Layer panel, their masking effect can still be seen in the Comp panel's image.

Figure 10.7 Masks appear in the layer outline in the order they were created.

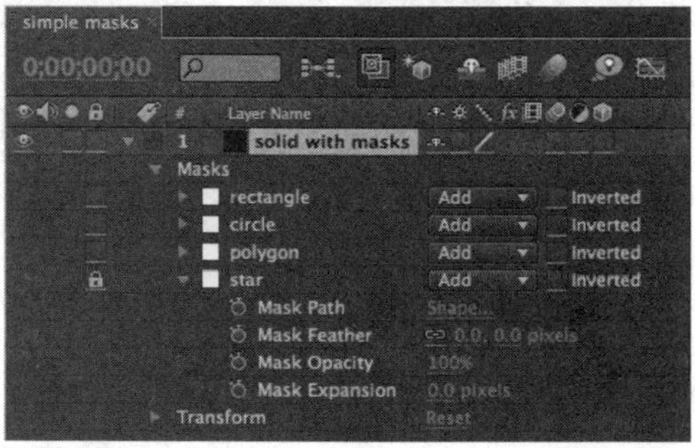

Figure 10.8 You can rename, reorder, and lock masks just like layers. Here, the default names have been replaced with more descriptive names, and the "star" mask has been locked.

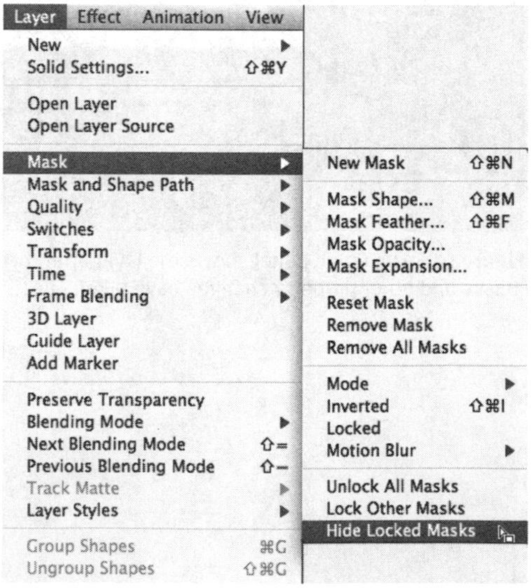

Figure 10.9 The Layer > Mask menu contains commands for applying motion blur and for hiding locked masks (selected here).

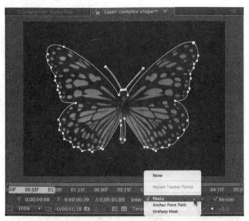

Figure 10.10 In the Layer panel's View pop-up menu, select Masks to make mask paths visible.

Figure 10.11 In the Comp panel, click the View Masks button...

Figure 10.12 ...to reveal the selected layer's masks.

Hiding and Showing Mask Paths

Because the Layer and Comp panels serve several purposes, sometimes you'll want to hide the mask paths from view. When you want to work with the layer masks, you can make them visible again. Creating a new mask reveals the masks for the selected layer automatically.

To view and hide masks in the Layer panel:

1. View a layer in a Layer panel.

2. In the Layer panel's View pop-up menu, select Masks to make mask paths visible (**Figure 10.10**).

   Selecting another option deselects the Masks option.

To view and hide masks in the Composition panel:

◆ In the Comp panel, click the View Masks button (**Figure 10.11**).

   Mask paths for selected layers can be viewed and edited in the Composition panel (**Figure 10.12**). Click the View Masks button again to hide mask paths.

✔ Tips

■ You can hide locked masks only by choosing Layer > Mask > Hide Locked Masks. Although invisible in the Layer panel, locked and hidden masks still function in the Comp panel.

■ By default, mask paths appear in yellow. You can double-click a mask's color swatch in the timeline to assign a unique color to each mask.

■ You can even have After Effects assign each subsequent mask a different color automatically by selecting the Cycle Mask Colors option in the User Interface Colors pane of the Preferences dialog.

Targeting Masks

Because you can apply numerous masks to a single layer, the Target menu at the bottom of the Layer panel provides one way to select the mask you want to use. Note that the Target pop-up menu appears only when the layer contains one or more masks.

To choose the target mask:

1. View a layer containing one or more masks in a Layer panel.

2. At the bottom of the Layer panel, choose a mask from the Target menu (**Figure 10.13**):

   ▲ Choose Target: None to create a new mask without changing an existing mask.

   ▲ Choose the name of an existing mask to target that mask for changes.

   The mask you choose appears, selected (**Figure 10.14**).

✔ Tip

■ To create an additional mask in the same Layer panel, make sure the Target pop-up menu is set to None. Otherwise, the new mask *replaces* the target mask.

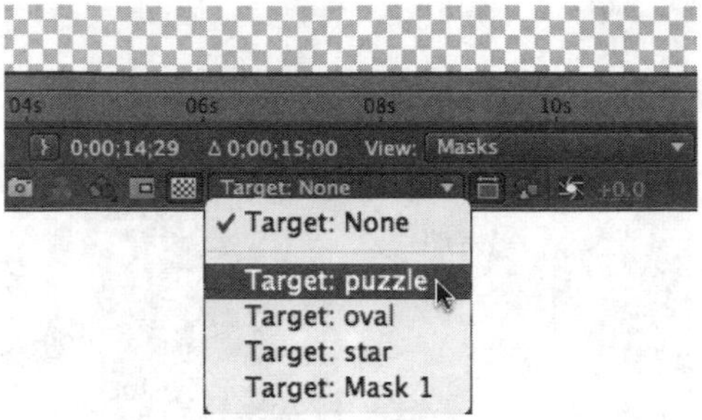

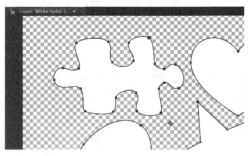

Figure 10.13 In the Target menu, choose a mask you want to select, or target, for changes.

Figure 10.14 The targeted mask appears, selected, with solid square vertices. If you create a new mask shape, it replaces the targeted mask.

Figure 10.15 In the Tools panel, choose a Shape tool.

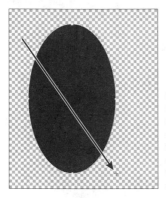

Figure 10.16
In the Layer or
Comp panel,
drag to define
the shape from
one corner of
the shape to its
opposite corner.

Figure 10.17
Shift-drag to
constrain the
shape to equal
proportions so
that you can
create a square
or circle.

Figure 10.18
Command-drag
(Ctrl-drag) to
create a mask
shape that
extends from the
center instead of
the corner.

Creating Paths Using Shape Tools

You can create simple mask paths quickly with one of the shape tools: Rectangle, Rounded Rectangle, Ellipse, Polygon, and Star. One of these simple shapes can also serve as the starting point of a more complex path. As you'll see in later sections, you can easily alter any path's shape. In addition, you can effectively combine masks using mask modes. You can use the same techniques to draw shape layers (see Chapter 14). Just remember that to mask a layer, the layer must be selected before you draw. If no layer is selected, the drawing tool creates a new shape layer.

To draw a mask path using a shape tool:

1. View the layer you want to mask in a Layer panel, or select it in the Composition panel.

   A layer must be selected to create a mask; if no layer is selected, using the tool will create a new shape layer, not a mask.

2. In the Tools panel, select a shape tool (**Figure 10.15**).

3. If you selected a shape layer in step 1, click the Tool Creates Mask button 🔲.

   You must click the appropriate button to specify whether you want to mask a shape layer or add another shape path to the shape layer.

4. In the Layer or Comp panel, drag to define the position and size of the mask on the layer.

5. To modify the shape as you drag, press the appropriate keyboard modifier (**Figures 10.16, 10.17,** and **10.18**).

   For a list of modifiers and their results, see **Table 10.1**.

6. Release the mouse when you've finished creating the mask.

In the Layer and Comp panels, the mask appears as a path with selected vertices (as long as you set the window to display masks; see "Hiding and Showing Mask Paths," earlier in this chapter). In the Composition panel, the areas of the layer outside the mask are concealed, whereas the areas inside the mask are visible. In the timeline, the layer's outline includes a Mask property.

✔ Tips

- To create a mask that fills the layer, double-click the Shape tool.

- To convert a text layer into a mask path, select the text layer and choose Layer > Create Masks from Text. Choosing Layer > Create Shapes from Text creates a shape layer (see Chapter 14, "More Layer Techniques," for more about shapes).

- To generate a mask around an image's contours, based on one of its channels, select the layer, choose Layer > Autotrace, and specify options in the Autotrace dialog.

Table 10.1

Keyboard Modifiers for Creating Masks

MODIFIER	ELLIPSES/RECTANGLE	ROUNDED RECTANGLE	POLYGON/STAR
Shift	Constrain proportions	Constrain proportions	Constrain rotation
Command (Ctrl)	Create from center	Create from center	Maintain inner radius
Option (Alt)	Render mask after releasing mouse		
Up Arrow	N/A	Increase corner roundness	Increase sides/points
Down Arrow	N/A	Decrease corner roundness	Decrease sides/points
Right Arrow	N/A	Minimum corner roundness	Increase star outer roundness
Left Arrow	N/A	Maximum corner roundness	Decrease star outer roundness
Page Up	N/A	N/A	Increase star inner roundness
Page Down	N/A	N/A	Decrease star inner roundness

Table 10.2

Keyboard Modifiers for Mask Paths	
TO DO THIS	PRESS THIS
Constrain new segment to 45 degrees	Shift
Temporarily switch to the Convert Vertex tool	Option (Alt)
Temporarily switch to the Selection tool	Command (Ctrl)

Building a Path with the Pen

As you know, a path consists of a series of connected line segments. The Pen tool lets you specify the location of each segment's endpoints, or vertices. A tangent extending from each vertex determines the curve of the corresponding segments.

The following task explains how to create a vertex that results in a certain type of path as you draw. If you're new to using the Pen tool, start by simply clicking to create vertices that are connected by straight lines. Then, try clicking and dragging to create vertices with tangents that create curves. As you become more comfortable, you'll be able to better anticipate the kind of curve you want and adjust each vertex's tangent as you draw the path. Once you're fluent in using the keyboard modifiers listed in **Table 10.2**, you've mastered making mask paths.

Note that the figures illustrate a heart shape, which uses different kinds of vertices and segments: the bottom vertex has no tangents; the side vertices have equal tangents; and the top has custom, discontinuous tangents. Don't worry if your path isn't perfect at first. You can always modify it afterward using the Selection and Pen tools.

To build a path:

1. *Do either of the following:*

   ▲ Open a Layer panel for the layer for which you want to create a mask.

   ▲ Select a layer in the Composition panel.

2. In the Tools panel, select the Pen tool ✒ (**Figure 10.19**).

3. In the Layer or Comp panel, *do one of the following:*

   ▲ To create a vertex without tangents, just click (**Figure 10.20**).

   ▲ To create a vertex with equal and opposite tangents extending from it, click and drag (**Figure 10.21**).

   ▲ To create a vertex with custom tangents, click and drag, then release the mouse and drag one of the tangents to change its length or angle (**Figure 10.22**).

4. Repeat step 3 to create straight and curved segments between vertices.

   Don't click an existing segment unless you want to add a vertex to the path. Don't click an existing vertex unless you want to convert it (toggle between a vertex with direction lines and without).

5. To leave the path open, stop clicking in the Layer or Comp panel.

Figure 10.19 In the Tools panel, select the Pen tool.

Figure 10.20 Click to create a vertex with no tangents.

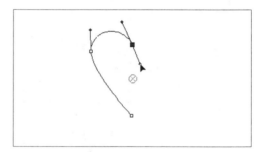

Figure 10.21 Click and drag to create a smooth vertex with two continuous tangents.

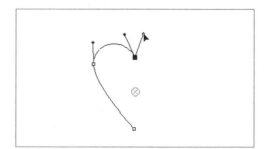

Figure 10.22 Drag a direction handle to break the relationship between the two handles, converting the point into a corner point.

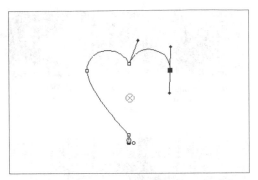

Figure 10.23 Continue clicking to create vertices that define straight and curved segments. You can leave the path open, or position the tool over the first point so that a circle appears next to the Pen tool...

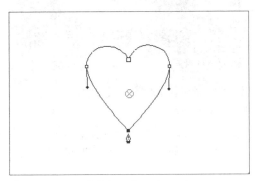

Figure 10.24 ...and click to close the path.

6. To close the path, *do one of the following:*

▲ Double-click in the Layer or Comp panel to create the final vertex and connect it to the first vertex.

▲ Position the Pen tool over the first vertex until a circle appears (**Figure 10.23**), then click (**Figure 10.24**).

▲ Choose Layer > Mask and Shape Path > Closed.

When you are finished, remember to choose the Selection tool, which is required for most other tasks.

✔ Tips

■ In most cases, you'll achieve the smoothest-looking curve if you make each tangent about one-third the length of the curve it influences.

■ Typically, using the minimum possible number of vertices results in a curve that's both smoother and easier to control.

■ The Pen tool 🖋 changes into the Add Vertex tool 🖋₊ when positioned over a path. It changes into the Convert Vertex tool ⋀ when positioned over a direction handle.

■ The first vertex you set is treated as just that. For example, the Stroke effect's Start property is set to the path's first vertex. When animating a path shape, one path's first vertex is mapped to another. The first vertex appears slightly larger than the others. You can designate any vertex as the first vertex by selecting it and choosing Layer > Mask and Shape Path > Set First Vertex.

Creating a RotoBezier Path

Even if you're a master of Bézier curves, you can often create a path more quickly and easily using a *RotoBezier path*. The Pen tool's RotoBezier option lets you define a curved path by clicking to create vertices; After Effects calculates curved segments automatically. You avoid using tangents, which can take time to adjust properly.

To create a RotoBezier path:

1. In the Tools panel, select the Pen tool ✒ and then click the RotoBezier check box to select this option (**Figure 10.25**).

2. In the Layer or Composition panel, click with the Pen tool to create the vertices of the path.

3. Repeat step 2 to create additional vertices connected by curved segments.

   Don't click an existing segment unless you want to add a vertex to the path.

4. To close the path, *do one of the following:*
   ▲ Double-click in the Layer panel to create the final vertex and connect it to the first vertex.
   ▲ Position the Pen tool over the first vertex until a circle appears ✒₀ (**Figure 10.26**), and then click.
   ▲ Choose Layer > Mask > Closed.
   The mask path closes (**Figure 10.27**).

5. To leave the path open, stop clicking in the Layer panel.

   You may want to choose a new tool, such as the Selection tool.

Figure 10.25 Select the Pen tool, and click the RotoBezier check box.

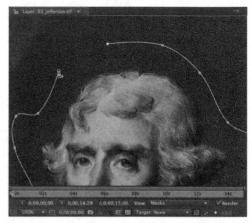

Figure 10.26 Click to create vertices. After Effects calculates the curved segments automatically. Position the mouse over the first vertex to make a small circle appear next to the Pen and then click...

Figure 10.27 ...to close the shape. Otherwise, you can leave the mask open and choose another tool.

Figure 10.28 The two figures started as identical RotoBezier masks. However, selecting vertices and then dragging with the Convert Vertex tool changed tension at the selected vertices in the figure on the right.

✔ Tips

■ You can convert a RotoBezier to a Bézier path and vice versa by selecting the mask and choosing Layer > Mask and Shape Path > RotoBezier. When the command is checked, the path is RotoBezier; when the command is unchecked, the path is standard Bézier. Selecting the command toggles it from checked to unchecked, and vice-versa.

■ Although RotoBezier curves are calculated automatically, you can adjust the relative amount of curves, or *tension*. Select the vertices you want to affect and then drag one with the Convert Vertex tool ⊼. Dragging right increases the tension until adjacent segments are flat, making sharp corners. Dragging left makes adjacent segments more curved (**Figure 10.28**).

Changing the Shape of a Path

Whether it's a mask path, shape layer path, or motion path, you can modify a path's shape at any time by applying the same Pen tool techniques summarized in, "Building a Path with the Pen," earlier in this chapter. And because the same techniques you use to add, remove, and convert keyframes in a motion path (covered in Chapter 9, "Keyframe Interpolation") also apply to mask and shape paths, those techniques aren't described here.

Although there's no need to reiterate the keyframing techniques covered in Chapter 7, "Properties and Keyframes," and Chapter 9, it's worth noting here that you can employ them to animate a path's shape over time, just as you would any layer property. An animated mask can serve many uses. For example, an animated mask can serve as a dynamic *garbage matte*, a mask used to cut the extraneous areas from a background you want to make transparent with a keying effect. Or you can animate a mask to transform graphical elements (see **Figures 10.29** and **10.30**).

✔ Tips

- This chapter covers the essentials of After Effects' powerful mask and path making features. When you're ready, you can explore on your own how Mask Interpolation can aid in animating mask shape.

- The way curves adjust to changes depends on whether the mask consists of Bézier or RotoBezier curves. As you learned in the earlier section, "Understanding Paths," Bézier curves use tangents you specify manually, whereas RotoBezier curves are calculated automatically. Each mask type's characteristic behavior continues to operate when you edit it.

Figure 10.29 You can keyframe the Mask Path property as you would any other layer property...

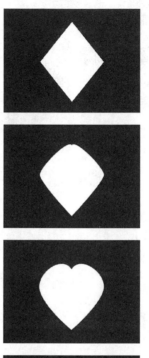

Figure 10.30
...to animate its shape over time.

- As you'll see in Chapter 14, "More Layer Techniques," shape layers don't necessarily consist of Bézier-based paths. They can also be parametric shapes, which you define and modify using a different set of parameters.

CHANGING THE SHAPE OF A PATH

Figure 10.31 In the Tools panel, choose the Selection tool.

Selecting Mask Path Vertices

To alter all or part of a path, you must first select its vertices—usually with the Selection tool. Selected vertices appear as solid squares; deselected vertices appear as hollow squares. To move, scale, or rotate the entire path, use the Free Transform Points command described in "Scaling and Rotating Paths," later in this chapter.

Although mask paths and other types of paths work the same in most other respects, the following task includes techniques unique to mask paths.

To select masks paths in a Layer or Comp panel:

1. In the Tools panel, choose the Selection tool if you haven't done so already (**Figure 10.31**).

2. Make sure the Layer or Comp panel is set to show masks.

   See "Viewing Masks in the Layer and Comp Panels" and "Viewing Masks in the Layer Outline," earlier in this chapter.

3. To select mask vertices in the Comp panel, select the layer containing the mask.

continues on next page

4. To select mask vertices in either the Layer panel or the Comp panel, *do any of the following:*

▲ Click a vertex on a mask to select it.

▲ To add to or subtract from your selection, press Shift as you click or drag a marquee around vertices.

▲ To select vertices at both ends of a segment, click the segment.

▲ To select an entire mask with the mouse, Option-click (Alt-click) the mask.

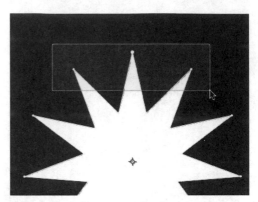

Figure 10.32 In the Layer panel, select several mask vertices simultaneously by dragging a marquee around them.

5. To select mask points in the Layer panel only, *do any of the following:*

▲ To select any or all vertices, drag a marquee around the vertices you want to select (**Figure 10.32**).

▲ To select all mask points, press Command-A (Ctrl-A).

▲ To select an entire mask by name, choose the mask from the Target pop-up menu in the Layer panel.

In the Layer or Comp panel, selected vertices appear as solid squares; vertices that are not selected appear as hollow boxes (**Figure 10.33**). Segments associated with the selected points also display tangents. When no vertices of a mask are selected, only the path is visible in the Layer or Comp panel.

Figure 10.33 Selected vertices appear as solid squares; deselected vertices appear as hollow boxes.

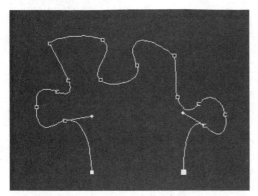

Figure 10.34 Choose the vertices at each end of an open path.

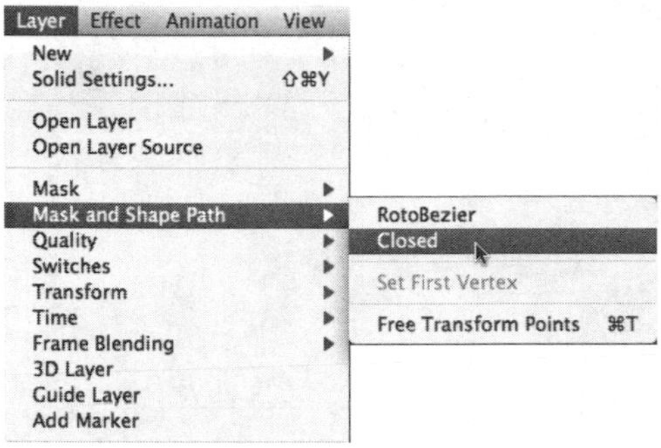

Figure 10.35 Choose Layer > Mask and Shape Path > Closed.

Opening and Closing Paths

You can use menu commands to close an open path or open a closed one.

To close an open path:

1. In a Layer panel, choose the vertices at each end of an open path (**Figure 10.34**).

2. Choose Layer > Mask and Shape Path > Closed (**Figure 10.35**).

   The vertices are connected, closing the path (**Figure 10.36**).

To open a closed path:

1. In a Layer panel, choose two adjacent vertices in a closed path.

2. Choose Layer > Mask and Shape Path > Closed.

   The Closed option is deselected, and the segment between the vertices disappears.

Figure 10.36 The open path becomes closed. You can use the same method to open a closed path.

Scaling and Rotating Paths

Using the Free Transform Points command, you can scale and rotate all or part of one or more mask (or shape layer) paths. As the word *free* suggests, these adjustments are controlled manually, not numerically, and they can't be keyframed to animate over time. Mask paths are rotated and scaled around their own anchor points, separate from the anchor point of the layer that contains them. Of course, you can still keyframe the rotation and scale of the layer containing the masks.

To move, scale, or rotate all or part of a path:

1. Open a Layer panel for the layer that contains the path you want to transform, or select the layer in the Comp panel.

2. *Do one of the following:*

   ▲ Select the mask or mask vertices you want to transform, and Choose Layer > Mask and Shape Paths > Free Transform Points.

   ▲ Double-click a path's line segment to transform the entire path.

   A bounding box and mask anchor point appear (**Figure 10.37**).

3. To reposition the anchor point for the mask's bounding box, drag the anchor.

   The mouse pointer changes from a Selection tool arrow into a Move Anchor Point icon when you position it over the anchor point (**Figure 10.38**).

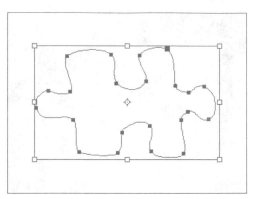

Figure 10.37 A bounding box and mask anchor point appear.

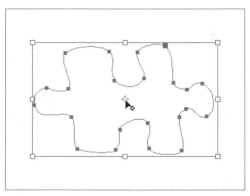

Figure 10.38 If you drag the mask's anchor point, the Selection tool becomes a Move Anchor Point icon.

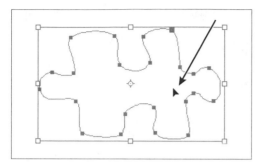

Figure 10.39 To move the mask or selected vertices, place the mouse pointer inside the bounding box and drag it to a new position.

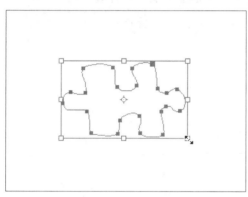

Figure 10.40 To scale the mask or selected vertices, place the cursor on one of the handles of the bounding box until it becomes a Scale icon, and then drag.

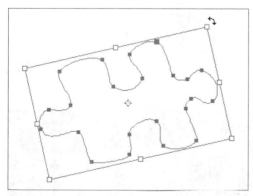

Figure 10.41 To rotate the mask or selected points, place the pointer slightly outside the bounding box until it becomes a Rotation icon, and then drag.

4. *Do any of the following:*

   ▲ To move the mask or selected vertices, place the mouse pointer inside the bounding box and drag it to a new position (**Figure 10.39**).

   ▲ To scale the mask or selected points, place the mouse pointer on one of the handles of the bounding box until it becomes a Scale icon, and then drag (**Figure 10.40**).

   ▲ To rotate the mask or selected points, place the mouse pointer slightly outside the bounding box until it becomes a Rotation icon, and then drag (**Figure 10.41**).

5. To exit Free Transform Points mode, double-click anywhere in the Layer or Comp panel, or press Return (Enter).

✔ Tips

■ As you can see, using the Free Transform Points command to scale and rotate a mask or mask points works much the same way as transforming a layer. You'll be happy to know that all the keyboard modifications—Shift, Command (Ctrl), Option (Alt)—also work the same.

■ You can copy paths from Adobe Photoshop or Illustrator and paste them as a layer mask in After Effects. By pasting a path as a layer mask, you can take advantage of After Effects' ability to animate its Shape, Feather, Opacity, and Expansion properties.

Converting Mask Paths into Motion Paths

Not only is an open mask path analogous to a motion path, but it can also be converted into one. Just make sure you paste the path into a compatible layer property, such as its Position property. If you paste a path into a Layer panel, it is pasted as a mask (as you saw in the previous section).

To paste a mask path as a motion path:

1. *Do either of the following:*

   ▲ Select an open mask path in a layer in After Effects.

   ▲ Select an open mask path in Photoshop or Illustrator.

2. Choose Edit > Copy, or press Command-C (Ctrl-C) (**Figure 10.42**).

3. In the Timeline panel, expand the layer outline to reveal the spatial property you want to paste the path into.

   You can use the Position, Effect Point, or Anchor Point property.

4. Select the property name.

   The property's keyframes are highlighted. If the property has no keyframes, the I-beam icon is highlighted.

5. Set the current time to the frame where you want the pasted keyframes to start (**Figure 10.43**).

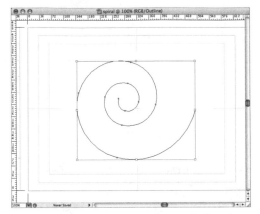

Figure 10.42 Select an open mask path in a layer in After Effects, or in Photoshop or Illustrator (shown here). Press Command-C (Ctrl-C).

Figure 10.43 In After Effects, select a layer property, and set the current time to the frame you want the pasted motion to start.

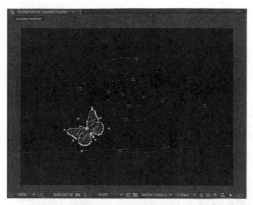

Figure 10.44 Pressing Command-V (Ctrl-V) pastes the path in the composition as a motion path...

6. Choose Edit > Paste, or press Command-V (Ctrl-V).

The path appears in the Comp panel as a motion path (**Figure 10.44**). In the property's track, keyframes begin at the current time and end two seconds later (**Figure 10.45**). The first and last key-frames are standard keyframes; the rest are roving keyframes (see Chapter 7).

7. Edit the motion path as you would any other.

Figure 10.45 ...and in the property's track as keyframes starting at the current time.

CONVERTING MASK PATHS INTO MOTION PATHS

Moving Masks Relative to the Layer Image

You can move a mask to reveal a different part of a layer in two ways: in a Layer panel or in a Composition panel.

When you move a mask in a Layer panel, its relative position in the Composition panel also changes (**Figures 10.46** and **10.47**). This approach works well if you want to change both the part of the image revealed by the mask and the mask's position in the composition. The mask moves, but the layer's position remains the same. Think of an iris effect at the end of a cartoon in which the circular mask closes in on the character for a final good-bye.

Alternatively, you can use the Pan Behind tool ![icon] in the Composition panel. Panning the layer behind the mask reveals a different part of the image without moving the mask's relative position in the composition. When you look back at the Layer panel, you can see that the mask has moved. However, After Effects recalculates the layer's position to compensate for this movement, maintaining the layer's position in the composition (**Figures 10.48** and **10.49**). Imagine a scene from a pirate movie in which a spyglass scans the horizon. The circle doesn't move, but the horizon pans through the viewfinder to reveal an island.

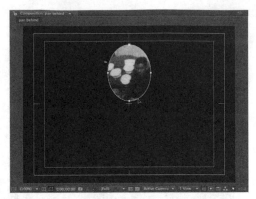

Figure 10.46 When you move a mask in a Layer or Comp panel...

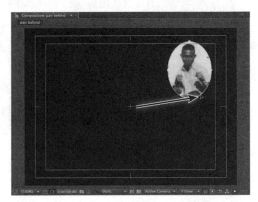

Figure 10.47 ...the mask's position changes in both the Layer and the Comp panel. The position value of the layer containing the mask doesn't change.

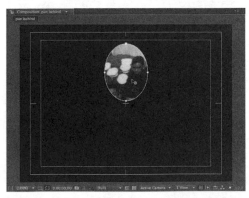

Figure 10.48 When you use the Pan Behind tool in the Composition panel...

Figure 10.49 ...the mask changes its position in the layer while maintaining its position in the composition. After Effects recalculates the layer's position value automatically. You can see the anchor point's new position in the Comp panel.

Figure 10.50 In the Tools panel, choose the Pan Behind tool.

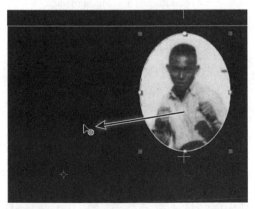

Figure 10.51 In the Comp panel, place the Pan Behind tool inside the masked area and drag.

To move a mask in the Layer panel:

1. Select an entire mask in the Layer panel.

2. Drag one of the vertices to move the entire mask to a new position.

   Make sure to drag a vertex, not a path segment. The mask changes position in both the Layer panel and the composition.

To pan a layer behind its mask:

1. In the Tools panel, select the Pan Behind tool ▥ (**Figure 10.50**).

2. In the Composition panel, position the Pan Behind tool inside the masked area of the layer, and then drag (**Figure 10.51**).

   In the Composition panel, the mouse pointer becomes the Pan Behind icon ✛ and the layer pans behind the masked area. After Effects calculates the layer's position in the composition and the mask's placement in the Layer panel.

Inverting a Mask

Ordinarily, the area within a closed layer mask defines the opaque parts of the layer's image; the area outside the mask is transparent, revealing the layers beneath it. However, just as you can invert a layer's alpha channel, you can invert a layer mask to reverse the opaque and transparent areas.

To invert a mask created in After Effects:

1. In the Layer, Comp, or Timeline panel, select the mask you want to invert.

2. *Do any of the following:*

   ▲ In the Timeline panel, click Inverted for the selected mask (**Figure 10.52**).

   ▲ Choose Layer > Mask > Invert.

   ▲ Press Shift-Command-I (Shift-Ctrl-I).

   Viewed in the Composition panel, the mask is inverted (**Figures 10.53** and **10.54**).

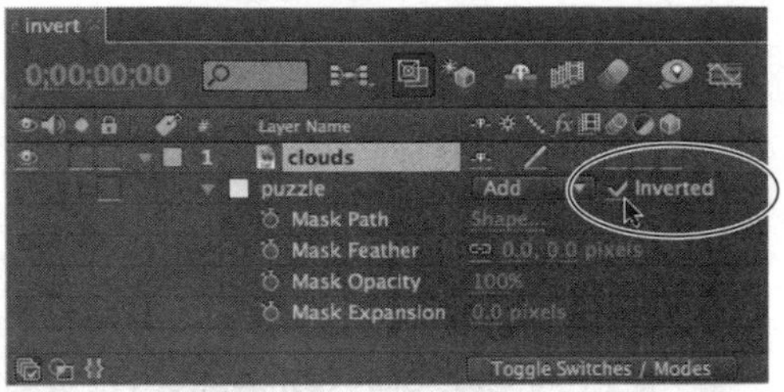

Figure 10.52 Click Inverted for the mask in the layer outline of the Timeline panel.

Figure 10.53 Ordinarily, the area within the mask defines the opaque parts of the layer's image.

Figure 10.54 Inverting the mask reverses the opaque and transparent areas of the layer.

Add

Subtract

Intersect

Lighten

Darken

Difference

Figure 10.55 This figure shows six different ways that a mask's mode setting changes how it interacts with other masks in the same layer. In each variation, two overlapping masks—a circle and a star—are applied to a black solid. The circle mask is higher in the stacking order than the star, and both masks are set to 75 percent opacity. But in each pairing, the star mask's mode is set to a different setting.

Mask Modes

When you add multiple masks to the same layer, you can determine how the masks interact by selecting a mask *mode*. Although modes don't create true compound paths (as do the Boolean functions in Illustrator), you can use them to achieve similar effects (**Figure 10.55**). Each mask's Mode pop-up menu includes the following options, which are illustrated using two masks:

None—Eliminates the effects of the mask on the layer's alpha channel. However, you can still apply effects (such as strokes or fills) to the mask.

Add—Includes the mask with the masks above it to display all masked areas. Areas where the mask overlaps with the masks above it use their combined opacity values.

Subtract—Cuts, or subtracts, areas where the mask overlaps with the mask above it.

Intersect—Adds the mask to all the masks above it so that only the areas where the mask overlaps with higher masks display in the composition.

Lighten—Adds the mask to the masks above it to display all masked areas. Areas where the mask overlaps with the masks above it use the highest opacity value, not the combined values.

Darken—Adds the mask to the masks above it to display only the areas where the masks overlap. Areas where multiple masks overlap use the highest opacity value, not the combined values.

Difference—Adds the mask to the masks above it to display only the areas where the masks don't overlap.

To set the mask mode:

1. Select the mask for which you want to set the mode.

2. *Do one of the following:*

   ▲ In the Timeline panel, choose a mode from the pop-up menu across from the mask (in the Switches/Modes panel) (**Figure 10.56**).

   ▲ Choose Layer > Mask > Mode > and select a mode from the submenu.

   The mode you choose affects how the mask interacts with the masks above it in the layer outline (for that layer only).

Figure 10.56 To the right of the mask in the Timeline panel, choose a mask mode from the pop-up menu.

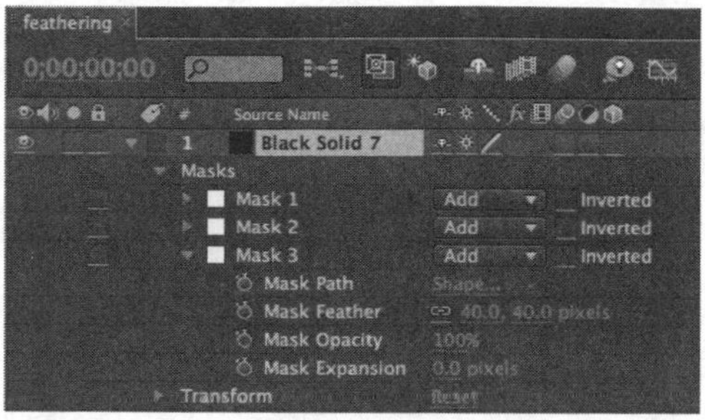

Figure 10.57 In addition to Mask Shape, properties include Mask Feather, Mask Opacity, and Mask Expansion.

Figure 10.58 These masks are identical except for their Mask Feather values.

Figure 10.59 In this figure, several masks in the same layer use different opacity values.

Figure 10.60 This figure shows three masks with identical shapes and feather values. However, each mask's expansion value is different.

Adjusting Other Mask Properties

In addition to Mask Shape, properties include Mask Feather, Mask Opacity, and Mask Expansion (**Figure 10.57**). Along with Mask Shape, you can view, adjust, and animate them as you would any layer property (as you learned in Chapter 7 and Chapter 9). For an explanation of Mask Feather, Opacity, and Expansion, consult the following list:

Feather—Controls the softness of a mask's edge; the Mask Feather value determines the width of the edge's transition from opacity to transparency. The feathered width always extends equally from each side of the mask edge—that is, a Feather value of 30 extends 15 pixels both outside and inside the mask edge (**Figure 10.58**).

Opacity—Controls the mask's overall opacity, that is, how solid the masked area of the layer appears. Mask Opacity works in conjunction with the layer's Opacity setting. If the layer is 100 percent opaque and a mask is 50 percent opaque, the masked area of the layer appears 50 percent opaque. Each mask's opacity also influences the net effect of mask modes, which are explained in the previous section, "Mask Modes." (**Figure 10.59**).

Expansion—Lets you expand or contract a mask's edges. This is particularly useful for fine-tuning the feathered edge of a mask (**Figure 10.60**).

✔ Tip

■ If you set the feather to extend beyond the perimeter of the layer containing the mask, the feather will appear cut off and the edges of the layer will be apparent. Make the mask or feather small enough to fit within the confines of the layer. If the layer is a solid or nested composition, you can also increase the size of the layer.

EFFECTS FUNDAMENTALS

At last, you come to the program's namesake: effects. As if you didn't already know, effects are used to alter the audio and visual characteristics of layers in countless ways. You can employ them to enhance, combine, or distort layers. You can simulate audio-visual phenomena from light to lightning. You can make changes that are subtle or spectacular. And, most important, you can animate these effects over time.

This chapter explains the process you use to apply effects to layers. It also describes how to use the Effect Controls panel as a complement or alternative to the property controls in the layer outline.

Using the Effects & Presets Panel

Although you can find and apply any effect using the Effects menu, it can be more convenient to use the Effects & Presets panel. As its name implies, it lists not only effects, but also animation presets.

By default, the effects are listed by category. As usual, you can click the triangle next to the item to expand it, revealing its contents in outline form. By expanding items, you can view effects contained in a category or see the components of a saved preset. Icons indicate the type of item listed (**Figure 11.1**).

To find an item in the Effects & Presets panel:

◆ In the Effects & Presets panel, type all or part of the name of the item you want in the search field, next to the Search icon (**Figure 11.2**).

As you type, the items on the list that don't match are hidden from view, leaving only the matching items (**Figure 11.3**).

To show all the items in the Effects & Presets panel:

◆ In the Effects & Presets panel's Contains field, click the Clear Search button .

The panel lists all items according to other sorting options you specify (explained in the following tasks). The Clear Search button appears only when you type in the search field.

✔ Tip

■ The Effects panel's pop-up menu includes other options for sorting and sifting effects. Instead of listing effects by category, you can list them alphabetically or according to how they're organized on your hard disk. And you can include or exclude certain types of effects (such as presets) from the list.

8 bpc effect

16 bpc effect

32 bpc effect

Audio effect

Effect preset

Figure 11.1 In the Effects & Presets panel, icons indicate the type of item listed.

Figure 11.2 As you type the name of the item you want in the Contains field...

Figure 11.3 ...the list sifts to show only the matching items. Click the Clear Search button (the X icon) to show all items.

Figure 11.4 Select a layer.

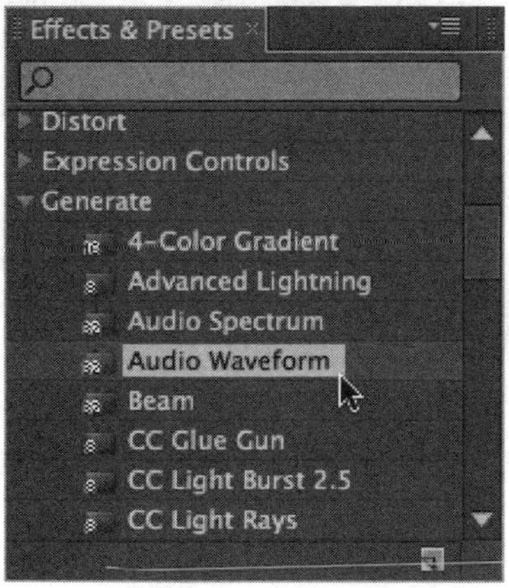

Figure 11.5 In the Effects & Presets panel, double-click the effect or preset you want.

Applying Effects

Although effects are numerous and varied, you apply all of them in essentially the same way.

You can also save any combination of effects (as well as animation keyframes) as a preset. To learn how to save and apply a preset, see the section "Saving and Applying Effect Presets" later in this chapter.

To apply an effect:

1. Select a layer in a composition (**Figure 11.4**).

2. *Do any of the following:*
   ▲ Double-click the effect or preset you want to apply in the Effects & Presets panel (**Figure 11.5**).
   ▲ Choose Effect, and then choose an effect category and an individual effect from the submenu.
   ▲ Control-click (right-click), and hold down the mouse button to access an Effects menu.

continues on next page

3. If an options dialog appears, select options for the effect and then click OK to close the dialog.

An Effect Controls panel appears with the effect selected (**Figure 11.6**).

4. Using controls in the Effect Controls panel or in the expanded layer outline of the Timeline panel, adjust the property values for the effect, and animate them if you want (**Figure 11.7**).

The applied effect appears in the composition (**Figure 11.8**). The quality and aspects (such as shading or shadows) of the effect depend on the preview options you specify; see Chapter 8, "Playback, Previews, and RAM," for more information.

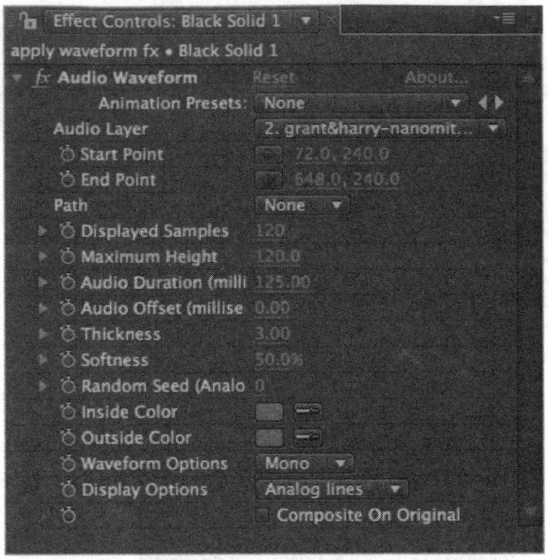

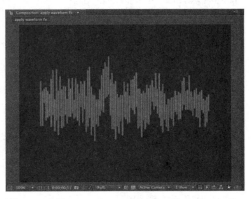

Figure 11.6 The effect appears selected in the Effect Controls panel. You can adjust the settings here...

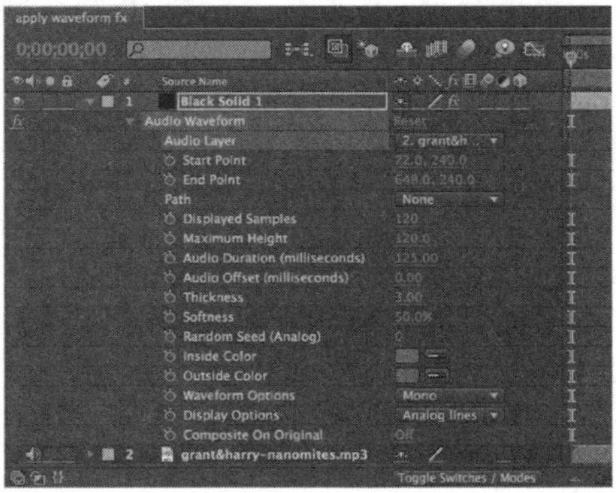

Figure 11.7 ...or in the layer outline of the Timeline panel.

Figure 11.8 You can view and preview the effect in the Composition panel.

APPLYING EFFECTS

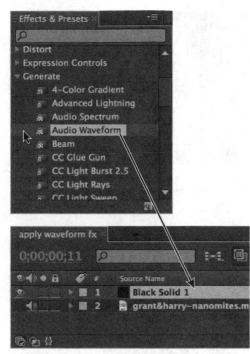

Figure 11.9 You can drag an effect or preset icon to the target layer in the timeline, dropping it on the layer's name, on the layer's effect property heading, or at any position in the layer's effect list.

To apply an effect or preset by dragging:

1. In the Effects & Presets panel, locate and select the effect or preset you want to apply.

2. Drag the selected effect or preset to any of the following places:

   ▲ The target layer's name in the Timeline panel.

   ▲ The target layer's effect list heading in the Timeline panel.

   ▲ Any position in the target layer's list of effects in the Timeline panel (**Figure 11.9**).

   ▲ Any position in the target layer's list of effects in the Effect Controls panel.

   ▲ The target layer in the Comp panel. The Info panel displays the name of the currently targeted layer as you drag over it.

   The effect is added to the layer when you release the mouse.

✔ Tips

■ After Effects includes a preset workspace for Effects. Where the Standard workspace has a Project panel, the Effects workspace places the Effect Controls panel.

■ Many effects are best applied to solid-black layers—particularly those that don't rely on a layer's underlying pixels, such as effects in the Generate category. This permits you to manipulate the layer containing the effect independently from other layers, which can give you more flexibility. Other times, you may want to use the effect to interact with a solid color to create graphical elements.

Viewing Effect Property Controls

Once you add effects to a layer, you can view their property controls in both the Timeline panel and the Effect Controls panel.

As you saw in Chapter 7, "Properties and Keyframes," you can view any layer property—including effects—by expanding the layer outline. Chances are, you even recall the keyboard shortcut: E for *effects*. However, you'll soon find that many effects include a long list of parameters—often too long to view in the layer outline conveniently (**Figure 11.10**).

For this reason, the Effect Controls panel is indispensable. Selecting a layer makes all of its effects appear in the Effect Controls panel (**Figure 11.11**). Or, if it's not open already, you can invoke the Effect Controls panel by double-clicking the effect in the layer outline. As in the Comp and Layer panels, a viewer pop-up menu in the Effect Controls panel's tab lets you open a new viewer (**Figure 11.12**); selecting the tab's Lock icon prevents it from toggling to a different layer's effects.

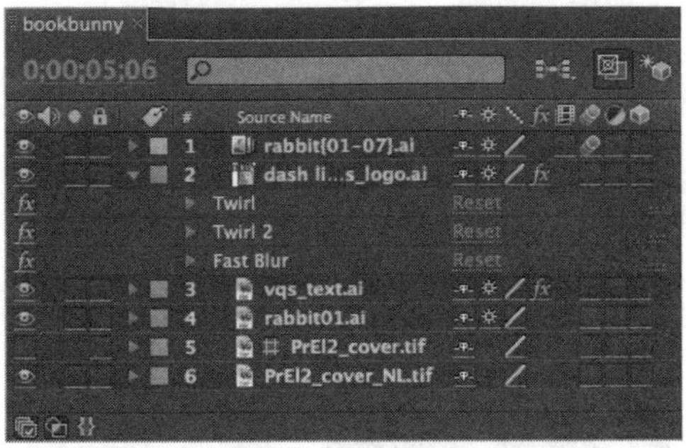

Figure 11.10 Pressing E reveals a selected layer's effect properties in the Timeline panel's layer outline...

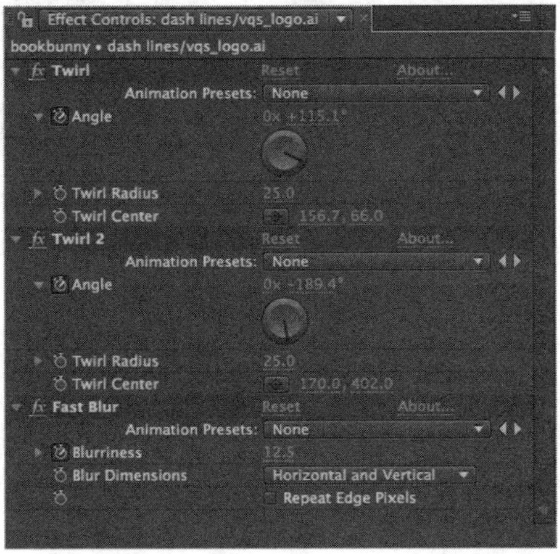

Figure 11.11 ...and selecting a layer containing effects reveals its effect properties in the Effect Controls panel. Typically, you use the two views in tandem to adjust and animate effects.

Figure 11.12 Much like the Comp and Layer panels, the Effect Controls panel's tab lets you open a new tabbed viewer; select Locked to prevent that viewer from toggling another layer's effects.

Figure 11.13 Some effects let you set a spatially based property (an effect point) by clicking directly in the Comp panel. Here, the center point of a lens flare effect is being placed using the mouse.

Generally, you use a Layer or Comp panel to view the result of your adjustments. However, some effects include a spatial property that you can set directly in the Layer or Comp panels by clicking where you want the *effect point* to be (**Figure 11.13**). See "Setting an Effect Point," later in this chapter.

As you can see, the Timeline panel's property controls are ideally suited for viewing the properties in time, whereas the Effect Controls panel provides a dedicated space for viewing and adjusting numerous effect properties at once. Naturally, you'll use both views in tandem. Don't forget that After Effects already includes a preset workspace called Effects that places an emphasis on both areas (see Chapter 1, "After Effects: The Big Picture," to review workspaces).

Removing and Resetting Effects

If you don't like an effect, remove it. If you need to restore the default settings, reset them.

To remove an effect:

1. In the Effect Controls panel, select the name of an effect.

2. Press Delete (Backspace).

   The effect is removed.

To remove all effects for a layer:

1. Select a layer containing one or more effects (**Figure 11.14**).

2. Choose Effect > Remove All, or press Shift-Command-E (Shift-Ctrl-E) (**Figure 11.15**).

   All effects are removed from the layer.

To reset an effect to its default settings:

◆ *Do either of the following:*

   ▲ In the Switches panel of the expanded Layer panel, click Reset for the effect.

   ▲ For the effect in the Effect Controls panel, click Reset (**Figure 11.16**).

   All the values for the effect are restored to the defaults.

✔ Tip

■ In addition to a Reset button, each effect includes an About button that displays the name and version number of each effect. A handful of effects also include a button to access additional options not listed in the Effect Controls panel. Depending on the effect, the button is labeled Options, Edit Text, or the like.

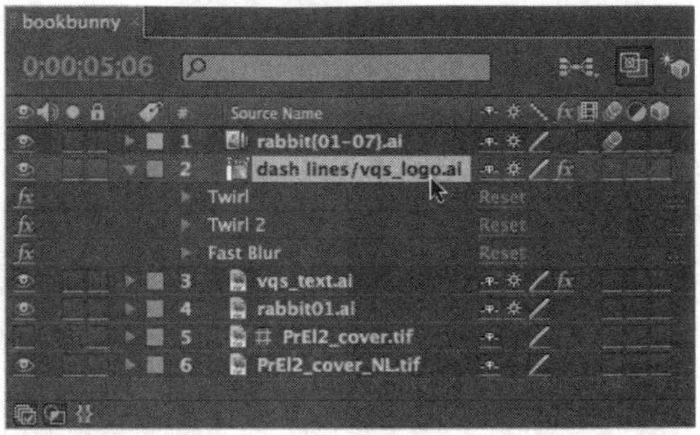

Figure 11.14 To remove all of a layer's effects, select the layer...

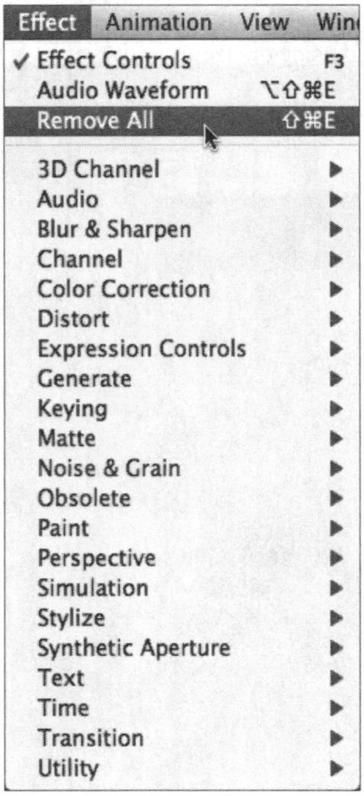

Figure 11.15 ...and choose Effect > Remove All, or use the keyboard shortcut.

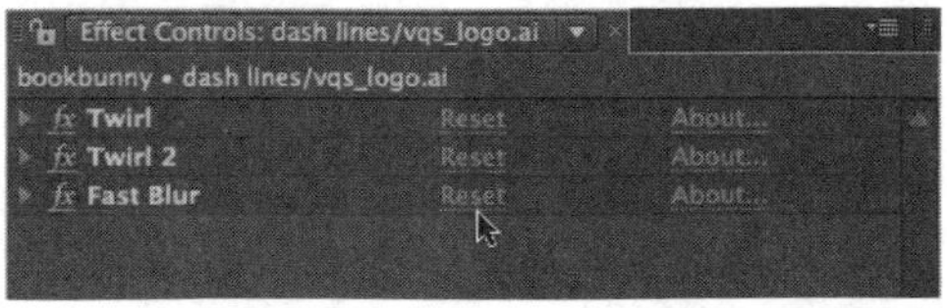

Figure 11.16 Clicking Reset returns all of the effects' properties to their defaults.

Disabling Effects Temporarily

You can turn off effects temporarily without removing them from the layer. Doing so is helpful when you're not certain you want to remove an effect (and the work you put into it), or when you want to see a single effect without other effects obscuring your view. Or, once you're satisfied with an effect's settings, you may want to disable it to speed up frame rendering.

To disable and enable individual effects:

◆ In the Timeline panel or the Effect Controls panel, click the Effect icon *fx* next to the effect's name.

When the icon is visible, the effect is enabled; when the icon is hidden, the effect is disabled (**Figures 11.17** and **11.18**).

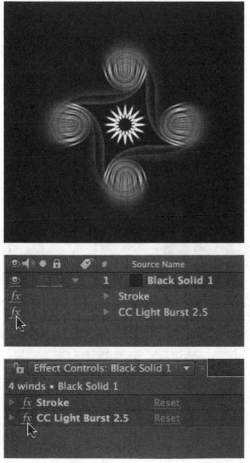

Figure 11.17 Clicking the Effect icon next to the effect name in the Timeline (middle) or Effect Controls panel (bottom)...

Figure 11.18 ...toggles the icon off and disables the effect.

To disable and enable all effects in a layer:

◆ In the Switches/Modes panel of the Timeline panel, click the Effect icon  next to a layer.

When the icon is visible, all effects for the layer are enabled; when the icon is hidden, all effects are disabled (**Figures 11.19** and **11.20**).

Figure 11.19 Clicking the Effect switch for a layer in the Switches/Modes panel of the Timeline panel...

Figure 11.20 ...toggles the icon off and disables all effects contained by the layer.

Adjusting Effects in the Effect Controls Panel

Although you can adjust effect properties in the layer outline just as you would any other layer property (using techniques covered in Chapter 7, "Properties and Keyframes"), the roomier Effect Controls panel can accommodate larger, more graphical controls for several effect properties. Most are intuitive or should already be familiar to you (**Figure 11.21**), so they won't be covered here. However, this chapter does discuss the slightly less intuitive effect point control (see the following section, "Setting an Effect Point").

Covering every possible graphical control is beyond the scope of this chapter. Other effects may offer a color range control (Hue/Saturation); a grid of control points (Mesh Warp); a histogram (Levels); or other graphs, such as those that represent an image's input/output levels (Curves) or an audio layer's frequency response (Parametric EQ). Some effects include an Options button to open a separate dialog, and third-party plug-ins may offer other exotic controls. Consult the documentation for each effect for detailed information on its individual controls.

✔ Tips

- By default, After Effects uses its own color picker for selecting colors. However, you can have After Effects use your system's color picker by selecting the appropriate option in the General pane of the Preferences dialog.

- Once you start dragging an angle control knob, you can drag the cursor outside the angle controller to move it with greater precision.

- You can set some property values using a slider control. However, the slider's range (say, 0 to 20) doesn't always represent the possible range of values (let's say 0 to 1000). Control-click (right-click) the property name and choose Edit Value to open a dialog and set the range of the slider.

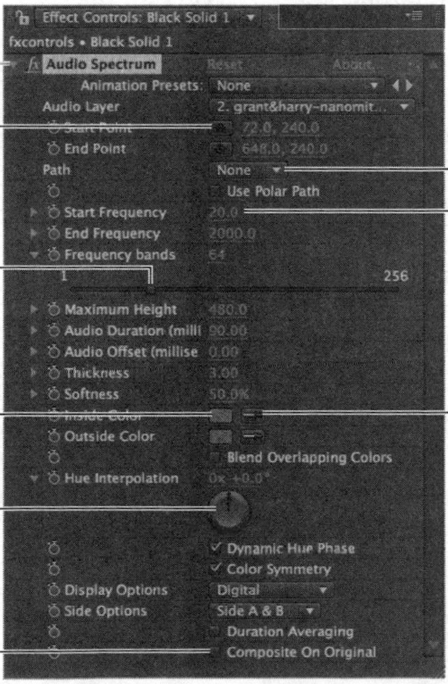

Figure 11.21 The Effect Controls panel furnishes you with a convenient alternative to the effect property controls in the layer outline, especially when the effect includes special graphical controls.

Setting an Effect Point

An *effect point* represents the position of an effect on a layer: It can be the focus of a Lens Flare effect, the center point of a Reflection effect, or the starting point for Path Text. Some effects require more than one effect point, such as the four corners of the Corner Pin effect.

You can set the effect point with the Effect Controls panel's Effect Point button or by manipulating it in the Composition or Layer panel. For an effect point to be visible in the Comp panel, Effect Controls must be selected in the Comp panel's View Options dialog (accessed from the Comp panel's pop-up menu). In the Layer panel, the effect's name must be selected in the Layer panel's View menu.

When you animate the effect point over time, you can view and manipulate its path in the Layer panel just as you would adjust an anchor point path or motion path in the Composition panel (**Figure 11.22**). In most ways, the effect point path works just like any other kind of motion path. Unlike a layer's position, however, the effect point's coordinates are unaffected by the layer's anchor point. (See "Animating Effects," at the end of this chapter; Chapter 7, "Properties and Keyframes," about basic animation; and Chapter 9, "Keyframe Interpolation," about adjusting a motion path.) And because effects are applied to a layer, the coordinates of an effect point refer to the layer, not the composition.

The following task explains how to set an effect point; you can animate it as you would any property.

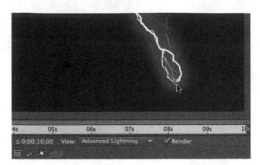

Figure 11.22 You can view and manipulate an effect point and its motion path in the Layer panel. Here, you can see the path of an Advanced Lightning effect's endpoint.

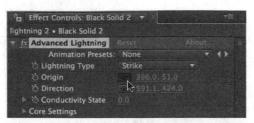

Figure 11.23 Click the Effect Point button for an effect property.

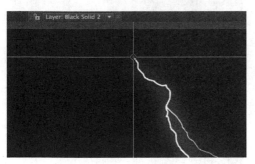

Figure 11.24 Position the cursor in a Layer or Comp panel (shown here), and click to set the effect point.

To set an effect point with the Effect Point button:

1. In the Effect Controls panel, click the Effect Point button for an effect property (**Figure 11.23**).

   Any effect property that uses layer coordinate values has an Effect Point button. When the button is active, the mouse pointer changes to an Effect Point icon -:- when positioned in a Composition or Layer panel.

2. Position the mouse pointer in a Composition or Layer panel, and click to set the effect point (**Figure 11.24**).

   The mouse changes back to the standard pointer, and the Effect Point button becomes deselected. The coordinate values reflect the effect point you chose. Even if you clicked the Effect Point icon in the Composition panel, the coordinate values correspond to the coordinate system of the layer that contains the effect.

SETTING AN EFFECT POINT

Saving and Applying Effect Presets

Occasionally, you'll create a complex effect that you're particularly proud of or that you need to reuse. You can save a combination of effect settings—including keyframes—as a *preset*.

You save preset effects as independent, cross-platform files, which use an .ffx extension. Because preset effects are independent files, you can store them separately from your project so that you can easily access them for other projects or share them with other After Effects artists.

By default, expanding an effect in the Effect Controls panel reveals an Animation Presets pull-down menu. This menu not only lists presets included with the effect, but also provides a command for saving your own preset.

To view presets in the Effect Controls pane:

1. In the Effect Controls panel, make sure the triangle next to an effect's name is pointing downward, so that its properties and, by default, its Animation Presets menu is visible.

2. To view built-in presets for the effect, *do any of the following:*

   ▲ Choose the name of the built-in preset in the Animation Presets menu (**Figure 11.25**).

   ▲ Click the Next Preset button ▶ to select the next preset in the list.

   ▲ Click the Previous Preset button ◀ to select the previous preset in the list.

   The Animation Preset menu is labeled with the preset's name.

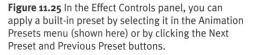

Figure 11.25 In the Effect Controls panel, you can apply a built-in preset by selecting it in the Animation Presets menu (shown here) or by clicking the Next Preset and Previous Preset buttons.

✔ Tip

■ Choosing Show Animation Presets from the Effect Controls panel's menu deselects the option and prevents the Animation Presets pop-up menu from appearing in the Effect Controls panel.

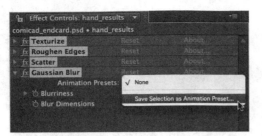

Figure 11.26 In the Effect Controls panel, select one or more of the effects you applied to the layer, and choose Save Selection as Animation Preset in the Animation Presets menu...

Animation	View	Window	Help
Save Animation Preset...			
Apply Animation Preset...			
Recent Animation Presets			▶
Browse Presets...			
Add Keyframe			
Toggle Hold Keyframe			⌥⌘H
Keyframe Interpolation...			⌥⌘K
Keyframe Velocity...			⇧⌘K
Keyframe Assistant			▶
Animate Text			▶
Add Text Selector			▶
Remove All Text Animators			
Add Expression			⌥⇧=
Separate Dimensions			
Track Motion			
Stabilize Motion			
Track this Property			
Reveal Animating Properties			U
Reveal Modified Properties			

Figure 11.27 ...or choose Animation > Save Animation Preset.

Figure 11.28 Specify the name and destination of the preset file in the "Save Animation Preset as" dialog.

To save effects as a preset:

1. Apply one or more effects to a layer in the composition.

   If you want, you can animate them over time using techniques explained in Chapter 7, "Properties and Keyframes."

2. In the Effect Controls panel, select one or more of the effects you applied to the layer.

3. *Do either of the following:*

   ▲ Select any effect, and then in the Animation Presets pop-up menu, choose Save Selection as Animation Preset (**Figure 11.26**).

   ▲ Choose Animation > Save Animation Preset (**Figure 11.27**).

   A "Save Animation Preset as" dialog appears.

4. Specify the name and destination of the preset file (**Figure 11.28**).

   The file uses the .ffx extension.

5. Click Save to save the settings and close the dialog.

   The preset is added to the appropriate categories in the Effects & Presets panel.

SAVING AND APPLYING EFFECT PRESETS

To apply a preset effect:

1. Select the layers to which you want to apply a preset, and set the current time to where you want keyframes (if included in the preset) to begin.

2. *Do one of the following:*

   ▲ In the Effects & Presets panel, double-click the name of the preset you want to apply to the selected layers (**Figure 11.29**).

   ▲ Choose Animation > Apply Animation Preset.

   ▲ Choose Animation > Apply Recent Preset, and select the name of a recently used preset.

   The preset is applied to the selected layers. Any animated properties' keyframes begin at the current time.

✔ Tips

■ You can often find the solution (or the inspiration) you need by viewing presets in After Effects Bridge. Choose Animation > Browse Presets, or in the Effect & Presets panel's pop-up menu, choose Browse Presets.

■ When the Show Preset Contents option is selected in the Effects & Presets panel's pop-up menu, the panel lists both the preset's name and the individual effects the preset contains. You can click the triangle to expand a preset and show its constituent effects. Moreover, you can apply any individual effect the preset contains to a layer.

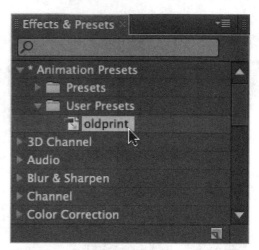

Figure 11.29 Select a layer, and apply a preset by using an option in the Animation menu or by double-clicking the preset in the Effects & Presets panel (shown here).

Figure 11.30 In the Effect Controls panel, select one or more effects, then press Command-C (Ctrl-C).

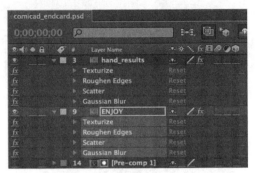

Figure 11.31 Selecting a target layer and pressing Command-V (Ctrl-V) pastes the effects, but it doesn't contain the same keyframes. (You can press E to view the selected layer's effects in the layer outline.)

Copying and Pasting Effects

To save time and labor, you can copy effects from one layer into another.

To copy a layer's effects into another layer:

1. In the Effect Controls panel, select one or more effects (**Figure 11.30**).

2. Select Edit > Copy, or press Command-C (Ctrl-C).

3. In the Timeline panel, select one or more layers.

4. Choose Edit > Paste, or press Command-V (Ctrl-V).

   The selected layer now contains the pasted effects; however, it doesn't contain the same keyframes (**Figure 11.31**).

✔ Tip

- You can also copy and paste keyframes from one property to another property that uses compatible values. For example, you can copy position keyframes to an effect point property.

Applying Multiple Effects

The Effect Controls panel lists effects in the order you add them, from top to bottom. Because each effect is applied to the result of the one above it, changing the order of effects can change the final appearance (or sound) of the layer (**Figures 11.32** and **11.33**). You can reorder effects in the Effect Controls panel as well as directly in the layer outline of the Timeline panel.

To reorder effects:

1. In the Effect Controls panel or in the layer outline of the Timeline panel, drag the name of an effect up or down to a new position in the effect stacking order.

   A dark horizontal line indicates the effect's new position when you release the mouse (**Figure 11.34**).

2. Release the mouse button to place the effect in its new position in the list (**Figure 11.35**).

   Changing the order of effects in the list changes the order in which they're applied to the layer.

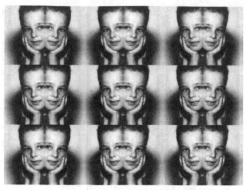

Figure 11.32 The Mirror effect followed by the Motion Tile effect results in this image...

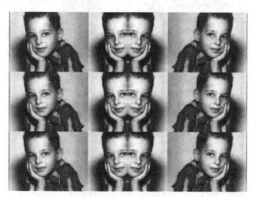

Figure 11.33 ...whereas reversing the order of the effects results in this image.

Figure 11.34 Drag the name of an effect up or down to a new position in the stacking order. A dark line indicates the effect's new position.

Figure 11.35 Release the mouse to place the effect in its new position in the list.

Figure 11.36 Masking an adjustment layer restricts its effects. Here, the Blur and Brightness & Contrast filters affect only masked areas (defined by an elliptical mask that's inverted).

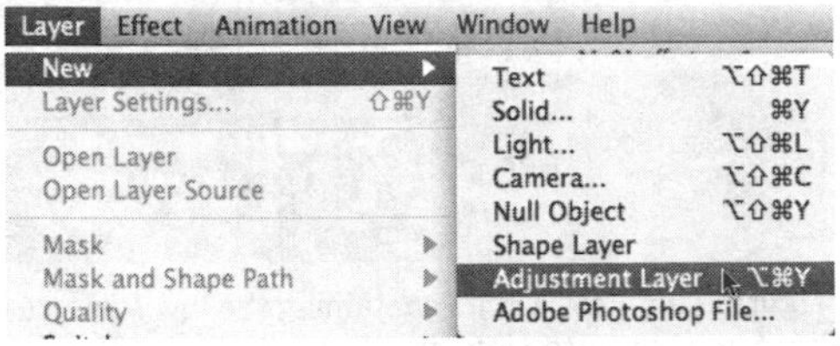

Figure 11.37 Choose Layer > New > Adjustment Layer.

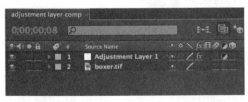

Figure 11.38 The adjustment layer appears as the topmost layer in the comp and uses the default still image duration.

Applying Effects to an Adjustment Layer

An *adjustment layer* contains effects, not footage. The effects contained in an adjustment layer are applied to all the layers below it. Adjustment layers save time and effort by letting you apply effects to a single layer rather than multiple layers.

You can also limit the areas affected by an adjustment layer by using a mask or by employing a layer's existing alpha channel.

Ordinarily, a mask modifies a layer's alpha channel to define opaque and transparent areas of a layer's image. Applying a mask to an adjustment layer—which by definition can't contain an image—allows the masked area of the effect to influence the lower layers; the areas outside the mask remain unaffected (**Figure 11.36**).

You can also use the alpha channel of any layer in a similar manner by converting the layer to an adjustment layer. As an adjustment layer, its image is ignored. However, any effects you add to the layer are restricted to the areas defined by its alpha channel.

To create an adjustment layer:

1. Open the Composition panel or Timeline panel for the composition in which you want to add an adjustment layer, or make sure one of these panels is active.

2. Choose Layer > New > Adjustment Layer (**Figure 11.37**).

   An adjustment layer appears in the composition. The adjustment layer starts at the current time and uses the default duration for still images (**Figure 11.38**).

To convert a layer to an adjustment layer:

◆ In the Switches area of the Timeline panel, click the Adjustment Layer switch for the layer you want to convert to make the icon appear or disappear.

When the Adjustment Layer icon is visible, the layer functions as an adjustment layer—its image disappears from the Composition panel, and its effects are applied to lower layers (**Figures 11.39** and **11.40**).

When the Adjustment Layer icon isn't visible, the layer functions as a standard layer, and its image appears in the composition. If the adjustment layer was created in After Effects, it becomes a solid layer. Any effects contained by the layer are applied only to that layer.

Figure 11.39 Alternatively, you can convert a layer into an adjustment layer by selecting its Adjustment Layer switch in the Timeline panel.

Figure 11.40 Here a solid containing the Invert effect has been converted into an adjustment layer. The solid isn't visible, but its effect alters the underlying layers, making the left side of this image look like a negative.

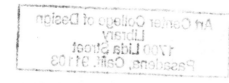

Understanding Compound Effects

Effects that require two layers to operate are called *compound effects*. Rather than appear in a separate category, compound effects are distributed among effects in various categories. Although some compound effects use the word *compound* in their names, you can identify others only by knowing their controls.

As with other effects, you apply compound effects to the layers you want to alter. Unlike other effects, however, compound effects rely on a second layer—an effect source or modifying layer—that acts as a kind of map for the effect. Typically, this takes the form of a grayscale image because many compound effects can be based on the modifying layer's brightness levels. In a Compound Blur effect, for example, the brightness levels of the modifying layer can determine the placement and intensity of the blurry areas of the target layer. The modifying layer can be a still image, movie, or nested composition (**Figure 11.41**).

✔ Tip

- You don't need ready-made footage to serve as an effect source; you can create your own within After Effects. You can use a combination of solids, masks, and effects to create a dynamic effect source. The effect source in Figure 11.41 was created by applying the Fractal Noise effect to a solid.

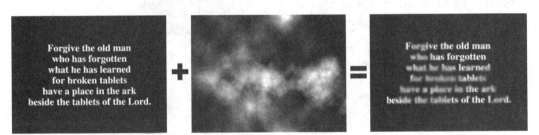

Figure 11.41 Compound effects rely on a second layer as a kind of map for the effect.

Using Compound Effects

Due to their peculiar nature, compound effects have certain unique features. This section summarizes those attributes. Other implications are addressed in Chapter 16.

Specifying an effect source

In compound effects, you must use a pop-up menu to specify the modifying layer; the name of the pop-up menu depends on the particular effect (**Figure 11.42**). Although the modifying layer must be included in the composition to appear in the list, you usually switch off its video in the Timeline panel. This is necessary because the modifying layer appears in the composition only as an effect source, not a visible layer.

Resolving size differences between source and target layers

Because compound effects use the pixels of the modifying layer as a map, that layer's dimensions should match those of the layer it affects (**Figure 11.43**). This way, your results will be more predictable and easier to control. If the dimensions of the two layers don't match, compound effects offer several ways to compensate (**Figure 11.44**).

Tile—The modifying layer is repeated to map the entire target layer. In some cases, the modifying layer won't tile evenly, cutting off some tiles. If images don't tile seamlessly, the edges may be evident in the effect.

Center—The modifying layer is positioned in the center of the target layer. If the modifying layer is smaller, the effect may appear to be cut off; if it's larger, the extraneous portions aren't used in the effect.

Stretch to Fit—The modifying layer is scaled to match the dimensions of the target layer. Sometimes, this can distort the modifying layer or make it difficult to position.

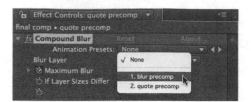

Figure 11.42 Compound effects contain a pop-up menu to specify the modifying layer, or effect source. In this Compound Blur effect, you specify the effect source in Blur Layer pop-up menu.

Figure 11.43 When the dimensions of the modifying layer match those of the layer it affects, the final result is more predictable. This example shows the effect source, target image, background image, and result of the Gradient Wipe effect.

Figure 11.44 If the dimensions of the two layers don't match, compound effects offer ways to compensate for the difference.

Figure 11.45 Compound effects refer directly to the effect source—before any mask, effect, or transform property changes have occurred. Apply the displacement map effect to this layer...

Using a nested composition as the effect source

It's important to understand that the three placement options described previously don't alter the modifying layer, only the way its pixels are mapped to the target layer. Conversely, scaling or positioning the modifying layer in the composition doesn't influence the compound effect. This is the case because the compound effect refers directly to the effect source, before any mask, effect, or transform property changes occur (**Figures 11.45, 11.46,** and **11.47**).

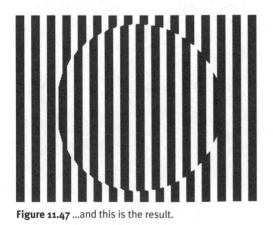

Figure 11.46 ...and use this layer as the effect source (the displacement map)...

Figure 11.47 ...and this is the result.

If a layer needs to be scaled (or otherwise treated) before it becomes an effect source, place it into another composition first. The nested composition, in turn, can serve as the modifying layer for the compound effect. This way, you can make any necessary changes to the layer within a composition—before it becomes the effect source. And unlike the layer it contains, the dimensions of the composition can be set to match the compound effect's target layer. As a result, the nested composition—and the layer it contains—maps perfectly to the target layer of the compound effect (**Figures 11.48** and **11.49**).

If all this talk of nesting sounds complicated, don't worry: Chapter 16, "Complex Projects," explains such topics as nesting and precomposing in greater detail.

Figure 11.48 If a layer requires treatment before becoming an effect source, place it into another comp first. Here, the effect source is scaled and repositioned.

Figure 11.49 You must use the nested comp as the effect source to achieve the desired result.

Animating Effects

Animating effect properties is no different than animating any other properties. As you learned back in Chapter 7, "Properties and Keyframes," once you activate the Stopwatch for a property, the procedure for creating keyframes is simple: Set the current time, set a property value, repeat.

But because many effects have a multitude of properties, they can easily overcrowd the layer outline—and force you to spend time adjusting the interface before you get to work. You can keep the workflow smooth by utilizing the controls in the Effect Controls panel.

The following task revisits the keyframing process—but this time using the Effect Controls panel in conjunction with the usual Timeline controls.

To set keyframes from the Effect Controls panel:

1. Select the layer containing the effect you want to keyframe, and reveal the effect in the Effect Controls panel.

2. Set the current time to the frame at which you want to set an effect property keyframe (**Figure 11.50**).

continues on next page

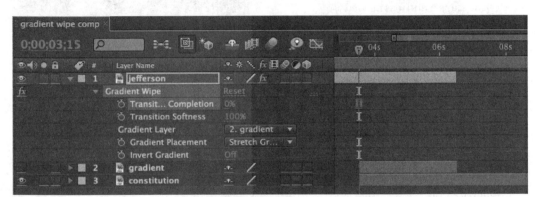

Figure 11.50 Set the current time to the frame at which you want to set an effect property keyframe.

3. In the Effect Controls panel, click the Stopwatch icon next to the name of the property you want to animate (**Figure 11.51**).

   Doing so activates the keyframing process. In the Timeline panel, a keyframe appears at the current time (**Figure 11.52**).

4. Adjust the value of the property in the Effect Controls panel.

5. Set the current time to the point at which you want to set another keyframe.

6. Using the controls in the Effect Controls panel, alter the property's values.

   In the Timeline, a new keyframe appears for the property at the current time.

7. Repeat steps 5 and 6 as needed.

✔ Tips

■ Control-clicking (right-clicking) a property's name in the Effect Controls panel invokes a context menu you can use to set and cue to keyframes.

■ To conserve space in the Timeline's layer outline, begin keyframing an effect using the Effects Controls panel, and then press U to reveal the selected layer's animated properties only.

■ The previous task illustrates keyframes explicitly, by showing their icons in the Timeline. But if you don't need the visual feedback of keyframe icons, feel free to animate the property without viewing keyframes. You can always expand the outline if you need to change the keyframes' timing, values, or interpolation, or make other keyframe-related commands (like copying and pasting them).

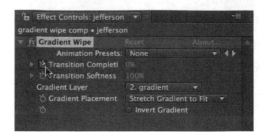

Figure 11.51 In the Effect Controls panel (shown here) or in the Timeline's layer outline select the Stopwatch icon next to the effect property you want to keyframe.

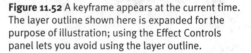

Figure 11.52 A keyframe appears at the current time. The layer outline shown here is expanded for the purpose of illustration; using the Effect Controls panel lets you avoid using the layer outline.

CREATING AND ANIMATING TEXT

With all its strengths in animation and compositing motion footage, you might expect After Effects to possess more limited text-creation tools, leaving serious typesetting to Photoshop or Illustrator. Not so. After Effects lets you create text with the same ease and flexibility as its siblings.

In After Effects CS4, you can create a text layer by typing directly in a Comp panel using a Type tool. Moreover, you can adjust the text using full-featured Character and Paragraph panels. You can even convert a text layer imported from Photoshop into a text layer you can edit in After Effects. And as in Illustrator, you can convert text into outlines you can manipulate as mask or shape paths.

You can animate text layers as you would any other layer in a comp. But you can also animate *the text itself.* Text layers include unique properties that allow you to change the content of the text over time and, yes, animate the text along a mask path you specify. But more amazingly, you can animate individual components of the text— a line, a word, a character—as though they made up their own layer. It's like having a text-based animation system within the layer-based animation system. And although the text-animation paradigm employs a unique feature called *animator groups*—each consisting of the properties and parts of the text you want to affect—it also uses the familiar keyframing process you learned about in Chapter 7, "Properties and Keyframes." Animator groups let you create intricate animations using relatively simple controls. Or, if you prefer, you can apply a canned text animation. After Effects includes an astonishingly varied, useful, and generous collection of preset animations you can apply to text with a click of the mouse. OK, *double-click.*

Creating Type

After Effects' Tools panel includes two tools for creating type: Horizontal Type and Vertical Type. Both tools occupy the same location in the panel, but you can access them by clicking and holding one tool to expand the panel and reveal the other (**Figure 12.1**). As you've guessed, the tool you choose depends on whether you want the type to be oriented horizontally or vertically (**Figure 12.2**).

Point text and paragraph text

Both tools let you create two kinds of text objects: *point text* and *paragraph text*. When you create point text, you use a Type tool to set the insertion point and start typing. When you create paragraph text, you first define a *text box* that contains the text.

Initially, there seems to be little difference between the two methods (**Figure 12.3**). But a practical distinction emerges when it's time to edit the text. With both kinds of text, changing the size of the text layer's bounding box transforms the text by scaling or stretching it (**Figure 12.4**). That happens because the bounding box consists of layer handles that work like any other layer's handles. But in contrast to point text, paragraph text also lets you resize its text box. Paragraph text reflows to fit in its text box, creating line breaks if necessary. This behavior is also known as *word wrap*.

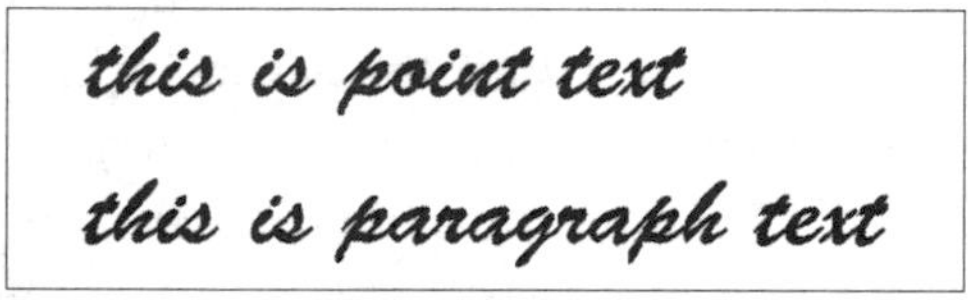

As its name suggests, paragraph text is better suited for lengthier messages that may need to be reflowed to better fit the comp or that require paragraph-style layout adjustments, such as margins.

Figure 12.1 Click and hold either Type tool to expand the panel and reveal the other.

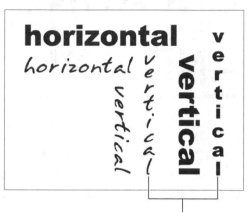

Standard Vertical Roman Alignment

Figure 12.2 The Horizontal Type tool created the horizontal text; the Vertical Type tool created the vertical text. The way characters appear in a vertical line depends on whether you specify Standard Vertical Roman Alignment.

this is point text

this is paragraph text

Figure 12.3 Although the point text on top doesn't look any different from the paragraph text on the bottom...

this is point text

this is paragraph text

Figure 12.4 ...resizing the point text's bounding box (its normal layer handles) scales the type, whereas resizing the paragraph text's text box reflows the type.

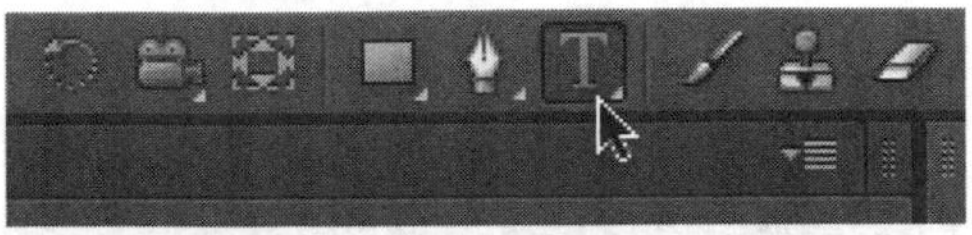

Figure 12.5 Choose the Vertical Type or Horizontal Type tool (shown here).

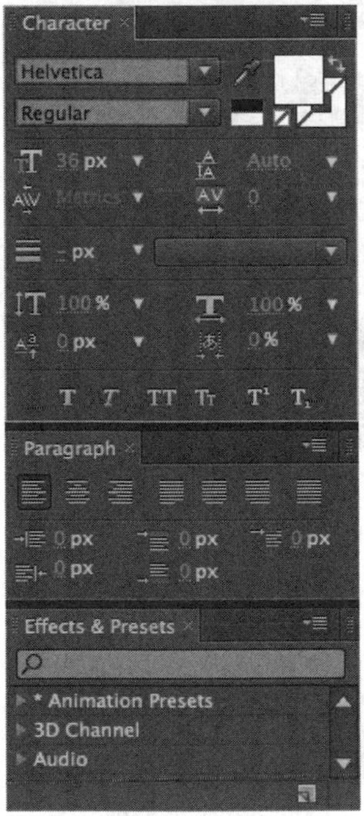

Figure 12.6 Specify how you want the text to look by choosing options in the Character and Paragraph panels.

✔ Tips

- The four corner handles of a layer's transform, or bounding, box appear as solid boxes, whereas all the corner handles of a text box appear hollow.
- The vertical orientation is particularly useful for Chinese, Japanese, and Korean text.

To create point text:

1. In the Tools panel, *choose either of the following tools:*
   - ▲ **Horizontal Type** —Creates horizontally oriented text (**Figure 12.5**)
   - ▲ **Vertical Type** —Creates vertically oriented text

   Both tools occupy the same location in the panel. To choose the hidden tool, click and hold the tool button to expand the panel, or use the keyboard shortcut Command-T (Ctrl-T).
2. Specify character and paragraph options using controls in the appropriate panel (**Figure 12.6**).

   You can select and modify the text at any time. See "Editing and Formatting Type," later in this chapter.
3. In the Composition panel, position the mouse where you want the text to begin.

   As you position the mouse pointer, it appears as an I-beam icon. The short horizontal line in the I-beam icon indicates the location of the text's baseline.
4. When the I-beam icon is where you want, click the mouse.

   A vertical line appears where you clicked, indicating the text's insertion point.

continues on next page

5. Type the text you want (**Figure 12.7**).

   Text appears at the insertion point, using the current character settings (font, size, fill color, and so on) and paragraph settings. The direction in which characters proceed from the insertion point depends on the current alignment or justification setting (see "Alignment and justification," later in this chapter).

6. When you're finished typing, choose the Selection tool ▶.

   In the Comp panel, bounding box handles indicate that the new text object is selected. In the Timeline panel, a text layer appears, and its name matches what you typed (**Figure 12.8**).

To create paragraph text:

1. In the Tools panel, *choose either of the following tools:*

   ▲ **Vertical Type**—Creates vertically oriented text

   ▲ **Horizontal Type**—Creates horizontally oriented text (**Figure 12.9**)

   Both tools occupy the same location in the panel. To choose the hidden tool, click and hold the tool button to expand the panel, or use the keyboard shortcut Command-T (Ctrl-T).

2. Specify character and paragraph options using controls in the appropriate panel (**Figure 12.10**).

   You can select and modify the text at any time. See "Editing and Formatting Type," and "Formatting Paragraph Text," later in this chapter.

Figure 12.7 Click to set the text's insertion point (indicated by a vertical line), and type the message you want.

Figure 12.8 When you choose the Selection tool, the new text layer is selected in the Comp panel. In the Timeline panel, its layer name matches what you typed.

Figure 12.9 Choose the Vertical Type or Horizontal Type tool (shown here).

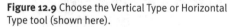

Figure 12.10 Specify character and paragraph options before you enter the text. You can reformat the text later if you want.

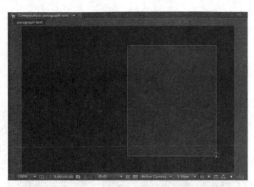

Figure 12.11 In the Comp panel, drag the mouse diagonally to define the size of the text box.

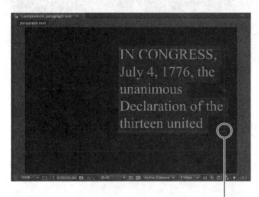

Indicates hidden text ⎯

Figure 12.12 When text reaches the side border of the text box, it flows to the next line automatically. If you type more than the text box can contain vertically, the text box's bottom-right handle displays a plus sign (+).

Figure 12.13 While in editing mode, you can drag the text box's handles to resize it and reveal hidden text.

3. In the Composition panel, drag the mouse diagonally to define a text box (**Figure 12.11**).

When you release the mouse, a text box appears with a vertical insertion point icon in the upper-left corner.

4. Type the text you want.

When the text box you defined can't contain the text horizontally, the text continues on the next line. Text that exceeds the vertical limit of its text box remains hidden until you resize the text box. When text is hidden this way, the bottom-right handle of the text box includes a plus sign (+) (**Figure 12.12**).

5. To resize the text box to include hidden text or reflow visible text, drag any of its eight handles.

The text reflows to fit within the text box. When the text box is large enough to hold all the text, the bottom-right handle no longer displays a plus sign (+) (**Figure 12.13**).

continues on next page

CREATING TYPE

6. When you're finished creating the message and resizing the text box, click the Selection tool .

In the Timeline panel, a text layer appears; its name matches what you typed (**Figure 12.14**). In the Comp panel, bounding box handles indicate that the new text object is selected. Note that resizing the text layer's bounding box scales the text object. To change the size of the text box and reflow the text, you must enter text-editing mode (as explained in the following task).

To resize a text bounding box:

1. *Do either of the following:*

▲ Select the Horizontal Type tool or Vertical Type tool, and click the paragraph text.

▲ Using the Selection tool, double-click the paragraph text (**Figure 12.15**).

An insertion point cursor appears, indicating that you can edit the text. Text box handles also appear. Note that all the handles in a text box are hollow, whereas the four corners of regular layer handles (bounding box handles) are solid (**Figure 12.16**).

Figure 12.14 Choosing the Selection tool exits editing mode, and the text layer appears selected in the Comp panel. In the Timeline panel, the layer's name matches the text.

Figure 12.15 Clicking text with a Type tool or double-clicking text with the Selection tool (shown here) activates text-editing mode. Layer handles are replaced by text box handles.

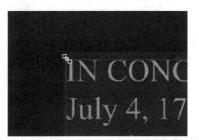

Figure 12.16 In text-editing mode, drag any of the text box handles to resize the box...

CREATING TYPE

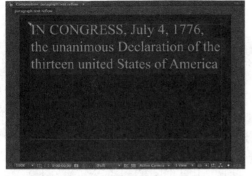

Figure 12.17 ...and reflow the text.

2. Drag any of the text box handles to resize the text box.

 The text contained in the box reflows to fit in the box horizontally (**Figure 12.17**). Text that doesn't fit in the text box vertically is hidden, and the text box's lower-right handle appears with a plus sign ⊞.

3. When you're finished editing the text box or text, be sure to choose the Selection tool to exit text-editing mode and select the text layer.

✔ Tips

■ You can convert point text to paragraph text and horizontal text to vertical text and vice versa by Control-clicking (right-clicking) the text object and choosing the appropriate option in the context menu.

■ By default, vertical text is aligned to a vertical baseline so that it appears sideways. You can make each letter in vertically oriented text appear upright by selecting the text and choosing Standard Vertical Roman Alignment from the Character panel's pop-up menu.

■ If you import a layered Photoshop file, you can convert its text layers to editable text in After Effects by choosing Layer > Convert to Editable Text.

Editing and Formatting Type

Chances are you're already familiar with the procedures for selecting text for modifying its content or format. This chapter won't cover those techniques, so you can spend more time learning text features unique to After Effects.

As in other Adobe programs, you format text with controls in the Character panel and Paragraph panel. Both panels let you choose settings by using buttons, specifying numerical values, or by choosing a preset option in a pop-up menu. (The following sections assume you know how to use these common controls.)

Font, style, fill, and stroke

Near the top of the Character panel you can specify the text's font, style, fill, and stroke using controls common to other programs, such as Photoshop and Illustrator (**Figure 12.18**). Controls for setting the stroke's width and how it's applied are located a bit farther down the panel.

Font—Provides a set of *typefaces*, or type designs, that determine the overall look of the text characters

Font style—Specifies a variation on the font, such as bold, italic, condensed, light, and so on

Fill—Specifies the color within a character's contours

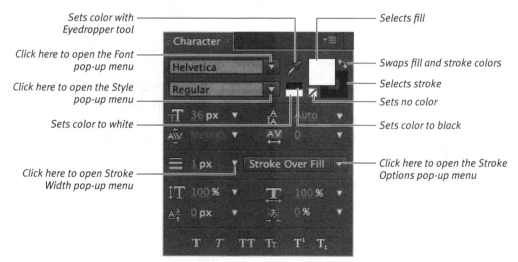

Figure 12.18 The Character panel includes standard controls for font, fill, and stroke.

Figure 12.19 Here, each line of text uses a different stroke width. (In the Character panel's pop-up menu, you can specify the stroke's Line Join type: Miter, Round, or Bevel.)

Stroke—Specifies the color of the character's contours: its outlines. You can detect the stroke color only if the stroke has a thickness greater than zero.

Stroke width—The thickness of a stroke in pixels (**Figure 12.19**)

Stroke options—Specifies whether the stroke is applied over the fill or vice versa for the selected characters or for all characters in the text object

✔ Tips

- For video output, avoid light text or text with fine features like *serifs* (the little tapering corners of letters in so-called old-style typefaces). Interlacing causes fine horizontal lines to flicker, making some text difficult to read. See Chapter 2, "Importing Footage Into a Project," for more about video interlacing.

- In the Character panel's pop-up menu, select Show Font Names in English to list foreign language fonts in English; deselect the option to list them in their native language.

- Starting with After Effects CS4, you can specify the type of line join used for strokes. In the Character panel's pop-up menu, choose Line Join and then select the type that you want: Miter, Round, or Bevel.

Font size, leading, kerning, and tracking

The second section of the Character panel contains controls for setting the font's size and for specifying the space between lines, letters, and pairs of characters (**Figure 12.20**).

Font size—Specifies the size of the font, expressed in pixels

Leading—Defines the space between lines of text

Kerning—The process of adjusting the value of *kern pairs*, spacing that the typeface's designer built into particular pairs of characters

Tracking—Adjusting the overall space between letters in a range of text (**Figure 12.21**)

✔ Tips

- When kerning characters, you can choose between two options in the Character panel. **Metrics** uses the kern pair values built into the font's design. **Optical** sets the value according to the shape of adjacent characters.

- By reducing kerning or tracking values, it's possible to make characters in the same text layer overlap. You can specify how overlapping letters interact by setting their Inter-Character Blending mode, found in the text layer's property outline under the heading More Options. Chapter 14, "More Layer Techniques," explains how Blending modes work.

- Options in the Character panel's pop-up menu let you specify how leading is calculated, whether to use smart quotes (" ")—also called *curly quotes*—instead of straight quotation marks, and foreign language features. For more about these options, consult After Effects Help.

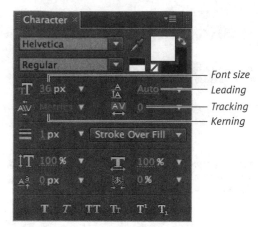

Figure 12.20 Specify values for font size and other options.

Figure 12.21 You can adjust tracking to tight (so tight that characters overlap) or loose.

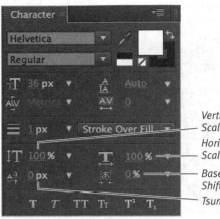

Figure 12.22 Specify scaling, baseline shift, or spacing for Chinese, Japanese, and Korean (CJK) fonts.

Vertical Scale
Horizontal Scale
Baseline Shift
Tsume

Figure 12.23 In this example, you can contrast the original text with the same text scaled vertically and horizontally.

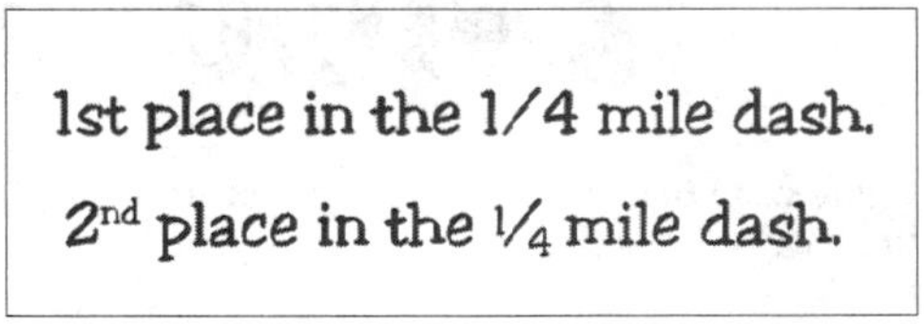

1st place in the 1/4 mile dash.

2nd place in the ¼ mile dash.

Figure 12.24 Here, the baselines of characters have been shifted to create the second fraction within the text. (The font size of the numerals has also been reduced.)

Scale, baseline shift, and tsume

The next set of controls lets you modify the text's horizontal and vertical scale, its baseline, and the spacing of text in languages that are typically vertically aligned (**Figure 12.22**).

Vertical Scale—Sets the vertical aspect of selected characters, making them relatively shorter or taller than the font size dictates (**Figure 12.23**)

Horizontal Scale—Sets the horizontal aspect of selected characters, making them relatively shorter or taller than the font size dictates

Baseline Shift—Offsets the selected character's baseline, the invisible "floor" on which the text rests. Adjusting the baseline can help you create mathematical notation or fractions (**Figure 12.24**).

Tsume—Sets the amount of space around each character in Chinese, Japanese, and Korean (CJK) vertically aligned text.

Faux bold, faux italics, all caps, small caps, superscript, and subscript

The bottom section of the Character panel contains controls for simulating typeface styles the selected font doesn't include by design (**Figure 12.25**).

Faux Bold—Simulates boldface for fonts that don't include a bold typeface

Faux Italics—Simulates italics for fonts that don't include an italic typeface

All Caps—Changes lowercase letters to uppercase, or capital, letters. For example, it would change a lowercase "a" to an uppercase "A."

Small Caps—Changes lowercase characters to a miniature version of uppercase characters.

Superscript—Makes characters appear higher than other characters on the text line. For example, the 2 in the familiar equation $E=Mc^2$ is superscript.

Subscript—Makes characters appear lower than other characters on the text line. For example, the 2 in the chemical notation for water, H_2O, is subscript (**Figure 12.26**).

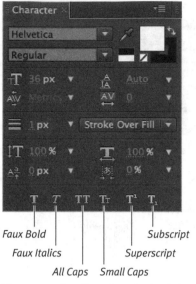

Faux Bold
Faux Italics
All Caps   Small Caps   Superscript   Subscript

Figure 12.25 Specify options for simulating typeface styles.

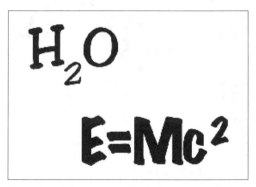

Figure 12.26 Here, the 2 in $E=Mc^2$ is superscripted, the 2 in H_2O is subscripted.

Formatting Paragraph Text

Whenever paragraph text reaches the edge of the text box, it flows into another line automatically. A new paragraph occurs when you press Return (Enter), also known as a *hard return*. You can format paragraph text using the Paragraph panel.

Alignment and justification

The topmost section of the Paragraph panel contains a number of buttons with icons that correspond to different alignment and justification options (**Figure 12.27**).

Alignment—Determines how the lines in a paragraph are positioned relative to the margins (the left and right sides of the text box) (**Figure 12.28**)

Justification—Alters the spacing in each line of text so that all the lines are flush with both the right and left margins. You can specify how After Effects aligns the last line, which is usually shorter than the others and doesn't lend itself to justification (**Figure 12.29**).

Align Left
Align Center
Align Right
Justify Last Left
Justify Last Center
Justify Last Right
Justify All
Paragraph
0 px
0 px
0 px
0 px
0 px

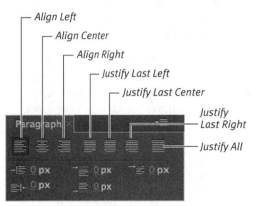

Figure 12.27 The Paragraph panel includes standard buttons for aligning and justifying paragraphs in a text box.

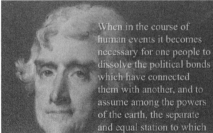

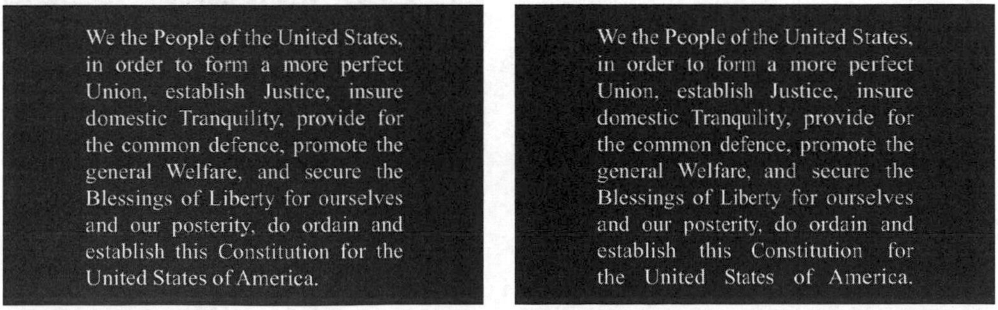

When in the course of human events it becomes necessary for one people to dissolve the political bonds which have connected them with another, and to assume among the powers of the earth, the separate and equal station to which
When in the course of human events it becomes necessary for one people to dissolve the political bonds which have connected them with another, and to assume among the powers of the earth, the separate and equal station to which

Figure 12.28 Compare the effect of different alignment options.

We the People of the United States, in order to form a more perfect Union, establish Justice, insure domestic Tranquility, provide for the common defence, promote the general Welfare, and secure the Blessings of Liberty for ourselves and our posterity, do ordain and establish this Constitution for the United States of America.
We the People of the United States, in order to form a more perfect Union, establish Justice, insure domestic Tranquility, provide for the common defence, promote the general Welfare, and secure the Blessings of Liberty for ourselves and our posterity, do ordain and establish this Constitution for the United States of America.

Figure 12.29 Choosing Justify Last Left (left) leaves the last line ragged. However, choosing Justify All (right) can result in awkward spacing.

Indent and spacing

The controls located in the bottom section of the Paragraph panel let you specify how to indent a paragraph's first line, and the spacing between paragraphs (**Figure 12.30**).

Indent—Increases one or both of its margins, shifting it away from the sides of the text box (**Figure 12.31**)

Spacing—Specifies the space before or after new paragraphs (hard returns), independent of the line spacing (leading) within each paragraph (**Figure 12.32**)

✔ Tips

- Hanging punctuation allows punctuation marks to appear outside the text box. To enable hanging punctuation, select the paragraph text and choose Roman Hanging Punctuation from the Paragraph panel's pop-up menu.

- After Effects determines line breaks in paragraph text using either of two methods you specify in the Paragraph panel's pop-up menu: Adobe Single-Line or Every-Line Composer. For more about these methods, consult After Effects Help.

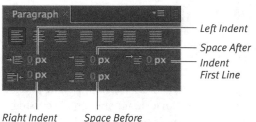

Left Indent
Space After
Indent First Line
Right Indent   Space Before

Figure 12.30 In the Paragraph panel, specify the amount you want to indent the text from the sides of the text box, and the space between paragraphs.

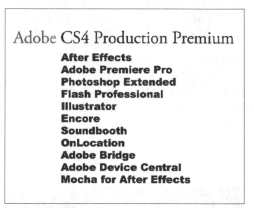

Adobe CS4 Production Premium

After Effects
Adobe Premiere Pro
Photoshop Extended
Flash Professional
Illustrator
Encore
Soundbooth
OnLocation
Adobe Bridge
Adobe Device Central
Mocha for After Effects

Figure 12.31 This example shows a single text layer, but the list is indented.

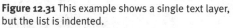

Need to learn Premiere Pro fast?
Try a Visual QuickPro!

Takes a visual, task-based approach to teaching Premiere Pro, using pictures to guide you through the software and show you what to do.

Works like a reference book -- you look up what you need and then get straight to work.

Concise, straightforward steps and explanations offer the fastest way to learn tasks and concepts.

Affordably priced, because buying a computer book shouldn't be an investment in itself.

Figure 12.32 Here, a single text layer contains several paragraphs. Increasing the default Space After Value creates extra space between paragraphs.

FORMATTING PARAGRAPH TEXT

Figure 12.33 Select the type you want to convert into paths, You can select characters or the entire text layer (shown here).

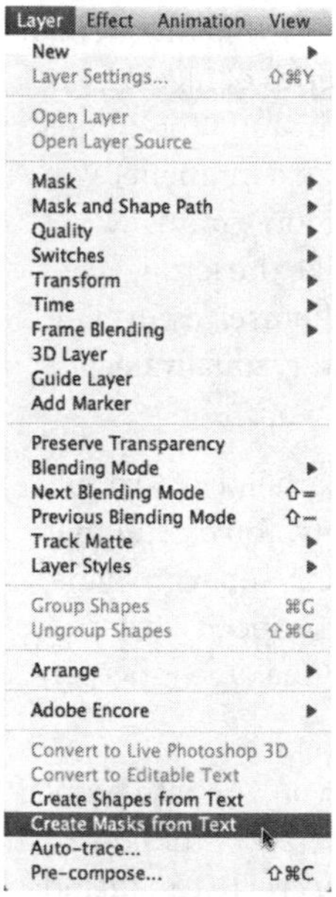

Figure 12.34 Choose Layer > Create Shapes from Text to create a shape layer from the selection; choose Layer > Create Masks from Text to create a solid containing a mask path of the selection.

Figure 12.35 Depending on your choice, After Effects creates a path-based shape layer based on the text (shown here)...

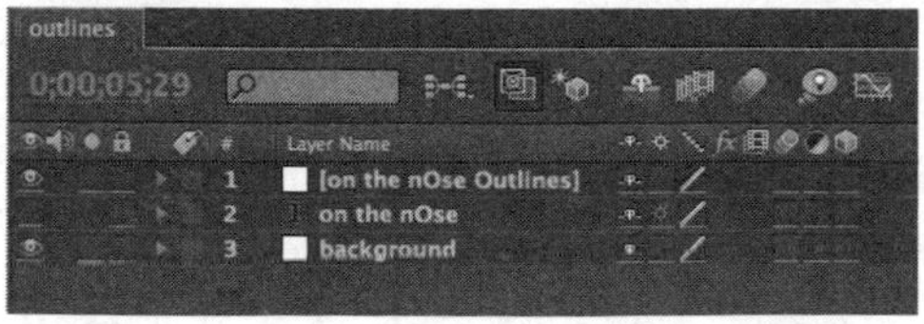

Figure 12.36 ...or a solid containing a mask path based on the text (shown here). In both cases, the text layer's video switch is turned off automatically.

Creating Masks and Shapes from Text

Converting text into mask or shape paths lets you use traditional text tools to work with type, and then enjoy the unique advantages of path-based shapes or masks. For example, you can copy a shape or mask path to a motion path (as you saw in Chapter 10, "Mask Essentials") or apply path-based effects. Or you can animate one mask path's shape into another. By converting type into a shape layer path, you can specify options unique to shapes. For example, unlike a text layer's stroke, a shape layer's stroke can become animated dashes, or a wiggly line. (To review mask paths, turn back to Chapter 10; for more about shape layers, read on through Chapter 14, "More Layer Techniques.")

To create mask or shape paths from text:

1. Create and format a text layer, and arrange the layer in the comp.

2. Select the text you want to convert into paths (**Figure 12.33**).You can select the entire text layer, or highlight any range of characters in the layer.

3. Choose either of the following (**Figure 12.34**):

   Layer > Create Shapes from Text to create a shape layer from the selection

   Layer > Create Masks from Text to create a solid with a mask path from the selection

   Depending on your choice, a new shape layer (**Figure 12.35**) or a solid containing a mask (**Figure 12.36**) appears above the text layer you selected in Step 1. The new layer uses the text layer's name with the word *Outlines* appended to it.

Animating Text

In most respects, text layers are just like other layers, and they include the same layer properties you learned about in Chapter 7, "Properties and Keyframes." But text layers have a number of unique text properties, as well. You can animate the layer and the text within the layer. But, unlike other layers, you can't open a text layer in a Layer panel.

Standard layer properties

Text layers include the same transform properties—Anchor Point, Position, Scale, Rotation, and Opacity—that you find in any layer (and learned about in Chapter 7). Text layers accept masks and effects; and, like other layers, you can make a text layer 3D. But the standard layer property controls affect the *layer as a whole*; they can't alter the content of the text (what it says) or apply to characters individually (not without using masks, anyway).

Text properties

A special set of text properties makes it possible to animate words or individual characters without complex keyframing, elaborate masking techniques, or resorting to using numerous text layers:

Source text—Lets you change the content of a text message over time. This way, a single text layer can convey a series of messages. Used in combination with animator groups and selectors (described in a moment), you can change the content more gradually. For example, you can make the letters in a word appear to encode themselves, cycling through other letters, and gradually decode themselves into another word.

Path text—Lets you make a line of text follow a path that you specify. You can animate the border to make the text appear to glide over the path. You can also specify other options, such as whether the type is perpendicular to the path.

Animator groups—Let you animate properties of any range of characters within the text. Each animator group you create can include any number or combination of properties, including both familiar transform properties and properties unique to text. You can specify the range of text affected by the animator properties with one or more *range selectors*. Numerous other options let you fine-tune the animation.

Figure 12.37 Create a text layer, and format and arrange it into its initial state (before animating it).

Animating Source Text

You can animate a text layer's *source text* (the content of the text message). Source text keyframes always use hold interpolation. As you can see in the section, "Interpolation Types," in Chapter 9, *hold interpolation* retains a keyframe value until the next keyframe value is reached. The message instantly changes to the text you specify at each keyframe. This way, a single layer can contain multiple text messages; you don't have to create multiple layers.

Note that you can change the source text while animating other properties. For example, by creating an animator group and animating the Character Offset property, you can change the characters in a word—encoding or decoding it. Changing an encoded word's source text during the animation lets you make one word change into another.

To animate source text:

1. Create and format a text layer, and arrange the layer in the comp (**Figure 12.37**).

   To create the text layer, use techniques described earlier in this chapter. To arrange the layer in the comp, use techniques covered in Chapter 5, "Layer Basics," and Chapter 6, "Layer Editing."

2. Set the current time to the frame where you want the message you created in step 1 to begin.

continues on next page

3. In the Timeline panel, expand the text layer's property outline, and click the Stopwatch icon ⬤ for the layer's Source Text property (**Figure 12.38**).

   An initial keyframe is created for the Source Text property. Source text keyframes always use the hold interpolation method (see Chapter 9, "Keyframe Interpolation").

4. Set the current time to the frame where you want a new message to appear.

5. Select the text, and type a new message (**Figure 12.39**).

   A new Hold keyframe appears at the current time for the layer's Source Text property (**Figure 12.40**).

6. Repeat steps 4 and 5 as needed.

   When you preview the animation, each message appears until the current time reaches the next source text keyframe.

✔ Tip

■ Another way to alter the shape of text (or any layer with an alpha channel) is to use the Puppet effect, covered in Chapter 14, "More Layer Techniques."

Figure 12.38 In the text layer's property outline, click the Source Text property's Stopwatch icon to create an initial keyframe.

Figure 12.39 Set the current time to the frame where you want the message to change, and edit the text...

Figure 12.40 ...to create a new Hold keyframe for the Source Text property (seen here in the layer outline).

Figure 12.41 Create a text layer and, with the layer selected, create a mask path.

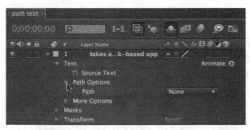

Figure 12.42 In the Timeline panel, expand the text layer's property outline to reveal its Path Options property heading.

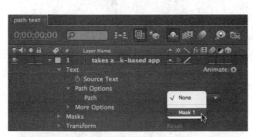

Figure 12.43 Choose the path you want the text to follow in the Path pop-up menu.

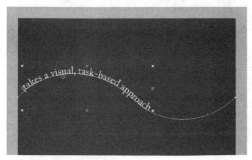

Figure 12.44 The text follows the path.

Making Text Follow a Path

You can make the type in any text layer follow a path you specify without sacrificing any of the formatting or text animation options available to the text layer.

To create path text:

1. Create and format a text layer.

   You can use any of the techniques discussed earlier in this chapter.

2. With the text layer selected, create a mask path to serve as the baseline of the text (**Figure 12.41**).

   Use any of the techniques described in Chapter 10, "Mask Essentials." In the Timeline panel, the mask you create appears in the text layer's property outline.

3. In the Timeline panel, expand the text layer's property outline; then, expand its Text property heading and Path Options property heading (**Figure 12.42**).

4. In the Path pop-up menu, choose the path you created in step 2 (**Figure 12.43**).

   The text uses the specified path as its baseline (**Figure 12.44**).

To animate path text:

1. Create path text as described in the previous task, "To create path text."

2. Set the current time to the frame where you want the animation to begin.

3. In the path text layer's property outline, set the First Margin value to specify the text's starting point on the path, and click the Stopwatch icon ![stopwatch] to set the initial keyframe (**Figure 12.45**).

4. Set the current time to the frame where you want the animation to end, and set the First Margin value to set the text's starting point on the path when the animation ends (**Figure 12.46**).

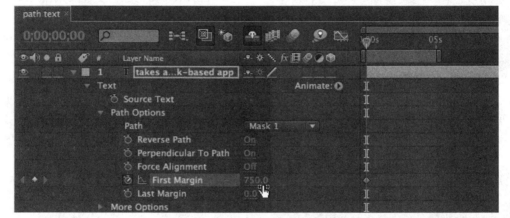

Figure 12.45 Set the current time to the frame where you want the animation to begin, and set a keyframe for the First Margin property value by clicking its Stopwatch icon.

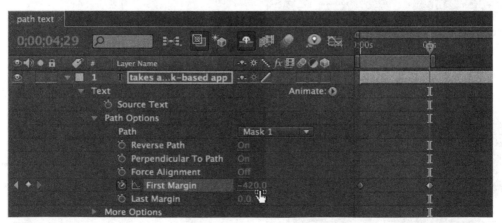

Figure 12.46 Set the current time to the frame where you want the animation to end, and change the First Margin property value to its final position along the path.

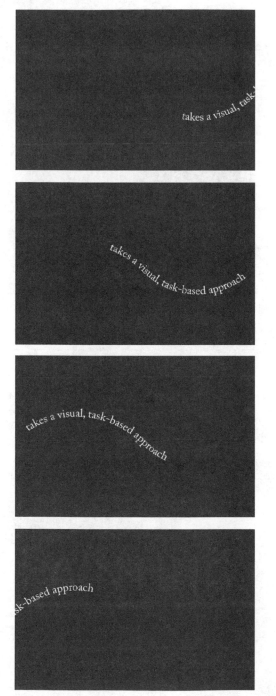

When you preview the animation, the text moves along the path (**Figure 12.47**). Use the techniques covered in Chapter 7, "Properties and Keyframes," and Chapter 9, "Keyframe Interpolation," to refine the animation.

Figure 12.47 Animating the First Margin property moves the text along the path.

Using Text Animation Presets

After Effects includes a generous and varied collection of text animation presets, conveniently sorted by category in the Effects & Presets panel (**Figure 12.48**). You're just as likely to modify one of these excellent presets as you are to build a text animation from scratch.

As you did with text animation, you should start by examining some of the presets. Once you see what text animation can do, dig into the sections on animator groups to find out what makes them tick and, ultimately, how to create your own.

To apply a text animation preset using Adobe Bridge:

1. Create and format a text layer, and select the layer (**Figure 12.49**).

   Make sure to select the entire text layer, not just a range of characters. To animate part of a text layer, you can use range selectors (as explained in the "Range Selectors" section, later in this chapter).

Figure 12.48 The Effects & Presets panel contains numerous preset text animations.

Figure 12.49 Create and format a text layer.

USING TEXT ANIMATION PRESETS

Animation	View	Window	Help
Save Animation Preset...			
Apply Animation Preset...			
Recent Animation Presets		▶	
Browse Presets...			
Add Keyframe			
Toggle Hold Keyframe		⌥⌘H	
Keyframe Interpolation...		⌥⌘K	
Keyframe Velocity...		⇧⌘K	
Keyframe Assistant		▶	
Animate Text		▶	
Add Text Selector		▶	
Remove All Text Animators			
Add Expression		⌥⇧=	
Separate Dimensions			
Track Motion			
Stabilize Motion			
Track this Property			
Reveal Animating Properties		U	
Reveal Modified Properties			

Figure 12.50 Choose Animation > Browse Presets.

2. Choose Animation > Browse Presets (**Figure 12.50**).

Adobe Bridge opens and displays the contents of the Presets folder within the After Effects CS4 folder.

3. To view text animation samples by category, click the appropriate link (**Figure 12.51**).

continues on next page

Figure 12.51 Click the category of text animations for which you want to see examples.

4. In Adobe Bridge, double-click the text animation preset you want to apply to the selected text (**Figure 12.52**).

The preset you specify is applied to the selected text (**Figure 12.53**). For more about using the Effects & Presets panel, see Chapter 11, "Effects Fundamentals."

You can modify the effect by changing the position or value of its keyframed text animation properties (as explained in Chapter 7, "Properties and Keyframes"). You can also add, delete, or modify the preset effect's animator properties or range selector values (as explained later in this chapter).

Figure 12.52 With the text layer selected, double-click the text preset you want in the Effects & Presets panel.

✔ Tips

■ If no text layer or type is selected when you select a text animation preset in Adobe Bridge, After Effects creates a new text layer containing the words, "Adobe After Effects," that uses the text animation. You can edit the content or animation as you would for any text layer.

■ As you learned in Chapter 11, "Effects Fundamentals." you can apply an animation preset—including a text animation preset—by selecting the layer and double-clicking the name of the preset in the Effects & Presets panel.

Figure 12.53 The preset is applied to the selected text layer.

Understanding Animator Groups

You animate type by adding one or more animator groups to a text layer. Animator groups appear in the layer outline under a text layer's Text property heading (**Figure 12.54**). You create an animator group by choosing a property you want to affect in the layer's Animator pop-up menu. You can add as many groups as you need to achieve the animation you want.

Each animator group consists of at least one *animator property* and one *selector*. You can add properties and selectors to a group by using its Add pop-up menu.

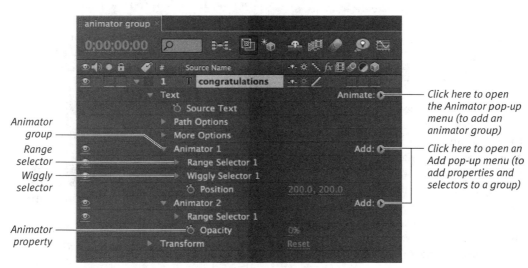

Animator group

Range selector

Wiggly selector

Animator property

Click here to open the Animator pop-up menu (to add an animator group)

Click here to open an Add pop-up menu (to add properties and selectors to a group)

Figure 12.54 Animator groups appear in the layer outline.

Animator properties

Animator properties include familiar trans-form properties (such as position, rotation, and so on). With type, however, each charac-ter, word, or line can possess its own anchor point. You can also animate properties unique to text (fill, stroke, tracking, and so on), as well as per-character blur. You can even set each character's value—the numerical code that determines which character is displayed. You can also enable Per-Character 3D, which endows text characters with the same 3D properties you can give layers.

Each animator group can have any number and combination of properties, which can be set to any value. But unlike when you're animating layers, you probably won't animate the property values to create the animation. Instead, you'll animate the range of charac-ters affected by the properties by keyframing a selector.

Range selectors

A selector lets you specify a *range*, or the part of the type that's affected by an anima-tor group's properties. Most animations are achieved by animating the range, not the properties. Selectors are comparable to layer masks in that they limit the areas affected by your adjustments. Just as you can add multiple masks to a layer, you can add multiple selec-tors to an animator group. Multiple selectors let you specify ranges that you couldn't define with a single selector (such as a noncontinuous range of characters). And like masks, you can specify how multiple ranges interact by choosing a mode. You can fine-tune the rate and manner in which the range includes units by specifying a number of options listed under the range selector's Advanced category in the expanded property outline.

In addition to a standard range selector, you can apply a *wiggly selector* to vary the selec-tion, giving it a more random or organic feel. You can also specify an *expression selector*, which can link the selection to another prop-erty or base it on a mathematical function.

As you might guess, the scope of this chapter prevents a detailed discussion of every animator group property and range selector option and their possible combinations. The following sections start with an overview of the text animation process and then go on to describe how to specify animator group properties and ranges. For a detailed expla-nation of the numerous options, see After Effects Help.

✔ Tip

■ In After Effects, an "expression" is a JavaScript-based formula that can gener-ate property values without keyframes. An expression selector controls an animator group's Amount property in a text layer. Expressions can be applied to any property in any layer, as explained in Chapter 16, "Complex Projects."

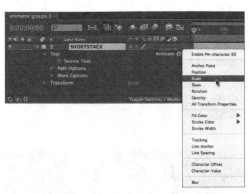

Figure 12.55 To create an animator group, choose a property in the Animate pop-up menu.

Figure 12.56 The new animator group includes the property you selected and a range selector.

Figure 12.57 Set the property values. Here, the type's vertical scale has been increased. Until you limit the range, the property value affects all of the text.

Animating Type with Animator Groups

As you gleaned from the previous section, "Understanding Animator Groups," animator groups grant you a great deal of control over text animation and can include numerous components.

The following task provides an overview of the steps required to create a simple text animation. The basic steps include creating an animator group, specifying its property value and range, and then animating the range. For the sake of clarity, the task doesn't mention particular property and selector options. It also doesn't include steps to add animator groups or to add properties or selectors to existing groups. Follow this task to create a simple animation, and then explore later sections to add complexity to your text animations.

To animate type with animator groups:

1. Create and format a text layer.

   Use the techniques explained earlier in this chapter.

2. In the Timeline panel, expand the text layer to reveal its Text property heading.

3. In the Timeline panel, choose the Text property you want to animate from the Animate pop-up menu (**Figure 12.55**).

   An Animator property heading appears under the layer's Text property heading. The Animator property contains a Range Selector property heading and the property you specified (**Figure 12.56**).

4. Set the values for the property you specified in step 3 (**Figure 12.57**).

   The values are applied to the entire text. You can limit the range of affected characters in step 5. Typically, you'll animate the range, not the property values (as explained in the next step).

   continues on next page

5. Set the current time, and specify values for the range selector.

   You can set the range by dragging the Range Start ◄ and Range End ► icons in the Comp panel (**Figure 12.58**) or by setting Start and End values in the property outline. For details, see "Specifying a Range," later in this chapter.

6. For the range properties you want to animate, click the Stopwatch icon to set the initial keyframe at the current time.

   You can set keyframes for any combination of the selector's Start, End, and Offset values (**Figure 12.59**).

7. Set the current time to another frame, and change the animated range property values to set another keyframe (**Figure 12.60**).

   For example, you can increase the range over time by animating the range's End property, or you can make the range travel through the characters by animating the Offset property.

8. If necessary, repeat step 7 to create additional keyframes.

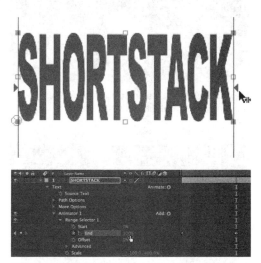

Figure 12.58 Set the current time, and specify values for the range. In this example, the range's end has been moved next to its start, so the property doesn't affect any of the characters at the beginning of the animation.

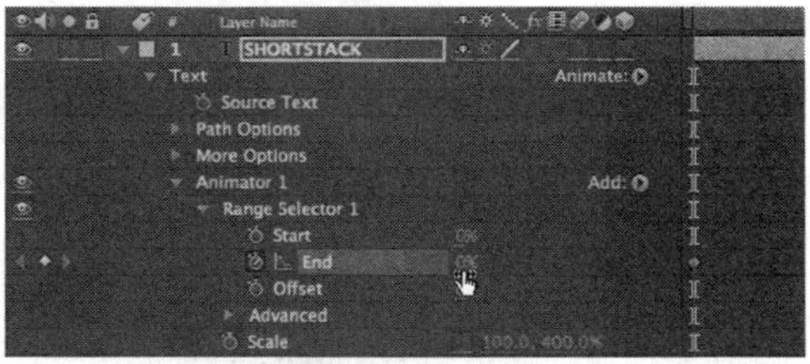

Figure 12.59 Click the Stopwatch icon to set the initial keyframe. Here, an initial keyframe is set for the end of the range.

Figure 12.60 Set the current time to another frame and change the range. Here, the current time is set 2 seconds later, and the end of the range has been moved from its original position (shown in Figure 12.58) so that all the characters are affected.

SHORTSTACK

SHORTSTACK

SHORTSTACK

SHORTSTACK

SHORTSTACK

SHORTSTACK

Figure 12.61 Previewing the animation shows how animating the range changes which parts of the text are affected by the animator property you set.

9. Preview the type animation using any of the techniques covered in Chapter 8, "Playback, Previews, and RAM."

As the range animates, different parts of the text are affected by the properties in the animator group (**Figure 12.61**).

✔ Tip

■ As with other elements in a project (comps, duplicate layers, expressions, and so on), it's a good idea to give animator groups and range selectors unique names. Doing so makes it easier to distinguish them and to ascertain their purpose at a glance. Select the animator or range selector, press Return (Enter), edit the name, and press Return (Enter) when you're finished.

Creating Animator Groups

You can add any number of animator groups to a text layer, and each animator group can contain any combination of properties and range selectors. However, each group must contain at least one property and one selector.

To create an animator group:

1. If necessary, expand the text layer's property outline in the Timeline panel.

2. In the Switches/Modes panel of the Timeline, choose a property from the text layer's Animate pop-up menu (across from the layer's Text property) (**Figure 12.62**).

   An Animator property heading appears under the layer's Text property heading. The Animator property (Animator 1 by default) contains a Range Selector property heading (Range Selector 1 by default) and the property you specified (**Figure 12.63**).

To add to an animator group:

1. If necessary, expand the layer outline of a text layer containing at least one animator.

2. In the Switches/Modes panel of the Timeline, choose an option from the animator's Add pop-up menu (**Figure 12.64**):

   ▲ **Property** adds a property to the specified animator.

   ▲ **Selector** adds a selector to the specified animator.

   The property or selector is added to the animator (**Figure 12.65**).

To remove a group, property, or selector:

◆ In a text layer's property outline, select an animator group, animator property, or selector, and press Delete.

   The selected item is removed from the layer.

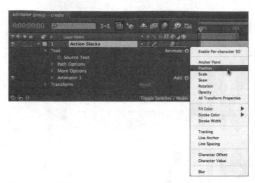

Figure 12.62 To create an animator group, choose a property from the Animate pop-up menu.

Figure 12.63 The animator group appears in the text layer's property outline; it contains the property and a default range selector.

Figure 12.64 To add a property or selector to an existing animator group, select the appropriate option from the group's Add pop-up menu.

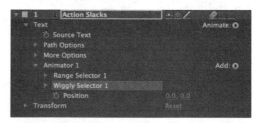

Figure 12.65 The group includes the added item. In this example, an additional selector has been added to the group.

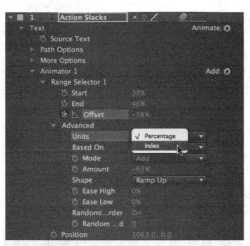

Figure 12.66 In the Units pop-up menu, choose whether range values are expressed as a percentage of the entire type or are expressed by indexing, or numbering, each unit.

Figure 12.67 For Based On, choose the units on which the range is based.

Specifying a Range

You can set a range either by dragging its left and right borders in the Comp panel or by using controls in the text layer's property outline. A range can be applied to different units of type: each character, word, or line. When you're specifying a range, these units are measured either in terms of a percentage of total units, or by the unit (1, 2, 3, and so on).

To specify how a range is measured:

1. In the layer outline of the Timeline panel, expand the range selector you want to adjust, and expand its Advanced property heading.

2. To specify how Start, End, and Offset range values are expressed, choose an option in the Units pop-up menu (**Figure 12.66**):

   ▲ **Percentage** expresses values in percentages.

   ▲ **Index** expresses values according to a numerical indexing scheme in which the first unit of text is assigned a value of 1, the next unit 2, and so on.

3. To specify the units on which a range is based (how the range is counted), choose an option in the Based On pop-up menu (**Figure 12.67**):

   ▲ **Characters**—Counts each character, including spaces, as a unit in the range.

   ▲ **Characters Excluding Spaces**—Counts each character as a unit in the range but excludes spaces.

   ▲ **Words**—Counts each word as a unit in the range.

   ▲ **Lines**—Counts each line (of a multi-line text layer) as a unit in the range.

The values for Start, End, and Offset are based on the option you specify.

To specify a range:

1. Expand the text layer animator group you want to adjust, and then expand the range selector you want to set.

2. To set the start of the range, *do either of the following:*
   ▲ In the text layer's expanded outline, specify a value for Start.
   ▲ With the text layer's Animator group heading selected in the expanded outline, drag the Range Start icon⁺ in the Composition panel (**Figure 12.68**).

3. To set the end of the range, *do either of the following:*
   ▲ In the text layer's expanded outline, specify a value for End.
   ▲ With the text layer's Animator property selected, drag the Range End icon⁺ in the Composition panel (**Figure 12.69**).

4. To change both the Start and End values by the same amount, specify an Offset value in the text layer's expanded outline (**Figure 12.70**).

Figure 12.68 With the range selected in the property outline, you can drag the start of the range in the Comp panel...

Figure 12.69 ...or drag the Range End icon to set the end of the range.

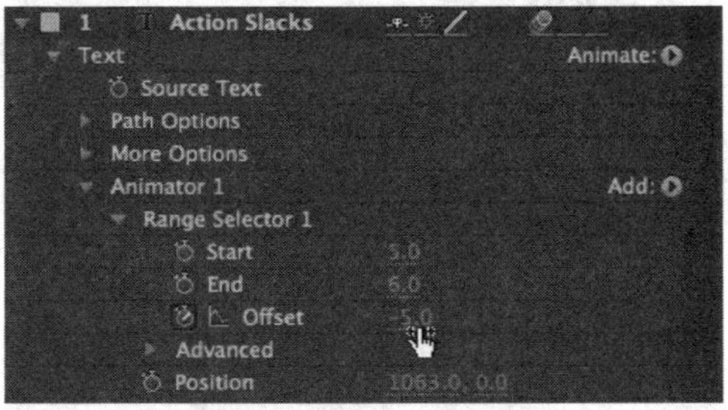

Figure 12.70 To change both the Start and End values by the same amount, change the Offset value in the property outline.

PAINTING ON A LAYER

Although it appears as a single effect in the layer's property outline, the Paint effect feels like an entirely separate set of features meriting a chapter of its own. The Tools panel includes several tools devoted to painting: the Brush, the Eraser, and the Clone Stamp. The Paint feature's numerous options require two specialized panels: the Paint panel and the Brushes panel. With the Brush and Eraser tools, you can simulate hand-writing, create hand-drawn graphics, or alter a layer's alpha channel to create (or fix) a track matte. Or you can make more subtle adjustments to an image with each stroke by using Blending modes. You can also use a Clone Stamp tool to retouch an image or to aid in tasks like wire removal.

Using your mouse—or, better yet, a tablet and stylus—you can record strokes directly onto a layer in real time, change their characteristics, and play them back in a number of ways. The Brushes panel includes a varied set of preset brushes and allows you to create and save your own variations—small or large, hard or soft-edged, round or ellipti-cal. Because strokes are vector-based, you can scale them without adversely affecting resolution. And like all effects, brush strokes are nondestructive, which means they don't alter your source files. Even strokes you make with the Eraser tool are nondestructive.

The Paint effect also deserves special attention because of its unique animation para-digm. Each stroke appears as its own layer within a layer—that is, each stroke appears as a duration bar within the Paint effect. This lets you toggle strokes on and off, control how they're layered, control how they interact with strokes lower in the stacking order, and precisely adjust when and how quickly they appear.

In this chapter, you'll learn this single effect's numerous options so you can explore its unlimited possibilities.

Using the Paint and Brushes Panels

After Effects includes two panels for controlling Paint: the Paint panel and Brushes panel. Both panels are nearly identical to their counterparts in other Adobe programs.

The panels are part of the Paint preset workspace. You can also summon the panels by clicking the Tools panel's Toggle Panels button  whenever the Brush, Clone Stamp, or Eraser tool is selected (**Figure 13.1**).

Figure 13.1 Clicking the Toggle Panels button when the Brush, Clone Stamp, or Eraser tool is selected...

To specify the Paint workspace:

◆ In the Tools panel's Workspace pop-up menu, select Paint (**Figure 13.2**).

   After Effects arranges the workspace automatically and includes the Paint and Brushes panels (**Figures 13.3** and **13.4**).

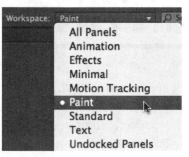

Figure 13.2 ...or selecting Paint from the Workspace pop-up menu...

Figure 13.3 ...opens the Paint panel...

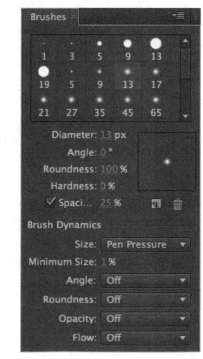

Figure 13.4 ...and the Brushes panel.

Figure 13.5 Opacity determines the paint's coverage strength; Flow determines the speed of coverage. Here, the words Opacity and flow are repeated, each time using a lower Opacity or Flow setting, respectively.

Specifying Paint Stroke Options

Before you start using the Brush and Eraser tools, take a moment to get a more detailed understanding of each option, starting with the options at the top of the Paint panel. These options not only allow you to control the character and color of each stroke but also let you specify which of the layer's channels are affected by each stroke and how long strokes appear.

Depending on the options you choose, you can make visible strokes, resembling those made by a loaded paintbrush or by an airbrush lightly applying each coat; or you can make strokes that affect the layer's alpha channel, effectively creating or modifying a matte. The strokes can appear for any length of time or reenact the painting process. Later, you'll specify many of the same options to determine the effects of the Clone Stamp tool.

Generally, you set these options before you paint a stroke. However, you can change these and most other options by selecting the stroke under the Paint effect and adjusting its values in the property outline.

Opacity and Flow settings

Opacity and Flow settings determine the paint's coverage strength and the speed of coverage, respectively. Together, they can make paint seem opaque or semitransparent (**Figure 13.5**). When you're using the Eraser, the same options determine how effectively and quickly pixels are removed:

Opacity—Sets the maximum opacity of each stroke, from 0 percent to 100 percent; opacity is analogous to how well a real-world paint covers a surface. (A brush's Hardness setting also contributes to a stroke's opacity near its edges.)

Flow—Determines how quickly paint is applied with each stroke, from 0 percent to 100 percent. Lower Flow settings apply less of the paint color in a stroke, making the paint appear more transparent; low Flow values also result in greater spaces between brush marks when the brush's Spacing option is active (see "Customizing Brushes," later in this chapter).

Brush tip

As you'd expect, the brush tip simulates the camel hair on the end of a brush (or the point of a pen, or the spray pattern of an airbrush). Brush settings define the character of strokes. The Paint panel displays the currently selected brush tip as an icon that represents its roundness, angle, and hardness settings; a number indicates the brush's size, in pixels (**Figure 13.6**). Clicking the current Brush Tip icon activates (or if necessary, opens) the Brushes panel, from which you can select a preset brush tip or create your own (see "Using Brushes," later in this chapter) (**Figure 13.7**).

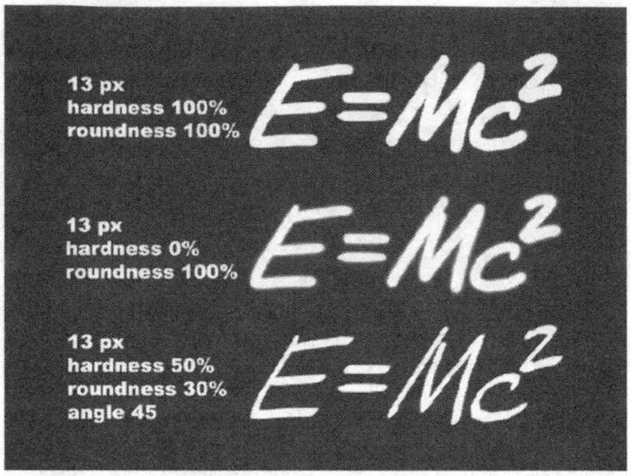

Figure 13.6 This figure shows strokes created by various brushes.

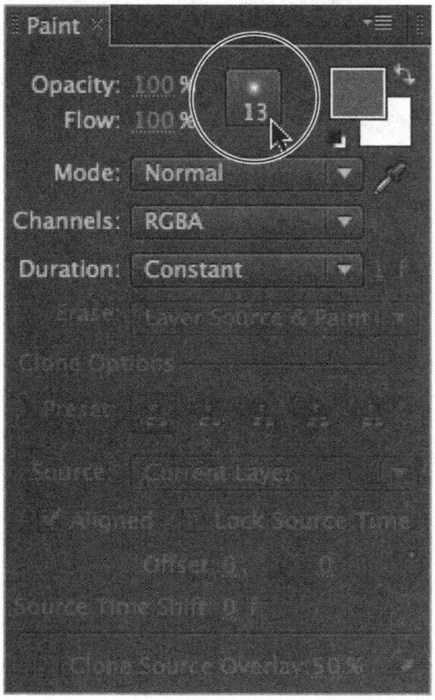

Figure 13.7 In the Paint panel, click the current Brush icon to reveal the Brushes panel.

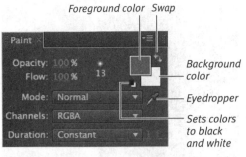

Figure 13.8 In the Paint panel, the upper-left swatch sets the foreground color; the lower-right swatch sets the background, or secondary color.

Figure 13.9 You can set how brushes interact with lower strokes or the underlying image with Blending modes. Here, a soft, transparent brush uses a Dodge mode to lighten shadows in this photo.

Figure 13.10 In this example, strokes are painted on the layer's alpha channel to reveal the parts of the layer's image (a tangerine) just as a mask or matte would do. The Paint effect's Paint on Transparent option is on.

Color

The Paint panel lets you choose the color you want to use. The upper-left swatch sets the *foreground color*, which specifies the paint applied by the brush; the lower-right swatch sets the *background color*, or secondary color. Clicking a swatch lets you choose a color from a color picker, or you can sample a color from the screen using a standard Eyedropper tool ▨. Click the smaller icon to reset the foreground and background colors to black and white, respectively; click the Swap icon ▨ to switch the colors (**Figure 13.8**).

Mode

The Mode pop-up menu lets you specify how each stroke interacts with underlying pixels (**Figure 13.9**). The menu's Blending mode options are summarized in Chapter 14, "More Layer Techniques." However, the stroke Blending mode menu doesn't include the Dissolve or Dancing Dissolve Blending modes. Note that each stroke can use a Blending mode, and the layer containing the paint effect (and all its strokes) can use a Blending mode also.

Channels

The Channels pop-up menu specifies which of the layer's channels are affected by a stroke. You can affect the visible red, green, and blue (RGB) channels, the alpha channel (which defines transparency), or all channels (RGBA). Painting on a layer's RGB channels creates visible strokes, whereas painting on its alpha channel affects its transparent areas. For example, you can animate strokes applied to a layer's alpha channel to reveal portions of the layer's image (**Figure 13.10**).

Duration

The Duration pop-up menu specifies how strokes are displayed over time. Duration options facilitate animating strokes the way you want—or if you prefer, keeping them static:

Constant—Displays all strokes from the current time to the end of the layer containing the stroke.

Write On—Reveals the stroke over time, from beginning to end, depending on the speed at which you paint it. You can change the speed of the effect by adjusting each stroke's End property; you can reverse or create a Write Off effect by adjusting the strokes' Start property (**Figure 13.11**).

Single Frame—Displays the stroke at the current frame only.

Custom—Displays the stroke for the number of frames you specify. Set the duration by adjusting the value that appears next to the Duration pop-up menu (**Figure 13.12**).

These options set each stroke's initial duration and, in the case of Write On, the stroke's initial End property's keyframes. After a stroke is created, you can't change the Duration setting in the property outline, per se; instead, you control when strokes are displayed by manipulating their duration bars and by keyframing properties such as Start and End.

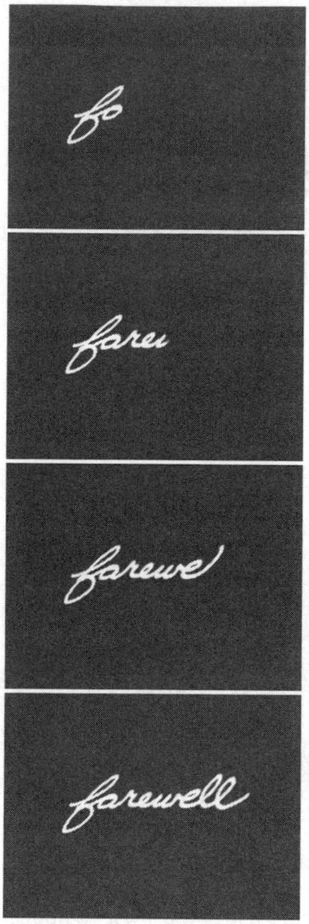

✔ Tips

- By applying certain modes, you can subtly retouch an image. Use a lightening mode (like Dodge) to brighten unwanted shadows. If necessary, animate the layer to follow the area you want to affect.

- By painting on the layer's alpha channel, you can use the advantages of various brush and duration options to affect the layer's transparency in ways that might be more difficult to do using masks or other methods.

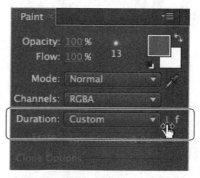

Figure 13.11 Strokes always start at the current time, but you can set how long they appear by setting a duration option. Here, the Write On option makes the strokes appear over time, to simulate handwriting.

Figure 13.12 When you choose a Custom duration, specify the number of frames for which you want the stroke to appear.

Figure 13.13 Select the Brush tool.

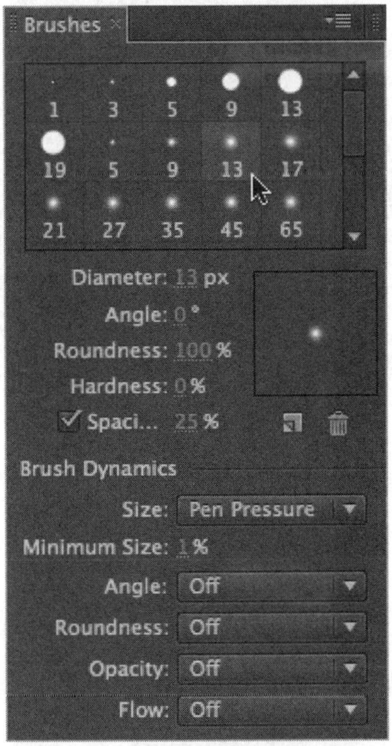

Brushes ×

1	3	5	9	13
19	5	9	13	17
21	27	35	45	65

Diameter: 13 px
Angle: 0 °
Roundness: 100 %
Hardness: 0 %
✓ Spaci... 25 %

Brush Dynamics

Size: Pen Pressure ▼
Minimum Size: 1 %
Angle: Off ▼
Roundness: Off ▼
Opacity: Off ▼
Flow: Off ▼

Figure 13.14 To change the current brush, choose a brush in the Brushes panel.

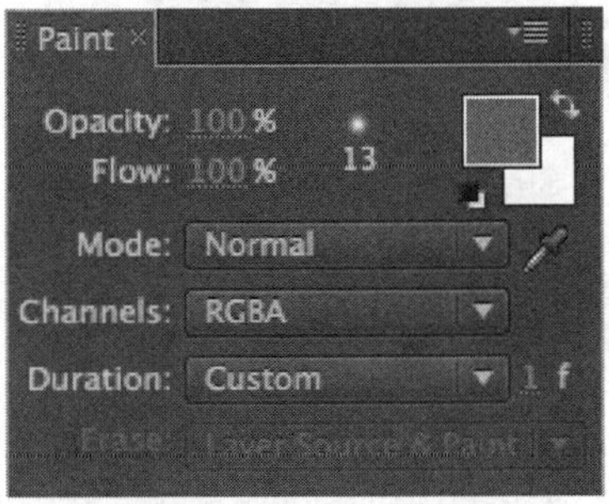

Paint ×

Opacity: 100 %
Flow: 100 %   13
Mode: Normal ▼
Channels: RGBA ▼
Duration: Custom ▼ 1 f
Erase: Layer Source & Paint ▼

Figure 13.15 In the Paint panel, specify the brush's Opacity, Flow, and Color.

Painting with the Brush Tool

Generally speaking, painting in After Effects is as easy as grabbing a brush and painting on the layer. But at the same time, this straightforward task includes numerous options. Not only can you change the characteristics of the brush, but you can also specify which channels the strokes modify and how long they appear on screen. (See the previous section, "Specifying Paint Stroke Options," for detailed descriptions of each menu option.)

To paint on a layer:

1. Open the layer you want to paint on in a Layer panel.

2. In the Tools panel, select the Brush tool ▨ (**Figure 13.13**).

   If the Auto Open Panels option is selected, the Paint and Brushes panels open.

3. In the Brushes panel, specify a brush (**Figure 13.14**).

   The selected brush becomes the current brush in the Paint panel.

4. In the Paint panel, specify options for the brush attributes (**Figure 13.15**):

   Opacity—Sets the relative opacity of pixels in a stroke.

   Flow—Sets the speed, or relative number of pixels applied with each stroke.

   Foreground Color—Sets the brush's color.

   Background Color—Sets a secondary color.

   continues on next page

5. To specify how brush strokes in the layer interact with the underlying image, choose a Blending mode from the Mode pop-up menu (**Figure 13.16**).

6. To specify the layer channels affected by the strokes, choose an option from the Channels pop-up menu (**Figure 13.17**).

7. To specify how strokes appear over time, choose an option from the Duration pop-up menu (**Figure 13.18**).

8. Set the current time to the frame where you want the first stroke to begin.

Figure 13.16 Choose a Blending mode from the Mode pop-up menu.

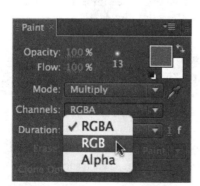

Figure 13.17 Specify the channels you want to paint on in the Channels pop-up menu. In this example, strokes are applied to the layer's RGB channels.

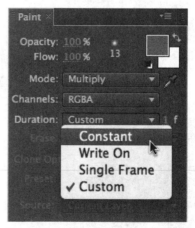

Figure 13.18 Choose how long you want the stroke to appear in the Duration pop-up menu. In this example, the strokes are set to appear from the current frame onward.

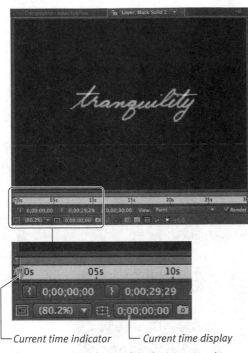

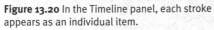

Current time indicator   *Current time display*

Figure 13.19 Drag the Brush in the Layer panel to create a stroke that starts at the current time. You can't paint in the Comp panel, but you can open a separate Comp panel to see the results.

Figure 13.20 In the Timeline panel, each stroke appears as an individual item.

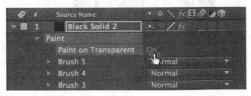

Figure 13.21 Under the Paint effect's property heading, set the Paint on Transparent option to On.

9. Using the Brush tool, drag in the Layer panel to paint strokes on the layer (**Figure 13.19**).

The mouse pointer appears as a circle that corresponds with the brush's size, angle, and roundness. Strokes use the options you specified. In the layer's property outline, the Paint effect appears. Expanding the Paint effect reveals that each stroke is listed separately and has a corresponding layer bar under the time ruler (**Figure 13.20**).

To make the painted layer transparent:

1. Select the layer containing the Paint effect.

2. In the layer's expanded property outline, expand the layer's Paint effect property heading.

or

Open the Effect Controls panel to view the layer's Paint effect.

3. Under the Paint effect's property heading, set the Paint on Transparent option to On (**Figure 13.21**).

The selected layer becomes transparent, leaving only the Paint effect visible.

✔ Tip

- The Paint effect discussed in this chapter must be applied to a layer in its Layer panel. After Effects also includes a Vector Paint effect that you can use to paint in the Comp panel. However, it uses a different toolset and procedures. See After Effects Help for details.

Erasing Strokes

In practice, the Eraser tool does just what you'd expect: It removes pixels from a layer. You can specify whether it affects the target layer's pixels and paint strokes, paint only, or just the most recent paint stroke.

It might be more accurate to say that the Eraser *negates* pixels rather than removes them. A look in the Paint effect's property outline reveals that Eraser strokes appear in the stacking order along with Brush strokes. Like the other paint options, Eraser strokes are nondestructive; they don't permanently affect either the layer or paint strokes. Turn off an Eraser stroke's video (by clicking its Eye icon 👁 in the timeline), and its effects disappear.

In most respects, the Eraser works like a brush—except it's an "anti-brush." The Eraser tool uses the same brushes as the Brush tool, but you can't apply a color to an eraser. And whereas a brush's Opacity and Flow settings control the strength of the brush—how thick you lay on the painted pixels—the same settings control how thoroughly the eraser removes pixels. Otherwise, the Eraser's settings are analogous to those of the Brush tool.

To use the Eraser tool:

1. In the Tools panel, select the Eraser tool ✎ (**Figure 13.22**).

2. In the Paint panel, specify values for Opacity and Flow (**Figure 13.23**).

   When you're using the Eraser tool, Opacity and Flow refer to the Eraser's strength.

3. To specify the layer channels affected by the strokes, choose an option from the Channels pop-up menu (**Figure 13.24**).

   ▲ **RGBA**—Erases pixels in the layer's red, green, blue, and alpha channels.

Figure 13.22 Select the Eraser tool.

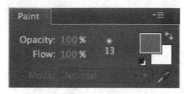

Figure 13.23 In the Paint panel, set the Opacity and Flow. These options help determine how completely pixels are removed with each stroke.

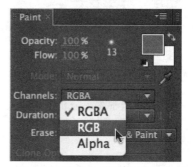

Figure 13.24 Choose which of the layer's channels are affected by the Eraser strokes in the Channels pop-up menu.

Figure 13.25 Choose how Eraser strokes remove pixels over time in the Duration pop-up menu.

ERASING STROKES

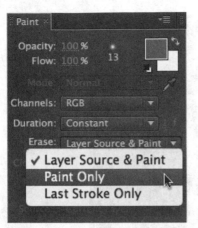

Figure 13.26 Specify the pixels affected by the eraser by choosing an option in the Erase pop-up menu.

Figure 13.27 Drag the eraser in the Layer panel to remove pixels.

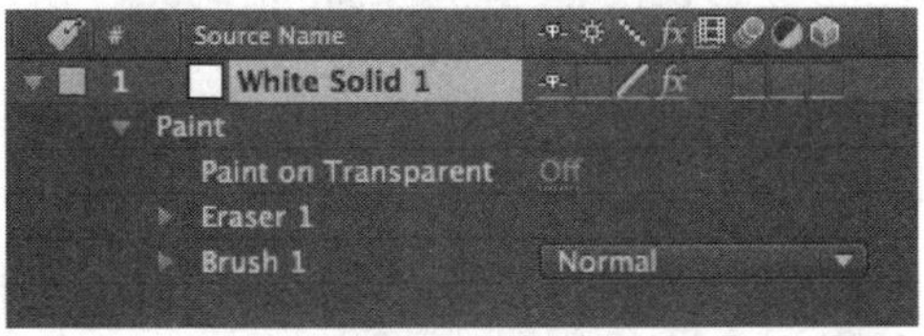

Figure 13.28 Like paint strokes, eraser strokes appear as individual items (including a layer bar) in the Paint effect's property outline.

▲ **RGB**—Erases pixels in the layer's red, green, and blue channels; alpha is unaffected.

▲ **Alpha**—Erases pixels in the layer's alpha channel (transparency information).

4. To specify how Eraser strokes remove pixels over time, choose an option from the Duration pop-up menu (**Figure 13.25**):

▲ **Constant**—Makes an Eraser stroke remain on the layer (and remove pixels) from the current time to the end of the layer containing the stroke.

▲ **Write On**—Draws the Eraser stroke over time, from beginning to end, depending on the speed at which you paint it.

▲ **Single Frame**—Allows the Eraser stroke to remove pixels at the current frame only.

▲ **Custom**—Allows the Eraser stroke to remove pixels for the number of frames you specify.

5. To specify the pixels affected by the eraser, choose an option from the Erase pop-up menu (**Figure 13.26**):

▲ **Layer Source & Paint**—Erases pixels in the source layer and any paint strokes at the same time.

▲ **Paint Only**—Erases pixels created by paint strokes.

▲ **Last Stroke Only**—Erases pixels created by the most recently painted paint stroke.

6. Using the Eraser tool, drag in the Layer panel to remove pixels from the layer (**Figure 13.27**).

Pixels are erased according to the options you specified. Expanding the Paint effect in the layer's property outline reveals that each eraser stroke is listed separately and has a corresponding layer bar under the time ruler (**Figure 13.28**).

Using Brushes

The brush you use determines the character of the strokes you paint with any of the paint tools (Brush, Eraser, or Clone Stamp). You can select from a number of preset brushes that appear in the Brushes panel. If the preset brushes aren't to your liking, you can create a brush that has a different "brush tip"—that is, one that has different characteristics, such as size, roundness, angle, and hardness. The following tasks explain how to choose, save, remove, and restore preset brushes. The section "Customizing Brushes," later in this chapter, covers each brush characteristic in detail.

To create a brush:

1. In the Brushes panel, specify the brush's attributes, including Diameter, Angle, Roundness, and so on (**Figure 13.29**).

   In the preview area of the Brushes panel, the brush's icon reflects your choices.

2. Click the Save icon .

   A Choose Name dialog box appears with a descriptive name for the brush already entered.

3. Leave the suggested name or enter a custom name for the new brush, and click OK (**Figure 13.30**).

   The brush appears selected among the other preset brushes (**Figure 13.31**). The new brush uses the attributes of the brush that was selected most recently. How presets appear in the panel depends on the option you choose in the Brushes panel's pop-up menu.

✔ Tip

- Options in the Brushes panel's pop-up menu let you customize the panel, such as the size of brush icons.

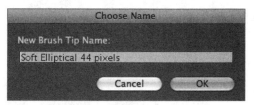

Figure 13.29 In the Brushes panel, set the brush's attributes and click the Save icon.

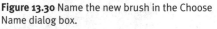

Figure 13.30 Name the new brush in the Choose Name dialog box.

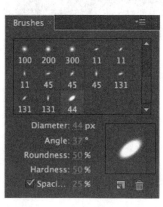

Figure 13.31 Your custom brush appears in the preset brushes area (shown here) and in Brushes Selector of the Paint panel.

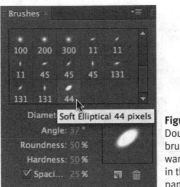

Figure 13.32
Double-click the brush you want to rename in the Brushes panel.

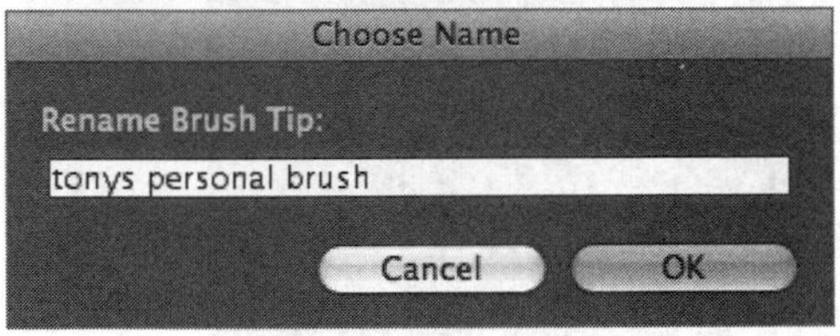

Choose Name

Rename Brush Tip:

tonys personal brush

Cancel   OK

Figure 13.33 Enter a new name in the Choose Name dialog box, and click OK.

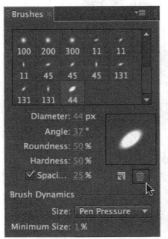

Figure 13.34
In the Brushes panel, click the brush you want to remove, and click the Delete (trash) icon.

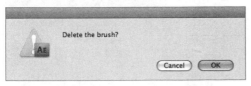

Delete the brush?

Cancel   OK

Figure 13.35 Confirm your choice by clicking OK.

To rename a preset brush:

1. In the Brushes panel, double-click the brush you want to rename (**Figure 13.32**). A Choose Name dialog box appears.

2. In the Choose Name dialog box, type a new name for the brush, and click OK (**Figure 13.33**).

To remove a preset brush:

1. In the Brushes panel, click the preset brush you want to remove, and click the Delete icon ▓ (**Figure 13.34**).

   After Effects prompts you to confirm your choice (**Figure 13.35**).

2. In the warning dialog box, click OK.

   The brush that you selected is removed from the list of presets (**Figure 13.36**).

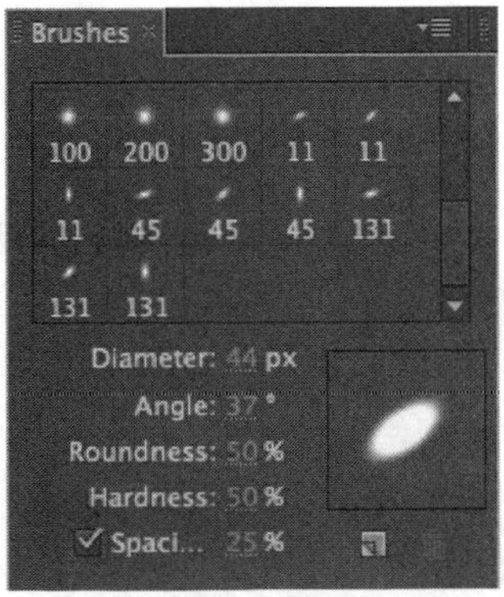

Figure 13.36
The selected brush is removed from the panel.

Customizing Brushes

Even though the Brushes panel includes a useful assortment of preset brushes, chances are you'll want to create your own brush to suit a particular task. As you learned in the previous section, "Using Brushes," you can save each of your special brushes as a preset that appears in the Brushes panel. Controlling a brush's attributes gives you a great deal of control over the character of the strokes it produces. This section covers the brush options; the next section, "Using Brush Dynamics," explains how to vary these qualities using a pen and tablet.

In the Brushes panel, you can specify the following attributes for each brush (**Figure 13.37**):

Diameter—The size, measured in pixels, across the diameter of the brush's widest axis (for elliptical brushes) (**Figure 13.38**).

Angle—The amount, measured in degrees, from which the widest axis of an elliptical brush deviates from the horizontal.

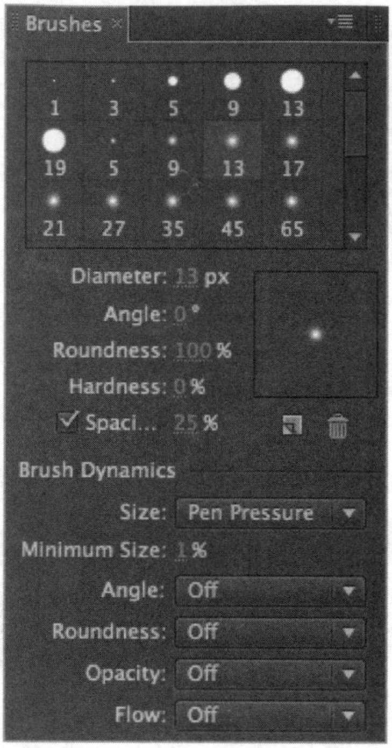

Figure 13.37 The Brushes panel includes several options that let you create custom brushes.

Figure 13.38 The strokes in this figure use different diameters.

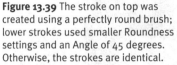

Figure 13.39 The stroke on top was created using a perfectly round brush; lower strokes used smaller Roundness settings and an Angle of 45 degrees. Otherwise, the strokes are identical.

Figure 13.40 These strokes are identical, except for their hardness settings.

Figure 13.41 These three words and their underlines are identical, except for their spacing values.

Roundness—The width of a brush's shortest diameter, expressed as a percentage of its widest diameter (determined by the Diameter value): 100 percent creates a circular brush; 0 percent creates a linear brush; intermediate values create an elliptical brush (**Figure 13.39**).

Hardness—The relative opacity of the brush's stroke from its center to the edges, analogous to feathering the edge of the brush. At 100 percent, the brush is opaque from its center to its edges (although the edge is antialiased); at 0 percent, the brush's edge has the maximum feather (although its center is opaque). Don't confuse hardness with the brush's overall opacity, which you can set in the Paint panel (**Figure 13.40**).

Spacing—The distance between brush marks within a stroke, expressed as a percentage of the brush's diameter. Setting Spacing to a relatively low value allows the brush to create continuous stroke marks; setting Spacing to a higher value causes the brush to make contact with the layer intermittently, creating a stroke with gaps between brush marks. The speed with which you paint the stroke also affects the spacing. Moving the brush more quickly as you paint results in greater spacing between marks (**Figure 13.41**). You can set the Spacing to values over 100 percent.

✔ Tip

- To restore the brush presets to their defaults, choose Reset Brush Tips in the Brushes panel's pop-up menu.

Using Brush Dynamics

You don't have to be a traditionalist to know that painting with a computer program isn't as tactile as using actual brushes and canvas. But swapping your mouse for a tablet and stylus can make you feel a lot more like a painter. Just as important, using a stylus makes your strokes look more painterly. That's because you can set the attributes of each stroke—its size, angle, roundness, opacity, and flow—to vary with the pressure you apply to the tablet or the tilt of the pen. If your stylus (sometimes referred to as a *pen*) has a wheel control, you can also use it to vary the brush.

To set Brush Dynamics options:

1. In the Brushes panel, make sure the Brush Dynamics options are visible.

2. For each of the attributes listed in the Brush Dynamics area, choose an option from the pop-up menu (**Figure 13.42**).

   Off—Disables the dynamic option and uses the static setting you specified elsewhere in the Brushes and Paint panels.

   Pen Pressure—Varies the attribute according to the pressure of the pen on the tablet; pressing harder increases the value.

   Pen Tilt—Varies the attribute according to the angle of the pen in relation to the tablet. For example, tilting the pen away from the angle perpendicular to the tablet can decrease the brush's roundness.

   Stylus Wheel—Varies the attribute when you scroll the pen's wheel control (a small roller on the side of the pen).

3. If you set the Size pop-up menu to an option other than Off, specify a Minimum Size (**Figure 13.43**).

   The brush's smallest possible diameter is limited by the value (1 percent–100 percent) you specify.

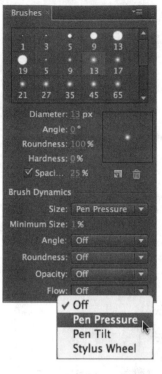

Figure 13.42 Specify which of the pen's characteristics affect each of the brush's attributes in the corresponding pop-up menu.

Figure 13.43 If you enabled Size, specify a Minimum Size.

Adjusting Strokes

As you learned in the chapter's introduction, Paint is an effect. It appears in the layer's property outline under its Effects category. But in contrast to other effects, the Effect Controls panel provides almost no controls for Paint. And whereas most effects include a single set of properties (however extensive they may be), the Paint effect lists each stroke individually, and each stroke contains its own set of properties.

Strokes are really layers within the layer containing the effect. Each stroke has its own duration bar, its own video switch, and its own set of properties that can be animated with keyframes (**Figure 13.44**). You can precisely control when each stroke appears and for how long. In the case of animated strokes, this paradigm lets you specify how quickly a stroke draws onto the screen and modify the stroke's shape.

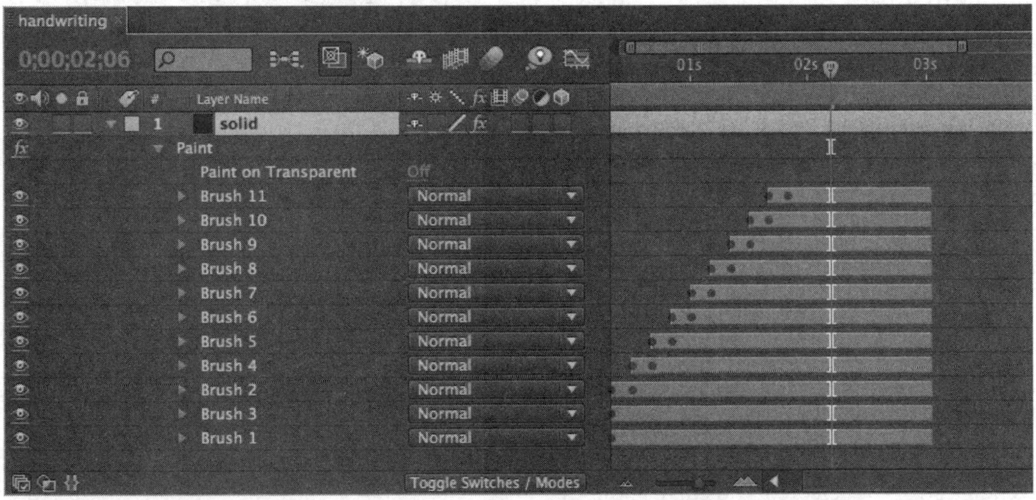

Figure 13.44 Each stroke has its own duration bar, its own video switch, and its own set of properties that you can animate with keyframes.

Strokes in the Timeline

Setting the current frame determines a stroke's initial In point. Its duration depends on the Duration option you specified in the Paint panel: Constant, Write On, Single Frame, or Custom (see the section "Specifying Paint Stroke Options" earlier in this chapter). As with layers, the strokes' stacking order in the property outline determines the order in which strokes are applied, and their Blending mode determines how they interact with strokes lower in the stack.

In general, you can manipulate strokes just as you would adjust layers: switch them on and off; change their stacking order; set their In and Out points and duration; and view, adjust, and keyframe their properties. However, the keyboard shortcuts you use with layers (cuing to or setting In and Out points, for example) don't work with strokes' duration bars.

In addition to all the properties that are unique to strokes, each stroke also includes its own set of Transform properties. You can use these to set each stroke's anchor point, position, scale, and rotation. Remember, for strokes, Opacity is listed in the Stroke Options property category (**Figure 13.45**).

Selecting strokes

Selecting a stroke in the layer's property outline makes it visible in the Layer panel. A stroke appears as a thin line running through the center of the painted line, much like a selected mask path is visible in the center of a stroked path. An Anchor Point icon appears at the beginning of the stroke (**Figure 13.46**). When a stroke is selected, you can use the Selection tool to drag it to a new position within the layer. (You can always move the layer within the comp, but doing so moves the entire layer—its image, its paint, and any other effects it contains.)

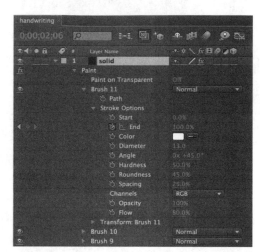

Figure 13.45 Each stroke includes Stroke Options and Transform properties.

Figure 13.46 A selected stroke (here, the "g") appears as a line in the center of the paint. An anchor point icon also appears at the beginning of each selected stroke.

Figure 13.47 To see and manipulate strokes in the Layer panel, choose the Paint effect in the Layer panel's View pop-up menu.

Figure 13.48 When the Layer contains more than one Paint effect, choose the one you want. Strokes of Paint effects higher in the stacking order are *visible*, but you can manipulate strokes in the selected effect only.

However, strokes appear in a Layer panel only when the Paint effect is selected in the Layer panel's View pop-up menu. This occurs automatically when you apply paint, but it can get confusing if you work on other tasks and return to the Layer panel to find the Paint effect is no longer selected—and no longer visible. The same holds true if the layer contains more than one Paint effect; make sure the Layer panel's View menu is set to the Paint effect you want.

Multiple Paint effects

Painting multiple strokes adds to the current Paint effect, and a single layer can contain more than one Paint effect. This can be useful when you want to treat sets of strokes as separate groups. For example, you can disable all of one Paint effect's strokes by clicking its Effect icon. However, the Layer panel can show only the Paint effect you specify in the View menu. The strokes of any Paint effects higher in the stacking order are *visible*, but you can't tell whether they're selected; Paint effects lower in the stacking order than the selected effect aren't visible in the Layer panel. You must choose a Paint effect in the View menu in order to view and drag its selected strokes in the Layer panel (**Figures 13.47** and **13.48**).

You can duplicate or add a Paint effect as you would any other effect. When you add strokes to a Paint effect, be sure to select the effect you want to modify in the layer's View menu.

✔ Tip

■ It can be useful to view the layer you're painting in a Layer panel and the composition that contains the layer in a separate Comp panel.

Animating Strokes

The following tasks apply what you learned in this chapter to achieve a few common Paint effects. The first employs the Duration option, Write On, to simulate natural writing. The next task explains how to adjust the timing of the strokes in the Timeline panel. The last task shows how to animate a stroke by keyframing its Shape property, making it appear as though one stroke is transforming into another.

These tasks focus on employing different animation techniques and don't cover other options (such as brushes, channels, and modes) in any detail. To find out about those options, refer back to the appropriate sections earlier in the chapter.

To animate strokes using the Write On option:

1. In the Tools panel, select a paint tool (**Figure 13.49**).

2. In the Paint panel, specify paint options, including Opacity, Flow, Color, Mode, and Channels.

   For a detailed explanation, see "Specifying Paint Stroke Options," earlier in this chapter.

3. In the Paint panel's Duration pop-up menu, choose Write On (**Figure 13.50**).

4. Set the current time to the frame where you want the first stroke to begin (**Figure 13.51**).

5. Using the Brush tool, drag in the Layer panel to paint strokes on the layer (**Figure 13.52**).

Figure 13.49 Select a paint tool: the Brush (shown here), Clone, or Eraser.

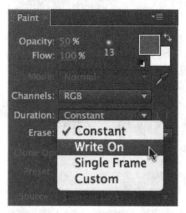

Figure 13.50 Choose Write On from the Paint panel's Duration pop-up menu.

Figure 13.51 Set the current time to the frame where you want the first stroke to begin.

Figure 13.52 Drag in the layer's Layer panel to draw or write. Lifting the mouse or pen ends the stroke, and because Write On is selected, the stroke disappears.

Figure 13.53 Each stroke appears in the layer's property outline under its Paint effect. The Write On option animates the stroke's End property automatically.

Figure 13.54 When you preview the animation, strokes appear in the same manner in which they were painted.

The speed at which you paint determines the duration and speed of the stroke animation. Lifting the mouse or pen to start a new stroke creates a separate brush layer in the Paint effect's property outline (**Figure 13.53**).

6. Preview the stroke animation in the Layer or Comp panel.

   Strokes appear gradually, as you painted them (**Figure 13.54**).

✔ Tips

- You can adjust the speed of the animation as you would any layer property by changing the timing of the keyframes—in this case, the End property keyframe. See Chapter 7, "Properties and Keyframes," for more about keyframes.

- Essentially, the Write On option animates the End property automatically. You can animate any stroke to create the same effect manually by animating the End property and duration of any stroke.

- The Write On option works effortlessly when animating a single stroke. However, lifting the mouse or pen creates multiple strokes that all begin at the current time. Therefore, multiple strokes will animate simultaneously, which doesn't simulate natural handwriting. To make each stroke animate sequentially, you must change the In points (and, possibly, the durations).

To animate a stroke by keyframing its shape:

1. Set the time you want the stroke to begin and, using a paint tool and the techniques described earlier in this chapter, create a stroke in a layer (**Figure 13.55**).

2. In the Timeline panel, expand the layer's property outline to reveal the stroke you want to animate.

3. Set the current time to the frame where you want the stroke's shape to begin changing, and click the Shape property's Stopwatch icon.

   A Shape keyframe appears at the current time for the stroke (**Figure 13.56**).

4. Set the current time to the frame where you want to paint a new stroke.

5. With the first stroke selected, paint a new stroke (**Figure 13.57**).

Figure 13.55 Set the current time and paint the stroke's initial shape.

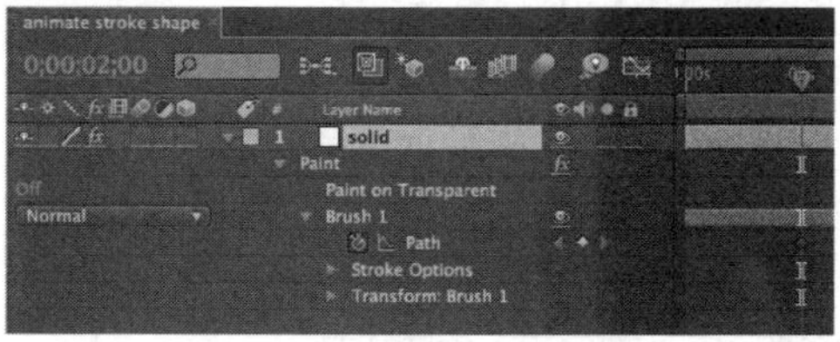

Figure 13.56 In the layer's property outline, expand the Paint effect and click the Shape property's Stopwatch icon to set the initial keyframe.

Figure 13.57 With the previous stroke selected, set the current time to the frame where you want the stroke to assume a new shape, and paint that shape.

Figure 13.58 Instead of creating a new stroke, the same stroke gets a new Shape keyframe at the current time.

Figure 13.59 When you preview the animation, the stroke transforms from one shape into another. In this example, the line that crosses the t was created as a separate stroke using the Write On option.

Instead of creating a new stroke layer, a new Shape keyframe appears in the selected stroke's property outline (**Figure 13.58**).

6. Repeat step 5, as needed.

7. Preview the stroke animation.

The stroke transforms from the shape defined by one keyframe to the shape defined by the next keyframe (**Figure 13.59**).

✔ Tip

■ You can keyframe any stroke or paint option that includes a Stopwatch icon in the Paint effect's property outline or Effect Controls panel.

Cloning

Like the Brush tool, the Clone Stamp tool adds pixels to a layer using the brush options you specify (Duration, Brush, and the like). But as the name implies, the Clone Stamp doesn't add pixels according to a specified color; instead, it copies, or *clones*, pixels from a layer's image. Photoshop veterans will instantly recognize the Clone Stamp tool and appreciate its value in retouching an image. They'll also have a big head start on using the tool; it works nearly the same in After Effects—except nondestructively, and over time.

As when you use the other paint tools, you must first specify brush options for the Clone Stamp tool. But instead of specifying a color, you specify the layer, frame, and location of the pixels you want to copy to the target layer. Once you've set these options, you paint pixels from the source to the target.

For the sake of clarity, the following sections break the cloning process into smaller tasks: setting the sample point, and then cloning. After that, you'll learn how to make cloning easier by superimposing the source image over the target image and saving clone options as convenient presets.

Setting the sample point for cloning

When cloning, pixels are copied, or *sampled*, from a particular layer, frame, and physical location in a source image. You can specify these three aspects of the clone source by using the Paint panel or by sampling manually. You can change the sample point at any time using either method, as needed.

You also need to understand the difference between setting a fixed sample point and one that maintains a consistent relationship with strokes in the target layer. In terms of space, you specify your choice with the Paint panel's Aligned option; in terms of time, you specify your choice with the Lock Source Time option.

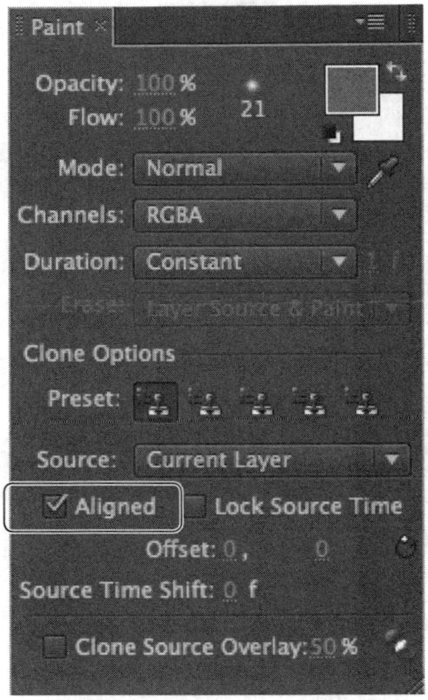

The Aligned option

The starting point for a clone stroke in the target layer always corresponds to the sample point you set in the source image. The Paint panel displays the distance between the stroke's starting point in the target and the sample point in the source as the Offset value. (When the target and source are different images, the distance is the difference in the corresponding points in each image's own coordinate system.)

However, the Aligned option determines which pixels are copied in subsequent strokes (**Figure 13.60**). By default, the Aligned option is selected, and pixels are always copied from a point in the source that is a consistent distance (the Offset value) from the corresponding location of the Clone Stamp in the target image (**Figure 13.61**). In contrast, when the Aligned option is not selected, pixels are copied using the initial sample as a fixed starting point (**Figure 13.62**).

Figure 13.60 The Aligned option determines whether pixels are copied from a fixed point or offset from a corresponding location of the Clone Stamp.

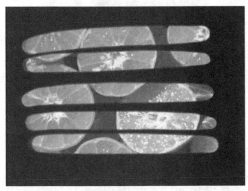

Figure 13.61 With Aligned checked, pixels are copied from a consistent distance from the corresponding location of the Clone Stamp.

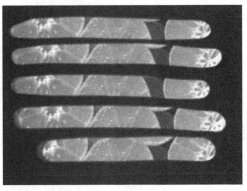

Figure 13.62 With Aligned unchecked, all strokes copy pixels from a fixed sample point in the source.

CLONING

The Lock Source Time option

The Lock Source Time option sets whether the Clone Stamp tool copies pixels from a fixed frame or maintains a time difference between the target frame and source frame (**Figure 13.63**). When Lock Source Time is selected, pixels are copied from a fixed frame that the Paint panel displays as the Source Time. If you change the target frame, the Source Time remains the same (unless you change it manually or sample from a different source frame). When Lock Source Time is not selected, the Paint panel displays a Source Time Shift value. This way, After Effects maintains a time difference between the target frame and source frame (**Figure 13.64**).

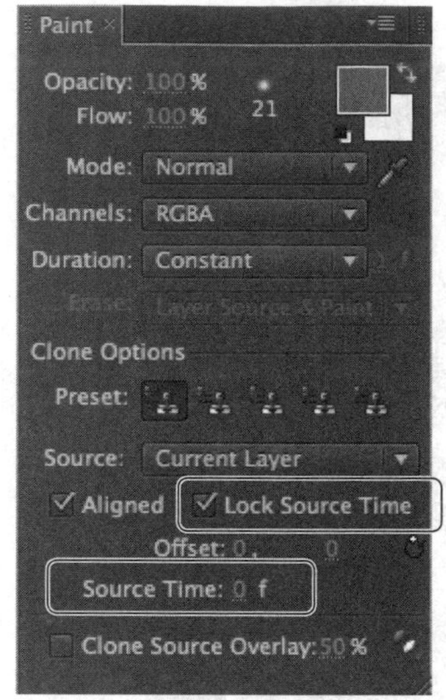

Figure 13.63 Checking Lock Source Time lets you specify a Source Time— a fixed frame from which to copy pixels.

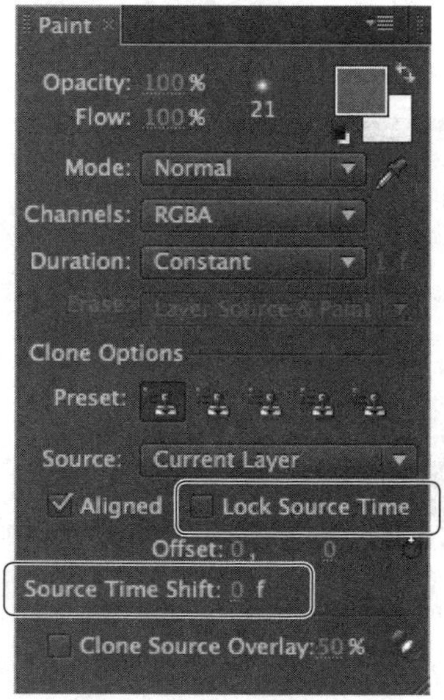

Figure 13.64 Unchecking Lock Source Time lets you specify a Source Time Shift—a consistent time difference between the target layer frame and source layer frame.

Figure 13.65 Select the Clone Stamp tool.

To set a clone source in the Paint panel:

1. If necessary, arrange the source and target layers in a composition.

2. Select the Clone Stamp tool (**Figure 13.65**). Clone Stamp options appear in the Paint panel.

3. In the Paint panel's Source pop-up menu, select the source layer from which the Clone Stamp tool will sample pixels (**Figure 13.66**).

4. *Do either of the following:*

   ▲ To clone from a point offset from the corresponding point in the target layer, check Aligned (**Figure 13.67**).

   ▲ To clone from the same starting point in the source layer with each new stroke, uncheck Aligned.

continues on next page

Figure 13.66 From the Paint panel's Source pop-up menu, specify the layer from which you want to clone.

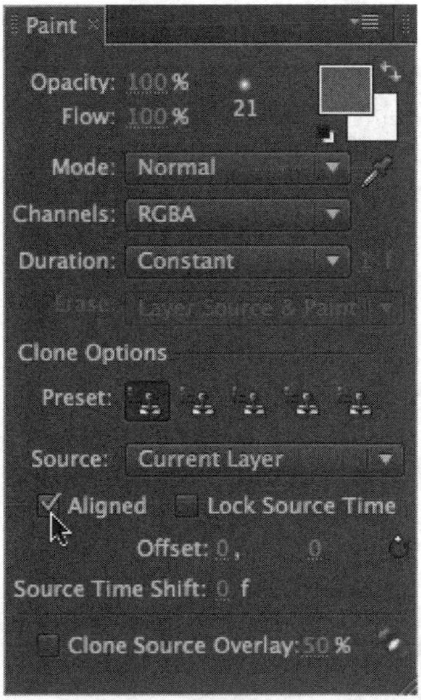

Figure 13.67 In the Paint panel, check Aligned if you want the sample point in the source to maintain a consistent relationship with each stroke in the target; uncheck Aligned to sample from the same point in the source layer with each stroke.

CLONING

5. Specify the difference, or *offset*, between the starting point of the sample (in the source layer) and the stroke (in the target layer) by setting X and Y values for the Offset value (**Figure 13.68**).

Offset values are expressed as the distance from the sample point to the stroke point in pixels, measured along the *X* and *Y* axes.

6. *Do either of the following:*

▲ To specify a specific source frame from which to sample, check Lock Source Time and specify a value for Source Time (**Figure 13.69**).

▲ To specify a consistent time difference between the target frame and source frame, uncheck Lock Source Time and specify a value for Source Time Shift (**Figure 13.70**).

Checking or unchecking Lock Source Time makes the corresponding time value appear in the Paint panel.

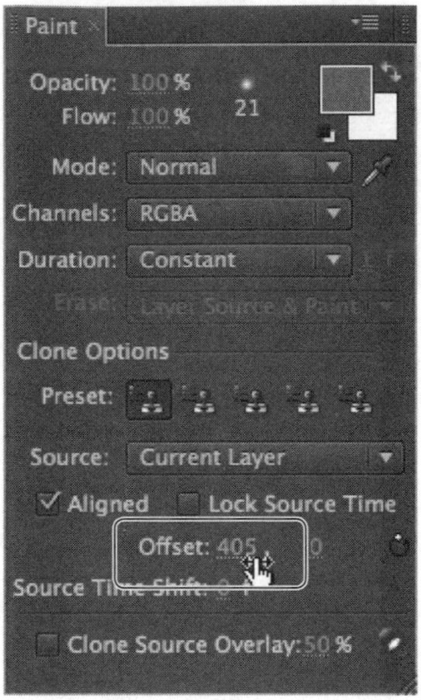

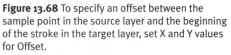

Figure 13.68 To specify an offset between the sample point in the source layer and the beginning of the stroke in the target layer, set X and Y values for Offset.

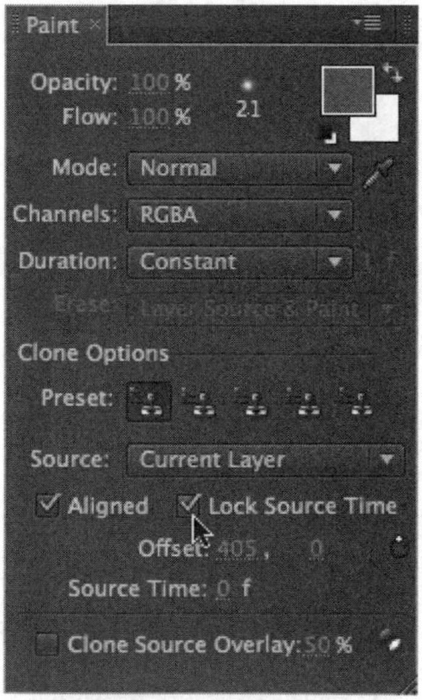

Figure 13.69 To sample from the same source frame regardless of the target frame, check Lock Source Time.

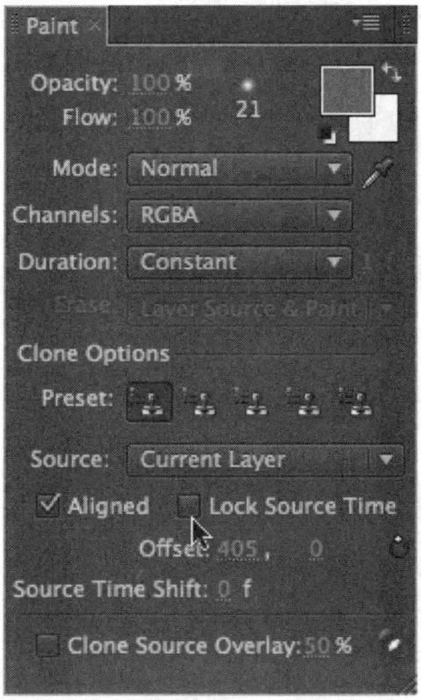

Figure 13.70 To maintain a consistent time difference between the source frame and the target frame, leave Lock Source Time unchecked and specify a value for Source Time Shift.

To set a clone source by clicking:

1. Follow steps 1 and 2 in the previous task, "To set a clone source in the Paint panel."

2. Specify options for the Aligned and Lock Source Time check boxes, as described in the previous task.

3. Set the current time to the frame from which you want to sample in the source layer, and Option-click (Alt-click) the sample point in the source layer's Layer panel (**Figure 13.71**).

   In the Paint panel, the source layer's name appears in the Source pop-up menu, and values appear for Offset. Values also appear for Source Time or Source Time Shift, depending on the options you chose earlier.

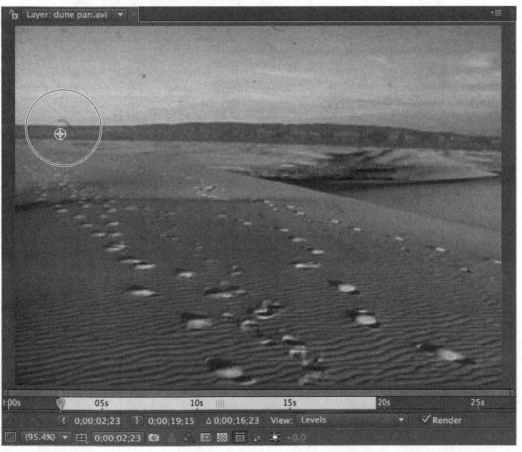

Figure 13.71 Option-click (Alt-click) to set the sample point in the source image. Here, the sample is taken from a future frame in order to eliminate an obtrusive string of dust on the lens.

CLONING

Using the Clone Stamp Tool

Now that you understand how setting a sample point works, you can integrate that knowledge into the overall cloning process. Once you master this task, move on to "Overlaying the Clone Source," and "Saving Clone Stamp Settings."

To clone pixels:

1. Arrange the clone source and target layers in a Comp panel, and open the target layer in a separate Layer panel (**Figure 13.72**).

2. In the Tools panel, choose the Clone Stamp tool (**Figure 13.73**).

3. In the Paint and Brushes panels, specify a brush and paint options, such as Opacity, Flow, Mode, and Duration (**Figure 13.74**).

   See the "Specifying Paint Stroke Options" and "Using Brushes" sections, earlier in this chapter.

Figure 13.72 This example uses the same layer for the target and source.

Figure 13.73 Choose the Clone Stamp tool.

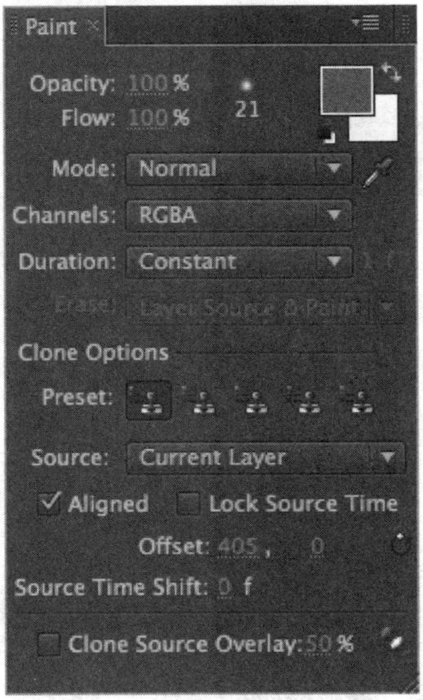

Figure 13.74 Specify paint options, such as Opacity, Flow, Mode, and Duration.

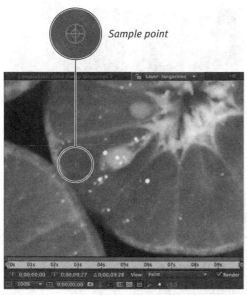

Sample point

Figure 13.75 Option-clicking (Alt-clicking) changes the cursor into crosshairs and sets the sample point (the layer, frame, and location of the source pixels).

Figure 13.76 Click or drag in the target layer with the Clone Stamp tool to copy pixels from the source layer. Here, cloning eliminates a distracting seed from the tangerine image.

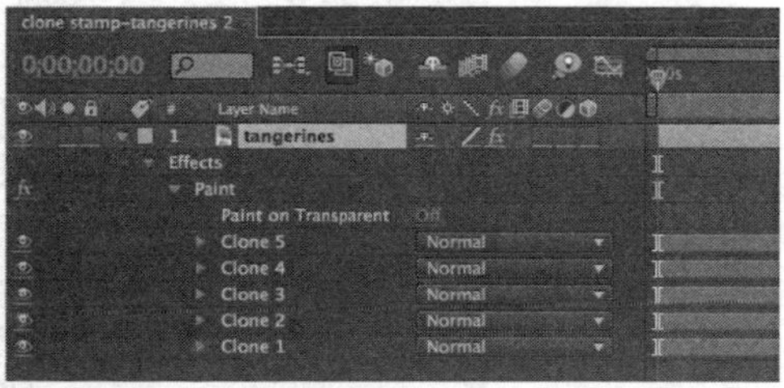

4. Specify the sample source by *doing either of the following:*

- ▲ Using the Clone Stamp tool, Option-click (Alt-click) in the source Layer panel at the frame and location you want to sample (**Figure 13.75**).

- ▲ In the Paint panel, specify the settings you want for the Source, Aligned, Lock Source Time (including the Source Time or Source Time Shift), and Offset options. (See the section "Setting the sample point for cloning," earlier in this chapter.)

5. Set the current time to the frame from which you want to clone pixels onto the target layer.

6. Click or drag in the target layer's Layer panel.

Pixels from the source layer are painted onto the target layer according to the options you specified (**Figure 13.76**). In the target layer's property outline, the Paint effect appears and includes each clone stroke you make (**Figure 13.77**).

✔ Tip

- ■ You can create a perfectly straight cloned stroke by clicking the stroke's starting point and Shift-clicking its ending point. This technique is great for cloning out linear elements such as wires or power lines.

Figure 13.77 In the target layer's property outline, the Paint effect appears and includes each clone stroke you make.

Overlaying the Clone Source

Although cloning can be painstaking, After Effects makes the process easier by letting you superimpose the source image over the target layer as you clone. This can help you see how the pixels copied from the source correspond to the target image.

To superimpose the source over the target layer as you clone:

1. Prepare layers for cloning and set options for the Clone Stamp tool, as explained in the previous task, "To clone pixels."

2. In the Paint panel, check Clone Source Overlay and specify the source layer's opacity (**Figure 13.78**).

   The overlay appears when the Clone Stamp tool is positioned over the target layer's image (**Figure 13.79**).

Figure 13.78 In the Paint panel, check Clone Source Overlay and specify the source layer's opacity.

Figure 13.79 The overlay appears when the Clone Stamp tool is positioned over the target layer's image.

OVERLAYING THE CLONE SOURCE

Figure 13.80 To see differences in the source and target layers more easily, click the Difference Mode button in the Paint panel.

3. To apply the Difference Blending mode to the superimposed source layer image, click the Difference Mode button (**Figure 13.80**).

   The Difference blending mode can help you identify differences between similar source and target frames. See Chapter 14, "More Layer Techniques," for more about blending modes.

✔ Tip

■ You can also toggle the overlay by pressing Option-Shift (Alt-Shift) as you use the Clone Stamp tool. This way, you can toggle the overlay on to see how the source and target image correspond, and toggle it off to see the target more clearly.

Saving Clone Stamp Settings

Meticulous retouching can require that you switch Clone Stamp tool settings often. Luckily, the Paint panel includes five Clone Stamp Preset buttons that you can use to store and quickly recall settings.

To save Clone Stamp settings:

1. In the Tools panel, select the Clone Stamp tool (**Figure 13.81**).

   The Clone Options become available.

2. In the Clone Options area of the Paint panel, click a Clone Stamp Preset button.

3. Specify the options you want (as described in the previous sections) to associate with the selected preset button (**Figure 13.82**).

   The options you specify are associated with the selected preset button.

To use a Clone Stamp preset:

1. In the Tools panel, select the Clone Stamp tool.

2. In the Clone Options area of the Paint panel, *do either of the following:*

   ▲ Click the Clone Stamp Preset button that corresponds to the preset you want to use.

   ▲ Press the number keyboard shortcut that corresponds to the preset you want: 3=first preset; 4=second preset; 5=third preset; 6=fourth preset; 7=fifth preset.

3. Use the Clone Stamp tool as explained in the previous tasks.

Figure 13.81 Select the Clone Stamp tool.

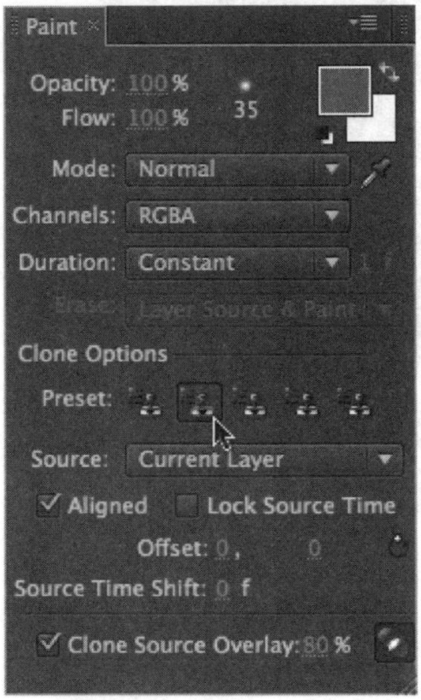

Figure 13.82 In the Paint panel, click a Clone Stamp Preset button and specify the settings you want associated with the button.

MORE
LAYER TECHNIQUES

This chapter tackles several techniques that encompass a wide range of topics: manipulating motion footage and its playback time, blending layers together, creating graphical objects, and distorting layers.

Specifically, you'll start by learning about a pair of layer switches—Frame Blending and Motion Blur—that influence how After Effects deals with motion between frames. Then, you'll play with the comp's frame rate using time remapping. From there, you'll take a closer look at the Transfer Controls panel, where you'll find a long list of modes you can use to blend a layer with underlying layers, expanding your repertoire of compositing tools. You'll also find out what the mysterious T option stands for, and, more important, how to use it. You'll complete your tour of the Transfer Controls by learning about yet another compositing option, Track Mattes. As you near the end of the chapter, you'll learn about two powerful features that merit their own dedicated tools. The first is a special kind of layer, called a shape layer. Shape layers let you create and animate graphical elements in countless variations. Finally, you'll animate layers using a powerful distortion effect that you control with a set of tools called, appropriately enough, Puppet tools.

Using Frame Blending

When the frame rate of motion footage is lower than that of the composition, movement within the frame can appear jerky—either because the footage's native frame rate is lower than that of the composition, or because you time-stretched the footage. Whatever the case, After Effects reconciles this difference by repeating frames of the source footage. For example, each frame of a 15-fps movie is displayed twice in a composition with a frame rate of 30 fps. However, because there aren't enough unique frames to represent full motion, the result can sometimes resemble a crude flip-book animation.

In these instances, you can smooth the motion by activating the Frame Blending switch. When frame blending is on, After Effects interpolates between original frames, blending them rather than simply repeating them (**Figures 14.1** and **14.2**). Motion footage that has been sped up can also benefit from frame blending.

You can specify either of two types of frame blending: Frame Mix and Pixel Motion. Comparing the two methods, Frame Mix renders faster but is lower quality; hence, the layer's Frame Blending switch ⬎ resembles a jagged backslash (which looks like the draft quality switch). Pixel Motion renders more slowly but can produce better results; it's indicated by a smooth slash ╱ (similar to the full quality switch).

Figure 14.1 Ordinarily, After Effects interpolates frames by repeating the original frames. Because this simple animation is interpreted as 15 frames per second, frames are repeated to compensate for a 30-fps composition.

Figure 14.2 When frame blending is applied and enabled, it blends the original frames to create interpolated frames.

Pixel Motion frame blending

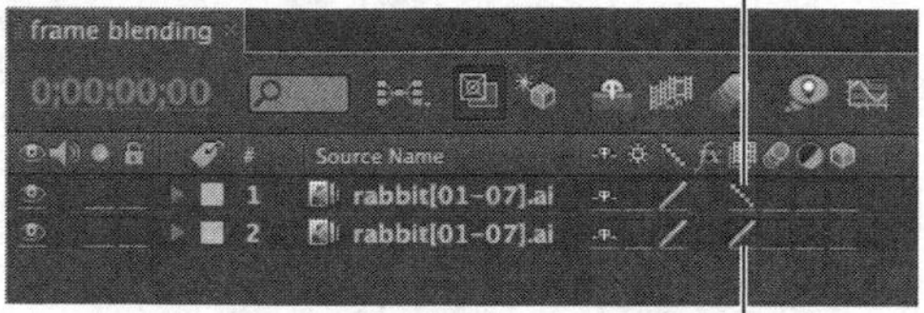

Frame Mix frame blending

Figure 14.3 Clicking a motion footage layer's Frame Blending switch repeatedly changes its state from no frame blending to frame mix to pixel motion.

Figure 14.4 Click the Enable Frame Blending button at the top of the Timeline panel.

To apply or remove frame blending in a layer:

1. If necessary, click the Timeline panel's Switches button to make the layer switches appear.

2. For a layer created from motion footage, click the Frame Blending switch to toggle its icon to the option you want:

No Icon—no frame blending applied

Frame Mix—blends frames using a faster but lower-quality method

Pixel Motion—blends frames using a slower but higher quality method

The layer uses the frame blending method you specify (**Figure 14.3**). Frame blending must be enabled for its effect to be rendered in the Comp panel (see the next task).

To enable or disable frame blending for all layers in a composition:

◆ *Do either of the following:*

▲ Click the Enable Frame Blending button ▦ at the top of the Timeline panel (**Figure 14.4**).

▲ Select Enable Frame Blending in the Timeline panel's pop-up menu.

When the Enable Frame Blending button is clicked, frame blending is enabled for all layers with frame blending applied.

✔ Tips

■ Because frame blending can significantly slow previewing and rendering, you may want to apply it to layers but refrain from enabling it until you're ready to render the final animation.

■ A layer with pixel motion frame blending uses frame mix frame blending when you set the layer's quality switch to draft quality.

USING FRAME BLENDING

Using Motion Blur

Ordinarily, an animated layer appears sharp and distinct as it moves through the frame of a composition (**Figure 14.5**). But this can appear unnatural, because we're accustomed to seeing moving objects as blurred—due to the limitations of either our eyes or our camera. To simulate this effect and make an animation appear more natural, you can activate an animated layer's Motion Blur switch (**Figure 14.6**).

Although you apply motion blur to individual layers, you must enable blur for the entire composition to see the results. This way, you choose whether you want to view the layers' motion blur, or disable it while you work and reduce rendering times. Because motion blur simulates the blur captured by a camera, it uses similar controls, which you can access in the Composition Settings dialog.

To apply or remove motion blur:

◆ Select the Motion Blur switch for a layer with animated motion (**Figure 14.7**).

When the Motion Blur switch is selected, motion blur is applied to the layer. The Motion Blur button determines whether motion blur is enabled (see the next task for details).

To enable or disable motion blur for all layers in a composition:

◆ *Do either of the following:*

▲ Click the Enable Motion Blur button at the top of the Timeline panel (**Figure 14.8**).

▲ Select Enable Motion Blur in the Timeline panel's pop-up menu.

When the Enable Motion Blur button is clicked or the Enable Motion Blur item is selected, motion blur is enabled for all layers with motion blur applied.

Figure 14.5 Ordinarily, an animated layer appears sharp and distinct as it moves through the frame of the composition.

Figure 14.6 To simulate a more natural-looking, blurred motion, activate the Motion Blur switch for an animated layer.

Figure 14.7 Select the Motion Blur switch for a layer with animated motion to apply motion blur.

Figure 14.8 Click the Enable Motion Blur button at the top of the Timeline panel to enable motion blur for the layers with motion blur applied to them.

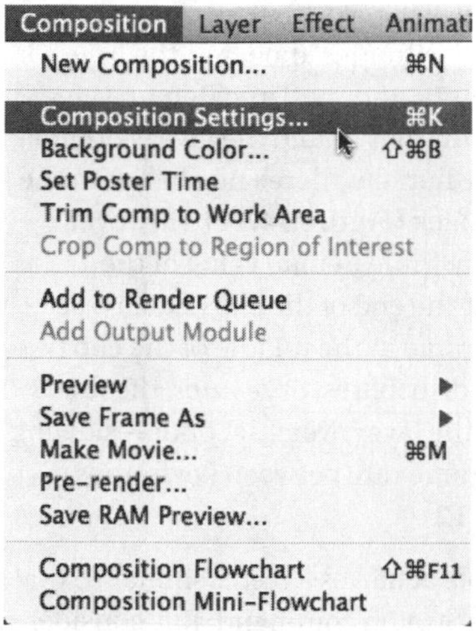

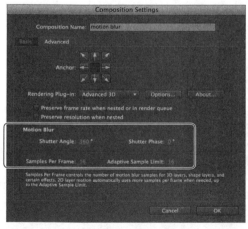

Figure 14.9 Choose Composition > Composition Settings.

Figure 14.10 In the Composition Settings dialog, enter a value for the Shutter Angle, Shutter Phase, Samples Per Frame, and Adaptive Sample Limit.

To set the amount of motion blur for previews:

1. Choose Composition > Composition Settings (**Figure 14.9**).

   The Composition Settings dialog appears.

2. In the Advanced panel of the Composition Settings dialog, specify values for any of the following (**Figure 14.10**):

   ▲ **Shutter Angle**—Simulates a camera's shutter angle, in degrees. Higher values (up to 360°) result in more blurry motion.

   ▲ **Shutter Phase**—Sets the position of the shutter relative to the start frame, in degrees.

   ▲ **Samples Per Frame**—Sets the number of samples used to calculate motion blur for 3D layers, shape layers, and some effects. Higher values result in a smoother motion blur.

   ▲ **Adaptive Sample Limit**—Sets the upper limit of samples used to calculate motion blur for 2D layers.

3. Click OK to close the Composition Settings dialog.

✔ Tips

- When you render the final output, you can choose whether to enable motion blur and frame blending in the Render Queue panel. This way, you don't have to return to your composition to check the setting. See Chapter 17, "Output."

- To reduce the time it takes to preview your animation, you may want to apply motion blur to layers but wait to enable it for all layers in the composition until you're ready to render.

- You can apply motion blur to a mask by selecting the mask, choosing Layer > Mask > Motion Blur, and choosing an option in the submenu.

Understanding Time Remapping

Back in Chapter 6, "Layer Editing," you learned how to change the speed of a layer using the Time Stretch command (or by changing the layer's Stretch value in the In/Out panel in the Timeline panel). Although it's useful, the Time Stretch command is limited to changing the layer's overall playback speed. To make the playback speed up, slow down, reverse, or come to a halt (or *freeze frame*), you need to use *time remapping*.

In a normal layer, a direct relationship exists between the layer's time and the frame you see and hear. In a time-remapped layer, the normal time controls show the layer's elapsed time but no longer dictate which frame is displayed (or heard) at that time. Instead, the Time Remap values determine the visible (or audible) frame at that time.

For example, when you first apply time remapping, keyframes appear at the layer's In and Out points, and the Time Remap values at those keyframes match the layer's original time values. Initially, there's no change in the layer's playback (**Figure 14.11**). However, changing the Time Remap value of the keyframe at the end of the clip (say, at 4 seconds) to a frame in the middle of the clip (2 seconds) redistributes, or *remaps*, the first 2 seconds of the layer over 4 seconds—slowing down the frame rate between keyframes (**Figure 14.12**).

This example achieves a result similar to that of the Time Stretch command. But consider that you can set additional time-remapped keyframes in the same layer and apply the temporal interpolation methods covered in Chapter 9, "Keyframe Interpolation."

Figure 14.11 Here, the Time Remap property values match the layer's original time values. The layer time is the top number; the remapped time is the lower number.

Figure 14.12 Here, the last Time Remap keyframe is still positioned at 04;00 into the clip, but its value has been changed to the frame at 02;00. The layer's frame rate slows between the keyframes.

Using the same layer as in the previous example, suppose you set a time-remap keyframe at 2 seconds into the clip and leave its value set to 2 seconds. The layer plays normally between the first and second keyframes (the first 2 seconds). But if you change the Time Remap value of the last keyframe—positioned 4 seconds into the clip—to 0 seconds (not the keyframe's position in time, just its value), then playback reverses between the second and third keyframes (**Figure 14.13**).

Although time remapping can sound confusing, it works just like keyframing other properties. But whereas most keyframes define a visible characteristic (like position) at a given frame, a time-remap keyframe specifies the *frame* you see (or hear) at a given point in the layer's time.

Figure 14.13 Here, the layer plays forward at twice the speed between the first keyframe and a second keyframe, set halfway through the layer's duration. The Time Remap value of the last keyframe—positioned at 04;00—has been changed to 00;00, which reverses the playback.

Controlling Time Remap Values

When you enable time remapping on a layer, the Layer panel displays additional controls for changing the frame rate. In addition to the layer's ordinary time ruler, current time indicator (CTI), and current time display, a corresponding remap-time ruler, marker, and display also appear (**Figure 14.14**). The lower CTI shows the (normal) time; the upper CTI shows the frame you specify to play at that time.

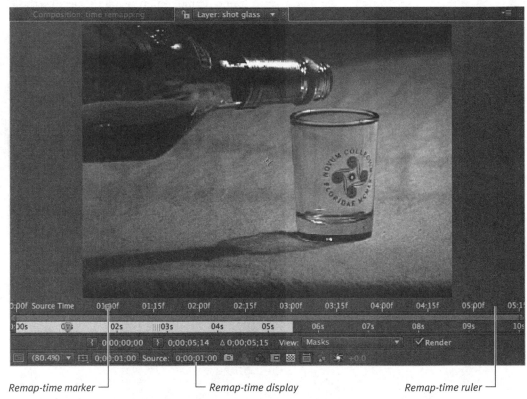

Remap-time marker ⌐   ⌐ Remap-time display   Remap-time ruler ⌐

Figure 14.14 Enabling time remapping makes additional controls appear in the Layer panel.

As is the case for any property value, you can set keyframes for the Time Remap property using controls in the Timeline panel (**Figure 14.15**). As usual, use the Add/ Remove Keyframe button in the property's keyframe navigator to set keyframes that use previously interpolated values. You can also view the property's value graph in the Graph Editor and drag control points on the graph to change the value of the corresponding keyframe. This technique lets you accelerate, decelerate, or reverse playback speed (see the task "To change playback speed over time," later in this chapter). For more about viewing and using a value graph and using interpolation methods (how After Effects calculates property values between keyframes), see Chapter 9, "Keyframe Interpolation."

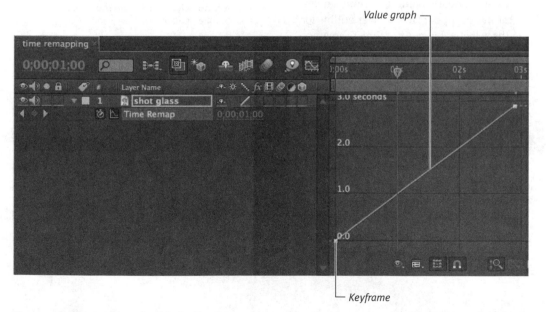

Value graph

Keyframe

Figure 14.15 You also use controls in the Timeline panel to set Time Remap values and keyframes. Here, the time remapping values are seen in the Graph Editor view.

Using Time Remapping

The tasks in this section explain how to enable time remapping for a layer and how to set keyframes to pause, reverse, or change the speed of playback. (The first three tasks use the Timeline panel and keyframes; the last task employs the Graph Editor.) Once you get the hang of these techniques, you can explore other ways to control playback using time remapping. You'll find that everything you've learned about keyframes and interpolation for other properties (in Chapter 7, "Properties and Keyframes," and Chapter 9, "Keyframe Interpolation") applies equally to time remap keyframes.

To enable time remapping:

1. Select a layer, and choose Layer > Time > Enable Time Remapping (**Figure 14.16**).

   In the Timeline panel, the Time Remap property appears in the layer outline for the selected layer. After Effects creates keyframes at the beginning and end of the layer automatically (**Figure 14.17**).

Figure 14.16 Select a layer, and choose Layer > Time > Enable Time Remapping.

Figure 14.17 After Effects sets a time-remap keyframe at the layer's In and Out points automatically. However, the values match the layer's original values, and the layer's frame rate remains unchanged.

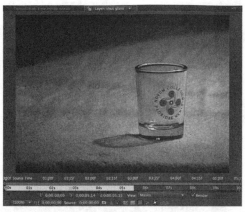

Figure 14.18 Double-click the layer in the Timeline panel to view it in a Layer panel and use the time-remapping controls.

Figure 14.19 Set the current time to the frame where you want playback to stop. There's no need to change the remap time; it should match the current time.

2. In the Timeline panel, double-click the layer to view it in a Layer panel.

   In addition to the standard controls, the Layer panel includes time-remapping controls (**Figure 14.18**).

To create a freeze frame with time remapping:

1. Select a layer and enable time remapping as explained in the previous task, "To enable time remapping."

   After Effects sets beginning and ending keyframes automatically.

2. Set the current time to the frame where you want the layer's playback to stop (**Figure 14.19**).

3. In the Timeline panel, select the keyframe navigator's Add/Remove Keyframe button (the diamond-shaped icon) for the layer's Time Remap property.

   A keyframe appears at the current time, using the previously interpolated value. In this case, the Time Remap value matches the frame's original value (**Figure 14.20**).

   continues on next page

Figure 14.20 In the Timeline panel, click the Add/Remove Keyframe button (the diamond-shaped icon in the Time Remap property's keyframe navigator to create a keyframe at the current frame.

4. With the new keyframe selected, choose Animation > Toggle Hold Keyframe (**Figure 14.21**).

The new keyframe uses Hold interpolation, evidenced by its Hold Keyframe icon (**Figure 14.22**). This holds the Time Remap value until the next keyframe is reached.

5. Select the last keyframe, and press Delete (Backspace).

The last keyframe is removed (**Figure 14.23**). It's no longer needed.

6. View the remapped layer in the Layer or Comp panel by dragging the CTI or pressing Play.

The layer's frames play back at normal speed; then, the layer freezes when it reaches the Hold keyframe. You can't use RAM previews to see the layer play back using the remapped frame rate.

✔ Tip

■ The Layer > Time > Freeze Frame command applies Time Remap and sets a Hold keyframe so that the current frame plays for the layer's entire duration.

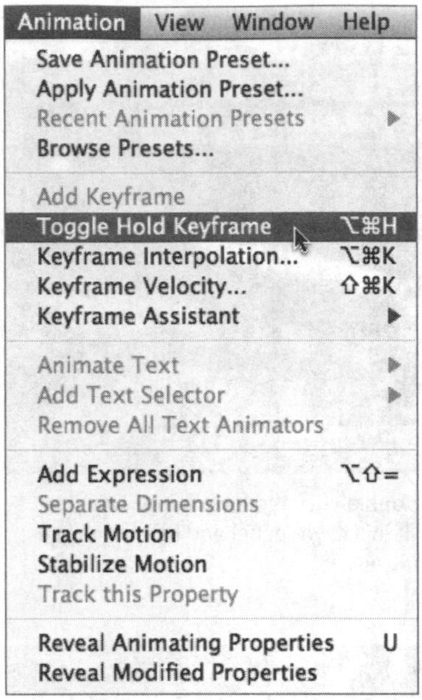

Animation	View	Window	Help

Save Animation Preset...
Apply Animation Preset...
Recent Animation Presets   ▶
Browse Presets...

Add Keyframe
Toggle Hold Keyframe   ⌥⌘H
Keyframe Interpolation...   ⌥⌘K
Keyframe Velocity...   ⇧⌘K
Keyframe Assistant   ▶

Animate Text   ▶
Add Text Selector   ▶
Remove All Text Animators

Add Expression   ⌥⇧=
Separate Dimensions
Track Motion
Stabilize Motion
Track this Property

Reveal Animating Properties   U
Reveal Modified Properties

Figure 14.21 With the new keyframe selected, choose Animation > Toggle Hold Keyframe.

Figure 14.22 The Keyframe icon changes to a Hold Keyframe icon, indicating that the property value will remain at that value until the next keyframe is reached.

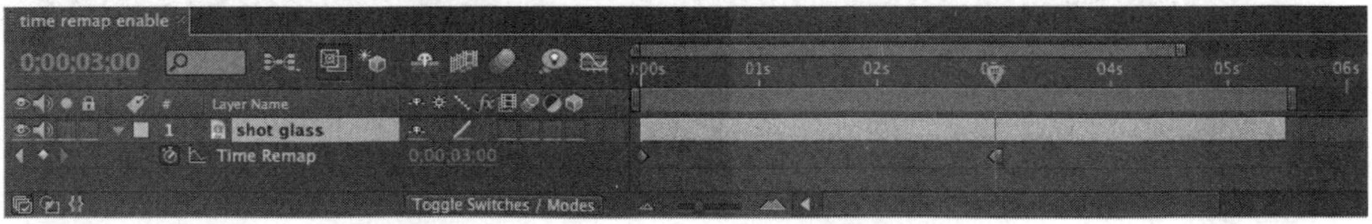

Figure 14.23 Select the last keyframe, and press Delete (Backspace). The layer's playback now freezes at the Hold keyframe you created in steps 3 and 4.

To reverse playback:

1. Select a layer, and enable time remapping as explained in the task, "To enable time remapping," earlier in this section.

2. Set the current time to the frame where you want the layer's playback direction to reverse, and select the Add/Remove Keyframe button in the Time Remap property's keyframe navigator.

   A keyframe appears at the current time, using the previously interpolated value. In this case, the keyframe's value matches the frame's original value (**Figure 14.24**).

3. Set the current frame later in time, to the point where you want the reversed playback to end (**Figure 14.25**).

continues on next page

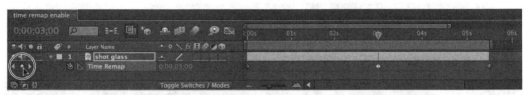

Figure 14.24 Set the current time to the point where you want the layer's playback to reverse, and click the box in the Time Remap property's keyframe navigator to set a keyframe.

Figure 14.25 Set the current time to the point where you want the reversed playback to end. Here, the current time is set to the Out point (which changes the keyframe value that was set automatically when remapping was applied).

USING TIME REMAPPING

4. In the Layer panel, drag the remap-time indicator to an earlier frame (**Figure 14.26**).

The layer's original frame value is mapped to the frame you specified with the remap-time indicator.

5. View the time-remapped layer in the Layer or Comp panel by dragging the CTI.

You can't use RAM previews to see the layer play back using the remapped frame rate. The layer's frames play back normally until the keyframe you set in step 2; the layer then plays in reverse until the keyframe you set in step 3. The remap frame you set in step 4 determines the actual frame played by the time the last keyframe is reached (**Figure 14.27**).

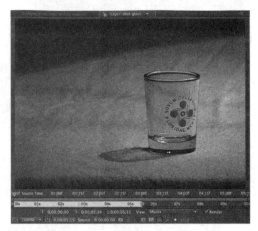

Figure 14.26 In the Layer panel, drag the remap-time marker to a time earlier than the one you chose in step 3.

Figure 14.27 The layer plays forward between the first and second keyframes and then plays in reverse between the second and last keyframes.

Using Time Remapping

Figure 14.28 In the Timeline panel, show the Time Remap property's value graph in the Graph Editor.

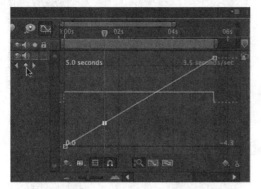

Figure 14.29 Set the current time when you want the speed change to begin, and click the Add/Remove Keyframe button (the diamond-shaped icon) in the keyframe navigator. (For illustration purposes, the Keys column—containing the keyframe navigator—is set to appear near the Graph Editor.)

To change playback speed over time:

1. Select a layer and enable time remapping as explained in the task, "To enable time remapping," earlier in this section.

2. In the Timeline panel, enable the Graph Editor and set the layer's Time Remap property to appear as a value graph (**Figure 14.28**).

   See Chapter 9, "Keyframe Interpolation," for more about using the Graph Editor.

3. Set the current time to the frame where you want the speed change to occur, and click the Add/Remove Keyframe button (the diamond-shaped icon) in the Time Remap property's keyframe navigator (**Figure 14.29**).

   A keyframe appears at the current time; its value matches the frame's original time value.

   continues on next page

4. In the Time Remap property's value graph, drag the control point that corresponds to the keyframe you set in step 3 in either of the following ways:

▲ To slow playback speed, drag the control point down (**Figure 14.30**).

▲ To increase playback speed, drag the control point up (**Figure 14.31**).

When the value is higher than the previous keyframe's value, the layer plays forward; when the value is lower, the layer plays in reverse. If the layer is already playing in reverse, drag the value graph's control point in the opposite direction.

5. Repeat steps 3 and 4 as needed.

The layer's playback speed and direction change according to your choices.

6. View the remapped layer in the Layer or Comp panel by dragging the CTI or pressing Play.

You can't use RAM previews to see the layer play back using the remapped frame rate.

✔ Tip

■ As with other properties, you can use keyframe assistants and interpolation methods to adjust the rate of change at time remap keyframes. For example, you could make a clip's playback speed change more gradually by changing its graph from a straight line to a curved one. Or you can use Hold keyframes to make a layer's playback "jump" from one frame to another instantaneously. To review the Graph Editor or interpolation types, see Chapter 9, "Keyframe Interpolation,"

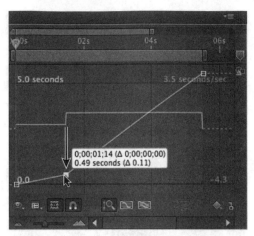

Figure 14.30 In the value graph, drag the control point corresponding to the keyframe. Decreasing the slope decreases speed; here, motion slows between the first and second keyframes. (In this figure, a reference speed graph is visible to better illustrate the result of the change.)

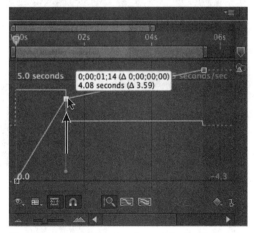

Figure 14.31 Increasing the slope of the line increases speed; here, motion between the first and second keyframe speeds up.

Upper Layer

Lower Layer

Result of Darker Color mode

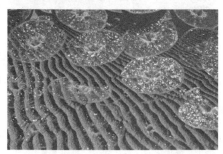

Result of Lighter Color mode

Figure 14.32 In this figure, the first image is the upper layer; the second image the lower layer. Subsequent images show the result of just a few Blending modes.

Using Blending Modes

In previous chapters, you learned that higher layers in the stacking order are superimposed on lower layers according to their alpha channel (which can also be modified with masks) or their Opacity property value. If you want to combine layers in more varied and subtle ways, you can use a variety of Blending modes.

A Blending mode changes the value of a layer's pixels according to the values of the corresponding pixels in the underlying image. Depending on how the values interact, the result often appears as a blend of the two (**Figure 14.32**). You may recognize most of the Blending modes from Photoshop; you'll find they work the same way here.

By default, a layer's mode is set to Normal. You can change the mode by selecting an option from a pop-up menu in the Transfer Controls panel of the timeline. When you do, the Video switch for the layer changes from a normal Eye icon ⊙ to a darkened Eye icon ⊙. Although most layer modes only blend color values (RGB channels), some—such as the Stencil and Silhouette modes—affect transparency (alpha channel) information.

This section describes how to set any Blending mode but doesn't describe all 33 modes or illustrate their results. (That would require a lot of pages, including ones in color.) After Effects Help provides a full-color gallery.

To apply a Blending mode:

1. If necessary, click the Timeline panel's Transfer Controls button to make the Modes panel appear (**Figure 14.33**).

   This panel includes controls for modes, preserving underlying transparency and track mattes.

2. Choose a mode from a layer's Mode pop-up menu (**Figure 14.34**).

   The Video switch for the layer becomes a darkened eye ▣. The mode you select affects how the layer combines with underlying layers.

✔ Tip

■ As you apply Blending modes, bear in mind that After Effects renders the bottommost layer first and works its way up the stacking order. Because a Blending mode determines how a layer interacts with the image beneath it, the resulting image becomes the underlying image for layer modes applied to the next higher layer in the stacking order, and so on. For more about render order, see Chapter 16, "Complex Projects."

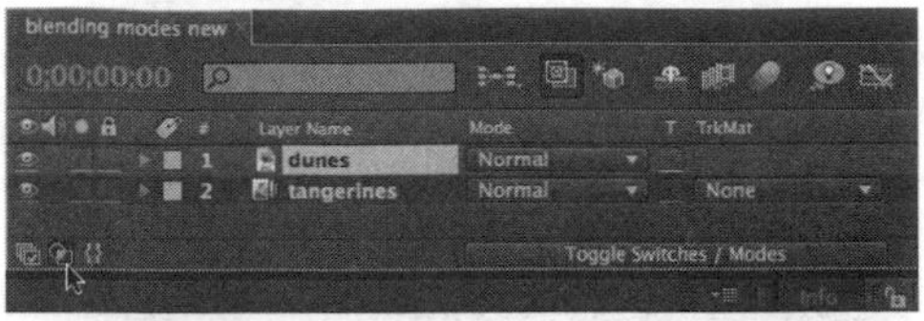

Figure 14.33 If necessary, click the Transfer Controls button to make the Mode panel appear.

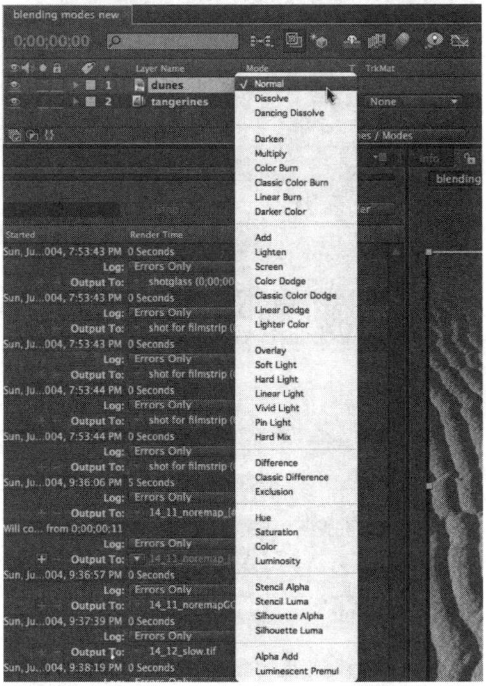

Figure 14.34 Choose a mode from a layer's Mode pop-up menu.

Figure 14.35 When composited without Preserve Underlying Transparency selected, the entire highlight layer is superimposed over the underlying image (the text).

Figure 14.36 When Preserve Underlying Transparency is selected, the opaque areas of the highlight layer appear only in the opaque areas of the underlying image.

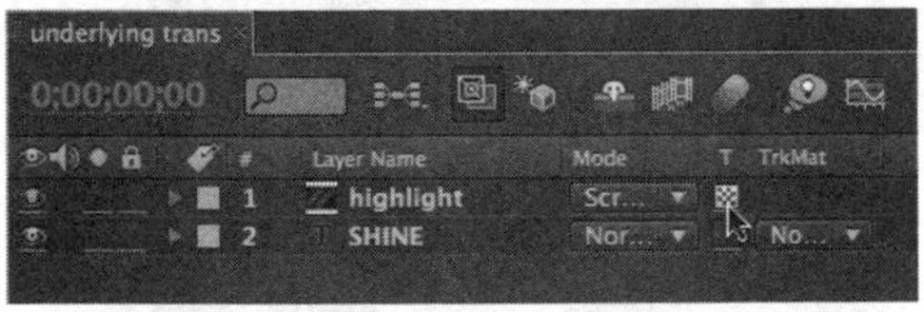

Figure 14.37 Click the box under the T heading to select Preserve Underlying Transparency.

Preserving Underlying Transparency

To the right of the Mode menu is a layer switch in a column marked *T*. This innocuous-looking T switch performs an important function: It preserves the underlying transparency. When you select this option, the opaque areas of a layer display only where they overlap with opaque areas in the underlying image (**Figures 14.35** and **14.36**).

The Preserve Underlying Transparency option is commonly used to make it appear as though light is being reflected from the surface of the underlying solid. You can use Preserve Underlying Transparency in conjunction with any layer mode or track matte. When you activate it, the Video switch becomes a darkened Eye icon.

To preserve underlying transparency:

1. Make sure the Mode column is visible in the Timeline panel.

2. For a layer you want to composite with the underlying image, click the box under the T heading (**Figure 14.37**).

   A transparency grid icon indicates that Preserve Underlying Transparency is active; no icon indicates that it's inactive. When you activate the option, the Video switch becomes a darkened Eye icon.

Track Mattes

So far, you've learned to define transparent areas in a layer by using the Opacity property, alpha channels, masks, and certain layer modes and effects—all options that are part of the layer. Sometimes, however, you won't want to use the transparency provided by the image, or you may find that creating a mask is impractical. This is especially true if you want to use a moving image or one that lacks an alpha channel to define transparency. Whatever the case, you may want to use a separate image to define transparency. Any image used to define transparency in another image is called a *matte*.

In After Effects, *track matte* refers to a method of defining transparency using an image layer, called the *fill*, and a separate matte layer. In the Timeline panel, the matte must be directly above the fill in the stacking order. Because the matte is included only to define transparency, not to appear in the output, its Video switch is turned off. The track matte is assigned to the fill layer using the Track Matte pop-up menu in the Switches panel. Transparent areas reveal the underlying image, which consists of lower layers in the stacking order (**Figures 14.38** and **14.39**).

Figure 14.38 Arrange the matte, the fill, and the background layers in the timeline. Note the settings in the A/V panel and the Mode panel.

Figure 14.39 The matte, the fill, the background, and the final composite.

Traveling Mattes

The term *track matte* often refers to a matte that's in motion, although in After Effects a track matte doesn't have to move. Animated mattes are also called *traveling mattes*, a term used when the same techniques were accomplished with film.

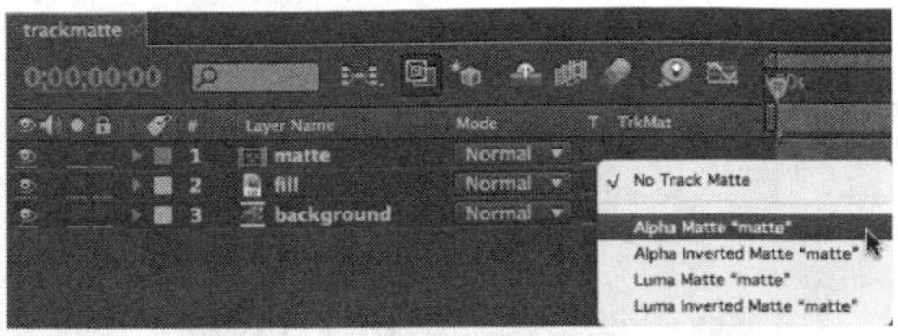

Figure 14.40 The Track Matte pop-up menu lists several options.

Figure 14.41 In the following example, the matte layer is an image of the moon...

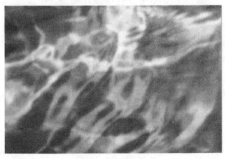

Figure 14.42 ...which also contains an alpha channel.

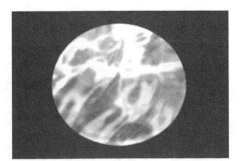

Figure 14.43 The water image serves as the fill layer, and black serves as the background.

Types of track mattes

The Track Matte pop-up menu lists several options (**Figure 14.40**). Each option specifies whether the matte's alpha or luminance information is used to define transparency in the fill layer. Ordinarily, white defines opaque areas, and black defines transparent areas. Inverted options reverse the opaque and transparent areas.

In the following example, a grayscale image of the moon serves as the matte layer (**Figure 14.41**). It also contains a corresponding circular alpha channel (**Figure 14.42**). A water image serves as the fill (**Figure 14.43**), and the background image is black. Subsequent figures show the result of setting the fill layer's track matte pop-up menu to the following options:

No Track Matte—No track matte is the default.

Alpha Matte—Defines the transparency in the fill (the alpha channel). White defines opaque areas; black defines transparent areas. Grays are semitransparent (**Figure 14.44**).

continues on next page

Figure 14.44 An alpha matte.

Alpha Inverted Matte—The inverted alpha channel of the matte. This defines the transparency in the fill. Black defines opaque areas; white defines transparent areas. Grays are semitransparent (**Figure 14.45**).

Luma Matte—Specifies the luminance values of the matte and defines transparency in the fill. White defines opaque areas; black defines transparent areas. Grays are semi-transparent (**Figure 14.46**).

Luma Inverted Matte—Specifies the inverted luminance values of the matte and defines transparency in the fill. Black defines opaque areas; white defines transparent areas. Grays are semitransparent (**Figure 14.47**).

Figure 14.45 An alpha inverted matte.

Figure 14.46 A luma matte.

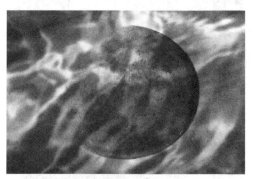

Figure 14.47 A luma inverted matte.

TRACK MATTES

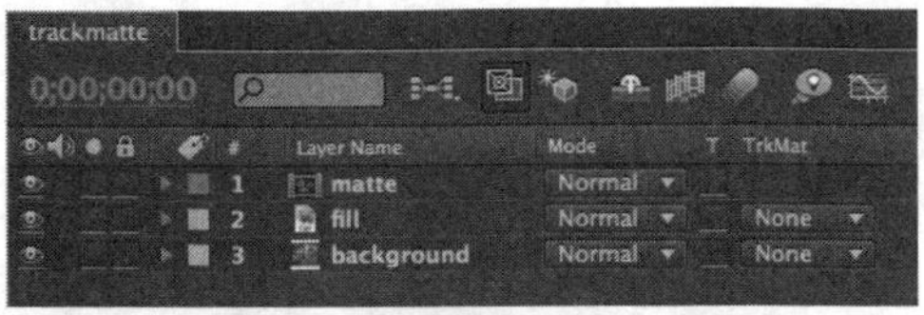

Figure 14.48 Arrange the fill and matte in the Timeline panel.

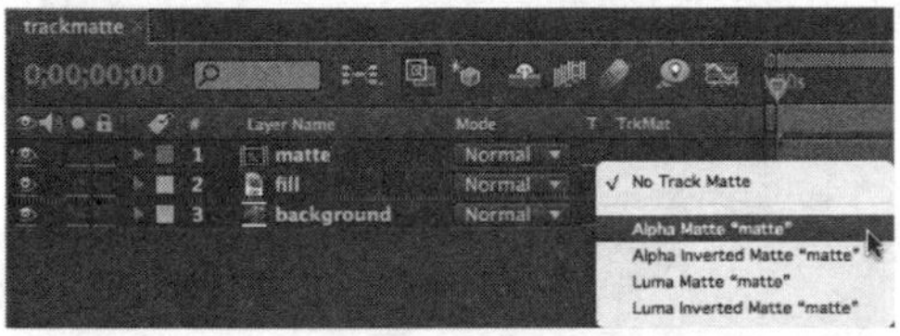

Figure 14.49 Choose an option in the Track Matte pop-up menu.

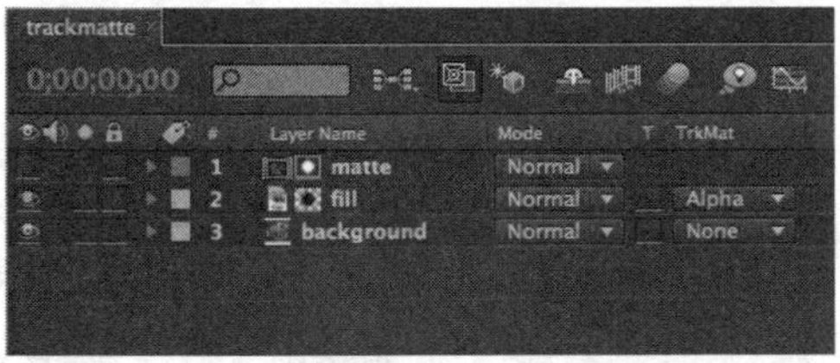

Figure 14.50 The layer directly above the fill layer in the stacking order becomes the track matte, and its Video switch is turned off automatically.

To create a track matte:

1. If necessary, click the Timeline panel's Transfer Mode button to display the Mode panel.

2. Arrange two layers in the Timeline panel so that the matte layer is directly above the fill layer in the stacking order (**Figure 14.48**).

3. In the Mode panel for the fill layer, choose one of the following options from the Track Matte pop-up menu (**Figure 14.49**):
   ▲ No Track Matte
   ▲ Alpha Matte
   ▲ Alpha Inverted Matte
   ▲ Luma Matte
   ▲ Luma Inverted Matte

   The layer directly above the fill layer in the stacking order becomes the track matte, and its Video switch is turned off automatically. In the Timeline panel, the thin border that usually appears between layers no longer appears between the fill and the matte layers (**Figure 14.50**).

4. If you want, place a layer lower in the stacking order to serve as the background.

✔ Tips

■ Because a luma matte doesn't utilize color, a matte is often a grayscale image—or to make the effect easier to visualize, an image is converted to grayscale.

■ You can use techniques you've learned throughout this book to create a matte from scratch. For example, using text as a matte allows you to fill it with an image instead of its fill color. Effects (such as Waveform, Block Dissolve, and Fractal Noise) can also generate animated mattes. Or you can use mask or shape layers (discussed in the next section) as mattes. Other effects can help you modify a layer into a suitable matte image.

TRACK MATTES

Using Shape Layers

In addition to video images and audio, After Effects animations often require purely graphical objects. At times, these elements are inconspicuous, serving as track mattes, effect sources, and the like. At other times, they take center stage. To help you create these elements, After Effects includes a special type of synthetic layer, called a shape layer.

Shape layers consist of one or more shapes you draw using the same drawing tools you use to create masks. But whereas masks are applied to a layer, shapes are layers in and of themselves. And whereas masks are always defined by Bézier curves, shapes can be either Bézier shapes defined by vertices or parametric shapes defined by a set of numerical parameters.

Either way, shapes are vector-based and possess a unique set of attributes you can modify and animate. In addition to the path that defines their, well, shape, shapes also possess fill and stroke properties (including blending modes). You can also add properties to modify each shape's path, fill, and stroke. These include some of the path and paint operations you can find in Illustrator.

A shape layer can contain multiple shapes that you can manipulate individually or in groups. And best of all, you can animate nearly every aspect of the shapes to create countless variations. With shape layers, you can achieve some effects easier than ever before and create other imagery never before possible (**Figures 14.51** and **14.52**).

As you might guess, the following sections won't attempt to explain every attribute or their countless combinations. But after you complete them, you'll know more than enough to start creating shape layers and explore the possibilities on your own.

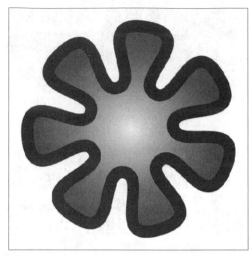

Figure 14.51 With shape layers, you don't have to turn to effects or a program like Illustrator to create graphical elements like this one.

Figure 14.52 Moreover, you can animate numerous shape properties to create more elaborate effects. This Brainstorm panel shows just a handful of variations on a shape layer's properties.

Figure 14.53 Bézier shapes work just like masks or motion paths. Because you can control each vertex in a Bézier shape, it's easy to create asymmetrical shapes.

Figure 14.54 Parametric shapes are defined by parameters you specify, such as the number of points in a star, and so on. This makes them well suited for creating and animating symmetrical, geometric shapes.

Bézier and parametric shapes

In shape layers, you can create two kinds of shapes: Bézier and parametric shapes.

Bézier shapes are defined by vertices (aka control points) connected by line segments. Invisible direction lines (or tangents) extending from each vertex influence the curve before and after the vertex. You modify a Bézier shape just as you would a mask or motion path, by adjusting control points and direction lines, or by using a transform box to scale or rotate it. When creating a shape with the Pen tool, you can have After Effects calculate continuous curves automatically by selecting the RotoBézier option. Typically, you would use Bézier shapes to create asymmetrical, organic looking shapes (**Figure 14.53**).

Parametric shapes are defined by a set of parameters (parametric, parameter, get it?) instead of Bézier curves. In After Effects, these parameters—for example, the number of points in a star—are listed in the shape layer's property outline. With parametric shapes, you can't manipulate individual points as you would in a Bézier shape, but you can more easily create and modify symmetrical, geometric shapes (**Figure 14.54**).

You can also see the difference between Bézier and parametric shapes in the layer's property outline; Bézier objects are defined by a Path property, whereas parametric objects list their parameters, depending on the type of shape (**Figure 14.55**).

Shapes you create with the Pen tool are always Bézier objects. Because you already learned about Bézier curves in Chapter 10, "Mask Essentials," the following sections focus on creating parametric objects using the shape tools.

✔ Tip

■ Because the shapes they create are similar in nature, both the Polygon and Star shape tools create a path identified in the shape layer's property outline as a *Polystar Path*.

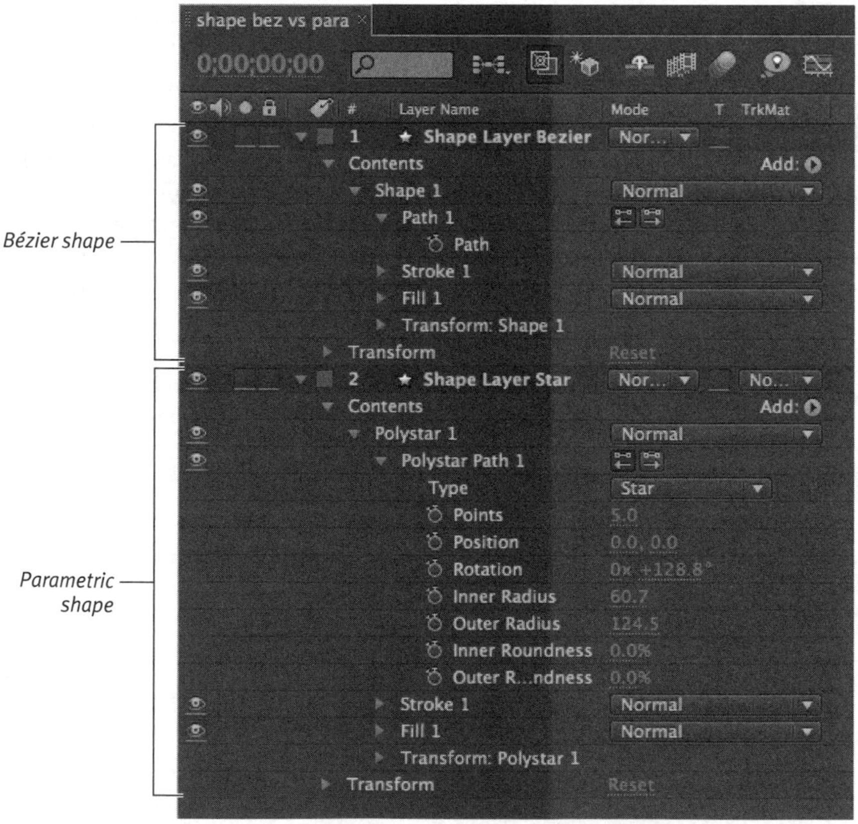

Bézier shape

Parametric shape

Figure 14.55 In a shape layer's property outline, a Bézier has a Path property, and a parametric object is defined by properties according to its type. Here, you can see the properties for a Polystar shape (created by using the Star).

Figure 14.56 Make sure no layers are selected, then choose a shape tool. In this example, the Star tool is selected.

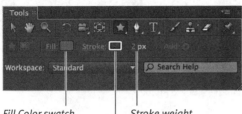

Fill Color swatch   *Stroke weight*

Stroke Color swatch

Figure 14.57 You can specify the shape's fill and stroke beforehand using controls in the Tools panel. You can change (and animate) these and other properties at any time.

Creating Shape Layers

You create shape layers in much the same way as you would create a mask. In fact, you can use the same tools and many of the same techniques you learned in Chapter 10, "Mask Essentials."

However, note the important differences between shapes and masks. By default, drawing with a shape tool creates a parametric object, not a Bézier object. (Drawing with the Pen always creates Bézier objects.) To create a shape layer, no other type of layer can be selected. Otherwise, drawing creates a mask path. If a shape layer is selected, you must specify whether you want to add a shape to the shape layer or mask the shape layer.

To create a new shape layer using a shape tool:

1. Make sure no layers are selected.

If a layer is selected, you will create a mask instead of a shape layer. If a shape layer is selected, you can decide whether to add the new shape to the shape layer or mask it.

2. In the Tools panel, select one of the shape tools (**Figure 14.56**).

As long as no layer is selected, the Create Shape button ★ and Create Mask button ▣ in the Tools panel are grayed out.

3. In the Tools panel, *do either of the following:*

▲ To specify the shape's fill or stroke color, click the corresponding color swatch icon to open a color picker (**Figure 14.57**).

▲ To specify the shape's stroke weight, specify a value, in pixels.

You can add fills and strokes (including gradients) and other attributes after you create the shape.

continues on next page

4. In the Comp panel, *do either of the following:*

▲ To create a parametric shape, drag with the tool (**Figure 14.58**).

▲ To create a Bézier shape, Option-drag (Alt-drag) with the shape tool.

Whether you create a parametric or Bézier shape, you can use other keyboard modifiers to determine the shape while you draw.

5. To complete the shape, release the mouse.

The shape layer appears in the Comp and in the Timeline panel's layer outline (**Figure 14.59**). By default, the shape layer contains a path, fill, and stroke property. It also possesses the usual transform properties that all image layers possess.

To add a shape or mask to a shape layer:

1. Select a shape layer (**Figure 14.60**).

2. In the Tools panel, select a drawing tool. You can select a shape tool or Pen tool.

Figure 14.58 Drag in the Comp panel to create a parametric shape (shown here). Pressing Option (Alt) creates a Bézier shape.

Figure 14.59 The shape layer appears in the layer outline and uses the default still image duration.

Figure 14.60 Select the shape layer to which you want to add a shape or mask.

Create Mask

Create Shape

Figure 14.61 Select a drawing tool, and then specify whether you want to draw a shape or mask.

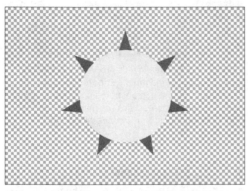

Figure 14.62 Drawing with Create Shape selected adds a shape to the shape layer. Here, an ellipse path has been added to the shape layer containing a star.

Figure 14.63 Drawing with Create Mask selected masks the shape layer. Here, an ellipse masks part of the star. The mask edge is feathered (shapes don't have a feather property).

3. In the Tools panel, *do either of the following* (**Figure 14.61**):

▲ To add a shape to the shape layer, select the Create Shape button

▲ To mask the shape layer, select the Create Mask button

4. In the Comp panel, draw the shape.

If you chose the Create Shape button, a new shape is added to the shape layer and is listed in the layer's property outline (**Figure 14.62**). If you chose the Create Mask button, the new shape masks the shape layer (**Figure 14.63**).

✔ Tips

■ You can deselect all layers by pressing F2 on the keyboard. This way, you'll be sure to create a shape layer and not a mask.

■ You can also create a shape layer using the Pen tool. As usual, you can check the RotoBézier option to have After Effects calculate curves automatically; leave RotoBézier unchecked to draw Bézier curves manually.

■ Shape creation tools retain the most recent settings. For example, drawing with the Star tool creates a polystar with the same number of points as the last time the tool was used.

Working with shape layer properties

When you first create a shape layer, it contains three shape property categories: a path (such as a polystar), a fill, and a stroke. But these properties are more comprehensive than you may expect. For example, you can specify the number of points in a star and its inner and outer radius and roundness (**Figure 14.64**). You can determine which part of a complex shape is filled; you can make strokes dashed and set the appearance of caps and joins.

The shape layer also possesses all the usual layer transform properties, such as position, anchor point, and so on.

Adding properties

What's more, you can add properties to a shape layer (**Figure 14.65**). (The process may remind you of adding properties to a text animator.) These properties can include additional paths, strokes, and fills. They can also specify other modifications, or operations. *Path operations* affect the path. For example, you can combine paths or add a random wiggle to a shape. *Paint operations* affect fill and stroke. For example, you can add gradients.

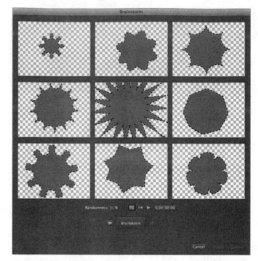

Figure 14.64 A shape layer's properties define its path, fill, stroke, and other attributes. Here, the Brainstorm feature demonstrates how changing some of a shape layer's properties (its number of points, and its inner and outer roundness properties) alters the shape layer.

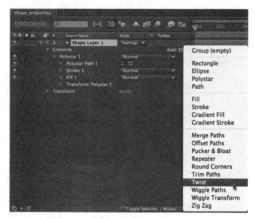

Figure 14.65 An Add pop-up menu lets you add attributes to the shape layer.

Figure 14.66 A single shape layer can contain multiple paths that you can arrange into groups. Selecting this shape layer depicting a gear...

Figure 14.67 ...reveals that it consists of several paths: a star, a polygon, rectangles, and circles.

Stacking order

Each shape and attribute behaves a lot like a layer within a layer. You can rename shapes and properties, and each one has a Blending mode pop-up menu and a video switch that lets you exclude or include it in output. Because the attributes listed in the shape layer's property outline are applied from the bottom of the list to the top, their relative order affects the final result. You can change the order by dragging in the shape's property outline (in much the same way as you would change the order of effects in the Effect Controls panel).

Groups

For an even greater degree of control, you can group shapes and properties. You can create an empty group using the Add pop-up menu, or simply drag items into a property heading. This way, each group is affected by its own set of attributes, yet each coexists in the same shape layer (**Figures 14.66** and **14.67**).

Paint and path operations

The bottom two sections of a shape layer's Add pop-up menu (also available in the Tools panel when the shape layer is selected) lists paint and path operations.

Paint operations are very useful and relatively straightforward: They let you apply additional fills, strokes, or gradients.

Path operations are more exciting; they include vector-based effects like the ones found in Illustrator. Path operations help you form more complex shapes (as you saw in Figure 14.67). Effects like pucker and bloat can transform a hexagon into a flower or curvy ornamentation (**Figures 14.68** and **14.69**). Wiggle or Zig Zag turns smooth contours into a vibrating squiggle (**Figure 14.70**).

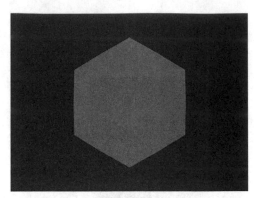

Figure 14.68 Start with a simple shape like this hexagon...

Figure 14.69 ...and use Pucker and Bloat to warp it into a flowerlike figure.

Figure 14.70 Adding Zig Zag turns it into this complex pattern.

CREATING SHAPE LAYERS

Figure 14.71 In the shape layer's property outline, click the Add button and select an option in the pop-up menu.

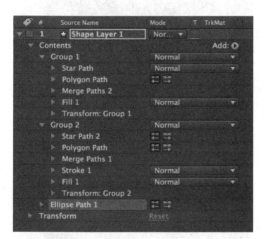

Figure 14.72 The property you specified appears in the selected category heading of the shape layer's property outline.

To add a group or property to a shape layer:

1. In the Timeline panel, expand a shape layer's property outline and select the property heading to which you want to add a property.

2. In the shape layer's property outline, click the Add button and select an item from the pop-up menu (**Figure 14.71**).

   The attribute appears as the bottommost property in the layer's property outline (**Figure 14.72**). If you add a group, a group heading appears but doesn't contain anything until you add items to the group, as explained in the following task, "To reorder or group shape properties."

To reorder or group shape properties:

1. In the Timeline panel, expand the shape layer's property outline.

2. In the shape layer's property outline, *do any of the following:*

   ▲ To group a property, drag it to highlight a property heading (**Figure 14.73**).

   The property is moved to the position you specified or becomes listed within the group heading (**Figure 14.74**).

   ▲ To change the stacking order of shape layer properties, drag the property to the position you want (**Figures 14.75** and **14.76**).

✔ Tip

■ The procedures for adding shape attributes may remind you of adding text properties and ranges to text animator groups; the concept of applying shape attributes up the stacking order reflects After Effect's overall process for rendering comps.

■ After Effects CS4 expands the repertoire of a shape layer's fill and stroke blend modes to include linear burn, darker color, linear dodge, linear color, linear light, vivid light, pin light, and hard mix.

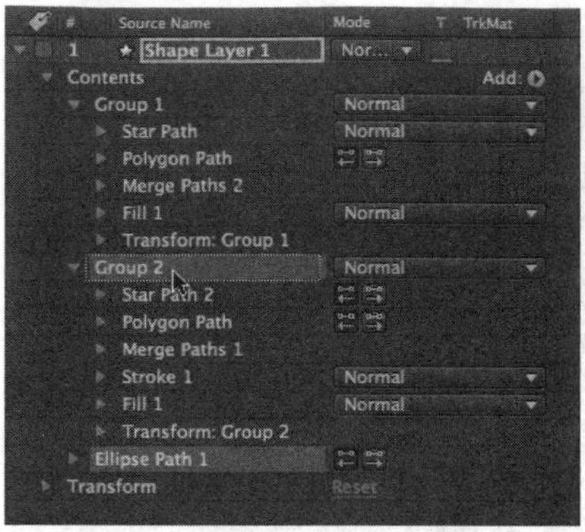

Figure 14.73 To group a shape or property, drag it to highlight another property heading and release the mouse button...

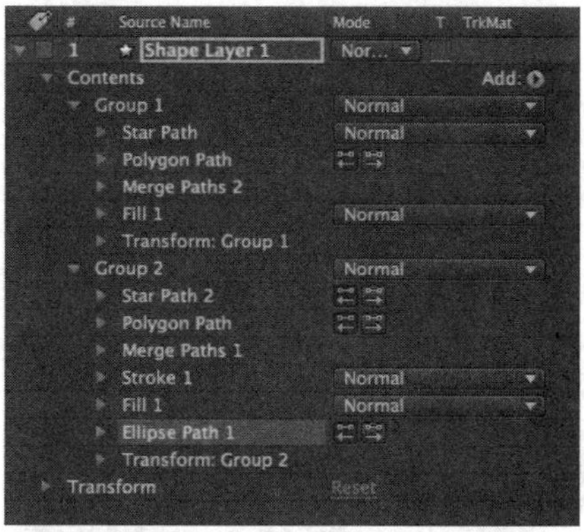

Figure 14.74 ... so that it appears within the property category.

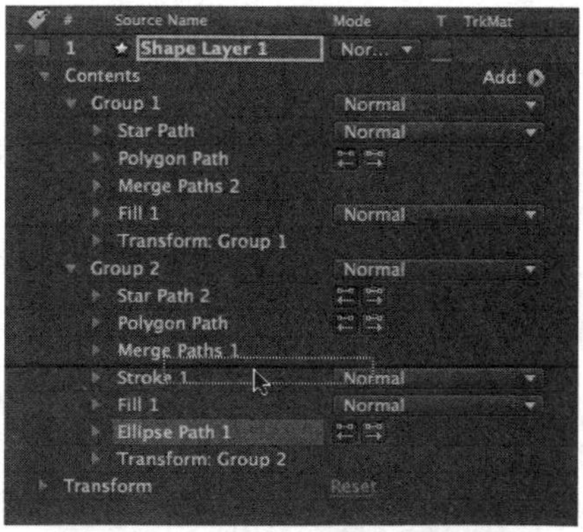

Figure 14.75 To change a shape attribute's place in the stacking order, drag it so that a black line indicates its new position...

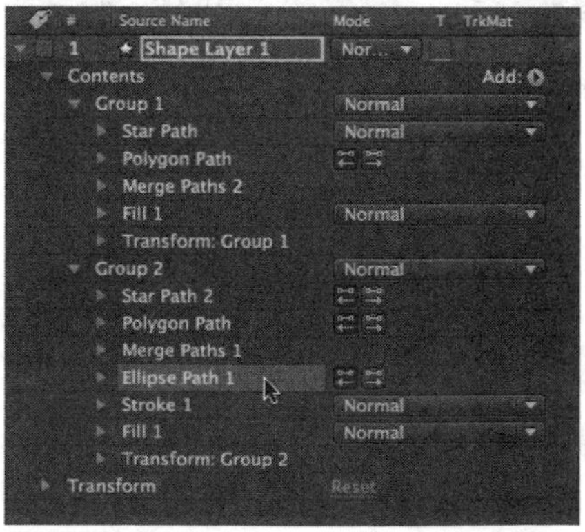

Figure 14.76 ...and then release the mouse button to place it in that position.

Figure 14.77 The Tools panel includes a new set of tools, Puppet tools.

Figure 14.78 A Puppet effect uses a mesh that interconnects points within the layer...

Figure 14.79 ...so that distortions seem organic and natural.

Using the Puppet Effect

Not every effect merits a section devoted to it. But the Puppet effect is so useful it deserves special treatment. The presence of a set of a special Puppet tools right in the Tools panel bespeaks the effect's special status (**Figure 14.77**).

Like Paint, you can apply the Puppet effect by just using its tools. However, you can still find the Puppet effect listed in the Effects & Presets panel under the Distort category. That's because the Puppet effect is essentially a kind of mesh warp effect. That is, it moves the pixels in a layer based on a *mesh*, an overlay of interconnected points that resembles a web, or a net (albeit one with a triangular weave) (**Figure 14.78**). Instead of moving a layer's pixels independent of one another, the mesh connects any given point on the layer to nearby points. This way, when you move a point on the layer, the rest of the layer responds in an organic, natural-looking way (**Figure 14.79**).

With the Puppet effect, you specify the points you want to manipulate with the Puppet Pin tool ▣. "Pinned" points don't move unless you move them. They act as the layer's pivot points to articulate the layer—your puppet, if you will. To control the malleability or stiffness of the mesh between pinned points, you can use the Puppet Starch tool ▣. And to specify whether part of the puppet appears in front of or behind an overlapping part, use the Puppet Overlap tool ▣.

By animating the position of the Pins (as well as the Starch and Overlap) you can move a puppet as though the layer were a bendable, poseable toy. You can even record your mouse movements as keyframes for even more natural movement.

When working with the Puppet effect, bear in mind that the mesh is based on the layer's alpha channel at its native size. And remember that as an effect, a Puppet effect renders after masks but before transformations. This means that in order to transform (scale, rotate, etc.) a puppet layer, you may have to use nesting or the Transform effect.

✔ Tip

■ For more about using nesting and the Transform effect to channel the rendering order, see Chapter 16, "Complex Projects."

To animate with Puppet tools:

1. Set the comp's current time to the point you want to begin animating a layer with the Puppet effect.

2. In the Tools panel, select the Puppet Pin tool.

3. In the Tools panel, specify any of the following options (**Figure 14.80**):

   Show Mesh—Displays the puppet mesh as you work.

   Expansion—Shrinks or expands the mesh area.

   Triangles—Sets the relative density of the mesh.

   You can change these settings at any time. See the section, "Refining Puppet Animations," later in this chapter.

4. Using the Puppet Pin tool, click the points on the layer you want to pin.

   A yellow dot or circle indicates a Puppet Pin (**Figure 14.81**). In the Timeline panel, the Puppet effect appears in the layer's property outline. A keyframe for each Puppet Pin's position is set at the current time automatically.

5. To view the Puppet Pin points in the layer's property outline, expand the Puppet effect until you reveal the Puppet Pin properties (**Figure 14.82**).

Figure 14.80 Set the current time to the point you want to start animating, and then choose the Puppet Pin tool and specify mesh options.

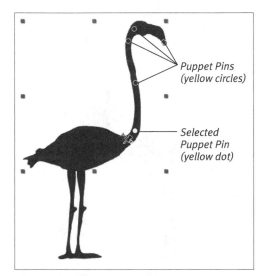

Figure 14.81 Clicking the layer sets Puppet Pins, indicated by yellow dots.

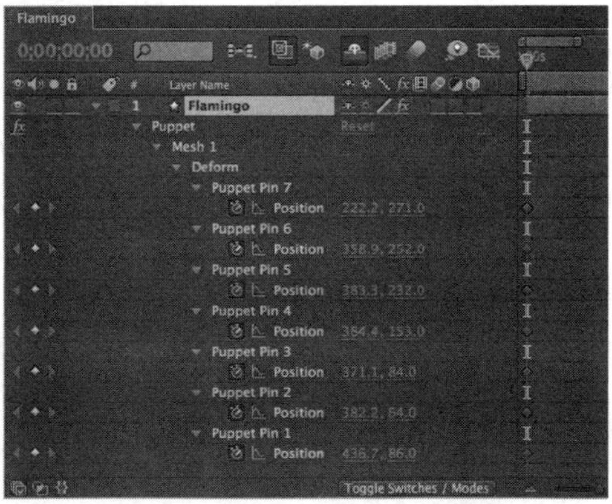

Figure 14.82 In the layer's property outline, you can see that a keyframe is set for each Puppet Pin's position automatically.

Figure 14.83 Set the current time to the frame in which you want to set a new Puppet Pin keyframe and move a Puppet Pin to a new position. The puppet distorts according to the pins.

6. Set the current time to the frame on which you want to set a Puppet Pin position keyframe.

7. *Do either of the following:*

▲ In the layer's property outline, click the Add Keyframe button to create a keyframe that uses the previously interpolated values for that frame.

▲ In the Comp panel, drag the Puppet Pin to a new position (**Figure 14.83**).

In the layer's property outline, you can see a new keyframe for the selected Puppet Pin (**Figure 14.84**).

8. Repeat steps 6 and 7 as needed and preview the animation.

✔ Tip

■ Once you set a Puppet Pin, you can't move it without also distorting the puppet layer. If you don't like the Puppet Pin's position relative to the mesh, select the Puppet Pin (so that the dot is solid) and then delete it.

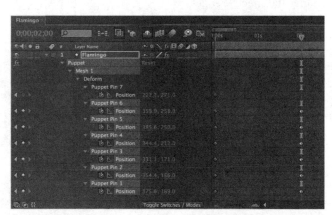

Figure 14.84 In the layer's property outline, a new keyframe is created.

USING THE PUPPET EFFECT

Refining Puppet Animations

The previous section explained the overall procedure for animating a layer with the Puppet effect; the following sections explain how to fine-tune the animation. First, you'll learn to refine the mesh. Then, you'll learn how the Puppet Starch and Puppet Overlap tools can make movement more convincing. Finally, you'll animate Pin points by recording the movements of the mouse.

Mesh triangles and expansion

Puppet distortions are influenced by the mesh's fundamental properties: its triangles and expansion. The Triangles property refers to the number of triangular areas described by the intersecting lines of the mesh. The more triangles a mesh has, the more points on which to base distortions. The result is greater precision, but also longer processing time. The Expansion property affects the mesh's coverage of the puppet layer. Although the mesh is based on the layer's alpha channel, you can expand or contract the mesh (just as you might change the effective edges of a mask). You might, for example, expand the mesh so that you can place Puppet Pin points outside the visible part of the layer. In some cases, this could prevent the Pin from causing unwanted distortions. Unlike other Puppet effect properties, you can't animate Triangles or Expansion.

Mesh: ☐ Show   Expansion: 9   Triangles: 600

Figure 14.85 You can customize the mesh according to your needs by setting a value for Triangles and for Expansion.

Figure 14.86 This mesh's Triangle and Expansion values are set to the defaults.

Figure 14.87 Here, the mesh's expansion is increased to 12; its density is increased to 700.

To set the mesh triangles and expansion:

1. To view the mesh options:
   - ▲ Select the layer containing the Puppet effect and select the Puppet Pin tool ⬛.
   - ▲ In the Timeline panel, expand the layer's property outline to reveal the Puppet effect and the properties it contains.

   The Comp panel shows Puppet Pin points.

2. To make the mesh visible, select Show Mesh in the Tools panel.

3. In either the property outline or the Tools panel, specify the following options (**Figure 14.85**):

   Triangles specifies the density of the mesh; higher values create more inter-sections in the mesh, thereby increasing precision and rendering times.

   Expansion specifies the mesh's size; lower values shrink the mesh, whereas higher values expand the mesh beyond the sides of the layer (determined by the layer's alpha channel).

   The mesh uses the values you specify (**Figures 14.86** and **14.87**).

REFINING PUPPET ANIMATIONS

Using Puppet Starch

Like its namesake, the Starch tool ⬛ makes areas on the mesh more stiff—or put another way, it makes parts of the mesh less responsive to distortions caused by the Puppet Pin points. By making some parts of the puppet less flexible than others, the puppet's movements can seem more natural (**Figures 14.88** and **14.89**).

Clicking on the mesh with the Starch tool sets Starch points, which appear as red dots on the puppet layer in the Comp panel. In the layer's property outline, Starch points appear under a category called Stiffness. You can control the size of the area affected by each starch point (the Extent), and the degree of stiffness (its Amount).

Whereas Pin points remain attached to a particular point on the mesh, Starch points can be moved relative to the mesh. You can animate a Starch point's Position, Amount, and Extent properties.

Figure 14.88 In this figure, the flamingo has no starch.

Figure 14.89 Here, the same puppet has starch in one part of its neck.

Figure 14.90 Select the Puppet Starch tool and specify values for Amount and Extent.

To make the mesh more or less flexible:

1. In the Tools panel, select the Puppet Starch tool 🔧.

2. In the Tools panel, specify the following options (**Figure 14.90**):

   ▲ **Show Mesh**—Lets you view the puppet effect's mesh as you work

   ▲ **Amount**—Specifies the relative stiffness of the mesh surrounding the Starch point; high values make the mesh more inflexible.

   ▲ **Extent**—Specifies the area surrounding the Starch point affected by the Starch Amount setting; higher Extent values affect a larger area of the mesh.

3. In the Comp panel, click the puppet layer where you want to affect the mesh's flexibility.

   Starch points appear as red dots; the Extent appears as a shaded area around the dot; the opacity of the shaded area correlates with the specified Amount value (**Figure 14.91**) so that 0% appears transparent and higher values appear gray.

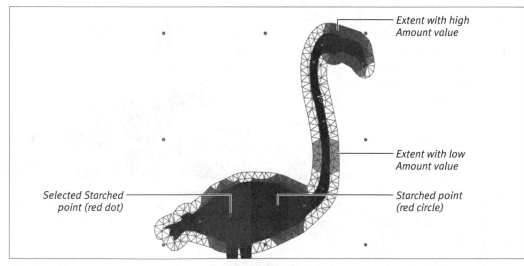

Figure 14.91 Clicking sets Starch points, indicated by red dots. The size and opacity of shaded areas correspond to the Extent and Amount values, respectively.

USING PUPPET STARCH

Using Puppet Overlap

It's possible to distort a puppet layer so that one area overlaps with another. When areas overlap, viewers expect one part to be in front, and the other behind—despite the fact all parts of the layer occupy the same plane and have no real depth (**Figure 14.92**).

Fortunately, you can specify layering with the Puppet Overlap tool. Clicking with the tool creates Overlap points, which appear as blue dots on the mesh. An Extent property determines the area surrounding the point affected by the In Front value. When a layer with a higher In Front value overlaps one with a lower value, it appears (predictably) in front—hence, creating the illusion of depth.

To specify how areas of the puppet overlap:

1. In the Tool panel, select the Puppet Overlap tool .

2. In the Tools panel, specify the following options (**Figure 14.93**):

   ▲ **Show Mesh**—Lets you view the puppet effect's mesh as you work.

   ▲ **In Front**—Specifies the area's apparent depth relative to other areas.

   ▲ **Extent**—Specifies the area surrounding the Overlap point affected by the In Front setting; higher Extent values affect a larger area of the mesh.

3. In the Comp panel, click the puppet layer where you want areas to control.

   Overlap points appear as blue dots; the Extent appears as a shaded area around the dot; the brightness of the shaded area correlates with the specified In Front value, so that higher values appear whiter (**Figure 14.94**).

Figure 14.92 In this example, points of the star with higher overlap values appear above points with lower values.

Figure 14.93 Select the Puppet Overlap tool and specify values for In Front and Extent.

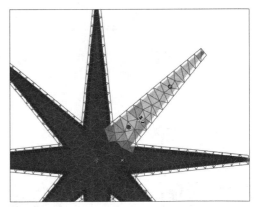

Figure 14.94 Clicking sets Overlap points, indicated by blue dots. The size and brightness of highlighted areas correspond to the Extent and In Front values, respectively.

Figure 14.95 Select the Puppet Pin tool and then click Record Options.

Figure 14.96 In the Puppet Record Options dialog, specify the settings you want and then click OK.

Animating Puppets by Sketching with the Mouse

A real-world puppet seems to come to life by the deft string-pulling of its puppet master. Puppet layers in After Effects don't have strings, but they do have the digital equivalent. Each tug—I mean drag—of the mouse on a Puppet Pin point can be recorded in real-time as keyframes. So instead of painstakingly and mechanically setting keyframes in the usual fashion, the puppet simply reenacts your puppeteering performance.

To animate puppets by sketching:

1. Set Puppet Pins points, Starch points, and Overlap points, as described in the previous sections.

2. In the Tools panel, select the Puppet Pin tool.

3. In the Tools panel, click Record Options (**Figure 14.95**).

continues on next page

Selecting and Modifying Puppet Properties

You can change the mesh's density and expansion at any time, but you can't keyframe those values. In contrast, you can change the position and properties of Starch and Overlap points at any time and keyframe their values.

To make Starch and Overlap points appear in the Comp panel, you must select a layer's Puppet effect and the corresponding tool. For example, select the Puppet effect and the Puppet starch tool to make Starch points appear in the Comp panel. Whatever kind of point you're viewing (Puppet Pin, Starch, or Overlap), selected points appear as solid dots; deselected points appear as hollow dots. When setting Starch or Overlap points, Puppet Pin points appear as small yellow "x"s. And remember that you can always toggle the mesh visibility by clicking the Show Mesh option in the Tools panel.

4. In the Puppet Record Options dialog, you'll find several settings (**Figure 14.96**):

▲ **Speed**—Specifies the recording speed relative to the playback speed of the motion; a value of 100% plays back motion at the same speed at which it was recorded; higher values play back the motion more slowly.

▲ **Smoothing**—Specifies how much to smooth the recorded motion by removing extraneous keyframes; higher values result in fewer recorded keyframes and smoother motion.

▲ **Use Draft Deformation**—Indicates that the distortion doesn't reflect Starch points; the preview outline can be less accurate, but the recording performance can be improved.

▲ **Show Mesh**—Makes the puppet mesh visible while you record mouse movements.

5. Click OK to close the Puppet Record Options dialog.

6. In the Comp panel, press Command (Ctrl) as you position the mouse pointer over a Puppet Pin.

The Puppet Pin tool appears with a Clock icon.

7. Pressing Command (Ctrl), drag the Puppet Pin in the manner you want the puppet to move (**Figure 14.97**).

After Effects records the mouse's movements as keyframes for the selected Puppet Pin (**Figure 14.98**).

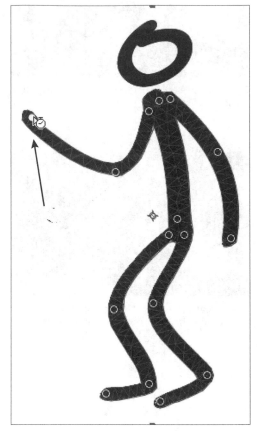

Figure 14.97 Pressing Command (Ctrl) as you drag a Puppet Pin...

Figure 14.98 ...records the movement as keyframes, according to the options you specified.

3D Layers

Up to now, you've dealt strictly with layers in two dimensions: horizontal and vertical, as measured on the X and Y axes. However, After Effects includes depth as well, measured along the Z axis. As in other 3D programs, you can create one or more cameras from which to view and render your 3D composition. You can also create lights to illuminate 3D layers that cast realistic shadows and have adjustable reflective properties. And despite their unique properties, you can adjust and animate 3D layers, cameras, and lights just as you would any 2D layer.

True, After Effects' 3D layers are just 2D panels in 3D space, and the program doesn't incorporate any of the modeling tools or other features you're likely to find in a dedicated 3D application. Even so, bringing the program into the 3D space *does* open a new frontier of creative exploration. For example, the sole ability to view the composition from custom camera views fundamentally alters how you would have approached a similar animation in the past. Similarly, 3D lighting features let you manipulate light and shadows in ways that were once difficult or impossible to achieve.

Using 3D

When you designate a layer to be three-dimensional, it acquires additional transform properties as well as "material" properties exclusive to 3D layers (**Figure 15.1**). (See "Using 3D Orientation and Rotation," "Using 3D Position," and "Using 3D Material Options," later in this chapter.) By default, 3D layers are positioned at a Z coordinate of 0.

With After Effects, you can use 2D and 3D layers in the same compositions, although doing so can add complexity to the rendering order. (See "Combining 2D and 3D," later in this chapter for more about rendering order.) Note that cameras and lights are inherently 3D objects and can't be transformed to 2D objects.

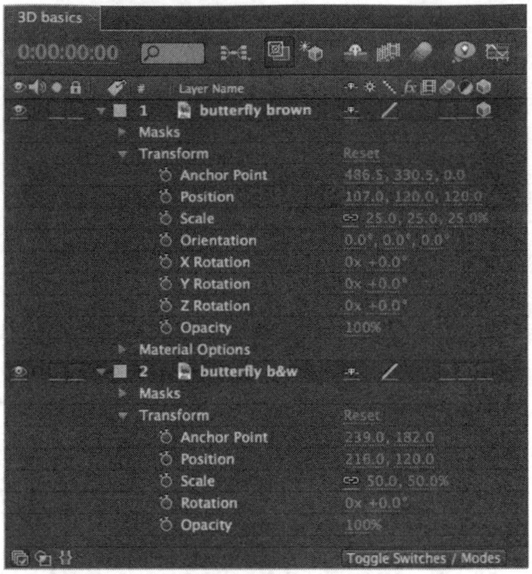

To designate a layer as 3D:

◆ On the Switches panel of the Timeline panel, click the 3D switch that corresponds to the layer you want to designate (**Figure 15.2**).

The Cube icon appears ▨. The layer becomes a 3D layer and acquires 3D transform and material properties.

To convert a 3D layer back to 2D:

◆ On the Switches panel of the Timeline panel, click the Cube icon ▨ to make it disappear and convert the layer back into a 2D layer.

The layer becomes a 2D layer and loses its 3D transform and material properties.

✔ Tip

■ Most effects that simulate three-dimensional distortions (like the Bulge effect) are really 2D effects. Thus, when you make a layer 3D, these effects remain 2D and won't distort the layer along the *Z* axis.

Figure 15.1 When you make a layer three-dimensional, it acquires new transform properties that take Z-depth and rotation into account. 3D layers also have a Material Options property category.

Figure 15.2 In the Switches panel of the Timeline panel, click the 3D switch for a layer to make a Cube icon appear.

Figure 15.3 Orthogonal views (Front, Left, Right, Back, Top, and Bottom) accurately represent lengths and distances at the expense of perspective. (Compare this Front view with Figure 15.5.)

Figure 15.4 By default, Custom View 1 shows the composition from above and to the left. Although Custom views aren't associated with an actual camera layer, you can adjust them using Camera tools.

Figure 15.5 Select a camera's name in the 3D View pop-up menu to see the composition through the lens of that camera.

Viewing 3D Layers in the Comp Panel

The presence of 3D objects in a composition activates additional viewing options in a 3D View pop-up menu in the Composition panel. By selecting different views, you can see and manipulate 3D layers, cameras, and lights from different angles. The views in this list fall into three categories: Orthogonal views, Custom views, and Camera views.

Orthogonal views show the composition from the six sides of its 3D space: front, left, right, back, top, and bottom. In an Orthogonal view, lengths and distances are displayed accurately at the expense of perspective (**Figure 15.3**).

Custom views show the composition from three predefined viewpoints, which you can adjust by using Camera tools (see "Adjusting Views with Camera Tools," later in this chapter). However, these views aren't associated with an actual camera layer in the composition (**Figure 15.4**).

Camera views show the composition from a camera layer you create or—if there's no camera—from a default Camera view (**Figure 15.5**).

Unlike Orthogonal views, both Custom views and Camera views represent the composition from a three-dimensional perspective. Distant objects look smaller; closer objects appear larger. Objects viewed at an angle are foreshortened so that right angles appear acute or obtuse, and lengths and distances appear compressed. The type of lens emulated by a camera also affects perspective. (See "Using Cameras," later in this chapter.)

To specify a 3D view:

◆ In the Composition panel, select a view from the Active Camera pop-up menu (**Figure 15.6**):

▲ **Active Camera**—Activates the Camera view listed at the top of the Timeline panel's layer outline. If no cameras are present, Active Camera uses a default view.

▲ **Front**—Shows the composition from the front, without perspective.

▲ **Left**—Shows the composition from the left side, without perspective.

▲ **Top**—Shows the composition from above, without perspective.

▲ **Back**—Shows the composition from behind, without perspective.

▲ **Right**—Shows the composition from the right side, without perspective.

▲ **Bottom**—Shows the composition from below, without perspective.

▲ **Custom View 1–3**—Shows the composition from a point of view you can adjust using the Camera tools. These views aren't associated with a camera layer.

▲ **[Custom Camera Name]**—Shows the composition from the view of the camera you create. Camera views appear in the 3D View pop-up menu when you create a camera layer.

The Composition panel shows the composition from the perspective of the selected view.

✔ Tips

■ You can assign a 3D view to keyboard shortcuts F10, F11, and F12. Set the 3D view and choose View > Assign Shortcut to [current view] > and in the submenu, choose the shortcut.

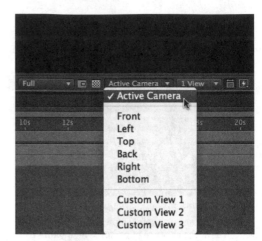

Figure 15.6 In the Composition panel, select a view from the Active Camera pop-up menu.

■ By default, the Mac OS uses F10, F11, and F12 as keyboard shortcuts. Disable them in the Keyboard and Mouse panel of the System Preferences to use these keys as shortcuts in After Effects.

■ As you progress through this chapter, view your 3D layers from different angles. After you grow accustomed to adjusting 3D layer properties, you'll learn how to adjust the views themselves using Camera tools. Finally, you'll create your own cameras and move them around the 3D composition. In other words, take it one step at a time.

Figure 15.7 If you're using a three-button mouse, you can take full advantage of the Unified Camera tool. Select the Unified Camera tool...

Adjusting Views with Camera Tools

Camera tools move the perspective of a 3D view much as you would move a real camera left, right, toward, or around a subject. Prior to After Effects CS4, you would switch among the Track XY, Track Z, and Orbit camera tools to accomplish these moves. With the new Unified Camera tool, you can switch to the tool you want by pressing the appropriate button on a three-button mouse.

When the 3D view is set to a Custom view, a camera tool changes its perspective for viewing purposes. When the 3D view is set to a camera layer you create, a camera tool moves the camera's position.

In this section, you'll use Camera tools to change the perspective of a 3D view, particularly a Custom view. By definition, the Orthogonal views prohibit camera angles other than their namesake (Front, Back, Left, Right, Top, or Bottom) and thereby prevent the use of the Orbit Camera tool. Orthogonal views do permit the Track XY and Track Z Camera tools, however.

Once you learn how to create and use camera layers, you can use Camera tools to move the camera (see the section "Moving Cameras with Camera Tools" later in this chapter).

To toggle the function of the Unified Camera tool:

1. In the Tools panel, select the Unified Camera tool (**Figure 15.7**).

continues on next page

ADJUSTING VIEWS WITH CAMERA TOOLS

2. *Do either of the following:*

▲ To adjust a 3D camera view, choose a Custom or Orthogonal view from the 3D View menu in the Composition panel.

▲ To adjust a camera, choose the name of the camera from the 3D View menu in the Composition panel.

3. Position the Unified Camera tool in the selected 3D view, and *do any of the following:*

▲ To toggle to the Orbit Camera function, press the left mouse button (**Figure 15.8**).

▲ To toggle to the Track XY Camera function, press the middle mouse button (**Figure 15.9**).

▲ To toggle to the Track Z Camera function, press the right mouse button (**Figure 15.10**).

The mouse pointer changes accordingly.

4. Drag the mouse to adjust the view or camera position (depending on your choice in step 2).

Figure 15.8 ...and toggle to the Orbit Camera function by pressing the right mouse button...

Figure 15.9 ...to the Track XY Camera function by pressing the middle mouse button...

Figure 15.10 ...and to the Track Z Camera function by pressing the right mouse button.

Figure 15.11 Select a Camera tool.

Figure 15.12 Dragging with the Orbit Camera tool...

To adjust a camera or view using Camera tools:

1. In the 3D View menu in the Composition panel, select a Custom or Orthogonal view.

   Note that you can't use the Orbit Camera tool in an Orthogonal view (which includes Front, Back, Left, Right, Top, or Bottom).

2. In the Tools panel, select a Camera tool (**Figure 15.11**):

   ▲ **Unified Camera** 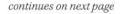—Dragging the tool in a 3D view functions as the Orbit Camera, Track XY Camera, or Track Z Camera tool, depending on the button you press on a three-button mouse.

   ▲ **Orbit Camera** —Dragging the tool in a 3D view rotates the perspective around its center in any direction (**Figures 15.12** and **15.13**). This tool can't be used in an Orthogonal view.

   ▲ **Track XY Camera** —Dragging the tool in a 3D view shifts the perspective along the view's *X* or *Y* axis (side-to-side or up and down) (**Figure 15.14**).

   continues on next page

Figure 15.13 ...rotates the view.

Figure 15.14 Dragging with the Track XY Camera tool lets you move the view or camera along its *X* and *Y* axes. Here, the camera has tracked left from its position in Figure 15.9.

▲ **Track Z Camera** ▦—Dragging the tool in a 3D view moves the perspective along the view's *Z* axis (similar to a camera dollying in or out) (**Figure 15.15**).

In an Orthogonal view, the 3D layers limit how far you can track in along the *Z* axis.

3. In the Composition panel, drag the mouse pointer.

The camera position or view changes according to the Camera tool you use.

To focus a 3D view on selected layers:

1. Set the Comp panel to the 3D view you want to adjust.

2. In a Comp panel or Timeline panel, select one or more 3D layers (**Figure 15.16**).

3. Choose View > Look at Selected Layers.

The 3D view adjusts so that the selected layers appear large and centered in the 3D view (**Figure 15.17**).

To reset a 3D view:

1. Set the Comp panel to the 3D view you want to reset.

2. Choose View > Reset 3D View.

The view's perspective adjusts to its default setting.

Figure 15.15 Dragging with the Track Z Camera tool lets you move the view or camera along its Z axis. Here, the view has dollied in from its position in Figure 15.14, closer to the star layer.

Figure 15.16 Select the 3D view you want to adjust, and select one or more 3D layers.

Figure 15.17 ...adjusts the view to frame-up that layer automatically.

Figure 15.18 Although you can change a single 3D view...

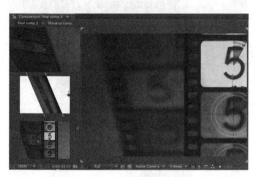

Figure 15.19 ...it's better to set the Comp panel's view layout to show several views at once.

Using Comp Panel Layouts

As you've seen, it would be practically impossible to work in 3D without being able to view layers from various perspectives. But the usefulness of 3D views would be severely limited if you could see only one at a time; having to switch from one view to another would make your progress awkward and slow (**Figure 15.18**). Fortunately, you can show several views in a single Comp panel by selecting a Comp panel layout (**Figure 15.19**).

You can make changes in the view best suited to the task. And by seeing the changes you make from different perspectives at once, it's easier to get them right the first time.

You can specify whether the views share Comp View Options and other settings (such as grids and guides, channels, and so on) or use individual settings. However, all views use the same Resolution setting. You can set each view's magnification setting and 3D view (Orthogonal, Custom, or Camera view) individually, and at any time.

To specify a view layout in the Comp panel:

1. In the Comp panel's View Layout menu (located next to the 3D View menu), choose an option (**Figure 15.20**):

   ▲ **1 View**

   ▲ **2 Views – Horizontal**

   ▲ **2 Views – Vertical**

   ▲ **4 Views**

   ▲ **4 Views – Left**

   ▲ **4 Views – Right**

   ▲ **4 Views – Top**

   ▲ **4 Views – Bottom**

   The Comp panel reflects your choice.

2. To make all views use the same view options, select Share View Options in the View Layout pop-up menu.

   Options include those in the View Options dialog (accessed via the Comp panel's pop-up menu) and other Comp view settings, except for Magnification and Resolution.

To specify the active view:

◆ In the Comp panel, click the view you want to use.

   Triangular highlights appear in the corners of the active view (**Figure 15.21**). Comp panel buttons affect the active view.

✔ Tip

■ If your mouse has a scroll wheel, you can hover the mouse over the view and use the scroll wheel to change the view's magnification setting, even if it's not the active view.

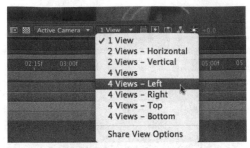

Figure 15.20 Choose a layout in the Comp panel's View Layout pop-up menu.

Figure 15.21 Clicking a view activates it, as evidenced by highlights in the view's corners. Comp panel buttons affect the active view.

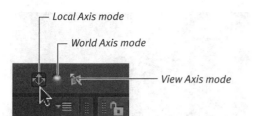

Local Axis mode

World Axis mode

View Axis mode

Figure 15.22 In the Tools panel, select an axis mode.

Figure 15.23 Here, the Local Axis mode aligns the axes to the selected object (a light). X is red, Y is green, and Z is blue. In Figures 15.25, 15.26, and 15.27, the axes are highlighted and labeled to make them identifiable in a black-and-white image.

Using Axis Modes

In the layer outline, the spatial transform properties (Position and Rotation) are expressed in terms of X, Y, and Z axes, which intersect at the center of your composition's 3D "world." When you transform a layer by dragging in the Composition panel, however, you won't always want changes to occur according to these world axes.

Axis modes let you specify whether transformations you make in the Comp panel are expressed in terms of the 3D object (Local Axis mode), the comp's X, Y, and Z planes (World Axis mode), or the current view (View Axis mode). Choosing how the axes are aligned makes moving and rotating 3D objects in the Comp panel a more flexible and intuitive process. The axis mode you employ doesn't affect transformations you make using the property controls in the layer outline; instead, these are expressed in terms of the world axis coordinate system.

To change axis modes:

1. Select a 3D layer, camera, or light.

2. In the Tools panel, select an axis mode (**Figure 15.22**):

   ▲ **Local Axis mode** ⬚—Aligns the axes used for transformations to the selected 3D object (**Figure 15.23**)

   continues on next page

▲ **World Axis mode** ■—Aligns the axes used for transformations to the 3D planes of the composition **(Figure 15.24)**

▲ **View Axis mode** ■—Aligns the axes used for transformations to the current 3D view **(Figure 15.25)**

The set of axes you select appears in the Composition panel. In Figures 15.25, 15.26, and 15.27, the axes are highlighted and labeled to make them identifiable in a black-and-white image.

3. Transform the selected object in the Composition panel by dragging it or by altering its transform properties in the layer outline.

Transformations occur according to the axes you selected. However, the transformation property values in the layer outline continue to be expressed in absolute terms, according to the world axis coordinate system.

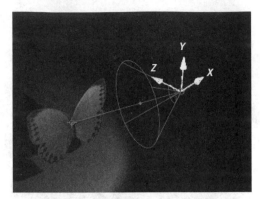

Figure 15.24 World Axis mode aligns the axes to the composition's X, Y, and Z planes.

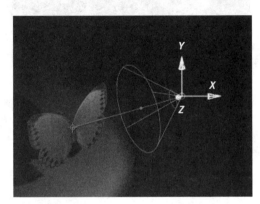

Figure 15.25 View Axis mode aligns the axes to the current 3D view.

Figure 15.26 In the Composition panel, position the mouse pointer over the axis along which you want to move the layer. The pointer should be labeled with the axis letter.

Figure 15.27 Drag the layer along the selected axis.

Using 3D Position

For 3D layers, position is expressed as a three-dimensional property with values for X, Y, and Z coordinates along the world axes. As with 2D position, 3D position corresponds to a layer's anchor point.

To move a 3D layer in the Comp panel:

1. In the 3D View pop-up menu, select a view.

2. In Tools, select an axis mode.

3. Select a 3D layer, camera, or light.

   The selected layer's axes appear. The X axis is red; the Y axis is green; the Z axis is blue. The axes align according to the axis mode you specified.

4. In the Composition panel, position the Selection tool over the axis along which you want to move the layer (**Figure 15.26**).

   The Selection tool icon includes the letter corresponding to the axis: $\blacktriangleright_X$ to move the layer along the X axis, $\blacktriangleright_Y$ to move the layer along the Y axis, or $\blacktriangleright_Z$ to move the layer along the Z axis.

5. Drag the layer along the selected axis (**Figure 15.27**).

   In the layer outline of the Timeline panel, the layer's Position property reflects the changes in terms of the world axis coordinate system.

✔ Tips

- You can change the anchor point of a 3D layer just as you would a 2D layer—except that the anchor point for 3D layers includes a value for its *Z*-axis coordinate. You will only be able to adjust the *X* and *Y* values of an anchor point in a Layer panel. To adjust an anchor point's position along the *Z* axis, use the property controls in the layer outline, or drag the anchor point in the Composition panel using the Pan Behind tool ▥. As you'll recall from Chapter 7, "Properties and Keyframes," the Pan Behind tool recalculates position as it transforms the anchor point, leaving the layer's relative position in the composition undisturbed.

- Lights and cameras can also have transform properties that define their point of interest. See "Using the Point of Interest," later in this chapter.

Separate X, Y, and Z Position Properties

As explained in the section, "Separating a Position's Dimensions," in Chapter 9, "Keyframe Interpolation," you can achieve certain animations more easily by treating each dimension (the X, Y—and in the case of 3D layers—Z values) of a layer's position as separate properties. This may be particularly true for 3D layers.

But also remember that although separating dimensions can make some tasks easier, it can also make it harder to make moves smooth, and it won't permit you to use roving keyframes. And because each dimension is independent, it can be more difficult to understand the layer's motion path.

Selecting the position property and choosing Animate > Separate Dimensions (or clicking the Separate Dimensions button in the Graph Editor) breaks the position property into its components.

You might compare the choice between animating a single position property and individual dimensions to animating a 3D layer's Orientation property versus its X, Y, and Z rotation properties—as explained in the next section.

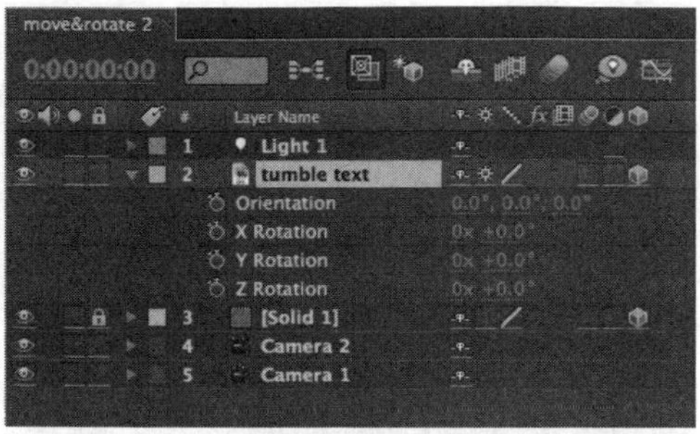

Figure 15.28 Three-dimensional layers, cameras, and lights can be rotated using a single Orientation property, or X, Y, and Z Rotation properties.

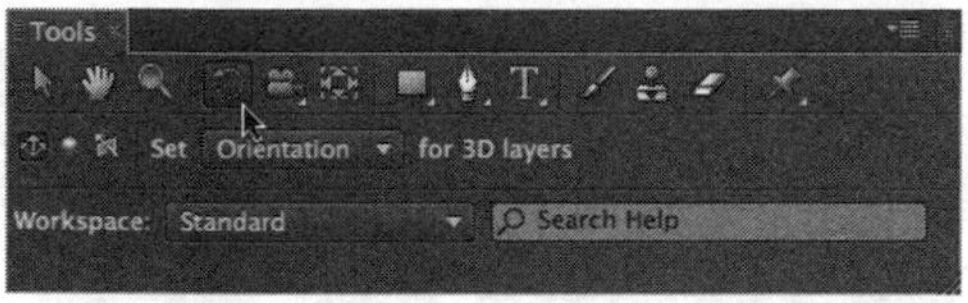

Figure 15.29 In the Tools panel, select the Rotation tool.

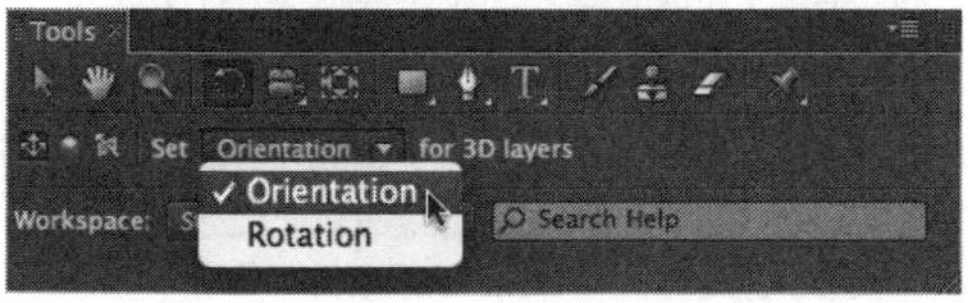

Figure 15.30 In the pop-up menu, choose Orientation.

Using 3D Orientation and Rotation

Making a layer three-dimensional adds a Z-axis dimension not only to its Position property but also to its Rotation property. And just as Position can be expressed in a single property or separate dimensions, the properties that control the way a layer rotates along its axes fall into two categories: Orientation and Rotation (**Figure 15.28**). The property you choose to adjust depends on the task at hand.

The Orientation property is expressed as a single three-dimensional value: X, Y, and Z angles. In the Comp panel, you adjust orientation with the standard Rotation tool.

You adjust rotation using three separate property values: X Rotation, Y Rotation, and Z Rotation. Unlike orientation, Rotation properties allow you to adjust the number of rotations in addition to the angle along each axis. You can adjust Rotation values in the Composition panel by using a Rotation tool option.

To adjust the orientation in the Comp panel:

1. In the 3D View pop-up menu, select a view.

2. In the Tools panel, select an axis mode.

3. Select a 3D layer, camera, or light.

   The selected layer's axes appear. The X axis is red; the Y axis is green; the Z axis is blue. The axes align according to the axis mode you specified.

4. In the Tools panel, select the Rotation tool ■ (**Figure 15.29**).

5. In the pop-up menu that appears, choose Orientation (**Figure 15.30**).

continues on next page

6. In the Composition panel, *do one of the following:*

▲ To adjust the orientation along all axes, drag the Rotation tool in any direction (**Figures 15.31** and **15.32**).

▲ To adjust the orientation along a single axis, position the Rotation tool over the axis you want to adjust so that the Rotation icon displays the letter corresponding to the axis, and then drag (**Figures 15.33** and **15.34**).

If the Orientation property's Stopwatch icon isn't activated, this will remain the Orientation value of the layer for the layer's duration. If the Stopwatch is activated, an orientation keyframe is created at this frame.

Figure 15.31 Drag the mouse pointer in any direction...

Figure 15.32 ...to adjust the orientation along all axes.

Figure 15.33 Position the mouse pointer over the axis you want to adjust so that the pointer displays the axis letter...

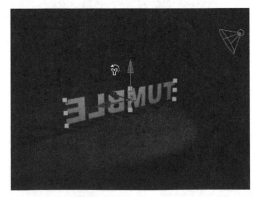

Figure 15.34 ...and drag to rotate the object around that axis.

USING 3D ORIENTATION AND ROTATION

Figure 15.35 In the Tools panel, select the Rotation tool.

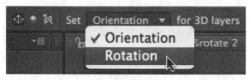

Figure 15.36 In the pop-up menu, choose Rotation.

Figure 15.37 Position the mouse pointer over the axis around which you want to rotate the 3D object, and then drag.

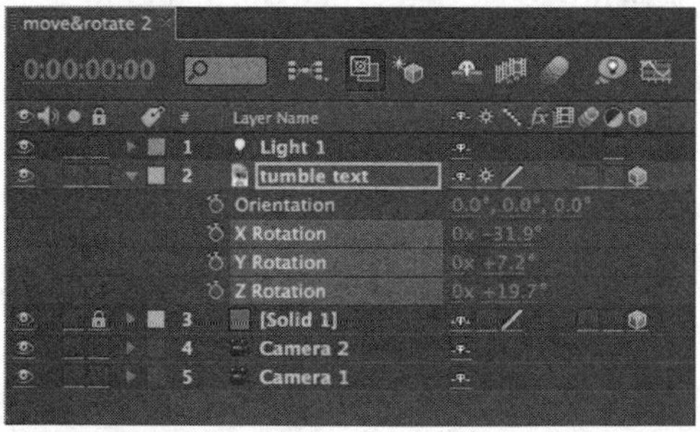

Figure 15.38 Dragging with the pointer adjusts the layer's 3D Rotation properties, not its Orientation properties.

To adjust 3D rotation in the Composition panel:

1. In the 3D View pop-up menu, select a view.

2. In the Tools panel, select an axis mode.

3. Select a 3D layer, camera, or light.

   The selected layer's axes appear. The X axis is red; the Y axis is green; the Z axis is blue. The axes align according to the axis mode you specified.

4. In the Tools panel, select the Rotation tool (**Figure 15.35**).

   A pop-up menu containing rotation options appears in the Tools panel.

5. In the pop-up menu, choose Rotation (**Figure 15.36**).

6. In the Composition panel, position the 3D Rotation tool over the axis around which you want to rotate the 3D object (**Figure 15.37**).

   The 3D Rotation tool displays the letter corresponding to the axis.

7. Drag to rotate the 3D layer, camera, or light around the selected axis.

   Dragging with the Rotation tool affects the layer's Rotation properties, not its Orientation property (**Figure 15.38**).

✔ Tip

■ As usual, don't forget to switch back to the Selection tool after you've finished using the Rotation tool (or any other tool). Otherwise, you could easily make accidental changes to layers.

USING 3D ORIENTATION AND ROTATION

Auto-Orienting 3D Layers

Using the Auto-Orientation command, you can make a 3D layer automatically rotate along its motion path or toward the top camera layer (see "Using Cameras," later in this chapter)—which saves you the trouble of keyframing the Orientation property manually. Alternatively, you can leave Auto-Orientation off and adjust the layer's rotation independently of other factors.

To specify an Auto-Orientation setting:

1. Select a 3D layer.

2. Choose Layer > Transform > Auto-Orient, or press Command-Option-O (Ctrl-Alt-O) (**Figure 15.39**).

Figure 15.39 Choose Layer > Transform > Auto-Orient.

Orientation vs. Rotation

When you're animating a layer's rotation in 3D, the Orientation property and the Rotation properties offer unique advantages and disadvantages. Choose the method best suited for the task at hand—and to avoid confusion, try not to use both methods simultaneously.

You may find that it's easier to achieve predictable results by animating the Orientation property rather than the Rotation properties, because interpolated Orientation values take the shortest path between one keyframe and the next. You can also smooth orientation using Bézier curves (just as you'd smooth a motion path for position). However, Orientation doesn't allow for multiple rotations along an axis. And although Orientation's speed graph allows you to ease motion, it doesn't display rates of change in rotations per second. Because of these limitations, some animators prefer to use Orientation to set rotational position—its angle or tilt in 3D space—and animate using the Rotation property.

Separate Rotation property values permit more keyframing options than Orientation does, but the results can be more difficult to control. Each Rotation property permits multiple rotations and can display a velocity graph that accurately measures the rotations per second at any frame.

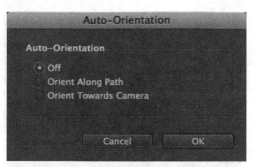

Figure 15.40 The Auto-Orientation dialog appears.

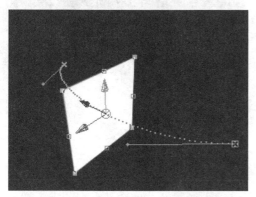

Figure 15.41 Orient Along Path makes the layer rotate so that its local *Z* axis points in the direction of the layer's motion.

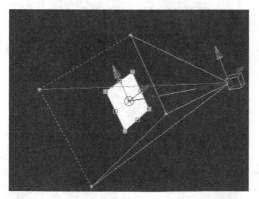

Figure 15.42 Orient Towards Camera makes the layer rotate so that its local *Z* axis points in the direction of the topmost camera in the Timeline's stacking order.

The Auto-Orientation dialog appears (**Figure 15.40**).

3. Select one of the following options:

▲ **Off**—Turns off Auto-Orient and adjusts rotation independently

▲ **Orient Along Path**—Makes the layer rotate so that its local *Z* axis points in the direction of the layer's motion path (**Figure 15.41**)

▲ **Orient Towards Camera**—Makes the layer rotate so that its local *Z* axis points in the direction of the topmost camera layer (that also has its video switch on) (**Figure 15.42**).

For more information, see "Using Cameras," later in this chapter.

4. Click OK to close the dialog.

✔ Tip

■ You can also apply special Auto-Orientation options to cameras and lights. See "Using the Point of Interest," later in this chapter.

AUTO-ORIENTING 3D LAYERS

Using 3D Material Options

Three-dimensional layers add a property category called Material Options that defines how 3D layers respond to lights in a comp. For more about lights, see "Using Lights," later in this chapter.

To set a 3D layer's Material Options:

1. Select a 3D layer.

2. Expand the layer outline to reveal the Material Options properties, or press AA (**Figure 15.43**).

   The layer's Material Options properties are revealed in the layer outline.

3. Set each Material Options property:

   s **Casts Shadows**—Turn on this option to enable the layer to cast shadows on other layers within the range of the shadow. This property can't be keyframed.

   Light Transmission—Adjust this value to set the percentage of light that shines through a layer. A value of zero causes the layer to act as an opaque object and cast a black shadow. Increasing the value allows light to pass through the object and cast a colored shadow, much like a transparency or stained glass does.

   Accepts Shadows—Turn on this option to enable shadows cast from other layers to appear on the layer. This property can't be keyframed.

   Accepts Lights—Turn on this option to enable the layer to be illuminated by lights in the composition. This property can't be keyframed.

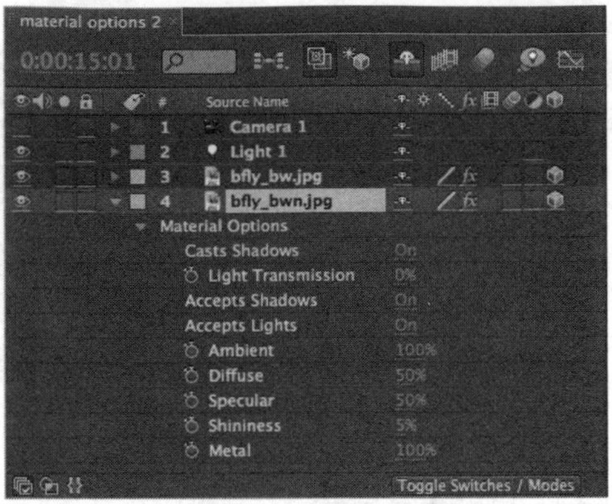

Figure 15.43 Expand the layer outline to reveal the Material Options properties, or press AA.

Figure 15.44 In this example, both 3D layers use the default material options, with Casts Shadows turned on.

Figure 15.45 Here, the Casts Shadows and Accepts Shadows settings are off on the left layer, and the Diffuse property on the right layer has been increased from 50 percent to 100 percent.

Ambient—Adjust this value to set the amount of *ambient*, or nondirectional, reflectivity of the layer. Higher values make the layer reflect more light from an ambient light source.

Diffuse—Adjust this value to set the amount of *diffuse*, or omnidirectional, reflectivity of the layer. A diffuse reflection implies the layer has a dull surface that reflects light equally in all directions. Higher values increase the layer's diffuse reflectivity.

Specular—Adjust this value to set the amount of *specular*, or directional, reflectivity of the layer. A specular reflection implies the layer has a smooth surface that reflects light in a single direction. Higher values increase the layer's specular reflectivity.

Shininess—Adjust this value to set the size of the layer's *specular highlight*, or shininess. This property is available only when the Specular property value is greater than 0 percent.

Metal—Adjust this value to specify the color of the specular highlight (as defined by the Specular and Shininess values). A value of 100 percent sets the color to match the layer, whereas a value of 0 percent sets the color to match the light source.

The layer in the Composition panel reflects your choices (**Figures 15.44** and **15.45**).

Using Cameras

You can view a composition from any angle by creating one or more 3D cameras. Cameras emulate the optical characteristics of real cameras. However, unlike real cameras, you can move these cameras through space unrestrained by tripods, gravity, or even union rules. This task summarizes how to create a new camera; the following sections explain each camera setting in detail.

To create a camera:

1. *Do either of the following:*

   ▲ Choose Layer > New > Camera (**Figure 15.46**).

   ▲ Press Shift-Option-Command-C (Shift-Alt-Ctrl-C).

   A Camera Settings dialog appears (**Figure 15.47**).

2. *Do one of the following:*

   ▲ Select a camera from the Preset pop-up menu (**Figure 15.48**).

   Presets are designed to emulate a 35mm camera of the specified focal length. Although presets are named for particular focal lengths, they set various camera settings automatically.

   ▲ Choose the custom camera options you want.

   See the next section, "Choosing Camera Settings," for a detailed description of each camera setting option.

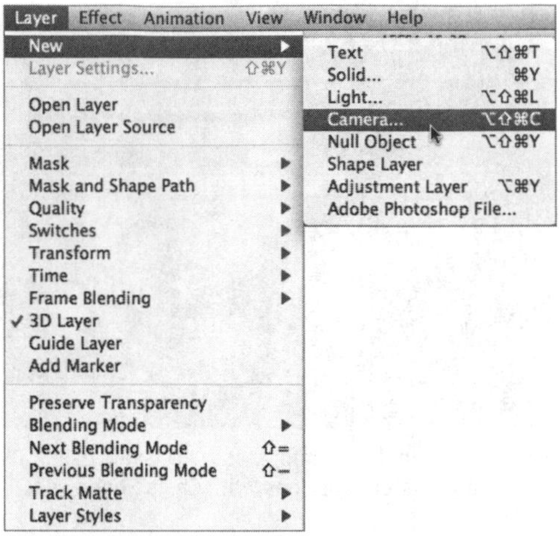

Figure 15.46 Choose Layer > New > Camera.

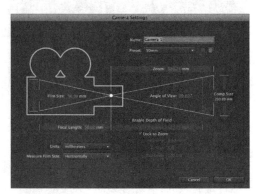

Figure 15.47 A Camera Settings dialog appears.

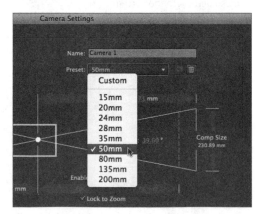

Figure 15.48 Select a camera from the Preset pop-up menu.

Figure 15.49 The new camera appears as the top layer in the composition, starting at the current time and using the default duration for still footage.

Figure 15.50 Changing the 3D view allows you to see the camera as a selectable object in the Composition panel.

3. To give the camera a custom name, enter one in the Name field of the Camera Settings dialog.

If you don't enter a name, After Effects uses the default naming scheme.

4. Click OK to close the Camera Settings dialog.

The new camera appears as the top layer in the composition, starting at the current time and using the default duration for still footage (**Figure 15.49**). The camera's default position depends on the camera settings you chose. Its default point of interest is at the center of the composition (see "Using the Point of Interest," later in this chapter). You can also switch the 3D view to see the camera's positioning in the Composition panel (**Figure 15.50**). (See "Viewing 3D Layers in the Comp Panel," earlier in this chapter.)

✔ Tips

■ If you don't name cameras, After Effects applies default names—Camera 1, Camera 2, and so on. When you delete a camera, After Effects assigns the lowest available number to the next camera you create. To avoid confusion, always give your cameras custom names. Note that always naming cameras will help you avoid problems when using expressions.

■ To revisit a camera's settings, double-click the camera's name in the Timeline panel's layer outline.

Choosing Camera Settings

When you create a camera, the Camera Settings dialog prompts you to set various attributes for it—such as focal length and film size—that emulate physical cameras.

You can choose from a list of presets, designed to mimic a number of typical real-world cameras. Or, if you prefer, you can customize the settings. The dialog provides a helpful illustration of the camera attributes (although it's not to scale, of course).

The following tasks divide an explanation of camera settings into two parts. The first explains the basic settings, which govern film size and most of the camera's optical attributes. The next task explains the Depth of Field settings, which can be activated to mimic the limited focus range of real-world cameras.

To choose basic camera settings:

1. *Do one of the following:*

   ▲ To create a new camera, press Shift-Option-Command-C (Shift-Alt-Ctrl-C).

   ▲ To modify a camera in the composition, double-click the name of the camera you want to modify in the layer outline of the Timeline panel.

   The Camera Settings dialog appears (**Figure 15.51**).

2. Enter a name in the Name field.

   If you don't enter a name, After Effects will use the default naming scheme in which the first camera is called Camera 1 and additional cameras are numbered in ascending order. If you delete a camera that uses this naming scheme, however, new cameras are named using the lowest available number.

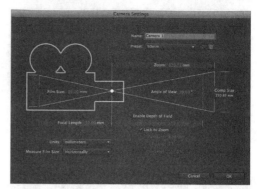

Figure 15.51 Customize the attributes of the camera in the Camera Settings dialog.

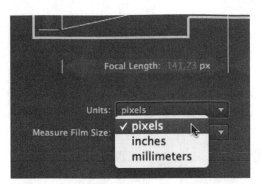

Figure 15.52 Select a unit of measure for the Camera Settings dialog in the Units pop-up menu.

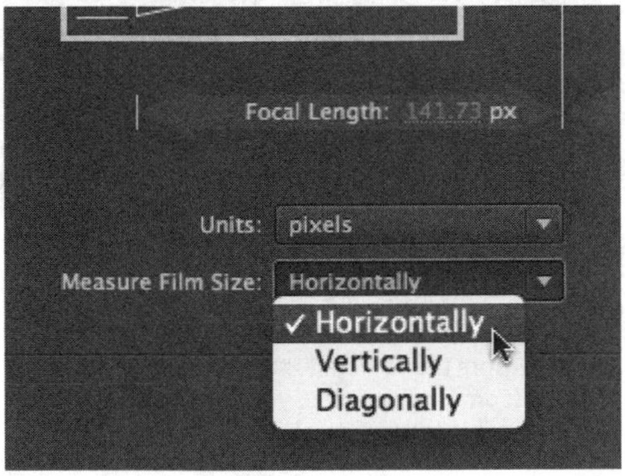

Figure 15.53 Select a unit of measure from the Measure Film Size pop-up menu.

3. If you want to use predefined camera settings, select a preset from the Preset pop-up menu.

Presets are designed to emulate a 35mm camera of the specified focal length. Although Presets are named for particular focal lengths, they set various camera settings automatically. You can also create a Custom camera by modifying individual settings manually.

4. In the same dialog, choose the units by which measurements are expressed:

Units—Sets whether the variables in the Camera Settings dialog are expressed in pixels, inches, or millimeters (**Figure 15.52**)

Measure Film Size—Measures film size horizontally, vertically, or diagonally (**Figure 15.53**).

Typically, film size is measured horizontally. In other words, 35mm motion picture film measures 35mm across the image area. Measured vertically, the image is about 26.25mm.

5. Enter the following variables:

Zoom—Sets the distance between the camera's focal point and the image plane.

Angle of View—Sets the width of the scene included in the image. Angle of View is directly related to Focal Length, Film Size, and Zoom. Adjusting this setting changes those variables, and vice versa.

Film Size—Controls the size of the exposed area of the film being simulated. When you change Film Size, Zoom and Angle are adjusted automatically to maintain the width of the scene in the camera's view.

continues on next page

Focal Length—Controls the distance between the focal point and the film plane of the camera. When you change Focal Length, the Zoom value changes automatically to maintain the scene's width in the camera's view.

6. Click OK to close the Camera Settings dialog.

To select Depth of Field options:

1. In the Camera Settings dialog, select Enable Depth of Field (**Figure 15.54**).

Selecting this option activates variables that affect the range of distance when the image is in focus, including Focus Distance, Aperture, F-Stop, and Blur Level.

2. To keep Focus Distance and Zoom the same, select Lock to Zoom.

Deselect this option to allow Focus Distance and Zoom to be adjusted independently.

3. In the same dialog, set the following options:

Focus Distance—Sets the distance from the camera's focal point to the focal plane (the plane of space that is in perfect focus) (**Figure 15.55**).

If Lock to Zoom is selected, adjusting Focus Distance also adjusts Zoom.

Aperture—Sets the size of the lens opening. Because the Aperture and F-Stop settings measure the same thing in different ways, adjusting one results in a corresponding change in the other. Aperture (or F-Stop) is directly related to depth of field.

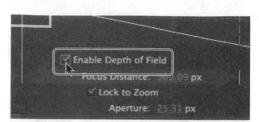

Figure 15.54 In the Camera Settings dialog, select Enable Depth of Field.

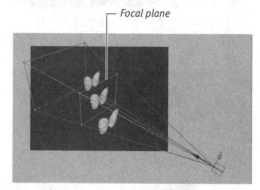

Figure 15.55 The Focus Distance value defines the distance from the camera to the focal plane. When Lock to Zoom isn't selected, you can see the focal plane represented in a selected camera's icon.

Figure 15.56 Here, the focal plane intersects the center butterfly, and objects outside the depth of field appear blurry.

F-Stop—Sets the aperture in terms of *f/stop*, a measurement system commonly used in photography. An f/stop is expressed as the ratio of the focal length to the aperture. On a real camera, increasing the f/stop by one full stop decreases the aperture to allow half the amount of light to expose the film; decreasing it by one stop doubles the amount of light. The term *stopping down* the lens refers to reducing aperture size.

Blur Level—Controls the amount of blur that results when a layer is outside the camera's depth of field. A value of 100 percent creates the amount of blur appropriate to the other camera settings. Lower values reduce the blur.

4. Click OK to close the Camera Settings dialog.

When viewed through the camera, objects outside the depth of field appear blurry (**Figure 15.56**).

✔ Tips

■ After Effects uses the term *position,* which is synonymous with the camera's Position property. In the physical world, the camera's position is synonymous with its focal point (**Figure 15.57**). In a real camera, the focal point defines where the light in the lens converges into a single point before it goes on to expose the film at the film plane. Distances associated with a camera are measured from its focal point.

■ The Camera Settings dialog includes buttons to save ⊡ and delete 🗑 camera presets. They look like the buttons you use to save and delete composition presets.

■ Photographers may wonder why the cameras in After Effects seem to have controls for everything but shutter speed and shutter angle. You'll find these controls in the Advanced panel of the Composition Settings dialog. See Chapter 4, "Compositions," for more information.

■ You can switch focus from one object in the scene to another, a technique cinematographers call *rack focus* or *pulling focus.* Make sure the Lock to Zoom camera setting is deselected, and animate the Focus Distance property.

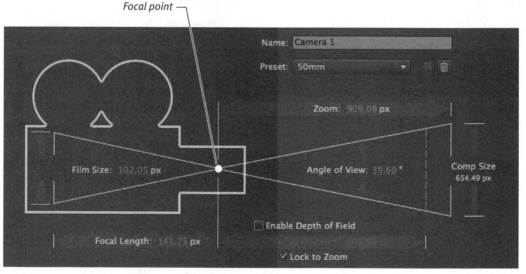

Focal point —

Name: Camera 1
Preset: 50mm
Zoom: 909.09 px
Film Size: 102.05 px
Angle of View: 39.60 °
Comp Size 654.49 px
Enable Depth of Field
Focal Length: 141.73 px
Lock to Zoom

Figure 15.57 The camera's position corresponds to the focal point, which is illustrated in the Camera Settings dialog but not labeled.

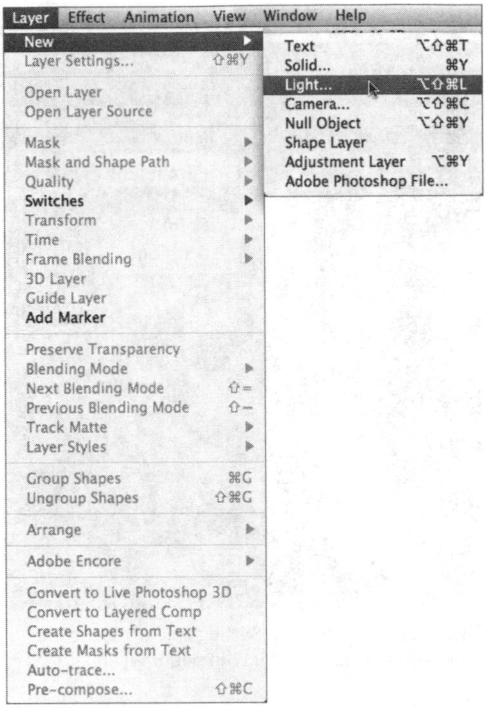

Figure 15.58 Choose Layer > New > Light.

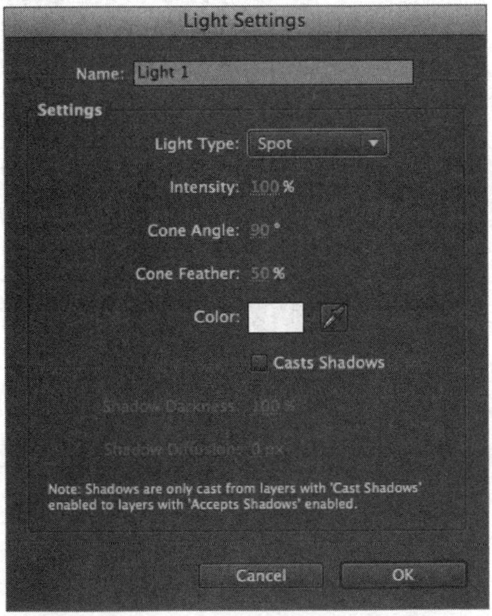

Figure 15.59 A Light Settings dialog appears.

Using Lights

You can create any number of lights to illuminate a 3D scene, and you can select and control these lights much as you would in the real world. Starting with After Effects CS4, you can identify each type of light by a unique icon that helps you position and point it (with the exception of Ambient lights, which light the scene from an indeterminate position). Unlike real-world lights, you can place a light anywhere you want without a lighting instrument appearing in the scene. Similarly, pointing a light into a camera won't cause a lens flare or overexposed image—in fact, you won't see anything at all. And you'll never blow a lamp or overload a circuit breaker.

As in the "Using Cameras" section, this section contains two tasks: The first summarizes how to create a light; the second describes light settings in more detail.

To create a light:

1. *Do either of the following:*
   - ▲ Choose Layer > New > Light (**Figure 15.58**).
   - ▲ Press Shift-Option-Command-L (Shift-Alt-Ctrl-L).

   A Light Settings dialog appears (**Figure 15.59**).

2. Enter a name for the light in the Name field.

   If you don't enter a name, After Effects uses the default naming scheme.

3. In the same dialog, select the type of
light you want from the pop-up menu
(**Figure 15.60**):

▲ **Parallel**—Radiates directional light
from an infinite distance. In this
respect, a parallel light simulates
sunlight (**Figure 15.61**).

▲ **Spot**—Radiates from a source positioned within an opaque cone, allowing the light to emit only through its
open end. Adjusting the cone's angle
changes the spread of the light. This
type of light emulates those commonly
used in film and stage productions
(**Figure 15.62**).

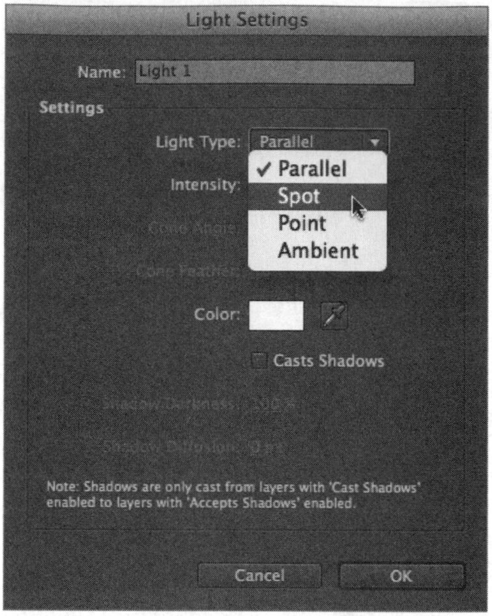

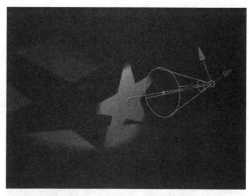

Figure 15.60 In the Light Settings dialog, select the
type of light you want from the pop-up menu.

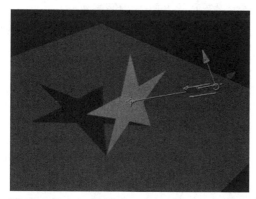

Figure 15.61 A parallel light radiates directional light
from a source infinitely far away, much like sunlight.

Figure 15.62 A spot light is constrained by a cone and
appears much like the lights used in film and stage
productions.

Figure 15.63 A point light emits an omnidirectional light, much like a bare bulb.

Figure 15.64 An ambient light contributes to the overall illumination of the 3D space. Here, an ambient light is set to 30 percent intensity.

Figure 15.65 The new light appears as the top layer in the composition, starting at the current time and using the default duration for still footage.

▲ **Point**—Emits omnidirectional light from its point of origin, comparable to a bare bulb or an signal flare (**Figure 15.63**).

▲ **Ambient**—Doesn't emanate from a specific source but rather contributes to the overall illumination of the scene. Ambient light settings only include those for intensity and color (**Figure 15.64**). Because they don't have a position, ambient lights don't have an icon in the Comp panel.

The type of light you select determines which options are available in the Light Settings dialog.

4. Specify the light settings available for the type of light you selected.

   See the next section, "Choosing Light Settings," for more information.

5. Click OK to close the Light Settings dialog.

   The new light appears as the top layer in the composition, starting at the current time and using the default duration for still footage (**Figure 15.65**). The light's default position depends on the type of light you select.

✔ Tips

■ You can revisit the Light Settings dialog at any time by double-clicking the name of a light in the layer outline of the Timeline panel.

■ If you need a lens flare or visible light beams, try an effect. After Effects includes a lens flare, and many third-party plug-in packages create light beams and other lighting effects.

Choosing Light Settings

The options available in the Light Settings dialog depend on the type of light you're using. They control the character of the light and the shadows it casts.

To select light settings:

1. *Do one of the following:*

   ▲ To create a new light, press Shift-Option-Command-L (Shift-Alt-Ctrl-L).

   ▲ To modify a light in the composition, double-click the name of the light you want to modify in the layer outline of the Timeline panel.

   The Light Settings dialog appears (**Figure 15.66**).

2. In the Light Settings dialog, specify the following options:

   Intensity—Sets the brightness of light. Negative values create *nonlight*—they subtract color from an already illuminated layer, in effect shining darkness onto a layer.

   Color—Selects the light's color; comparable to placing a colored gel over a light. You can use the color swatch or eyedropper control.

   Cone Angle—Sets the angle of the cone used to restrict a spot type of light. Wider cone angles emit a broader span of light; smaller angles restrict the light to a narrower area (**Figure 15.67**).

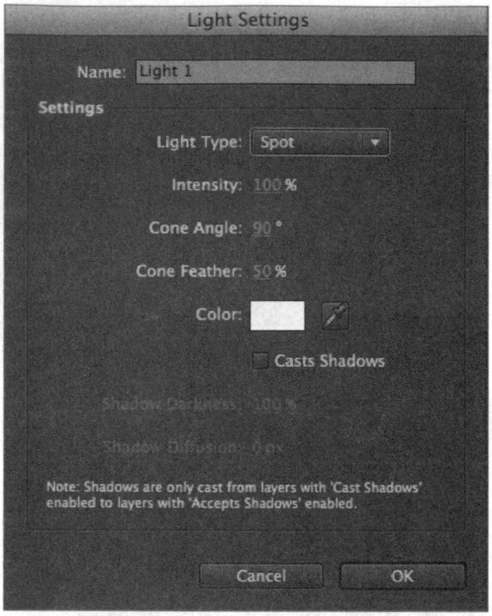

Figure 15.66 In the Light Settings dialog, specify the settings available for the type of light you're using.

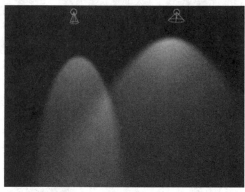

Figure 15.67 Both spot lights are the same intensity and distance from the layer. The light on the left uses a 45-degree cone angle; the light on the right uses a 90-degree cone angle.

CHOOSING LIGHT SETTINGS

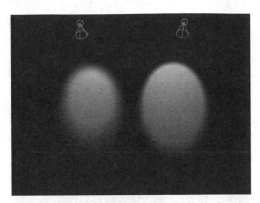

Figure 15.68 Both spot lights here are identical, except the light on the right uses a Cone Feather setting of 25, whereas the light on the left uses a Cone Feather setting of 50.

Cone Feather—Sets the softness of the edges of a spot type of light. Larger values create a softer light edge (**Figure 15.68**).

Casts Shadows—When selected, makes the light cast shadows onto layers with the Accepts Shadows property selected. See "Using 3D Material Options," earlier in this chapter, for more information.

Shadow Darkness—Sets the darkness level of shadows cast by the light. This option is available only when the light's Casts Shadows option is enabled.

Shadow Diffusion—Sets the softness of shadows, based on the apparent distance between the light and the layers casting shadows made by the light. Larger values create softer shadows. This option is available only when the light's Casts Shadows option is enabled.

Making a Light an Adjustment Layer

Like 3D layers, a light's position in the layer outline's stacking order doesn't determine whether it's in front of or behind other 3D layers. Where it shines depends on its position in 3D space, and on the type of light (**Figure 15.69**). However, its position in the stacking order does make a difference when you make the light an adjustment layer—or if you prefer, an *adjustment light*.

Just as an adjustment layer's effects are applied to all the layers below it in the stacking order, an adjustment light illuminates only 3D layers below it in the layer outline's stacking order. 3D layers higher than the adjustment layer in the stacking order won't be lit—regardless of their relative positions in 3D space or their settings (**Figure 15.70**). By making a light an adjustment layer, you can limit its effects to certain 3D layers in the comp, while excluding others.

To make a light an adjustment layer, just select its Adjustment Layer switch ◢:

◆ Under the Switches heading of the Timeline panel, click the layer's Adjustment Layer switch so that the Adjustment layer icon appears (**Figure 15.71**).

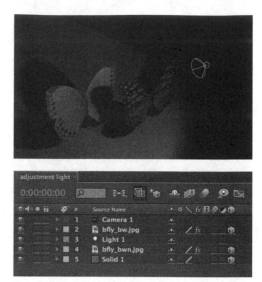

Figure 15.69 Whatever the light's position in the layer outline's stacking order, it affects other 3D layers according to its relative position in space (as well as the light's settings, and the layers' material options).

Figure 15.70 As an adjustment layer, the same light doesn't illuminate 3D layers higher in the layer outline's stacking order—regardless of their relative position in space.

Figure 15.71 To make a light an adjustment layer, select its Adjustment layer switch in the switches area of the Timeline panel so that the Adjustment Layer icon appears.

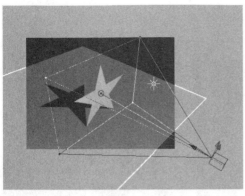

Figure 15.72 In the Composition panel, the point of interest appears as a crosshair at the end of a line extending from a camera or light.

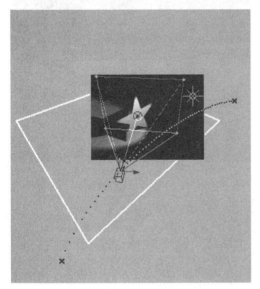

Figure 15.73 You can set a camera or light to automatically orient toward its point of interest as it moves.

Using the Point of Interest

Point of Interest is a transform property unique to cameras and lights. It defines the point in space at which the camera or light is pointed. By default, a new camera's or light's point of interest is at the center of the composition (at the coordinates (0,0,0) in terms of the world axes). In the Composition panel, the point of interest appears as a crosshair at the end of a line extending from a camera or light (**Figure 15.72**).

As you can see, a camera's or light's Point of Interest value is closely related to its other transform property values: A change in position or rotation can affect the point of interest, and vice versa.

Because of its relationship to other transform properties, the Point of Interest property is available only when you activate a 3D object's Auto-Orient option. When you animate the position of a light or camera, auto-orienting a layer saves you the effort of setting rotation keyframes manually.

By default, cameras and lights are set to orient toward the point of interest automatically. That is, moving a camera or light causes it to rotate so that it always points toward its point of interest. When applied to a camera, this setting may create a point of view similar to that of careless drivers who turn their head to see an accident as they drive by (**Figure 15.73**).

You can also set each light or camera to auto-orient along its motion path. When applied to a camera, this setting may mimic the view from a roller coaster, automatically rotating the camera to point in a 3D tangent to the motion path (**Figure 15.74**).

Finally, you can turn off the Auto-Orient setting so that the light's or camera's orientation isn't automatically adjusted to maintain a relationship with its motion path or point of interest. When you set Auto-Orient to off, the light or camera loses its Point of Interest property.

To choose the Auto-Orient setting for cameras and lights:

1. Select the camera or light you want to adjust.

2. Choose Layer > Transform > Auto-Orient (**Figure 15.75**).

   An Auto-Orientation dialog appears (**Figure 15.76**).

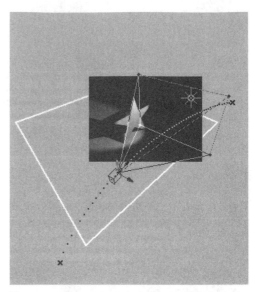

Figure 15.74 Or you can set a camera or light to automatically orient along its motion path.

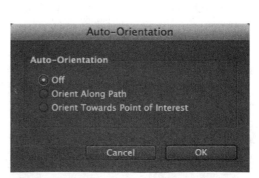

Figure 15.75 Choose Layer > Transform > Auto-Orient.

Figure 15.76 An Auto-Orientation dialog appears.

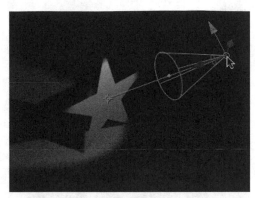

Figure 15.77 If Orient Towards Point of Interest is active...

3. Choose an option:

   ▲ **Off**—Turns off Auto-Orient so that the camera or light rotates independently of its motion path or point of interest. Selecting this option eliminates the camera's or light's Point of Interest property.

   ▲ **Orient Along Path**—Makes the camera or light rotate automatically so that it remains oriented to its motion path.

   ▲ **Orient Towards Point of Interest**— Makes the camera or light rotate automatically as you move it so that it remains oriented toward the point of interest.

To move a light or camera without changing the point of interest:

1. Select a camera or light.

2. In the 3D View pop-up menu, select a view.

   You may also want to choose a different magnification setting in the Composition pop-up menu so that you can see the light or camera in the Composition panel.

3. In the Tools panel, select an axis mode. The selected layer's axes appear. The X axis is red; the Y axis is green; the Z axis is blue. The axes align according to the axis mode you specified.

4. If necessary, make sure Auto-Orient is set to Orient Towards Point of Interest.

   This is the default setting.

5. *Do any of the following:*

   ▲ In the Composition panel, drag the camera or light (**Figure 15.77**).

   Make sure the Selection tool icon doesn't include an axis letter. If it does, you'll move the camera or light by an axis, and the point of interest will move in tandem with the camera or light.

continues on next page

▲ In the Composition panel, position the Selection tool over an axis (so that the mouse pointer displays the letter corresponding to the axis), and Command-drag (Ctrl-drag).

▲ In the layer outline, adjust the light's or camera's Position property.

The selected camera's or light's position changes, but rotates so that its point of interest remains stationary (**Figure 15.78**).

To move a camera or light and the point of interest:

1. Select a camera or light.

2. In the 3D View pop-up menu, select a view.

   You may also want to choose a different magnification setting in the Composition pop-up menu so that you can see the light or camera in the Composition panel.

3. In the Tools panel, select an axis mode.

   The selected layer's axes appear. The X axis is red; the Y axis is green; the Z axis is blue. The axes align according to the axis mode you specified.

4. If necessary, make sure Auto-Orient is set to Orient Towards Point of Interest.

   This is the default setting.

5. In the Composition panel, position the Selection tool over a camera's or light's axes.

   The Selection tool icon appears with a letter that corresponds to the axis (**Figure 15.79**).

6. Drag the camera or light along the selected axis (**Figure 15.80**).

   As you move the camera or light, its point of interest moves accordingly.

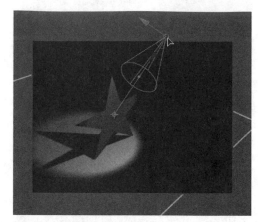

Figure 15.78 ...dragging the camera or light orients it automatically.

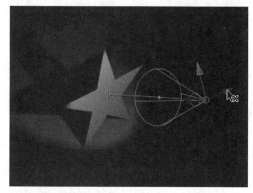

Figure 15.79 Command-dragging (Ctrl-dragging) the camera or light by one of its axes also activates the Orient Towards Point of Interest command...

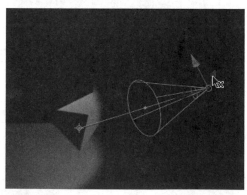

Figure 15.80 ...but dragging the camera or light by one of its axes doesn't allow it to auto-orient. Here, moving the light also moves its point of interest away from the star layer.

Figure 15.81 Select the Camera tool you want to use.

Figure 15.82 When Auto-Orient is set to Orient Towards Point of Interest, dragging with the mouse pointer...

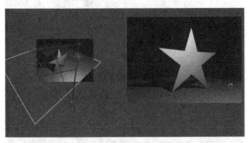

Figure 15.83 ...rotates the camera around its point of interest.

Figure 15.84 Otherwise, the camera rotates around its position.

Moving Cameras with Camera Tools

Camera tools provide you with another way to easily adjust Camera views. In contrast to dragging the camera's icon from a separate Camera view, Camera tools let you change a camera's Position property while viewing the composition from the camera's point of view. Although it's harder to see the camera's motion path, you get to see the movement from the camera's perspective. You can also use Camera tools to adjust one of the Custom 3D views (see "Viewing 3D Layers in the Comp Panel," earlier in this chapter).

To adjust a camera using Camera tools:

1. In the Composition panel's 3D View pop-up menu, select a Camera view.

   Selecting another 3D view adjusts that view, not a camera layer's Position property.

2. If necessary, set the camera's Auto-Orient option to determine how the Orbit Camera tool functions.

3. In the Tools panel, select a Camera tool (**Figure 15.81**):

   Unified Camera ▦—Rotates or moves the camera according to the button you press on a three-button mouse as you drag. Pressing the left button toggles to the Orbit Camera tool; pressing the center mouse button toggles to the Track XY Camera tool; pressing the right button toggles to the Track Z Camera tool.

   Orbit Camera ◙—Rotates the camera around its point of interest when Auto-Orient is set to Orient Towards Point of Interest. Otherwise, the camera rotates around its position (much like a camera panning on a tripod) (**Figures 15.82, 15.83,** and **15.84**).

continues on next page

Track XY Camera ⊕—Moves the camera along its *X* and *Y* axes (similar to a real-world camera tracking right or left, or craning up or down). Regardless of the Auto-Orient setting, the camera's rotation is unaffected (**Figure 15.85**).

Track Z Camera ⊟—Moves the camera along its *Z* axis (similar to a camera dollying in or out). Regardless of the Auto-Orient setting, the camera's rotation remains unaffected (**Figure 15.86**).

4. In the Composition panel, drag the selected Camera tool.

   The camera position or view changes according to the Camera tool you use.

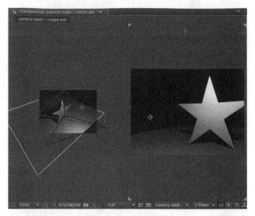

Figure 15.85 Dragging with the Track XY Camera tool selected lets you move the camera along its *X* and *Y* axes. Here, the camera is tracking left (from its position in Figure 15.84).

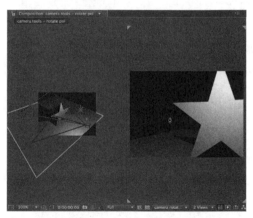

Figure 15.86 Dragging with the Track Z Camera tool selected lets you move the camera along its *Z* axis. Here, the camera is dollying back from its position in Figure 15.85.

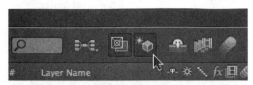

Figure 15.87 In the Timeline panel, click the Draft 3D mode button.

Figure 15.88 With Draft 3D mode on, the Composition panel doesn't preview lights, shadows, or depth-of-field blur.

Figure 15.89 When Draft 3D mode is off, the Composition panel displays lights, shadows, and depth-of-field blur.

Previewing 3D

Draft 3D disables lights and shadows as well as blur caused by camera Depth of Field settings. As you've made your way through this book, you've encountered several ways of reducing a composition's preview quality so that you can increase rendering speed. The increased processing demands of 3D compositing will make you appreciate this trade-off even more.

To enable or disable Draft 3D mode:

◆ In the Timeline panel, click the Draft 3D mode button ▓ (**Figure 15.87**).

The image in the Composition panel no longer previews 3D lights, shadows, or depth-of-field blur. Click the button again to deselect it and turn off Draft 3D (**Figures 15.88** and **15.89**).

Understanding 3D Layer Order

As you learned in Chapter 5, "Layer Basics," layers listed higher in the Timeline panel's layer outline appear in front of other layers in the Composition panel. After Effects always renders 2D layers in order, from the bottom of the layer stacking order to the top. (See "Rendering Order" in Chapter 16, "Complex Projects.")

However, the simple 2D stacking order becomes irrelevant in 3D compositing, where object layering is determined by objects' relative positions in 3D space according to the current 3D view.

For 3D layers, After Effects renders from the most distant layer (with the highest Z-coordinate value) to the closest (with the lowest Z-coordinate value).

Combining 2D and 3D

When a composition contains both 2D and 3D layers, the rendering order becomes even more complex, combining aspects of both 2D and 3D rendering. Once again, layers

are rendered from the bottom of the stacking order to the top. However, 3D layers are rendered in independent sets, separated by 2D layers.

In other words, placing a 2D layer so that it doesn't separate the 3D layers in the Timeline's stacking order allows the 3D layers to interact geometrically. 3D layers appear in front of one another and interact with lights and shadows according to their position in 3D space (as well as according to light settings and material options). The 2D layers neither share the same space as 3D layers nor interact with lights or cameras (**Figure 15.90**).

In contrast, positioning a 2D layer between 3D layers in the stacking order splits the 3D layers into separate groups. Although the 3D layers share the same lights and cameras, they exist in identical but separate 3D "worlds" and are rendered independently of one another (**Figure 15.91**).

✔ Tip

- For more on working effectively with the rendering order, see "Rendering Order" in Chapter 16.

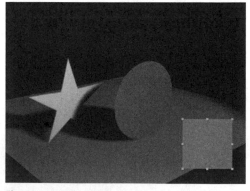

Figure 15.90 In this example, the 2D layer is higher in the stacking order than the 3D layers, allowing the 3D layers to be rendered together.

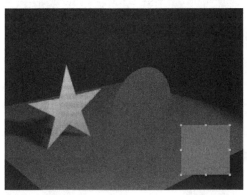

Figure 15.91 In this example, the 2D layer is between the circle and star in the stacking order, causing the 3D layers to be rendered separately. Notice how the circle no longer casts a shadow.

16

COMPLEX PROJECTS

As your projects become more ambitious, their structures will grow increasingly complex as well. After Effects includes several features that help you create complex projects without resorting to complicated procedures.

A typical project contains not only layers created from individual footage items, but also layers created from other compositions—*nested compositions.* Nesting comps makes it possible to group elements and to arrange them into a hierarchical structure, creating effects you couldn't achieve otherwise. You can survey the project's structure in a flowchart view, and step through the hierarchy of nested comps using navigational tools new in After Effects CS4.

You can also create relationships among elements using the Parenting feature, which puts the spatial properties of one or more layers in terms of another layer, the *parent layer.* By shifting the layers' context from the child comp to the parent, you can more easily make the layers act as a single system.

Using another powerful feature—expressions—you can create relationships between layer properties in the same layer, in different layers, even in layers contained within different compositions. Rather than keyframing multiple properties independently, you can link one property's values to another property's values using a JavaScript-based instruction, or *expression.* (Don't worry: you can work with expressions without being a JavaScript programmer.)

But before you tackle nesting, parenting, or expressions, you'll get the lowdown on *rendering order,* the scheme for rendering frames in After Effects. You'll learn how rendering order influences your results as well as how you can use the rendering order to your advantage.

Rendering Order

When After Effects renders frames for playback or output, it calculates each attribute in a particular sequence referred to as the *rendering order*.

Having interpreted the source footage according to your specifications, After Effects processes each frame layer by layer. Starting with a composition's bottom layer, After Effects renders layer properties in the order they're listed in the layer outline: masks, effects, and transform. Then the program processes layer modes and track mattes before combining the layer with the underlying layers. Rendering proceeds in this fashion for successively higher layers in the stacking order until the frame is complete (**Figures 16.1**, **16.2**, **16.3**, **16.4,** and **16.5**).

Figure 16.1 Starting with the bottom layer...

Figure 16.2 ...After Effects renders the masks first...

Figure 16.3 ...then applies effects in the order they appear in the Effect Controls panel...

Figure 16.4 ...then calculates transform properties...

Figure 16.5 ...and finally calculates track mattes and modes before combining the layer with the underlying image.

For audio layers, rendering proceeds in the same sequence: effects followed by levels. If you were to change the audio speed, time remapping would be calculated first and time stretch would be calculated last.

When compositing 3D layers, rendering order is determined by each layer's relative Z-coordinate value as well as by whether the composition contains a mix of 2D and 3D layers. See "Understanding 3D Layer Order" in Chapter 15, "3D Layers," for more information.

To identify most problems you're likely to encounter with an animation, you need to understand its rendering order and how to circumvent it.

Channeling the Rendering Order

If you were to strictly adhere to the rendering order, certain effects would be impossible to achieve. For example, you might want to use the Motion Tile effect to impart a digitized look to a rotating object. However, rendering order dictates that the Motion Tile effect be rendered before the rotation, a transform property. Unfortunately, this causes the layer to rotate after tiling—which will not have the effect you desire (**Figure 16.6**). To solve the problem, you must defy the rendering order so that the effects are calculated after transformations (**Figure 16.7**).

Although you can't alter the rendering order directly, you can do so indirectly. For example, you can subvert rendering order by using the Transform effect or an adjustment layer, or by nesting or precomposing. In some cases, you can use an expression to make continual adjustments to a property automatically, effectively defeating limitations imposed by the rendering order.

Figure 16.6 Because After Effects calculates effects before transform properties, a mosaic effect is applied to the butterfly image before it's rotated. The squares produced by the mosaic are tilted so they become diamonds—which, in this case, isn't the result we want.

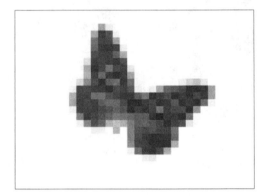

Figure 16.7 To create the desired effect, the effect must be calculated before the rotation. Note how the mosaic squares remain level, parallel to the sides of the comp.

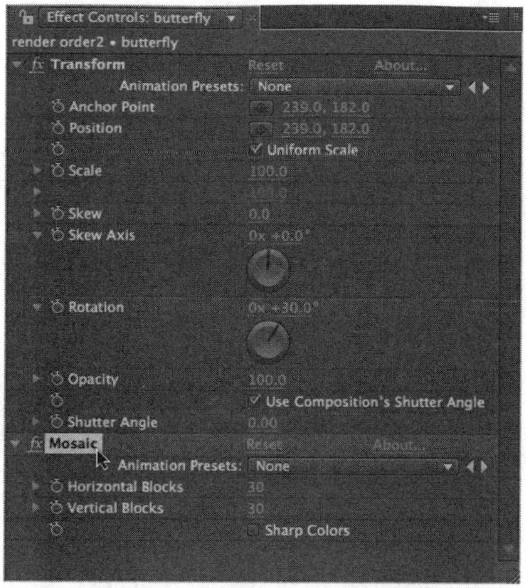

Figure 16.8 The Transform effect emulates the transform properties. To render it before other effects, you can place it higher in the list in the Effect Controls panel.

Figure 16.9 You can postpone the rendering of an effect by placing it in an adjustment layer higher in the layer stack.

Figure 16.10 You can also use a nested composition to effectively change the rendering order. Before After Effects renders the nested composition (top) as a layer, it must complete the rendering sequence within the nested composition (bottom).

Transform effect

In many instances, you'll need a transform property to render before an effect property. Fortunately, all the transform properties (as well as the Skew and Shutter Angle properties) are also available in the form of an effect, the Transform effect. By placing the Transform effect at the top of the list in the Effect Controls panel, you can render it before subsequent effects on the list (**Figure 16.8**).

Adjustment layer

Because the rendering order proceeds from the bottom of the layer stack, you can postpone rendering an effect by placing it in an adjustment layer. After Effects then calculates the properties in the lower layers before the adjustment layer affects them (**Figure 16.9**).

As you'll recall from the "Adjustment Layer" section in Chapter 11, the effects contained in an adjustment layer are applied to all the underlying layers. To limit an adjustment layer's effects to just some of those lower layers, you must nest or precompose them with the adjustment layer. (*Precomposing* refers to another method of creating a nested composition—you might think of it as nesting retroactively—so it works the same way.)

Nesting or precomposing

Another way to effectively change the rendering order is to place layers in a nested composition.

Nesting describes the process of using a composition as a layer in another composition. Before After Effects can render the nested composition as a layer, however, it must complete the rendering sequence within the nested composition. In other words, the properties of the layers contained by the nested composition are calculated first. Then the nested composition is treated like the other layers, and its properties are processed according to the rendering order (**Figure 16.10**).

CHANNELING THE RENDERING ORDER

445

Expressions

In some cases, an expression can compensate for the unwanted effects of the rendering order. For example, an expression can link an effect property to a transform property so that the effect adjusts dynamically to compensate for the fact that it's calculated before the transformations (**Figures 16.11** and **16.12**). (In contrast to putting the effect in an adjustment layer, this approach also lets you scale or reposition the layer and maintain the effect.)

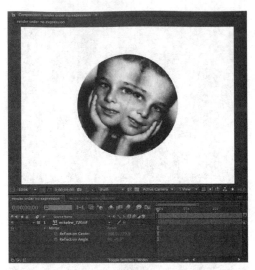

Figure 16.11 Here, the Mirror effect is applied to a rotating layer to achieve a kind of kaleidoscopic effect. Because the effect is calculated first, the angle of reflection rotates with the layer.

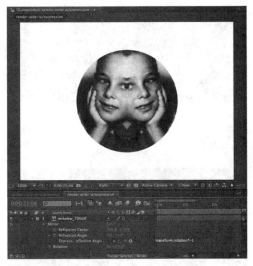

Figure 16.12 Using an expression, the angle of reflection changes opposite of the layer's rotation. The angle of reflection remains vertical even as the image is rotated.

Figure 16.13 Merely rotating each layer in this composition doesn't achieve the desired effect.

Figure 16.14 Nesting the composition makes it a single layer in another composition, which can be rotated as a single element.

Nesting

To achieve many effects, you must make a composition a layer in another composition—a process called *nesting*. Put briefly, nesting can do the following:

Group Layers—When a comp becomes a layer in another comp, all the layers contained in the nested comp can be treated as a single element. This technique is frequently convenient to use, and it is often necessary to get the results you want (**Figures 16.13** and **16.14**). You can easily reuse a complex comp by nesting it in one or many comps, and if you alter the contents of the source comp, the changes are evident whenever that comp is nested.

Channel the Rendering Order—After Effects processes each layer's properties in a strict order, often called the rendering order. In broad terms, After Effects renders masks, then effects, then transformations (position, scale, and so on). Yet there are times when you need to render, say, transformations before effects. Although you can't change the rendering order, you can channel it, so to speak, with nesting. That's because After Effects must apply the rendering order to the layers within a nested comp before applying it to the nested comp itself. This way, it's possible to perform the transformation (to a layer within the nested comp) before applying the effect (to the nested comp itself). (See "Channeling the Rendering Order," earlier in this chapter.)

Control Compound Effects—In much the same way nesting exploits a loophole in the rendering order, it can also circumvent the rules governing a type of effect known as a *compound effect*. Although you apply a compound effect to one layer, the effect's placement or intensity is dictated by another layer, called an *effect source*. However, a compound effect refers to the effect source directly, bypassing any masks, effects, or transformations that you may have applied. To retain the property changes in the effect source, you must place the altered layer in a nested comp. This way, the changes are rendered within the nested comp before the nested comp is referenced by the compound effect. To see this in action, see "Understanding Compound Effects" in Chapter 11.

To nest a composition:

1. Display the Composition panel or Timeline panel of the composition that will contain the nested composition.

2. Drag a composition you want to nest from the Project panel to any of the following (**Figure 16.15**):

   ▲ Composition panel of the target composition

   ▲ Timeline panel of the target composition

   ▲ Name or icon for the target composition in the Project panel

   The composition becomes a layer in the target composition, beginning at the current time and having the same duration as the original composition.

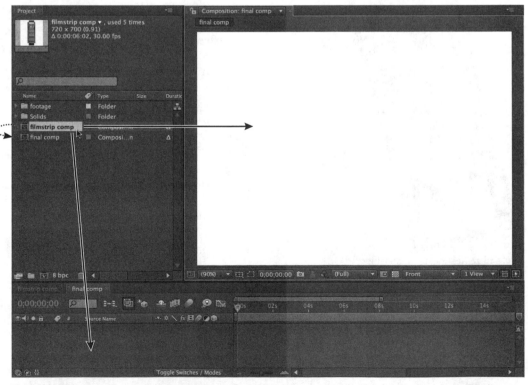

Figure 16.15 Drag a composition you want to nest from the Project panel to the Composition panel, the Timeline panel, or the icon for the target composition.

Figure 16.16 Dragging a composition to the Composition icon nests the composition in another composition that has the same settings.

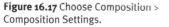

Figure 16.17 Choose Composition > Composition Settings.

To nest one composition in a new composition with the same settings:

◆ Drag a composition in the Project panel to the Composition icon at the bottom of the Project panel (**Figure 16.16**).

The composition becomes a layer in a new composition that uses the same composition settings as the nested one.

✔ Tips

■ When you drag a comp (or other footage item) to the timeline, you can drag it to a specific starting time and position in the stacking order.

■ To find out how to turn selected layers into a nested composition retroactively, see "Precomposing," later in this chapter.

Nesting options

In the composition's settings, nesting options dictate whether nested compositions retain their own frame rate and resolution settings or assume those of the composition in which they're nested.

To set nesting options:

1. With a comp selected, choose Composition > Composition Settings or press Command-K (Ctrl-K) (**Figure 16.17**). The Composition Settings dialog appears.

2. In the Composition Settings dialog, click the Advanced tab.

continues on next page

NESTING

3. In the Advanced panel of the Composition Settings dialog, select one or both of the following options (**Figure 16.18**):

▲ **Preserve frame rate when nested or in render queue**—Choosing this option allows nested compositions to retain their frame rates regardless of the frame rate of the composition that contains them.

▲ **Preserve resolution when nested**—If this option is selected, nested compositions retain their resolution settings regardless of the resolution of the composition that contains them.

If you select neither option, nested compositions will take on the frame rate and resolution of the composition in which they're nested.

4. Click OK to close the Composition Settings dialog.

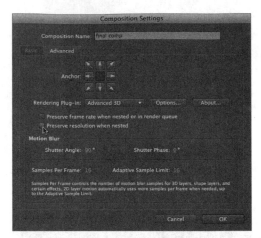

Figure 16.18 In the Advanced Panel of the Composition Settings dialog, select the nesting options you want.

✔ Tips

■ By preserving the frame rate of a nested composition, you can achieve results similar to those produced by the Posterize Time effect.

■ The Render Queue dialog allows you to use the current resolution settings or to reset them for all nested comps. See Chapter 17, "Output," for more about the render queue.

Nesting Preferences

When working with nested comps, you should consider a few options you can find by choosing After Effects > Preferences > General (File > Preferences > General).

When viewing a comp alongside a comp nested within it, you can specify whether the time in their respective panels are synchronized by selecting, "Synchronize Time of All Related Items."

When the "Switches Affect Nested Comps," is selected, switches operate *recursively*. That is, setting a switch for a composition also sets the switch for the comps nested within it. These switches include Collapse Transformations, Continuously Rasterize, and Quality. The composition's Resolution, Enable Motion Blur, and Enable Frame Blending settings also operate recursively.

In general, recursive switches can save you time and effort. Sometimes, however, recursive switches can produce undesired results. For example, recursive switches could prevent you from enabling Motion Blur selectively in a series of nested compositions. As a rule, use recursive switches. If using a switch has unintended consequences, disable recursive switches.

NESTING

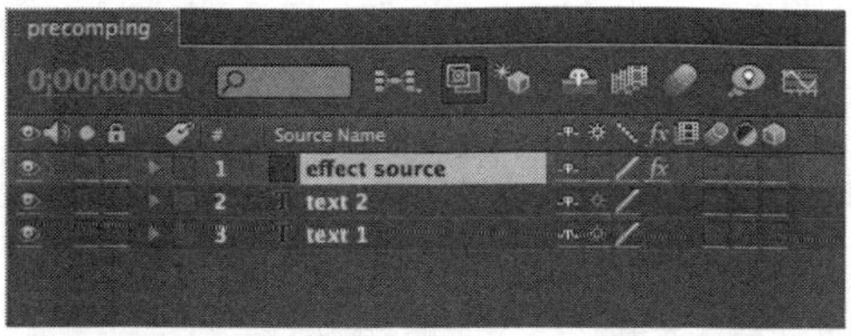

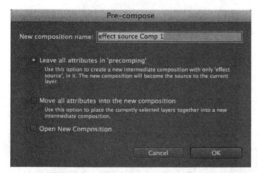

Figure 16.19 Precomposing allows you to select one or more layers...

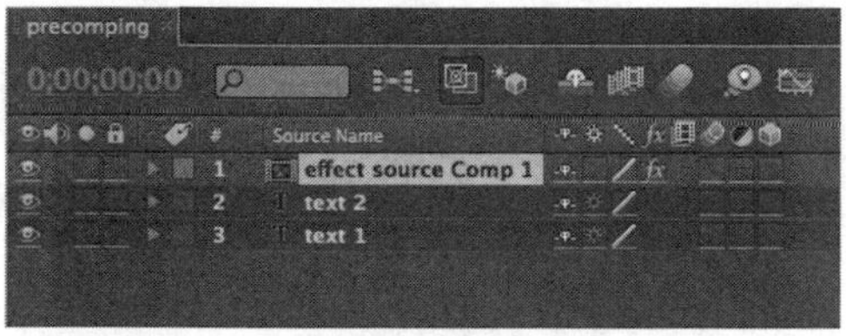

Figure 16.20 ...and place them into a nested composition.

Figure 16.21 When you precompose one or more layers, After Effects prompts you with a dialog of options.

Precomposing

You can't always anticipate the need to nest. Often, you realize that layers should be contained in a nested composition only after they're part of the current composition. Fortunately, you can repackage layers of an existing composition into a nested composition by using a method called *precomposing*.

The Precompose command places one or more selected layers in a nested composition (or, if you prefer, a *precomp*), thus accomplishing in a single step what could otherwise be a tedious reorganization process (**Figures 16.19** and **16.20**).

When you precompose more than one layer, the layers' properties (masks, effects, transform) and associated keyframes are retained and moved into the nested composition. When you precompose a single layer, however, you may choose whether its properties and keyframes move with it or remain in the current composition (becoming properties of the nested composition). After Effects prompts you with a dialog that lists your choices (**Figure 16.21**):

Leave all attributes in [current composition] —This moves a single layer into a nested composition. The nested composition has the size and duration of the layer, and it acquires the layer's properties and keyframes.

Move all attributes into the new composition—Choose this to move one or more layers into a nested composition, which has the size and duration of the current composition. All properties and keyframes are retained by the layers and move with them into the nested composition.

Open New Composition—This opens the newly created nested composition automatically. Leaving this option deselected creates a nested composition but leaves the current composition open.

To precompose one or more layers:

1. Select one or more layers in the Timeline panel (**Figure 16.22**).

2. *Do either of the following:*

   ▲ Choose Layer > Pre-compose (**Figure 16.23**).

   ▲ Press Shift-Command-C (Shift-Ctrl-C).

   A Pre-compose dialog appears (**Figure 16.24**).

3. Select an option:

   ▲ Leave all attributes in [current composition]

   ▲ Move all attributes into the new composition

   ▲ Open New Composition

   If you're precomposing more than one layer, only the second option is available.

4. To have After Effects open the nested composition automatically, select Open New Composition.

5. Click OK to close the Pre-compose dialog.

   The selected layers are moved into another composition, which is nested in the current composition (**Figure 16.25**). The nested composition is also listed in the Project panel.

Figure 16.22 Select one or more layers in the Timeline panel.

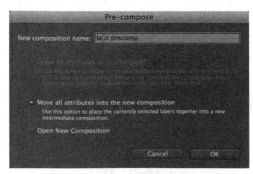

Figure 16.23 Choose Layer > Pre-compose.

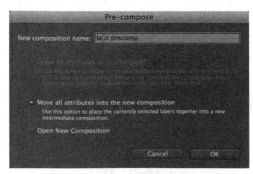

Figure 16.24 In the Pre-compose dialog, select an option.

Figure 16.25 The selected layers are moved into another composition, and that composition replaces the layers in the current composition.

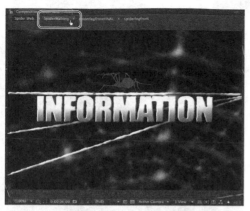

Figure 16.26 Buttons at the top of the Comp panel correspond to successively nested comps from left to right. Clicking a button...

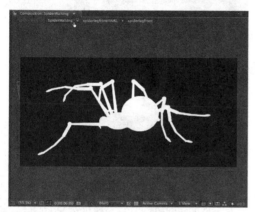

Figure 16.27 ... makes it visible in the Comp panel's viewer.

Viewing Composition Hierarchy as a Flowchart

A complex project can begin to resemble a labyrinth of nested comps. Luckily, After Effects CS4 furnishes you with new tools to visualize the project's structure and navigate your way through it. When the current comp is part of a hierarchy of nested comps, buttons along the top of the Comp panel represent each successive comp, from left to right. Clicking the comp's name makes it the current comp and visible in the viewer.

After Effects can also represent the hierarchical structure of comps graphically, in flowchart form. A flowchart view acts as both map and vehicle, showing the relationship among elements and transporting you to any given point with just a click or two of the mouse.

In the Comp and Timeline panels, you can quickly invoke a mini-flowchart that lets you view and navigate through comps. Alternatively, you can open a Flowchart panel that shows either a whole project's structure or a particular comp's place in a hierarchy of comps. The Flowchart panel also includes options for viewing each comp's constituent parts, such as individual layers and effects. But be aware that you can't use a Flowchart panel or a mini-flowchart to change the way the project is organized.

To navigate through comps in the Comp panel:

◆ At the top of the Comp panel, click the name of the comp you want to view (**Figure 16.26**).

The selected comp becomes the current comp in the viewer (**Figure 16.27**). Comp names are arranged from left to right, so that the highest comp in the hierarchy appears in the leftmost position, and the most deeply nested comp appears farthest to the right.

To display the Flowchart panel:

◆ *Do one of the following:*

▲ To view a flowchart for the entire project, click the Flowchart View button in the Project panel (**Figure 16.28**).

▲ To view a flowchart for the current composition, click the Flowchart View button  in the Composition panel (**Figure 16.29**).

▲ A Flowchart panel appears, depicting a flowchart view of the project or current comp, depending on your choice (**Figure 16.30**).

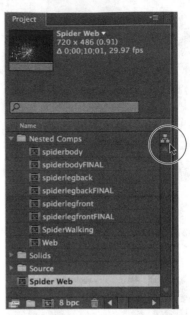

Figure 16.28 Click the Flowchart View button in the Project panel to view a flowchart of the entire project...

Figure 16.29 ...or click the Flowchart View button in the Composition panel to view a flowchart of the composition...

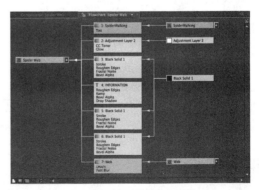

Figure 16.30 ...and the Flowchart panel displays the structure of a project or composition (shown here).

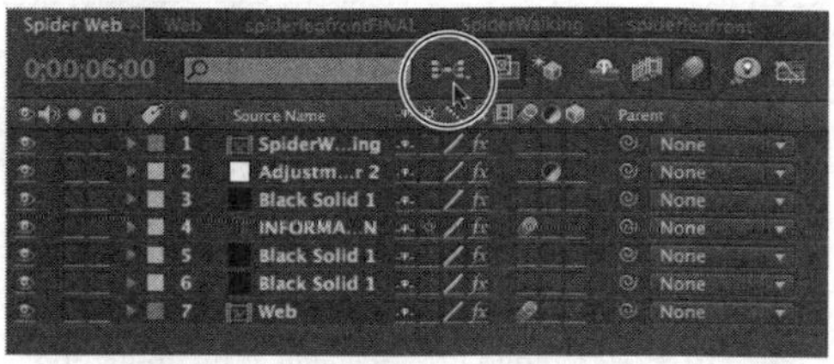

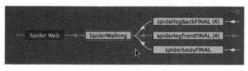

Figure 16.31 Select a comp in the Timeline panel and then click the Mini-Flowchart button...

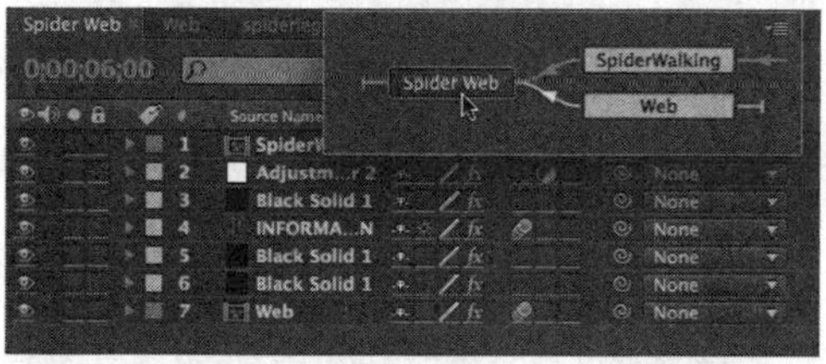

Figure 16.32 ...to view the comp's structure in a Mini-Flowchart view.

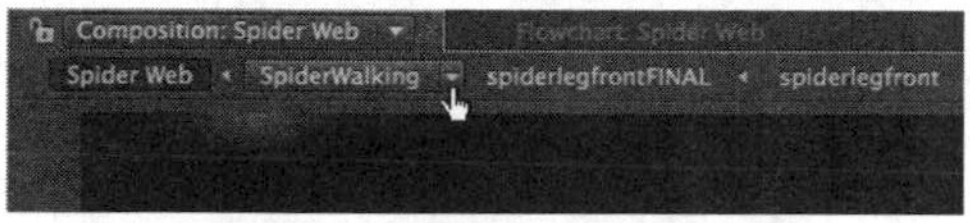

Figure 16.33 In the Comp panel, position the mouse pointer to the right of a comp's name and click the arrow...

Figure 16.34 ...to view that comp's structure in a Mini-Flowchart view.

To toggle a comp's mini-flowchart in the timeline:

1. In the Timeline panel, select the comp's tab.

2. *Do either of the following:*
   - ▲ Click the Mini-Flowchart button (**Figure 16.31**).
   - ▲ Press Shift on the keyboard.

   A mini-flowchart appears (**Figure 16.32**).

3. To close the mini-flowchart, click an empty area of the Mini-Flowchart panel, or press Shift on the keyboard.

To toggle a comp's mini-flowchart in the Comp panel:

1. Open a comp in the Comp panel.

2. *Do either of the following:*
   - ▲ To view a mini-flowchart for the current comp, press Shift on the keyboard.
   - ▲ To view a mini-flowchart, position the mouse pointer to the right of a Comp's name and click the arrow that appears (**Figure 16.33**).

   A mini-flowchart opens (**Figure 16.34**).

3. To close the mini-flowchart, click an empty area of the Mini-Flowchart panel, or press Shift on the keyboard.

To toggle a mini-flowchart using a keyboard shortcut:

◆ Select a comp in the Timeline panel or Comp panel and then press Shift on the keyboard.

A mini-flowchart appears for the current comp. Pressing Shift again hides the mini-flowchart.

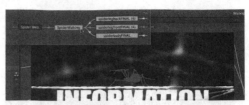

Figure 16.35 In a Mini-Flowchart, click the name of a comp you want to view...

To open a comp from a mini-flowchart:

◆ Open a mini-flowchart and then click the comp you want to view (**Figure 16.35**).

The comp you selected becomes the current comp (**Figure 16.36**).

✔ Tips

■ Unlike a mini-flowchart, the Flowchart panel lets you open both Comps and Layers from the flowchart. Clicking an item once selects it (so that you can, for example, reposition it in the view); double-clicking an item opens it in a Comp or Layer panel.

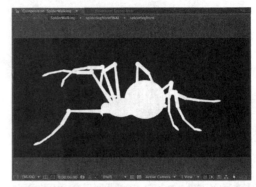

Figure 16.36 ...to make it the current comp.

■ Options in the Mini-Flowchart pop-up menu (in the Flowchart panel's upper right corner) let you change the flowchart's layout.

■ The Flowchart View panel includes several buttons and options for showing and hiding types of items in the flowchart, and for changing the flowchart's layout. See After Effects Help for details.

Figure 16.37 When an image at one resolution...

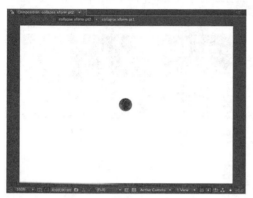

Figure 16.38 ...is scaled down, it's rasterized at the new size.

Figure 16.39 Scaling the image up again in a subsequent composition doesn't restore the original resolution.

Collapsing Transformations

Sometimes the rendering order in nested compositions can cause image resolution to degrade. This happens because transform properties, such as Scale, are calculated at every tier in the project hierarchy: first in the most deeply nested composition, then in the next, and so on. At each level, the image is *rasterized*—its resolution is defined and then redefined in successive compositions.

Scaling down an image in a nested composition rasterizes the image at the smaller size and, consequently, at a lower resolution (**Figures 16.37** and **16.38**). Because the smaller image becomes the source for successive compositions, scaling it up again makes the reduced resolution more apparent (**Figure 16.39**).

This rescaling process is sometimes unavoidable, especially when a boss or client dictates revisions. In such circumstances, you can maintain image quality by *collapsing transformations*.

By collapsing transformations, you prevent After Effects from rasterizing the image in every successive composition, instead forcing it to calculate all the transform property changes and rasterize the image only once (in the composition with the Collapse Transformations switch selected). This way, the composition uses the resolution of the source image rather than that of intermediate versions (**Figure 16.40**, see next page).

To collapse transformations:

1. If necessary, click the Switches/Modes button in the Timeline panel to display the Switches panel.

2. For a nested composition, select the Collapse Transformations switch ▓ (**Figure 16.41**).

   The same switch is used to continuously rasterize a layer created from path-based artwork.

✔ Tips

■ When applied to a layer created from a path-based illustration (such as an Illustrator file), the Collapse Transformations switch functions as the Continuously Rasterize switch. See "Continuously Rasterizing a Layer" in Chapter 5 for more information.

■ The Opacity settings for the nested compositions are retained and combine with the opacity of the layer that uses collapsed transformations.

Figure 16.40 By collapsing transformations, you can postpone rasterization until rendering reaches the nested composition in which the switch is selected.

Figure 16.41 Click the Collapse Transformations switch for a nested composition.

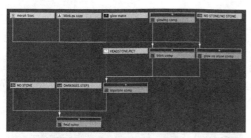

Figure 16.42 By prerendering, you avoid rendering every element of a nested composition (here, the layers contained in the nested "Topstone" comp)...

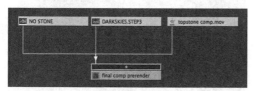

Figure 16.43 ...and replace the nested comp with a rendered version. (This flowchart illustrates the process; the actual Flowchart view continues to show the nested composition.)

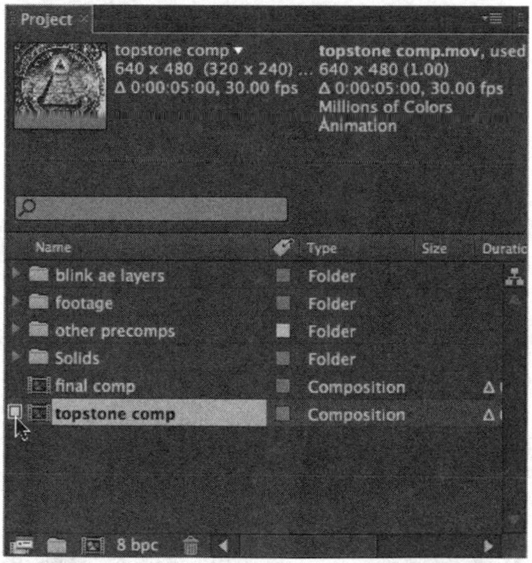

Figure 16.44 Because the prerendered movie is a proxy, you can always switch back to the nested composition.

Prerendering

It seems that if you're not occupied with making the project better, you're preoccupied with making it render faster. A process known as *prerendering* is one strategy you can use to reduce rendering times.

Typically, you'll complete work on nested compositions long before the final composition is ready—which makes it all the more frustrating to wait for the nested comps to render (not to mention unnecessary).

With prerendering, you can render nested compositions and use the movie file as a proxy. Thereafter, render times are reduced because After Effects refers to the movie instead of calculating every element in the nested composition (**Figures 16.42** and **16.43**). If you decide you need to make changes, you can stop using the proxy and switch back to the source composition (**Figure 16.44**). Prerender the composition again to save the changes in the proxy. When exporting, the Render Queue lets you prerender a comp and set the rendered file as a proxy in a single step, using something called a *postrender action*.

To reduce render times for the final output, make sure that the Prerender settings are compatible with the settings of your final file and that you've set the Render settings to Use Proxies.

To use prerendering, consult Chapter 17, "Output," as well as the "Proxies" section in Chapter 3, "Managing Footage."

Parenting Layers

Often, you need layers to act as a group or an integrated system. For example, if you wanted to simulate a planetary system, you can establish a relationship between one layer's transformation properties and the transformation properties of one or more other layers—a technique fittingly known as *parenting* (**Figures 16.45**).

Changing a parent layer's transformation properties (with the exception of its Opacity property) provokes a corresponding change in its related child layers. For example, if you were to change a parent layer's position, the child layers' positions would change accordingly. Although you can animate child layers independently, the transformations occur relative to the parent, not the composition. In the layer outline of the timeline, note that child layers' property values don't reflect the layer's actual appearance, which is a product of the parent's property values. For example, scaling the parent layer also scales the child layer—even though the child layer's Scale property continues to display the same value (**Figures 16.46** and **16.47**).

It may be helpful to compare parenting to traveling in a vehicle, such as an airplane. In this analogy the plane is like the parent layer. Relative to the earth, a plane moves hundreds of miles per hour. And as a passenger on the plane, so do you. However, sitting in your cramped coach seat, you think of yourself as motionless. You're like the child layer; relative to the plane, you're not going anywhere. Just as the child layer can move relative to the parent layer, you can get up and move about the cabin and stretch your legs. But as long as you're on the plane, you'll measure movements relative to say, your seat on the plane—and not the ground far below.

Figure 16.45 In this example, the logo and book cover are separate layers, but parenting links them so they move as one.

Figure 16.46 When the child layer's (the rabbit logo's) and parent layer's (the book cover's) transform properties are linked...

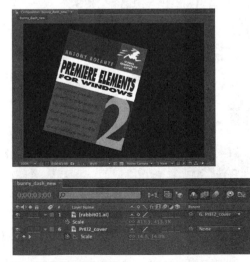

Figure 16.47 ...changing the parent's property value isn't reflected in the child layer's property value display.

Figure 16.48 Ordinarily, assigning a parent-child relationship leaves the child layer's relative transform properties unchanged in the Comp panel.

Jumping

When you assign (or remove) a parent-child relationship, you can specify whether the child layer *jumps*—changes its transform properties relative to its parent layer. Ordinarily, assigning a parent-child relationship leaves the child layer's transform properties unchanged until you make subsequent alterations to either the parent or child layers (**Figure 16.48**). In contrast, when you set the child layer to jump, its transformation properties are immediately altered relative to the parent layer (**Figure 16.49**). Conversely, you can make a child layer jump when you remove the parent-child relationship, so that its transform properties immediately shift relative to the composition.

Figure 16.49 In contrast, when you have the child layer jump, its transformation properties are altered relative to the parent layer immediately.

To assign a parent-child relationship:

1. If necessary, reveal the Parenting panel in the Timeline panel by choosing Panels > Parent in the Timeline pop-up menu.

2. For the child layer, do either of the following:

   ▲ Choose the layer you want to assign as the parent in the Parent pop-up menu (**Figure 16.50**).

   ▲ Drag the Pickwhip to the layer you want to designate as the parent (**Figure 16.51**).

   You can drag the Pickwhip anywhere in the layer's horizontal track in the layer

outline to select it. The name of the parent layer appears in the Parenting pop-up menu for the child layer.

To remove a parent from a layer:

◆ In the Parent pop-up menu for the child layer, choose None (**Figure 16.52**).

The parent-child relationship is removed, and you can now transform the layer.

To make a child jump when assigning or removing a parent:

◆ Press Option (Alt) when you select a layer name in the Parent pop-up menu, or select a layer with the Parent Pickwhip ⊙.

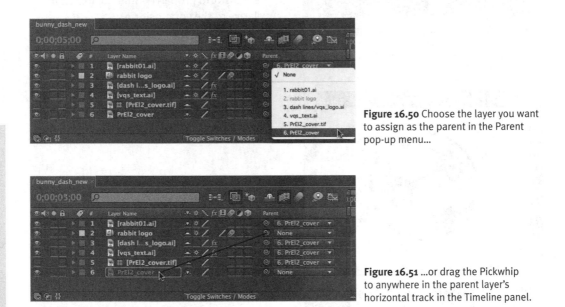

Figure 16.50 Choose the layer you want to assign as the parent in the Parent pop-up menu...

Figure 16.51 ...or drag the Pickwhip to anywhere in the parent layer's horizontal track in the Timeline panel.

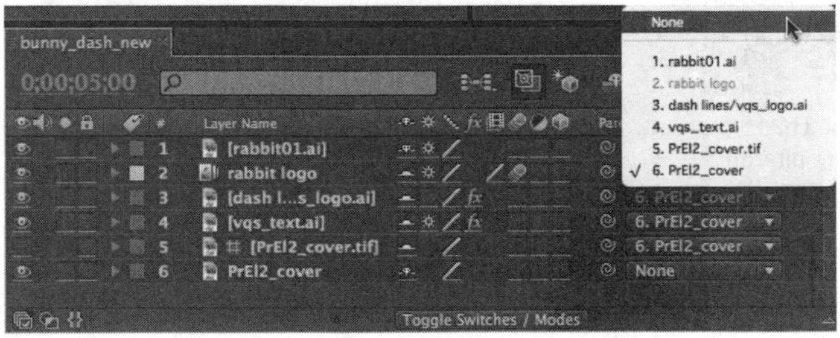

Figure 16.52 In the Parent pop-up menu for the child layer, choose None to cut the apron strings.

Figure 16.53 Here, a null layer (named "3D control") is the parent of the other layers in the comp so that animating the null animates the other layers as an interconnected system.

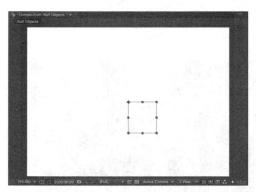

Figure 16.54 When selected, a null object appears in the Composition panel as a framed outline (but it won't ever appear in an exported image). A null object's anchor point is positioned in its upper-left corner.

Using Null Objects

You can add invisible layers, called *null objects,* to a composition to create sophisticated animations that don't rely on the movement of visible layers. For example, a null object can serve as a parent layer, exerting an invisible influence over several child layers (**Figure 16.53**). Because these layers aren't visible in previews or output, you can't apply effects to them. When selected, a null object appears in the Composition panel as a framed outline. A null object's anchor point is positioned in its upper-left corner (**Figure 16.54**). Otherwise, null objects behave like other layers.

To create a null object:

◆ Choose Layer > New > Null Object
(**Figure 16.55**).

A Null Object layer appears as the top
layer in the timeline, beginning at the current time and using the specified default
duration for still images (**Figure 16.56**).

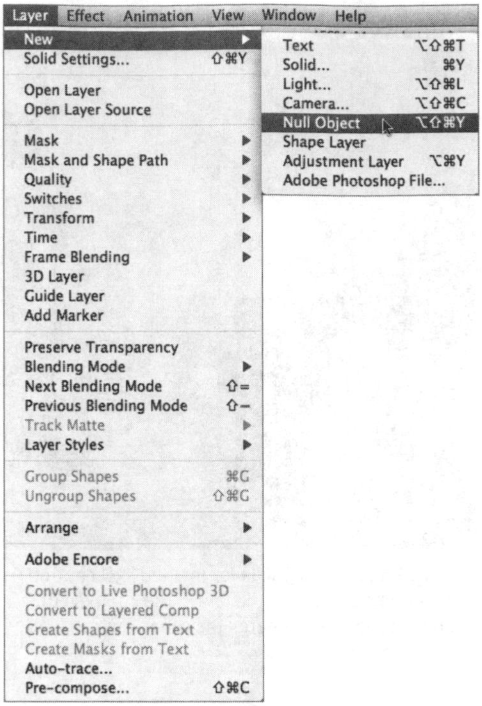

Figure 16.55 Choose Layer > New > Null Object.

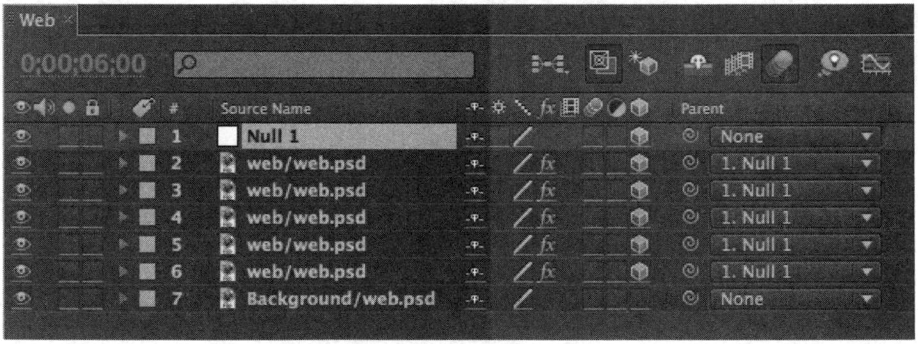

Figure 16.56 A Null Object layer appears as the top layer, beginning at the current time and using the specified default duration for still images. Here, the null layer has been assigned as the parent to other layers.

Figure 16.57 Expressions are especially useful in depicting the parts of a machine. Here, the rotation of the small center gear is linked to the large gear's rotation via an expression.

Using Expressions

Expressions are a set of instructions that can generate and animate property values without necessarily using keyframes. Frequently, an expression generates a property's values based on another property (in the same layer, in a different layer, or even in a layer that resides in different compositions). This way, expressions allow you to create sophisticated relationships between properties that you could otherwise produce only through painstaking keyframing. Alternatively, an expression can generate values independently, via a set of instructions akin to a mathematical formula.

Expressions are especially useful for depicting the parts of a machine: wheels turning as a car moves, a small gear turning in response to a larger gear, or a meter increasing in height as a dial is turned (**Figure 16.57**). Because you can link all kinds of properties using simple or complex formulas, expressions afford endless possibilities. And because you can change the timing of the whole system by modifying a single element, you save time and effort as well.

Because expressions are based on JavaScript, experience with that language or a similar scripting language gives you a definite head start. However, even with no knowledge of JavaScript and only basic math skills, you can create useful expressions. Using the Pickwhip tool, you can generate a basic expression automatically. You can then modify your basic expression by appending a little arithmetic. When you're ready to write your own scripts, After Effects supplies the terms you need in a convenient pop-up menu.

To create an expression using the Expression Pickwhip:

1. Expand the layer outline to reveal the properties you want to link via an expression (**Figure 16.58**).

2. With the property selected, *do either of the following:*

   ▲ Choose Animation > Add Expression (**Figure 16.59**).

   ▲ Press Shift-Option-= (Shift-Alt-=).

   An Equal Sign icon ▬ appears next to the property to indicate an expression is enabled. The property also expands to reveal buttons in the Switches panel of the timeline. Under the time ruler, the expression script appears selected (**Figure 16.60**).

3. In the Switches panel, click the Expression Pickwhip button ⊚, and drag the Pickwhip to the name of the property value to which you want to link the expression (**Figure 16.61**).

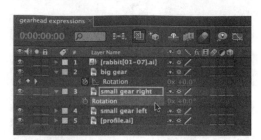

Figure 16.58 Expand the layer outline to reveal the properties you want to link using an expression.

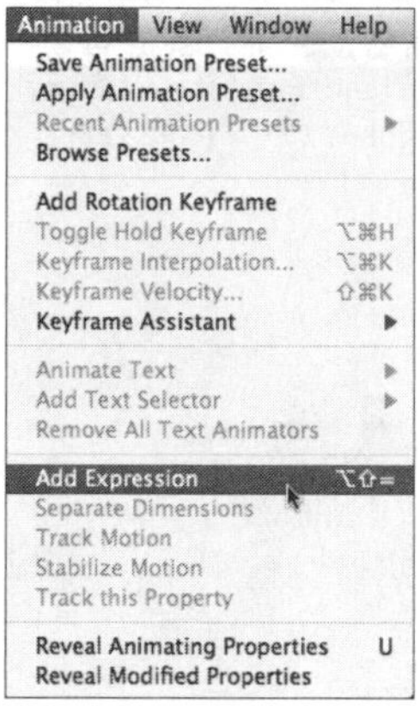

Figure 16.59 Choose Animation > Add Expression, or press Shift-Option-= (Shift-Alt-=).

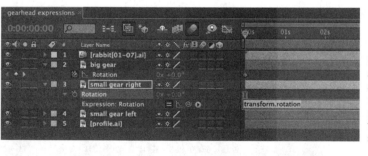

Figure 16.60 An Equal Sign icon appears next to the property, and the property expands to reveal buttons in the Switches panel. In the time ruler area, the expression script appears selected.

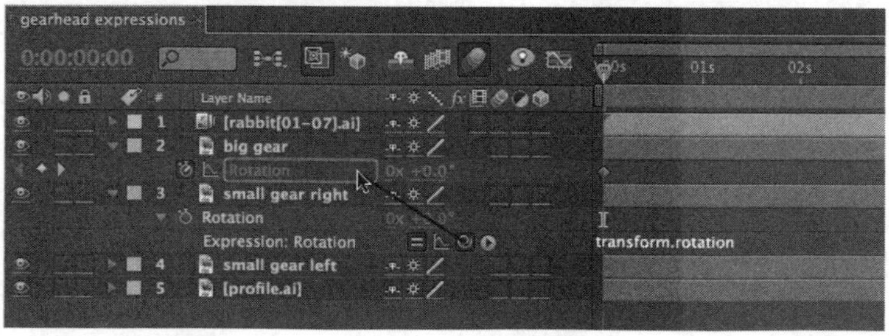

Figure 16.61 In the Switches panel, drag the Pickwhip to the name of the property value to which you want to link the expression.

The property's name becomes highlighted when the Pickwhip touches it. When you release the mouse, the expression script is entered in the script area under the time ruler (**Figure 16.62**).

4. Modify the script by *doing either of the following* (**Figure 16.63**):

▲ Enter changes or additions to the script using standard JavaScript syntax.

▲ Use the Expressions pop-up menu to select from a list of common scripting terms.

If you make a mistake, After Effects prompts you with a warning dialog and advises you to correct the script.

5. Keyframe the linked property (the one without the expression) using the methods you learned in Chapter 7, "Properties and Keyframes."

The property using the expression changes automatically according to the relationship defined by the expression (**Figure 16.64**).

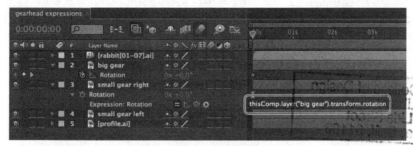

Figure 16.62 When you release the mouse, the expression script is entered in the script area under the time ruler.

Figure 16.63 If necessary, modify the script manually. Here, *-2 is added to the script to multiply the rotation value by -2.

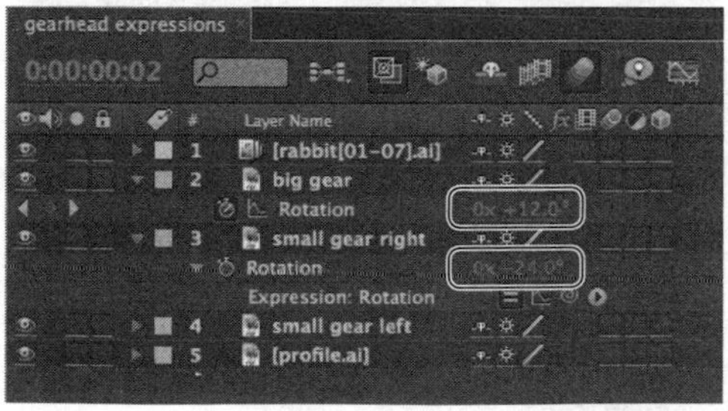

Figure 16.64 The property using the expression changes automatically, according to the relationship defined by the expression.

To disable and enable expressions:

◆ In the layer outline, click the Expression icon next to the property containing the expression to toggle it on and off.

An Equal Sign icon ▬ indicates the expression is enabled; a crossed-out Equal Sign icon ▬ indicates the expression has been temporarily disabled (**Figure 16.65**).

✔ Tips

■ Despite their similar names, JavaScript isn't related to Java.

■ After Effects includes a project template called Expression Sampler. See Chapter 2, "Importing Footage into a Project," for more about importing project templates.

Expression disabled

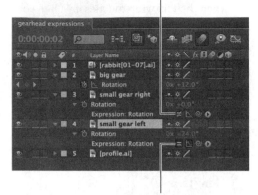

Expression enabled

Figure 16.65 An Equal Sign icon indicates that the expression is enabled; a crossed-out equal sign indicates that the expression is temporarily disabled.

Expression Errors

If you exit expression editing mode before the expression is complete, or if the expression uses incorrect syntax, an error dialog appears containing a description of the problem (**Figure 16.66**). When you close the dialog, a Warning icon appears in the Switches panel, and the expression is disabled automatically (**Figure 16.67**). You must correct the expression language to enable it. Click the Warning icon to reopen the Warning dialog.

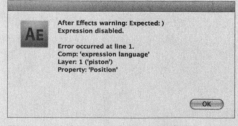

Figure 16.66 If you exit editing mode before the expression is complete or if the expression uses incorrect syntax, an error dialog appears.

Figure 16.67 When you close the dialog, a Warning icon appears in the Switches panel, and the expression is disabled automatically. Click the Warning icon to reopen the Warning dialog.

Viewing Expressions

Although expressions don't create keyframes, you can still see how an expression modifies the property in a property graph.

In contrast to the Graph Editor Set button, which appears to the left of a property, the button that reveals how an expression affects a property appears to the right of the property in the Switches panel's column. Otherwise, the button looks and works just like the Graph Editor Set button. (See Chapter 9, "Keyframe Interpolation," for more about reading property graphs.) This book always refers to the icon as a Graph Editor Set button, even though a tool tip identifies the icon next to an expression as the Show Post-Expression Graph button.

To view an expression graph:

1. Expand the layer outline to reveal the layer property containing the expression.

2. In the Switches panel, click the Graph Editor Set icon █ (**Figure 16.68**).

3. In the Timeline panel, select the Show Graph Editor button 📈.

   In the Graph Editor, a graph shows the property's value or speed/velocity after the expression has been applied (**Figure 16.69**).

✔ Tips

■ To view expressions for all layers in the composition, select the layers and press EE.

■ You can convert property values calculated by an expression into keyframed values by choosing Animation > Keyframe Assistant > Convert Expression to Keyframes.

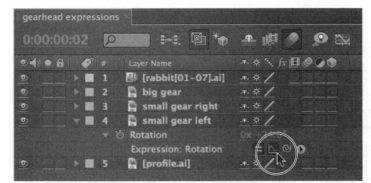

Figure 16.68 In the Switches panel, click the Expression's Graph Editor Set icon...

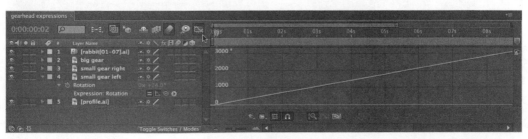

Figure 16.69 ...and then click the Timeline panel's Show Graph Editor button to view how the expression affects the property.

Using the Expression Language Menu

When you start writing your own expressions, you'll discover that the language's vocabulary is extensive. Fortunately, you can plug in most of the terms you'll need automatically by selecting them from a categorized list contained in a convenient pop-up menu.

To use the Expression pop-up menu:

1. Expand the layer outline to reveal the property you want to adjust with an expression.

2. With the property selected, *do either of the following:*

   ▲ Choose Animation > Add Expression.

   ▲ Press Shift-Option-= (Shift-Alt-=).

   An Equal Sign icon ▣ appears next to the property, and a default expression appears under the time ruler. The default expression won't modify the property values. The property also expands to reveal buttons in the Switches panel of the timeline.

3. In the Switches panel of the timeline, click the Expressions pop-up menu.

   A categorized menu of expression language terms appears (**Figure 16.70**).

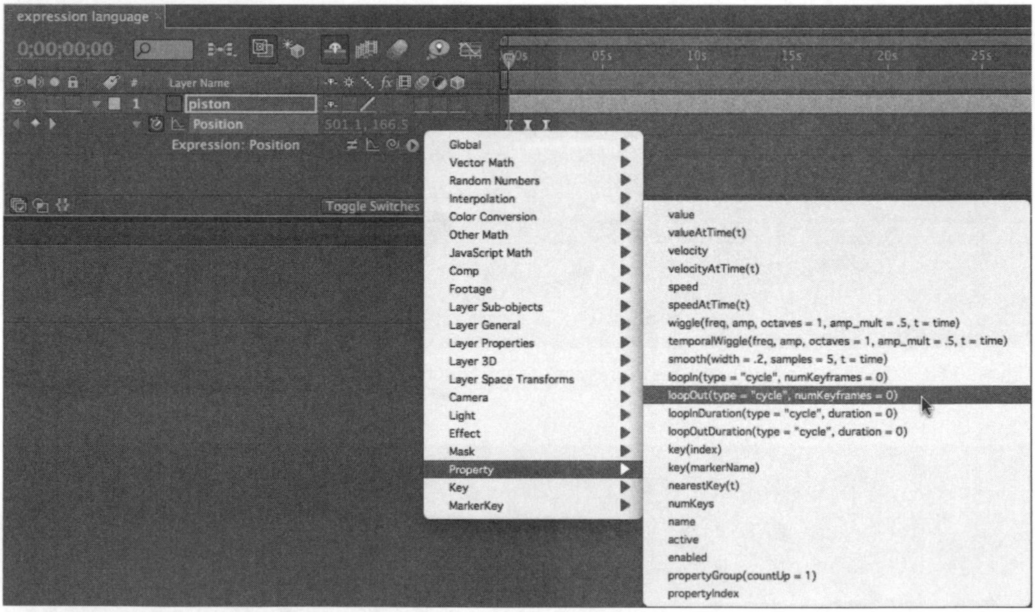

Figure 16.70 In the Switches panel of the timeline, click the Expressions pop-up menu to see a categorized menu of expression-language terms.

4. In the pop-up menu, select the term you need.

In the time ruler area of the timeline, the term appears in the expression text. A cursor appears at the end of the text, indicating the insertion point for additional expression terms (**Figure 16.71**).

5. If necessary, enter expression language manually.

6. Repeat steps 3–5 as needed.

7. Click anywhere outside the expression text field to get out of edit mode.

Figure 16.71 The term appears in the expression text. A cursor appears at the end of the text, indicating the insertion point for additional expression terms.

USING THE EXPRESSION LANGUAGE MENU

Writing Expressions

Once you've created a few simple expressions with the Pickwhip, you'll probably want to try writing some of your own—a process that can appear daunting if you don't have experience with JavaScript or scripting in general (especially because After Effects discourages your early attempts with warning dialogs about syntax errors, bad arguments, and the like).

Once you understand a few basic concepts, however, you should feel confident enough to experiment a bit. You'll also find it easier to decipher Adobe's Expressions guide (or an entire book on the subject of JavaScript) and to analyze other expressions.

Translating a simple expression

Consider the following example, which was created by dragging the Expression Pickwhip ◎ to a Rotation property:

```
this_comp.layer("panel1").rotation
```

This simple expression links a layer's property (in this case, Rotation) to the Rotation property of a layer called panel1. A plain-English translation would read something like the following: "To set Rotation values for this property, look in this composition, find the layer called panel1, and take its Rotation value." Adjusting panel1's Rotation property results in a corresponding change in the layer containing the expression.

Typically, you would modify the expression:

```
this_comp.layer("panel1").rotation+60
```

The +60 adds 60 to the rotational value, which is measured in degrees. Setting panel1's Rotation value to 30 degrees would cause the layer containing the expression to rotate 90 degrees (30+60=90).

✔ Tips

- You may be familiar with JavaScript as it applies to Web design. Expressions are based on the same core JavaScript language but not particular JavaScript interpreters, which are browser-specific.

- Throughout this book, you've been advised to give your layers and comps descriptive names (rather than use the default names) and to refrain from changing them. The former habit helps you make clear expressions; the latter keeps your expressions from losing their links and becoming disabled.

- Although the term property is used in JavaScript, After Effects' Expressions reference substitutes the term attribute to avoid confusion with layer properties (which can be attributes in an expression).

OUTPUT

Finally.

The beginning of this book likened your project and compositions to a musical score. Now that you've written and rehearsed that score, it's time to put on the show!

In your case, that show is a comp rendered and exported to a particular format. You can export all or part of a comp to a multitude of formats—each one containing an extensive number of variable settings. The number of choices can be daunting.

But with few exceptions, the procedures to export any format are essentially the same: Add the comp to the Render Queue panel and specify the render settings and one or more output modules.

The typical export option is a movie file, saved in a format tailored for a particular playback device or medium: videotape, DVD, Blu-ray Disc, the Web, or a mobile device (such as a video-capable phone). Some workflows require exporting a still-image sequence for transferring (usually high-resolution) images from After Effects to an editing system or even to film. On the other hand, you may need to export just a single image or audio-only file.

Your particular output goals (and, unfortunately, your equipment's limitations) will help determine a wide range of output settings; this chapter will guide you through those myriad options. You'll start by familiarizing yourself with the panel dedicated to rendering and output: the Render Queue panel. You'll learn the overall process for exporting a movie and still image frame, as well as how to tailor the render and output options to any goal. To deal with the thornier formats, you'll start from a list of presets designed for particular scenarios. Although this chapter can't cover every output specification, it can provide you with enough information so that you know which questions to ask to derive your own answers.

The Render Queue Panel

You control the rendering process from the Render Queue panel, listing the items you want to render and assigning their rendering settings (**Figure 17.1**). This section provides an overview of the Render Queue panel; following sections explain each feature in more detail.

Figure 17.1 You control and monitor the rendering process from the Render Queue panel.

Rendering progress

The top of the panel contains buttons to start, stop, or pause the rendering process. During rendering, the top of the panel also shows how long the current item in the queue has been rendering, and how long it has to go. Clicking the triangle next to Current Render reveals more information (**Figure 17.2**). This information not only lets you compare an estimate of the completed file size to the available disk space, but it also helps you identify the areas of the composition that render more slowly than others. The bottom of the Render Queue panel displays information regarding all renders in the queue: which of the total number of items in the queue is being processed, when the render was started, the time elapsed so far, and any errors.

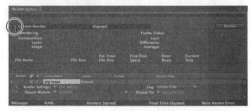

Figure 17.2 Clicking the triangle next to Current Render reveals detailed information about the current render.

Rendering settings

Most of the Render Queue panel is devoted to the render queue itself, where you list items in the order you want to render them. You can assign rendering settings to each item as well as render the same item with different settings. By default, the triangle next to each item's name is set to reveal four types of information (**Figure 17.3**).

On the left side of the Render Queue panel, the settings you assign each item in the queue are grouped into two categories: Render Settings and Output Module. The first step, Render Settings, calculates each frame for

Figure 17.3 By default, the triangle next to the name of each item points down to reveal four categories of information.

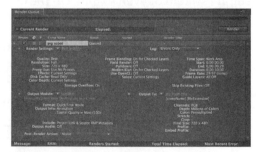

Figure 17.4 Clicking the arrow next to the Render Settings and Output Module options reveals a summary of each group of settings.

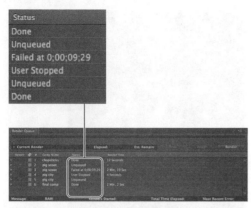

Figure 17.5 When the view of the items in the queue is collapsed, it's easier to see customizable columns of information, including the Render Status column.

Figure 17.6 Control-click (right-click) to use a pop-up menu to customize the panel headings.

output. Once the attributes of the frames have been rendered, Output Module determines how they're saved to disk. Clicking the triangle next to each setting category reveals a summary of the setting (**Figure 17.4**).

On the right side, you can specify the type of record After Effects generates in the Log pop-up menu; you can also specify a name and destination for Output To.

Panel headings and the Render Status column

In the Render Queue panel, clicking the triangle next to each item collapses the queue information, making several columns of information more apparent (**Figure 17.5**). Although most panel headings are self-explanatory, Render Status merits special attention because it indicates the current state of each item in the queue:

Queued—The item is ready to be rendered.

Unqueued—The item is listed but not ready for rendering, meaning you need to assign a name and destination to it, or select the Render option by clicking its check box.

Failed—The render was unsuccessful. Check the render log generated by After Effects to determine the error.

User Stopped—This indicates that you stopped the rendering process.

Done—The item has been rendered successfully.

After an item is rendered or stopped, it remains in the render queue until you remove it. Although you can't change the status of rendered items, you can duplicate them as other items in the queue. You can then assign new settings to the new item and render it.

✔ Tip

- Customize the headings of the Render Queue panel just as you would the Project panel headings. Control-click (right-click) for options (**Figure 17.6**).

Making a Movie

This section explains how to add a composition to the render queue by dragging or by using the Make Movie command. Later sections focus on the Render Queue panel and choosing specific settings.

To make a movie from a composition:

1. *Do either of the following:*

   ▲ Select a composition and then choose Composition > Make Movie

   ▲ Drag the composition's icon from the Project panel to the Render Queue panel (**Figure 17.7**).

   The composition appears as an item in the Render Queue panel (**Figure 17.8**).

2. In the Render Queue panel, choose render settings by *doing one of the following:*

   ▲ Choose a template from the Render Settings pop-up menu (**Figure 17.9**).

   ▲ Click the name of the current render settings to open the Render Settings dialog.

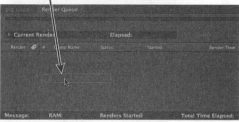

Figure 17.7 Drag the Comp's icon from the Project panel to the Render Queue panel.

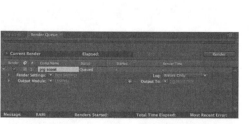

Figure 17.8 The composition appears as an item in the Render Queue panel.

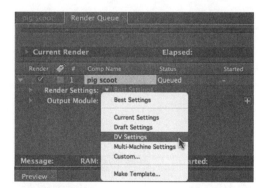

Figure 17.9 Choose a template from the Render Settings pop-up menu, or click the underlined name of the current settings to open a dialog.

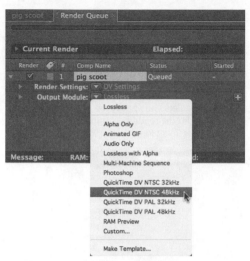

Figure 17.10 Choose a template from the Output Module pop-up menu, or click the underlined name of the current settings to open a dialog.

Figure 17.11 Select the type of log After Effects will generate in the Log pop-up menu.

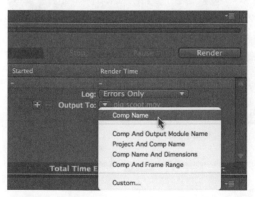

Figure 17.12 Choose a naming scheme from the Output To pop-up menu.

3. In the Render Queue panel, choose output options by *doing one of the following:*
   - ▲ Choose a template from the Output Module pop-up menu (**Figure 17.10**).
   - ▲ Click the name of the current output options to open the Output Options dialog.

4. In the Render Queue panel, choose an option from the Log pop-up menu (**Figure 17.11**):
   - ▲ Errors Only
   - ▲ Plus Settings
   - ▲ Plus Per Frame Info

5. In the Render Queue panel's Output To pop-up menu, choose an option for naming the exported file (**Figure 17.12**):
   - ▲ Comp Name
   - ▲ Comp and Output Module Name
   - ▲ Project and Comp Name
   - ▲ Comp Name and Dimensions
   - ▲ Comp and Frame Range
   - ▲ Custom

6. Click the exported file name to specify a destination for the exported file (**Figure 17.13**).

   An Output Movie To dialog appears.

continues on next page

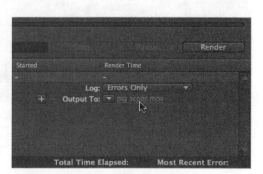

Figure 17.13 Clicking the name...

MAKING A MOVIE

477

7. In the Output Movie To dialog, specify a destination for the exported file (**Figure 17.14**).

If you want to save the movie as a single file, make sure your chosen destination has sufficient storage space to contain it.

8. Click the Render button near the top of the Render Queue panel (**Figure 17.15**).

After Effects begins to render the composition. A progress bar and rendering-time data indicate the elapsed render time as well as the estimated time remaining in the rendering process. After Effects sounds a chime when rendering is complete.

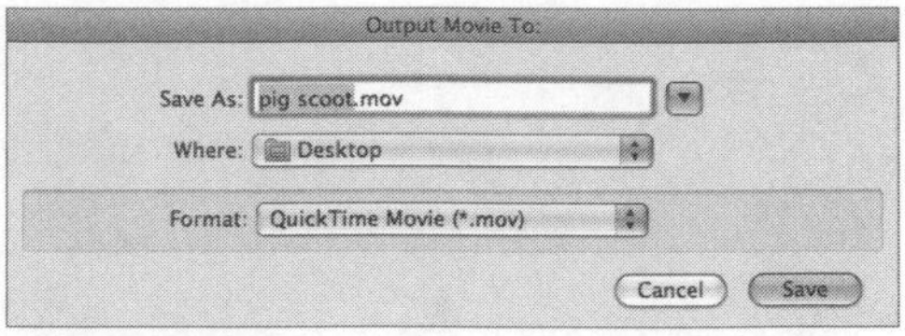

Figure 17.14 ...lets you specify the name and destination for the rendered composition in an Output Movie To dialog.

✔ Tips

■ The first time you use the Make Movie command, After Effects prompts you to specify a name and destination for the exported file in an Output To dialog. Thereafter, the command adds the comp directly to the Render Queue panel, where you can specify another destination by clicking the comp's name next to the Output To pop-up menu.

■ Whereas exporting to a movie file format is generally an all-or-nothing affair, exporting a still-image sequence allows you to stop rendering and resume where you left off. Better yet, you can make changes to the comp and then render the changes only (numbering them accordingly). This can spare you hours of rendering entire movie files again.

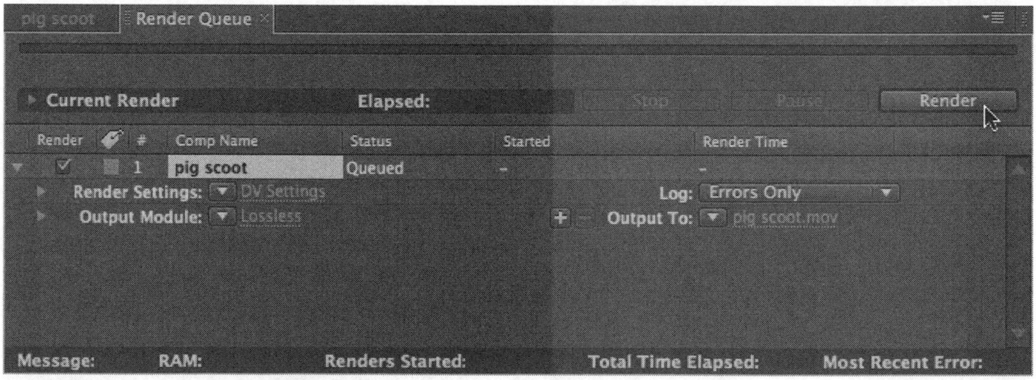

Figure 17.15 Make sure the Render column is checked for the item, and click Render.

Using the Render Queue Panel

Among other things, the render queue is just that: a queue, or line, of compositions waiting to be rendered.

To manage items in the render queue:

◆ In the Render Queue panel, *do any of the following:*

▲ To add a composition to the queue, drag a Composition icon from the Project panel to the Render Queue panel (**Figure 17.16**).

▲ To remove a composition from the queue, select a composition in the queue and press Delete.

▲ To change the order of the compositions in the queue, drag a composition up or down (**Figure 17.17**).

A dark horizontal line indicates where the composition's new position in the queue will be when you release the mouse.

▲ To prevent a composition in the queue from rendering, click the Render check box to deselect it (**Figure 17.18**).

The composition remains in the list, but its status changes to Unqueued; it won't render until you select the Render option box.

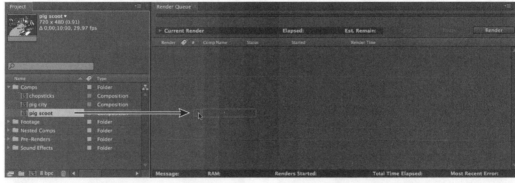

Figure 17.16 To add a composition to the queue, drag a Composition icon from the Project panel to the Render Queue panel.

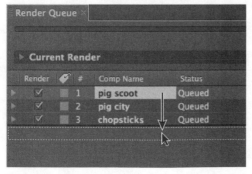

Figure 17.17 To change the order of the compositions in the queue, drag an item up or down.

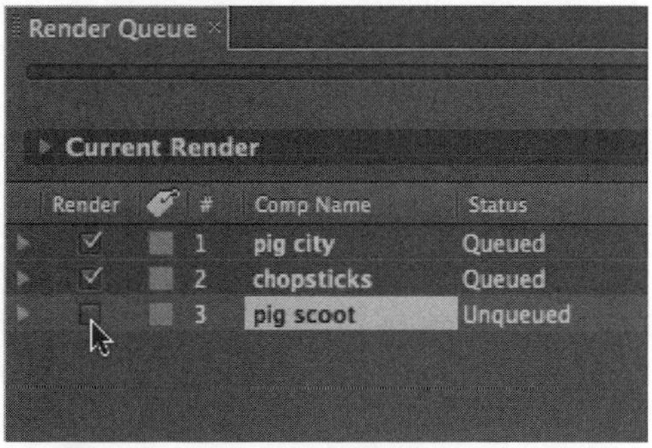

Figure 17.18 To remove a composition from the render queue, click the Render check box to deselect it.

Pausing and Stopping Rendering

After you click the Render button, the Pause and Stop buttons become active. Pausing a render comes in handy if you need to access other programs, or if you didn't plan ahead and find you need to clear some drive space for the render. You should avoid clicking Stop when exporting a movie file, however. A movie file ends at the point that you stop the render, and when you resume, After Effects renders the remaining part of the composition as a second movie file. Stopping a render won't adversely affect a frame sequence, though: you can pick up where you left off.

To pause rendering:

1. After the composition has begun to render, click the Pause button in the Render Queue panel (**Figure 17.19**).

   During the pause in rendering, you can use other applications or manage files on the desktop. However, you can't do anything in After Effects (not even close a window) except restart the render.

2. To resume rendering, click Continue.

   After Effects continues to render to the same file from where it left off.

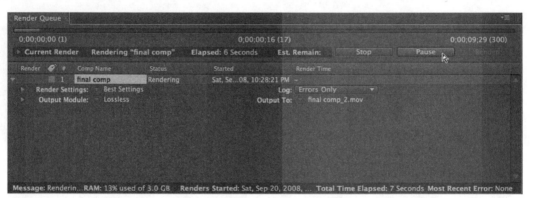

Figure 17.19 Click the Pause button in the Render Queue panel to pause rendering and use the desktop or other programs.

To stop rendering:

◆ After the composition has begun rendering, click the Stop button in the Render Queue panel (**Figure 17.20**).

When rendering stops, the composition's status changes to User Stopped. A new item—with an Unqueued status—is added to the queue. If you render this item, it will render a new movie, starting with the next unrendered frame of the interrupted movie (**Figure 17.21**).

✔ Tip

■ Pausing allows you to use other programs or the desktop but not After Effects. If you want to hide the Composition panel, do so before you start rendering.

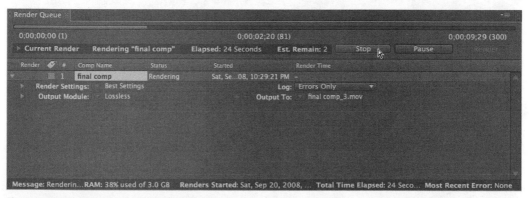

Figure 17.20 Click Stop to halt rendering completely.

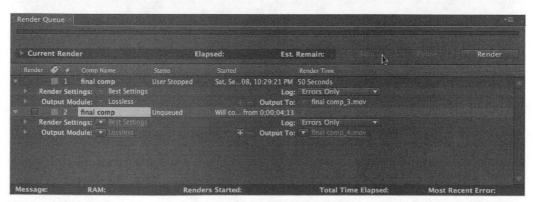

Figure 17.21 When you stop the rendering, the item's status changes to User Stopped, and a new item is added with the status Unqueued. This item will start rendering at the next unrendered frame.

Assigning Multiple Output Modules

You can assign more than one output module to a single item in the queue—a capability that allows you to easily create multiple versions of the same composition.

To assign additional output modules:

1. Make sure an item in the Render Queue panel is expanded so that its render settings and output module are visible.

2. Click the Add Output Module button ⊞ (located to the left of the Output Module label) (**Figure 17.22**).

   Another output module appears for the item in the queue (**Figure 17.23**).

3. Specify settings or a template for the output module, and render the items in the queue (as explained earlier in the section "Making a Movie").

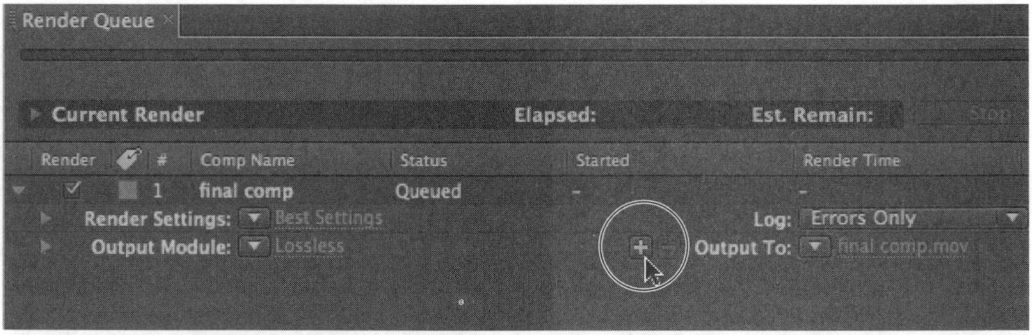

Figure 17.22 Click the Add Output Module button (circled).

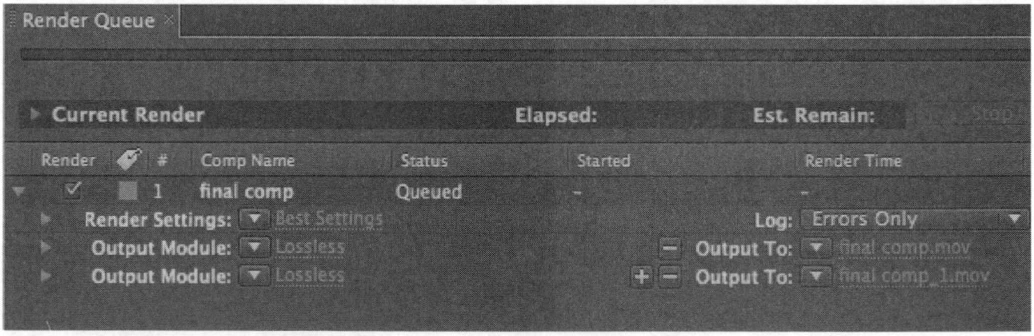

Figure 17.23 Another output module appears for the item in the queue.

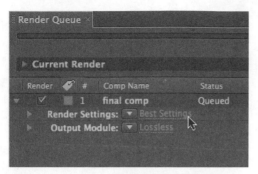

Figure 17.24 In the Render Queue panel, click the underlined name of the render settings.

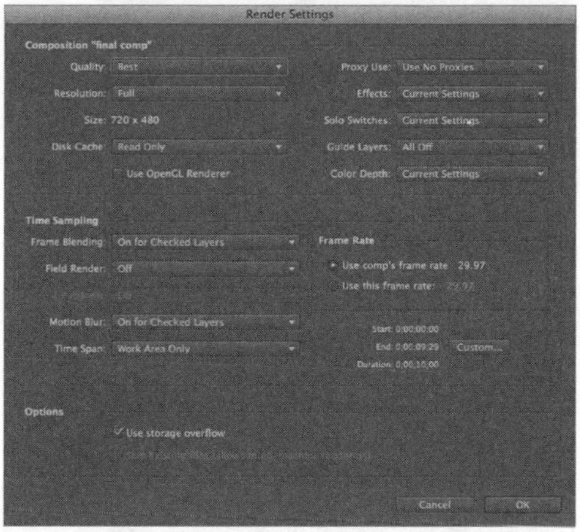

Figure 17.25 In the Render Settings dialog, specify various settings for rendering the frames of the composition.

Choosing Render Settings

Determining render settings is the first step in the rendering process. These settings dictate how each frame of a composition is calculated for the final output, in much the same way that composition settings calculate frames for playback in the Composition panel.

You can specify the render settings manually or by choosing from a list of preset templates. The names of the included templates indicate their purpose: "Current" renders frames using the comp's current settings, while "Best" renders at the highest quality, resolution, and so on. You can also save settings you set manually as a template that appears in the Render Settings pop-up menu.

This section shows you how to choose render settings manually and explains each setting. You'll learn how the preset template settings work and will be able to create your own template (covered in the section, "Creating Templates," later in this chapter).

To choose render settings manually:

1. In the Render Queue panel, click the underlined name next to Render Settings (**Figure 17.24**).

   A Render Settings dialog appears (**Figure 17.25**).

   continues on next page

2. Make a selection for each of the following options:

Quality—Sets the quality for all layers (**Figure 17.26**). (See "Quality Setting Switches" in Chapter 5.)

Resolution—Sets the resolution for all layers in a composition. (See "Setting a Comp's Viewing Resolution" in Chapter 4.) Setting the resolution to Half, for example, renders every other pixel, resulting in an image with half the dimensions of the full-sized composition (**Figure 17.27**).

Disk Cache—Specifies whether After Effects uses the current cache settings—the ones you specified in the Memory & Cache pane of the Preferences dialog. Setting this option to Read Only specifies that no new frames are written to the cache during rendering (**Figure 17.28**).

Use OpenGL Renderer—Utilizes an OpenGL graphics card to render (see "Using OpenGL" in Chapter 8, for more information) (**Figure 17.29**).

Figure 17.26 Set the Quality setting for all layers from the Quality pop-up menu.

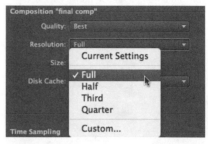

Figure 17.27 Set the resolution for all layers in the composition in the Resolution pop-up menu.

Figure 17.28 Specify an option for Disk Cache.

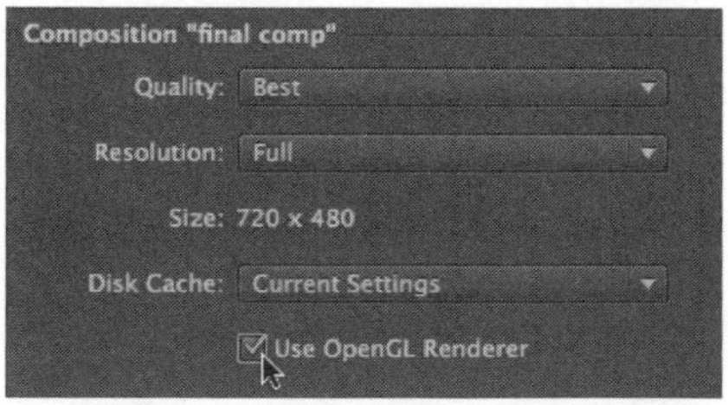

Figure 17.29 To employ OpenGL hardware, click the Use OpenGL Renderer check box.

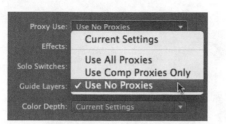

Figure 17.30 Specify whether proxies or source footage are used for output in the Proxy Use pop-up menu.

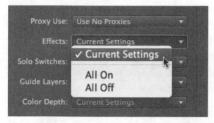

Figure 17.31 In the Effects menu, specify whether effects appear in the output.

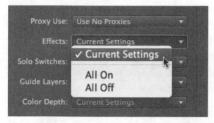

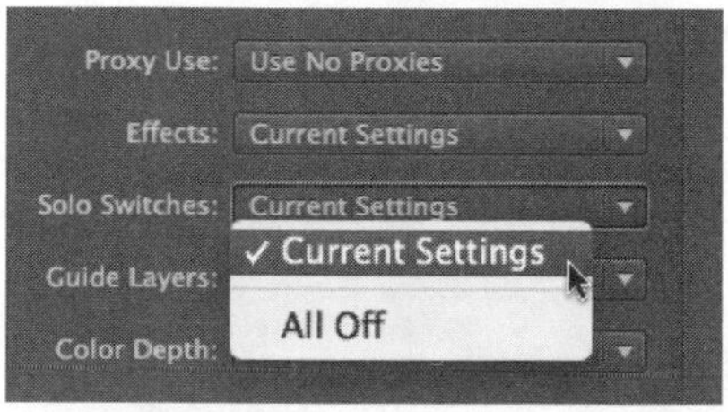

Figure 17.32 In the Solo Switches pop-up menu, specify whether to render layers with the Solo switch activated or to render layers without regard to their Solo switch.

Figure 17.33 In the Guide Layers pop-up menu, specify whether to render guide layers or to turn off guide layers.

Proxy Use—Specifies whether proxies or source footage are used for output (**Figure 17.30**). (See "Proxies" in Chapter 3.)

Effects—Specifies whether effects appear in the output. (See "Disabling Effects Temporarily" in Chapter 11.) Set Effects to All On to enable all effects, including ones you had disabled temporarily; set it to Current Settings to exclude effects you disabled deliberately (**Figure 17.31**).

Solo Switches—Specifies whether After Effects renders only layers with their Solo switch on (see "Switching Video and Audio On and Off" in Chapter 5) or turns off all Solo switches and renders all the layers in the comp (**Figure 17.32**).

Guide Layers—Specifies whether After Effects renders guide layers or deactivates all guide layers (**Figure 17.33**).

continues on next page

Color Depth—Specifies color bit depth which can be set to 8, 16, or 32 bits per channel (bpc) (**Figure 17.34**). For more about color bit depth, see the sidebar, "Choosing a Color Bit Depth Mode," in Chapter 2.

Frame Blending—Specifies whether frame blending is applied to layers with the Frame Blending switch enabled (regardless of a composition's Frame Blending setting) (**Figure 17.35**). (See "Using Frame Blending" in Chapter 14.)

Field Render—Specifies whether to field-render the output movie and, if so, which field is dominant. (See the section "Interpreting Interlaced Video" in Chapter 2.) Set this option to Off unless the output is destined for video (**Figure 17.36**).

3:2 Pulldown—Specifies whether to reintroduce pulldown to the footage and determines the phase of the pulldown. Phase refers to the cadence of whole and split frames created when transferring film footage to video. You need to set the proper phase only if the movie will be cut back into the original footage (**Figure 17.37**). For more information about pulldown and phase, see After Effects Help.

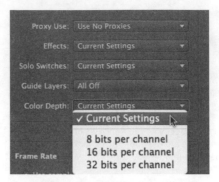

Figure 17.34 In the Color Depth pop-up menu, specify the color depth for the exported file.

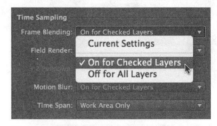

Figure 17.35 In the Frame Blending pop-up menu, specify whether frame blending is applied to layers with the Frame Blending switch enabled.

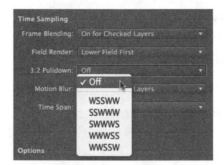

Figure 17.37 To reintroduce pulldown to the footage, choose an option from the 3:2 Pulldown menu.

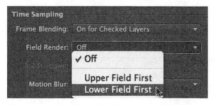

Figure 17.36 In the Field Render pop-up menu, choose whether to field-render the output.

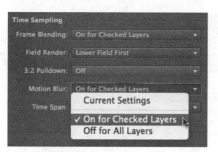

Figure 17.38 In the Motion Blur pop-up menu, specify whether motion blur is applied to layers with the Motion Blur switch enabled.

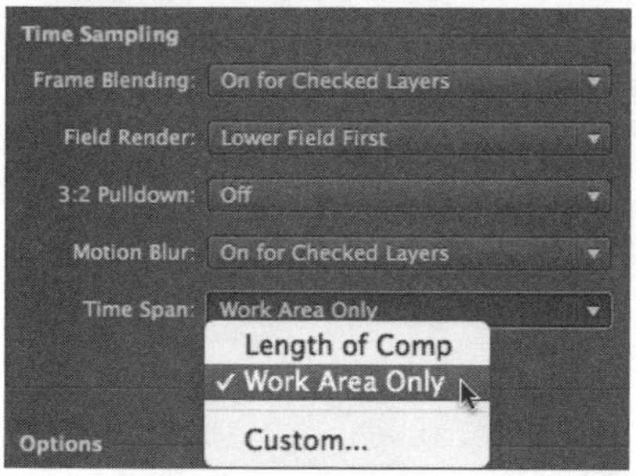

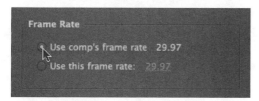

Figure 17.39 Define the part of the composition for output in the Time Span pop-up menu. Choosing Custom lets you specify a custom time span in a dialog.

Motion Blur—Specifies whether motion blur is applied to layers with the Motion Blur switch enabled regardless of a composition's Motion Blur setting. Or, you can set this option to respect the composition's current Motion Blur setting. When you enable motion blur, it uses the settings you specified in the Composition settings (see "Using Motion Blur," in Chapter 14). Alternatively, you can select "Override shutter angle" and enter the shutter angle to be used instead. A setting of 360 degrees results in the maximum motion blur (**Figure 17.38**).

Time Span—Defines the part of the composition for output (**Figure 17.39**). Choosing Custom from the Time Span pop-up menu or clicking the Set button opens a Custom Time Span dialog. (See "Previewing the Work Area" in Chapter 8.)

Frame Rate—Sets the frame rate used to render the composition. You can select the composition's frame rate or enter a custom frame rate (**Figure 17.40**).

continues on next page

Figure 17.40 Select the frame rate of the composition, or enter a custom frame rate.

Use storage overflow—Determines whether rendering continues to an overflow volume when the output file exceeds the capacity of the first storage volume (**Figure 17.41**). You can set the Overflow Volumes in the Output pane of the Preferences dialog. See the sidebar "Overflow Volumes" below.

Figure 17.41 Click the "Use storage overflow" check box to ensure that rendering continues to an overflow volume when the output file exceeds the capacity of the first storage volume.

Skip existing files—Enables After Effects to render frames of an existing frame sequence. This option also allows multiple computers to render parts of the same image sequence to a Watch folder (**Figure 17.42**). (Consult your After Effects documentation for more about network rendering features.)

Figure 17.42 Click the "Skip existing files" check box to enable After Effects to render or rerender frames of an existing frame sequence.

3. Click OK to close the Render Settings dialog and return to the Render Queue panel.

Overflow Volumes

If a file or sequence exceeds either the file size limit imposed by the computer's operating system or the size of the storage volume, you can instruct After Effects to continue rendering into a folder on the root level of another volume on a hard disk, called an *overflow volume*.

To set overflow volumes, choose After Effects > Preferences > Output (Edit > Preferences > Output). In the Output pane of the Preferences dialog, you can specify up to five volumes and set the disk space that remains before rendering to the subsequent volume. For sequences, you can set the maximum number of files each volume contains; for movie files, you can set the maximum size before segmenting the file. Finally, you can set a movie file's audio block size and whether to use the default filename and folder.

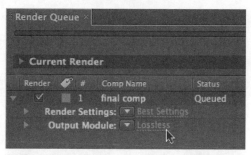

Figure 17.43 In the Render Queue panel, click the underlined name of the output module.

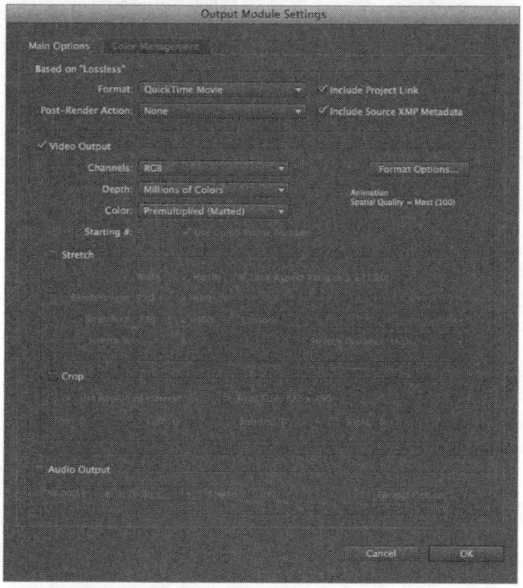

Figure 17.44 An Output Module Settings dialog appears.

Choosing Output Module Settings

Choosing output module settings is the second step in the movie-making process. These settings determine how processed frames are saved. In the Output Module menu, you can choose from a list of templates named for particular output types, such as Lossless or DV NTSC 48kHz. This section explains how to modify the current output module settings manually, so you'll understand how the templates were designed and be able to create an output module template of your own (as explained in the section, "Creating Templates," later in this chapter).

To choose an output module manually:

1. In the Render Queue panel, click the underlined name of the output module (**Figure 17.43**).

   An Output Module Settings dialog appears (**Figure 17.44**).

   continues on next page

2. Make a selection for each of the following options:

Format—The output's file format includes a variety of movie and still-image-sequence formats (**Figure 17.45**).

Include Project Link—This option determines whether After Effects embeds a project link into the output movie. When opening the output file in a program that supports project links—such as Adobe Premiere Pro—you can use the Edit Original command to reopen the source project and make any necessary changes to it (**Figure 17.46**).

Include Source XMP Metadata—This selection determines whether After Effects includes metadata present in the comp's source files in the exported file (**Figure 17.47**).

Post-Render Action—Choose this to specify whether After Effects utilizes the rendered movie in the project. You can instruct After Effects to import the movie, replace the source composition (including its nested instances) with the movie, or use the movie as a proxy in place of its source (**Figure 17.48**). This way, you can replace complex, processing-intensive elements with a single, easy-to-render footage item—thereby reducing render times. Using a postrender action is part of a strategy called *prerendering*; see "Prerendering" in Chapter 16, "Complex Projects."

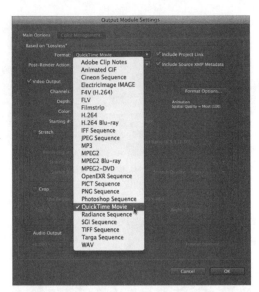

Figure 17.45 Choose the format of the saved file in the Format pop-up menu.

Figure 17.46 Clicking the Include Project Link check box embeds a link into the exported movie that allows the project to be reopened in other Adobe applications with the Edit Original command.

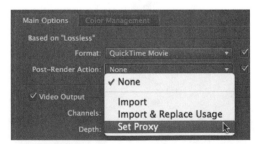

Figure 17.48 In the Post-Render Action pop-up menu, choose whether you want to use the rendered movie in the project. You can import the rendered movie, use it in place of its source footage, or set it as a proxy for its source footage.

Figure 17.47 Clicking the Include Source XMP Metadata check box adds the source footage's metadata to the exported file.

Figure 17.49 Click Format Options to open a dialog containing format-specific settings.

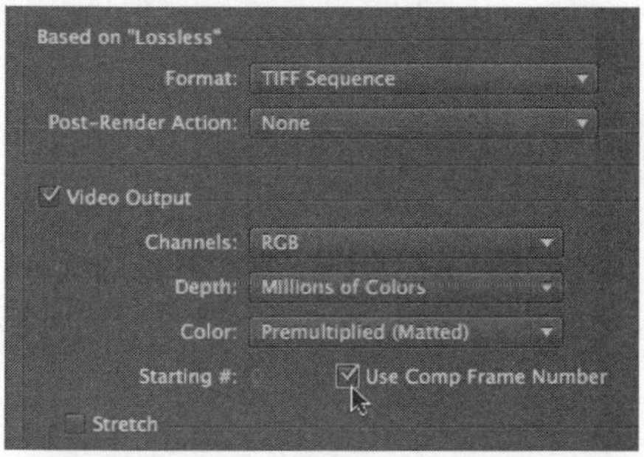

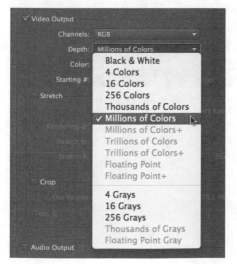

Figure 17.50 When you're exporting a still image sequence, specify the starting number, or select Use Comp Frame Number.

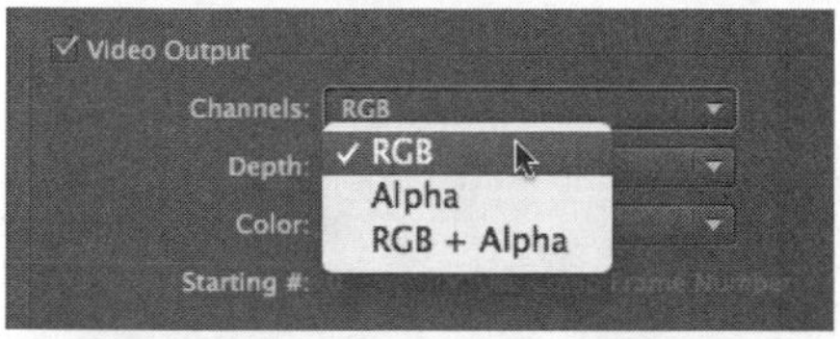

Figure 17.51 Specify the channels present in the output in the Channels pop-up menu.

Figure 17.52 The options available in the Depth menu depend on the format and channels you selected.

Format Options—Select this option to open a dialog that includes options associated with particular formats (**Figure 17.49**). For example, if you choose QuickTime Movie as the format, the Format Options button opens a Compression Settings dialog for QuickTime movies.

Starting #—Use this to specify the starting frame number in the filenames when you're exporting an image sequence. Alternatively, you can select Use Comp Frame Number to match exported frame numbers to the frame numbering in the comp (the option is selected by default) (**Figure 17.50**).

Channels—This option lists the channels present in the output (**Figure 17.51**). Depending on the format, you can choose to export the RGB channels, the Alpha channel, or RGB + Alpha.

Depth—The available color depth options depend on the format and channels you selected (**Figure 17.52**).

Color—This setting specifies how color channels factor in the alpha channel (if one is present), determining whether the output uses a straight alpha or is premultiplied with black (**Figure 17.53**).

continues on next page

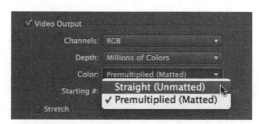

Figure 17.53 If you chose to output an alpha channel, use the Color pop-up menu to choose between straight alpha or premultiplied with black.

Stretch—By selecting this option, you can choose common frame sizes for your output from the Stretch To pop-up menu or enter custom dimensions (**Figure 17.54**).

You may also choose between a low- and high-quality resizing method in the Stretch Quality pop-up menu. Stretch resizes the image after it has been rendered.

Crop—You can add pixels to or, more likely, remove pixels from the edges of the image frame (**Figure 17.55**). Cropping is useful for removing black edges from video footage.

Audio Output—Choose this option to specify the audio-track attributes (if any) of your output. Settings include sample rate, bit depth, and format (mono or stereo) (**Figure 17.56**). Clicking the Format Options button opens a dialog to apply audio compression to the exported file.

Color Management—Select options that can modify color values of the comp's images according to the presentation medium's color space (**Figure 17.57**). Color management options are available only when you enable Color Management in the Project Settings dialog. For more about color management, see the After Effects Help system.

3. Click OK to close the Output Module dialog and return to the Render Queue panel.

Figure 17.54 Select Stretch options to resize the image after it has been rendered. Several common options are available in the Stretch To pop-up menu.

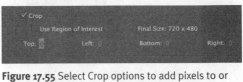

Figure 17.55 Select Crop options to add pixels to or remove pixels from the edges of the frame.

Figure 17.56 Specify the sample rate, the bit depth, and whether the audio track is stereo or mono.

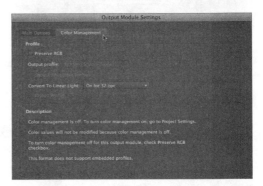

Figure 17.57 If you enabled Color Management in the Project Settings dialog, the Color Management tab contains options for modifying the color values on export.

Figure 17.58 Choose Make Template in the Render Settings pop-up menu.

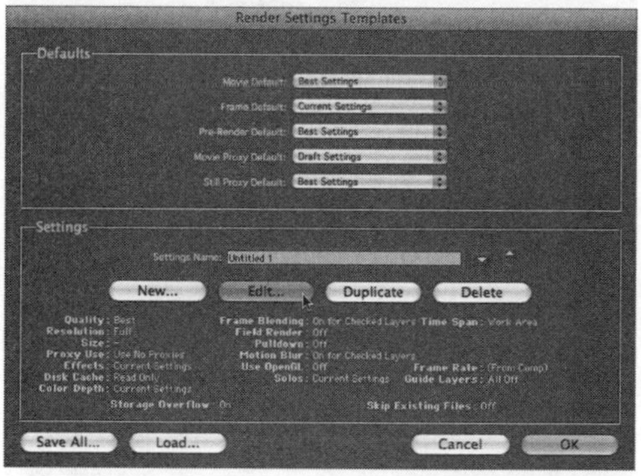

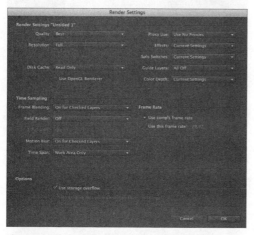

Figure 17.59 In the Render Settings Templates dialog, click Edit to specify settings for the untitled template.

Figure 17.60 In the Render Settings dialog, choose the options you want to save as a template, and click OK to return to the Render Settings Templates dialog.

Creating Templates

You should save your most commonly used settings as templates so that you can apply them by selecting templates in the Render Settings and Output Module pop-up menus in the Render Queue panel. You can also make your most useful render settings and output module templates your default settings. You can even save templates as stand-alone files that you can then move to other systems or share with other users.

To create a template:

1. *Do one of the following:*
   ▲ To create a render settings template, choose Make Template in the Render Settings pop-up menu (**Figure 17.58**).
   ▲ To create an output module template, choose Make Template in the Output Module pop-up menu.

   Depending on your choice, a Render Settings Templates or Output Module Templates dialog appears. An untitled template appears in the Settings Name field.

2. Click Edit in the Render Settings Templates (**Figure 17.59**) or Output Module Templates dialog.

   Depending on the type of template you're creating, the Render Settings (**Figure 17.60**) or the Output Module dialog appears.

continues on next page

3. Choose the render-settings or output-module options you want to save as a template.

4. When you've finished selecting settings, click OK to close the Render Settings or Output Module dialog and return to the Render Settings Templates or Output Module Templates dialog.

5. In the Render Settings Templates or Output Module Templates dialog, enter a settings name for the new template (**Figure 17.61**).

6. Click OK to close the dialog and save the template.

   From now on, the template will appear in the appropriate pop-up menu in the Render Queue panel (**Figure 17.62**).

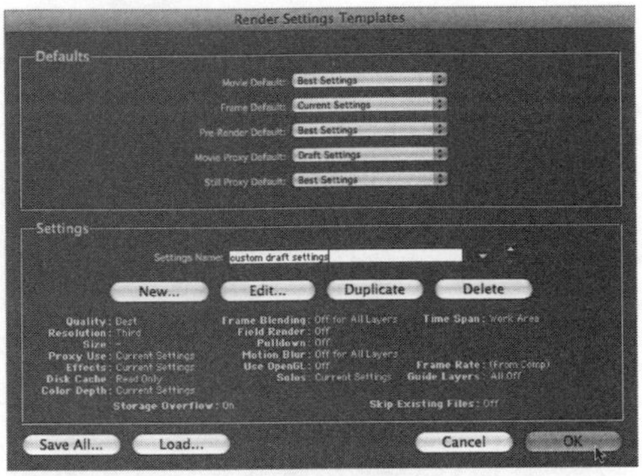

Figure 17.61 In the Render Settings Templates dialog, enter a name for the new template and click OK.

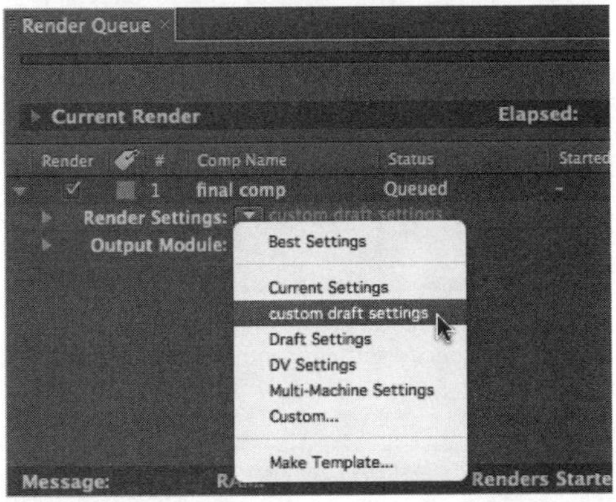

Figure 17.62 From now on, the template will appear in the appropriate pop-up menu in the Render Queue panel (the Render Settings menu is shown here).

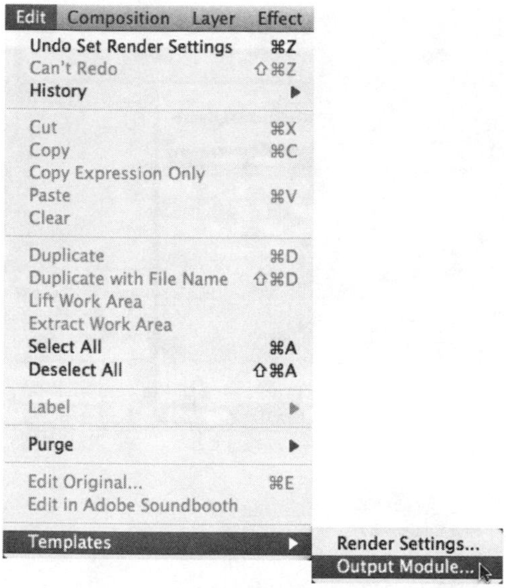

Figure 17.63 Choose Edit > Templates and select whether you want to manage templates for Render Settings or Output Module settings (shown here).

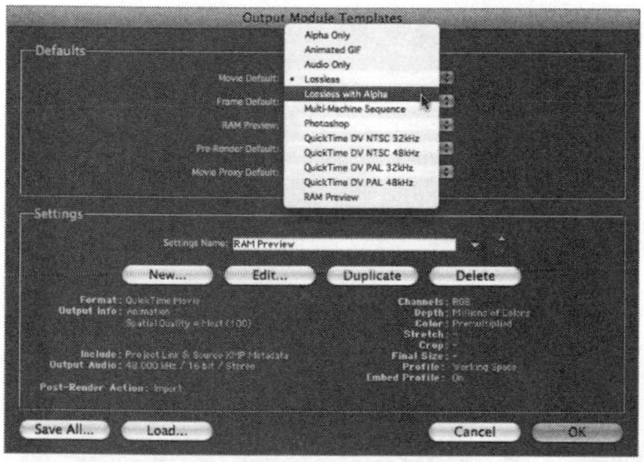

Figure 17.64 In the Render Settings Templates dialog or Output Module Templates dialog (shown here), specify a template in each output type's pop-up menu. Here, a template is assigned as the new Movie Default.

To set a default template:

1. *Do one of the following:*

   ▲ To set the default render settings template, choose Edit > Templates > Render Settings.

   ▲ To set the default output module template, choose Edit > Templates > Output Module (**Figure 17.63**).

   Depending on your choice, the Output Module Templates or the Render Settings Templates dialog appears.

2. In the Defaults area of the dialog, specify a template for each output type in the corresponding pop-up menu.

   For example, choose the template you want to be the default settings for rendering or exporting movies in the Movie Default pop-up menu (**Figure 17.64**).

3. Repeat step 2 to set templates for other defaults.

   Pre-Render and Movie Proxy defaults affect movies created using post-render actions, explained in "Choosing Output Module Settings," earlier in this chapter.

4. Click OK to close the dialog.

   The selected templates become the default templates for the corresponding output types.

Saving Single Frames of a Composition

Frequently, you'll want to render a single frame of a composition. For example, when an animation halts its motion, substituting a single still image for multiple static layers can lighten the rendering load. Or you may need a still for a storyboard or client review. After Effects lets you save a single frame using the default frame settings or as a layered Photoshop file.

To save a composition frame as a still-image file:

1. Set the current time of the composition to the frame you want to export (**Figure 17.65**).

2. Choose Composition > Save Frame As > File (**Figure 17.66**).

   The composition appears selected in the Render Queue panel (**Figure 17.67**).

3. To change the destination of the saved image, click the name of the file next to Output To.

   An Output Frame To dialog opens.

Figure 17.65 Set the current time of the composition to the frame you want to export.

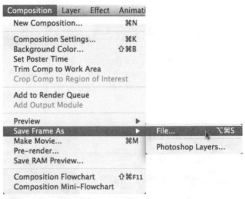

Figure 17.66 Choose Composition > Save Frame As > File.

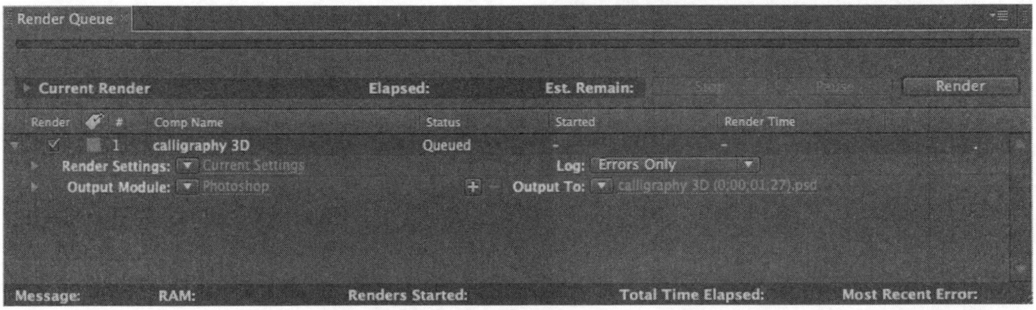

Figure 17.67 The item appears selected in the Render Queue panel.

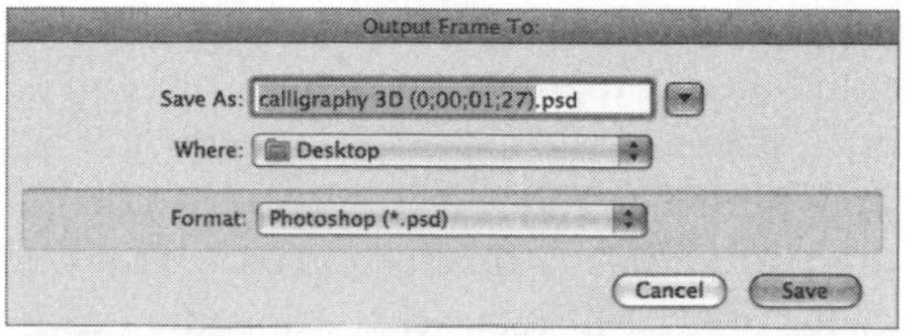

Figure 17.68 To change the destination of the saved file, click its name next to Output To; in the Output Frame To dialog, specify the destination and name of the saved frame.

4. Specify the destination and name of the saved frame (**Figure 17.68**).

5. Click Save to close the Output Frame To dialog.

6. To change the default settings for frames, select render settings and output module settings, or choose templates.

7. In the Render Queue panel, click Render.

✔ Tips

- If you want to use the still frame in the project, be sure to specify a postrender action in the Output Module Settings dialog. See "Choosing Output Module Settings," earlier in this chapter, and "Prerendering" in Chapter 16.

- You can export the current frame as a layered Photoshop file in a similar manner by choosing Composition > Save Frame As > Photoshop Layers.

SAVING SINGLE FRAMES OF A COMPOSITION

Clip Notes

Exporting to the Adobe Clip Notes format isn't essentially different than exporting to any other movie format—but what you can do with a Clip Notes file is unique.

Exporting to Clip Notes creates a draft-quality movie that is embedded into (or linked to) a PDF file (Adobe's Portable Document Format). Using the free Adobe Reader software, colleagues can enter comments into the PDF that are linked to specific points in the movie. When imported into the originating project, reviewers' comments appear as markers at corresponding points in the comp's timeline. Just double-click the markers to see the comments and make adjustments accordingly. The Clip Notes feature (also found in Adobe Premiere Pro) facilitates a collaborative process—though coming to an agreement is still up to you.

Using the Adobe Media Encoder Dialog

Several movie formats—particularly those designed for encoding video to DVD or for Web delivery—include numerous settings that merit a specialized export dialog, generally referred to as the Adobe Media Encoder. But strictly speaking, *Adobe Media Encoder* refers to the output mechanism, not the name of the dialog.

In After Effects, choosing certain formats in the Output Module Settings dialog invokes the appropriate variation of the Adobe Media Encoder, which bears the name of the specified format and contains options particular to that format.

However, the Adobe Media Encoder is also a stand-alone program for encoding files into other formats, and for exporting sequences from Adobe Premiere Pro and compositions from After Effects. This section covers the dialog in After Effects. See the documentation for the Adobe Media Encoder for more information on the stand-alone program.

In After Effects, the encoder's options vary according to format, but the overall appearance of the dialog is consistent. General settings appear in the upper part of the dialog; the lower part of the dialog consists of tabbed panels that organize settings by category (**Figure 17.69**).

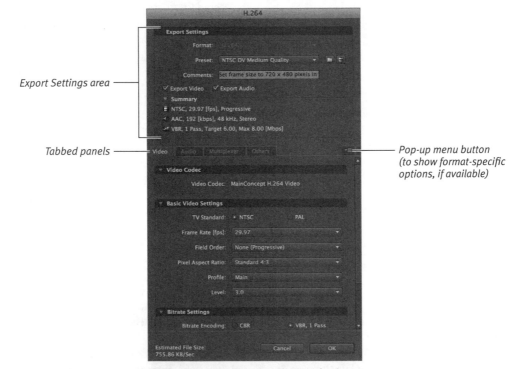

Export Settings area

Tabbed panels

Pop-up menu button
(to show format-specific options, if available)

Figure 17.69 Choosing certain formats (such as MPEG2, Windows Media, or H.264) as the export format invokes a specialized export dialog for that format. This figure shows the dialog for H.264.

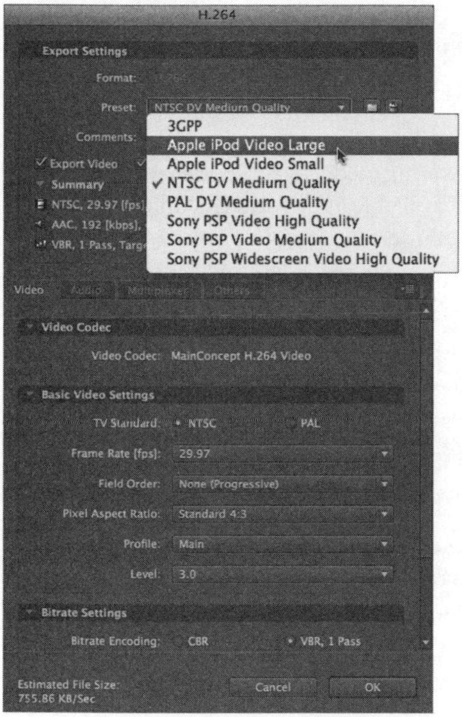

Figure 17.70 A Preset pop-up menu automatically optimizes extensive settings for a particular goal.

Settings for these formats are extensive and can require an in-depth understanding of file compression. Fortunately, you can select from a list of presets designed for particular delivery media (**Figure 17.70**). (You can also save custom presets or delete ones you don't need.) For a detailed explanation of each setting, consult After Effects Help and the documentation provided by the format's developer.

✔ Tips

- When you export to a format designed for playback on mobile devices, you can test for compatibility using Adobe Device Central, which is part of Adobe Production Premium.

- The Adobe Media Encoder program allows you to add Adobe Premiere Pro sequences and other files to an After Effects rendering queue. As a stand-alone program, it can render while you continue to do other work in After Effects.

Notable Output Formats

In addition to the standard Video for Windows (AVI) and QuickTime Movie (MOV) file formats, other common output formats include the following:

Flash Video (FLV)—Format chiefly intended for delivering media over the Web using Flash Player (or compatible player software). Flash Player is available as free stand-alone software but is even more widespread as a Web browser plug-in. You can export a comp to the Adobe Flash (SWF) or Adobe Flash Professional (XFL) formats by choosing File > Export and selecting the appropriate option.

MPEG2—Variations on this format are commonly used to encode video for burning to DVD media or the newer Blu-ray Disc format. Note that MPEG-2 formats are supported on Windows and Intel-based Macs only (not PowerPC-based Macs).

H.264—A relatively new and versatile standard capable of encoding video for a wide range of applications—from highly compressed video for playback on mobile devices to HD video on Blu-ray Disc media. H.264 is also known as MPEG-4 Part 10, and AVC (Advanced Video Coding).

Windows Media—Microsoft's standard for low-data rate applications, particularly downloading and streaming audio and video over the Web.

INDEX

H

H.264 format, 500
handles, layer, 98
headings in Project panel, 52–53
hiding/showing mask paths, 239
hold interpolation, 202, 305
Horizontal Scale control (text), 299
Horizontal Type, 290–292

I

icons, keyframe, 163, 204
Illustrator files, Adobe
    importing as compositions, 38
    importing as single footage item, 35–36
images
    magnifying, 65–66
    RAM calculation formula for, 27
    rasterizing, 457
    saving composition frames as still-image files,
        496–497
importing
    with Adobe Bridge, 41–43
    Adobe Premiere Pro projects, 39–40
    After Effects projects, 39–40
    files with alpha channels, 31–33
    layered files as compositions, 37–38
    layered files as single footage items, 34–36
    motion footage, 44–45
    still-image sequences, 30
In points, setting, 124–126
incoming and outgoing interpolation
    defined, 198
    mixing linear and Bézier, 204
Indent control (text), 302
Info panel, defined, 9
intelligent caching, 175–176
interface, After Effects
    Audio panel, 10
    Brushes panel, 11
    Character panel, 10–11
    Composition panel, 7
    Effect Controls panel, 9
    Effects & Presets panel, 10
    Flowchart panel, 9
    Footage panel, 8
    Info panel, 9

Layer panel, 8
Mask Interpolation panel, 12
Metadata panel, 12–13
Motion Sketch panel, 12
Paint panel, 11
Paragraph panel, 11
Preview panel, 10
Project panel, 7
Smoother panel, 12
Timeline panel, 8
Tools panel, 9
Tracker panel, 12
Wiggler panel, 12
workspaces setting up, 14–16
interlaced video, interpreting, 46
interpolation
    auto Bézier, 200
    Bézier, 201
    continuous Bézier, 200
    default spatial interpolation, 205
    of frame values, 160
    fundamentals of, 196
    Graph Editor. See Graph Editor
    hold, 202
    incoming and outgoing, 198
    incoming and outgoing, mixed, 204
    keyframe icons and, 204
    linear, 199
    no interpolation, 199
    spatial, 196, 206–209
    temporal, 197, 225–229
inverting masks, 258
items
    finding with Project panel, 51
    removing from Project panel, 57

J

jumping, child layer, 461
Justification option (text), 301

K

kerning control, 298
keyboard shortcuts
    nudging layer properties with, 159
    for playback and preview, 191
    for property dialogs, 159

INDEX

INDEX

INDEX

W

Z

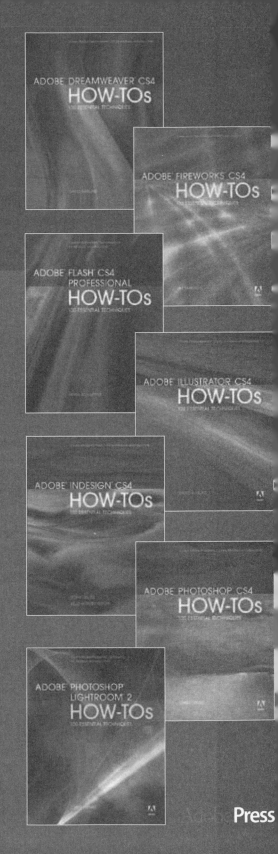

Get free online access to this book!

And sign up for a free trial to Safari Books Online to get access to thousands more!

With the purchase of this book you have instant online, searchable access to it on Safari Books Online! And while you're there, be sure to check out the Safari on-demand digital library and its Free Trial Offer (a separate sign-up process)—where you can access thousands of technical and inspirational books, instructional videos, and articles from the world's leading creative professionals with a Safari Books Online subscription.

Simply visit www.peachpit.com/safarienabled and enter code OCKHMZG to try it today.